DRUMVOICES

EUGENE B. REDMOND, a native of East St. Louis, Illinois, is a graduate of Southern Illinois University and Washington University (St. Louis) and has achieved distinction in several areas of writing, including poetry, drama, journalism, and criticism. He has published five books of poetry and recorded an album reading his own verse to musical accompaniment. Cofounder and publisher of Black River Writers Press, Redmond is also literary executor for the estate of the late poet and fiction writer Henry Dumas. Currently Redmond is professor of English and poet-in-residence at California State University, Sacramento, and is one of the co-ordinators of the Annual Third World Writers and Thinkers Symposium held on that campus. He is in demand as a speaker, lecturer, reader, and consultant to various workshops, symposia, and conferences, having appeared before audiences at UCLA, UC Berkeley, in Harlem, in Watts, Howard University, Southern University, and many more.

DRUMVOICES:

The Mission of Afro-American Poetry

A CRITICAL HISTORY

BY EUGENE B. REDMOND

ANCHOR BOOKS
ANCHOR PRESS / DOUBLEDAY
GARDEN CITY, NEW YORK 1976

IN MEMORIAM:
GEORGIA DOUGLAS JOHNSON, MELVIN TOL-
SON, LANGSTON HUGHES, CONRAD KENT
RIVERS, HENRY DUMAS, ARNA BONTEMPS
AND FOR THE STILL-BURNING LAMPS:
STERLING BROWN, OWEN DODSON, MAR-
GARET WALKER, GWENDOLYN BROOKS, ROB-
ERT HAYDEN

Library of Congress Cataloging in Publication Data

Redmond, Eugene.
  Drumvoices: the mission of Afro-American poetry.

  Bibliography: p. 423
  Includes index.
  1. American poetry—Afro-American authors—
History and criticism. I. Title.
PS310.N4R4   811'.009
ISBN: 0-385-06168-4
Library of Congress Catalog Card Number 75-6171

ACKNOWLEDGMENTS

Many thanks are due the following poets, editors, publishers, and survivors of poets for use of cited material. All efforts have been made
to secure the proper permission for each selection. However, if some
of the selections are not properly acknowledged, please contact Doubleday & Company, Inc., in order to clarify the situation.
Lewis Alexander for lines from "Nocturne Varial" from *The Poetry of
the Negro*, copyright 1949, 1970 by Anna L. Thompson. Published by
Doubleday & Company, Inc. Reprinted by permission of Mrs. Anna L.
Thompson.

Margaret Walker Alexander for lines from "Bad-Man Stagolee," "For My People," "Pappa Chicken," "The Struggle Staggers Us," and "We Have Been Believers" from For My People, copyright 1942 by Margaret Walker and Yale University Press. Reprinted by permission of Margaret Walker Alexander.

J. Mord Allen for lines from "The Psalms of Uplift" from Negro Poets and Their Poems, edited by Robert Thomas Kerlin. Copyright 1923, 1935 by the Associated Publishers, Inc. Reprinted by permission of the Associated Publishers, Inc.

Samuel Allen (Paul Vesey) for lines from "To Satch," copyright 1962 by Samuel Allen. Reprinted by permission of Samuel Allen (Paul Vesey).

Russell Atkins for lines from "At War," which first appeared in American Weave, copyright 1962 by Russell Atkins, and "Irritable Song," which first appeared in Naked Ear, copyright 1958 by Russell Atkins. Reprinted by permission of the author.

Imamu Amiri Baraka for lines from "Black Art," "Black People," "leroy," and "Sterling Street September" from Black Magic: Poetry 1961–1967, copyright 1969 by LeRoi Jones. Reprinted by permission of the publisher, the Bobbs-Merrill Company, Inc.

Austin Black for "Asexual Flight" from The Tornado in My Mouth: Poems by Austin Black, copyright 1966 by Austin Black. Reprinted by permission of Exposition Press, Inc., Hicksville, N.Y. 11801.

Arna Bontemps for lines from "Golgotha Is a Mountain" from Personals, copyright 1963 by Arna Bontemps. Reprinted by permission of Harold Ober Associates.

Gwendolyn Brooks for lines from "The Anniad," "The Ballad of Rudolph Reed," "Beverly Hills, Chicago," "the children of the poor," "Of De Witt Williams on his way to Lincoln Cemetery," "do not be afraid of no," "The Last Quatrain of the Ballad of Emmett Till," "Negro Hero," "The Preacher: Ruminations Behind the Sermon," and all of "We Real Cool," from The World of Gwendolyn Brooks, copyright 1971 by Gwendolyn Brooks; for lines "Langston Hughes," "Riders to the Blood-Red Wrath" and "Of Robert Frost," from Selected Poems by Gwendolyn Brooks, copyright 1963 by Gwendolyn Brooks. Reprinted by permission of Harper & Row, Publishers, Inc.; for lines from "Speech to the Young" from Family Pictures, copyright 1970 by Gwendolyn Brooks Blakley. Reprinted by permission of Broadside Press.

Sterling Brown for lines from "Memphis Blues" from Southern Road, Beacon Press reprint, copyright 1975, and "Old Lem," copyright 1975 by Sterling Brown. Used by permission of Sterling Brown.

Benjamin Burrell for lines from "A Negro Mother" from Negro Poets and Their Poems, edited by Robert Thomas Kerlin, copyright 1923, 1935 by The Associated Publishers, Inc. Reprinted by permission of The Associated Publishers, Inc.

Marcus B. Christian for lines from "McDonogh Day in New Orleans" from The Poetry of the Negro, copyright 1949 by Langston Hughes and Arna Bontemps. Copyright 1970 by Arna Bontemps. Reprinted by permission of Doubleday & Company, Inc.

Lucille Clifton for lines from "Lately" and "Mary" from Good News About the Earth, copyright 1972 by Lucille Clifton, and "God's

Mood" from *An Ordinary Woman*, copyright 1974 by Lucille Clifton. Reprinted by permission of Random House, Inc.

Sam Cornish for lines from "Middleclass Girls with crippled fingers waiting for me to light their cigarettes" from *People Beneath the Window*, copyright 1968 by Sam Cornish. Published by Sacco Publishers. Reprinted by permission of the author.

Jayne Cortez for lines from "Festivals and Funerals" from *Festivals and Funerals*, copyright 1971 by Jayne Cortez. Reprinted by permission of the author.

Joseph Seamon Cotter, Sr., for lines from "The Don't Care Negro" and "The Negro Child" and Joseph Seamon Cotter, Jr., for lines from "Rain Music," from *Negro Poets and Their Poems*, edited by Robert Thomas Kerlin. Copyright 1923, 1935 by The Associated Publishers, Inc. Reprinted by permission of The Associated Publishers.

Countee Cullen for lines from "Heritage," "Scottsboro, Too, Is Worth Its Song," and "Yet Do I Marvel" from *On These I Stand*. Copyright 1927, 1955 by Harper & Row, Publishers, Inc. Reprinted by permission of Harper & Row, Publishers, Inc.

Waring Cuney for lines from "Hard Times" and "No Images" from *Storefront Church*, copyright 1973 by Waring Cuney. Reprinted by permission of Waring Cuney.

James Cunningham for lines from "St. Julien's Eve: For Dennis Cross" from *Jump Bad*, edited by Gwendolyn Brooks. Copyright 1971 by Broadside Press. Reprinted by permission of Broadside Press.

Walter Delegall for lines from "Psalms for Sonny Rollins" from *Burning Spear: An Anthology of Afro-Saxon Poetry*, copyright 1963 by the Dasein Literary Society. Reprinted by permission of Jupiter Hammon Press of Dasein Literary Society.

Alexis DeVeaux for lines from *Spirits in the Streets*, copyright 1973 by Alexis DeVeaux. Reprinted by permission of Doubleday & Company, Inc.

Charles Dinkins for lines from "Invocation" from *Negro Poetry and Drama*, copyright 1969 by Sterling Brown. Reprinted by permission of Atheneum.

Owen Dodson for lines from "Countee Cullen," *Divine Comedy*, "Guitar," "Jonathan's Song," "Lament," "Open Letter," and "Poems for My Brother Kenneth" from *Powerful Long Ladder*, copyright 1946 by Owen Dodson and copyright renewed 1974 by Owen Dodson. Reprinted by permission of Farrar, Straus & Giroux, Inc. For lines from "The Confession Stone," "Let me rock him again in my trembling arms," and "Mary Passed This Morning" from *The Confession Stone*, volume 13 in the Heritage Series, published by Paul Bremen Limited, London, 1970. Copyright 1970 by Owen Dodson. Reprinted by permission of Owen Dodson.

W. E. B. Du Bois for lines from "A Litany of Atlanta," copyright 1906 by W. E. B. Du Bois, and "Hymn of Hate," from *Darkwater: The Twentieth Century Completion of Uncle Tom's Cabin*, copyright 1920 by W. E. B. Du Bois; for lines from "Song of the Smoke," copyright 1899 by W. E. B. Du Bois. Reprinted by permission of Mrs. Shirley Graham Du Bois.

Henry Dumas for "I Laugh Talk Joke" and lines from "Jackhammer," "Ngoma," "Play Ebony Play Ivory," "Rite," "Root Song," and "A Song of Flesh" from *Play Ebony Play Ivory*, copyright 1974 by

Loretta Dumas and edited by Eugene B. Redmond. Reprinted by permission of Random House, Inc.

Alice Dunbar-Nelson for lines from "The Lights at Carney's Point" from *Negro Poets and Their Poems*, edited by Robert Thomas Kerlin. Copyright 1923, 1935 by The Associated Publishers, Inc. Reprinted by permission of The Associated Publishers, Inc.

Ray Durem for "Broadminded" from *Take No Prisoners*, volume 17 in the Heritage Series, published by Paul Bremen Limited, London, 1971. Copyright 1971 by Dorothy Durem. Reprinted by permission of Paul Bremen Limited.

Mari Evans for lines from "Who Can Be Born Black" and "The Rebel" from *I Am a Black Woman*, copyright 1970 by Mari Evans and published by William Morrow & Company, Inc., 1970. Reprinted by permission of Mari Evans.

B. Felton (Elmer Buford) for lines from "An Elegy to Eternity" from *Conclusions*, copyright 1971 by B. Felton and reprinted by permission of the author.

Julia Fields for lines from "Aardvark" from *Nine Black Poets*, edited by R. Baird Shuman and copyright 1968 by Moore Publishing Company. Used by permission of Moore Publishing Company, P. O. Box 3143, West Durham Station, Durham, N.C. 27705.

Sherman Fowler for lines from "Thinking" from *Sides of the River: A Mini-Anthology of Black Writing*, edited and copyright 1969 by Eugene Redmond. Reprinted by permission of Black River Writers Press.

Nikki Giovanni for lines from "Concerning One Responsible Negro with Too Much Power," "Of Liberation," "Nikki-Rosa," and "The True Import of the Present Dialogue, Black vs. Negro" from *Black Feeling, Black Talk, Black Judgement*, copyright 1968, 1970 by Nikki Giovanni; lines from "Africa" from *My House*, copyright 1972 by Nikki Giovanni. All reprinted by permission of William Morrow & Company, Inc.

Oswald Govan for lines from "The Lynching" from *Burning Spear: An Anthology of Afro-Saxon Poetry*, copyright 1963 by the Dasein Literary Society. Reprinted by permission of Jupiter Hammon Press of Dasein Literary Society.

Angelina Grimké for lines from "The Black Finger" from *American Negro Poetry*, edited and copyright 1963 by Arna Bontemps. Reprinted by permission of Farrar, Straus & Giroux, Inc.

Michael S. Harper for lines from "Dear John, Dear Coltrane." Reprinted from *Dear John, Dear Coltrane* by Michael S. Harper by permission of the University of Pittsburgh Press. Copyright 1970 by University of Pittsburgh Press.

John Wesley Holloway for lines from "Calling the Doctor" and "Miss Merlerlee" from *From the Desert*, copyright 1919 by John Wesley Holloway. Reprinted in *The Book of American Negro Poetry*, edited by James Weldon Johnson. Copyright 1922, 1931 by Harcourt, Brace & World, Inc. Copyright 1950, 1959 by Mrs. Grace Nail Johnson. Source for reprint rights could not be found at publication time.

Lucy Ariel Williams Holloway for lines from "Northboun'" in *The Book of American Negro Poetry*, copyright 1926 by Lucy Ariel Williams Holloway. Reprinted by permission of the National Urban League.

Langston Hughes for lines from "Mother to Son" and "The Negro Speaks of Rivers" from *Selected Poems*, copyright 1954 by Langston Hughes. Reprinted by permission of Random House, Inc.; for lines from "Harlem" from *The Panther and the Lash: Poems of Our Times*, copyright 1967 by Langston Hughes. Reprinted by permission of Random House, Inc.; for lines from "Jazzonia" from *The Weary Blues*, copyright 1926 by Alfred A. Knopf, Inc., and renewed by Langston Hughes. Reprinted by permission of Alfred A. Knopf, Inc.

Lance Jeffers for lines from "Black Soul of the Land" and "My Blackness Is the Beauty of This Land" from *My Blackness Is the Beauty of This Land*, copyright 1970 by Lance Jeffers. Reprinted by permission of Broadside Press.

Charles Bertram Johnson for lines (no title given) from *Negro Poets and Their Poems*, edited by Robert Thomas Kerlin. Copyright 1923, 1935 by The Associated Publishers, Inc. Reprinted by permission of The Associated Publishers, Inc.

Georgia Douglas Johnson for lines from "Dreams of the Dreamer" from *Caroling Dusk*, edited by Countee Cullen. Copyright 1955 by Harper & Row, Publishers, Inc. Reprinted by permission of Harper & Row, Publishers, Inc.

Helene Johnson for lines from "Magulu" from *Caroling Dusk*, edited by Countee Cullen. Copyright 1955 by Harper & Row, Publishers, Inc. Reprinted by permission of Harper & Row, Publishers, Inc.

James Weldon Johnson for lines from "My Lady's Lips Am Like de Honey" and "O Black and Unknown Bards" from *Saint Peter Relates an Incident* by James Weldon Johnson, copyright 1917, 1935 by James Weldon Johnson, copyright renewed 1963 by Grace Nail Johnson. Reprinted by permission of Viking Penguin, Inc.; for lines from "The Creation" and "The Prodigal Son" from *God's Trombones* by James Weldon Johnson, copyright 1927 by The Viking Press, Inc. Copyright 1955 renewed by Grace Nail Johnson. All rights reserved. Reprinted by permission of The Viking Press, Inc.

Percy Johnston for lines from "Fitchett's Basement Blues, Opus 5" from *Burning Spear: An Anthology of Afro-Saxon Poetry*, copyright 1963 by Dasein Literary Society. Reprinted by permission of Jupiter Hammon Press of Dasein Literary Society.

June Jordan for lines from "Uncle Bull-Boy" from *Some Changes by June Jordan*, copyright 1967 and 1971 by June Meyer Jordan. Reprinted by permission of the publishers, E. P. Dutton & Co., Inc.

Norman Jordan for lines from "High Art and all that Jazz" from *Destination-Ashes*, copyright 1970 by Norman Jordan. Reprinted by permission of Third World Press, 7524 South Cottage Grove, Chicago, Ill. 60619.

Bob Kaufman for lines from "Heavy Water Blues" from *Golden Sardine*, copyright 1967 by Bob Kaufman. Reprinted by permission of City Lights Books.

Etheridge Knight for lines from "The Bones of My Father" from *Belly Song*, copyright 1973 by Etheridge Knight, and "Haiku 9" from *Poems from Prison*, copyright 1968 by Etheridge Knight. Reprinted by permission of Broadside Press.

Pinkie Gordon Lane for lines from "Griefs of Joy" from *Wind Thoughts*, copyright 1972 by Pinkie Gordon Lane. Published by South & West, Inc. Reprinted by permission of Pinkie Gordon Lane.

Wayne Loftin for lines from "Reality" from *Sides of the River: A Mini-Anthology of Black Writing*, edited and copyright 1969 by Eugene Redmond. Reprinted by permission of Black River Writers Press.

Audre Lorde for lines from "Black Mother Woman" from *From a Land Where Other People Live*, copyright 1973 by Audre Lorde and reprinted by permission of Broadside Press; for lines from the "Moon-minded the Sun" from *Sixes and Sevens*, copyright 1962 by Audre Lorde, and "Rites of Passage" from *Cables to Rage*, copyright 1970 by Audre Lorde. Used by permission of the author.

Claude McKay for lines from "Baptism," "If We Must Die," and "The Lynching" from *Selected Poems of Claude McKay*, copyright 1953 by Twayne Publishers, Inc. Reprinted by permission of Twayne Publishers, a division of G. K. Hall & Company.

Haki R. Madhubuti for lines from "First Impressions of a Poet's Death" from *Think Black*, copyright 1967 by Don L. Lee, and "The Self-Hatred of Don L. Lee" and "Don't Cry, Scream" from *Directionscore: Selected and New Poems*, copyright 1971 by Don L. Lee. Reprinted by permission of Broadside Press.

George Reginald Margetson for lines from *The Fledgling Bard and the Poetry Society*, copyright 1916 by George Reginald Margetson. Reprinted in *The Book of American Negro Poetry*, edited by James Weldon Johnson. Copyright 1922, 1931 by Harcourt, Brace & World. Copyright 1950, 1959 by Mrs. Grace Nail Johnson. Source for reprint rights could not be found at publication time.

G. C. Oden for lines from ". . . As When Emotion Too Far Exceeds Its Cause" from *Kaleidoscope*, edited by Robert Hayden. Copyright 1967 by G. C. Oden. Reprinted by permission of the author.

Pat Parker for lines from "Brother" from *Child of Myself*, copyright 1972 by Pat Parker. Reprinted by permission of the author.

Dudley Randall for "Iwo Jima" from *More to Remember*, copyright 1971 by Dudley Randall. Reprinted by permission of Third World Press, 7524 South Cottage Grove, Chicago, Ill. 60619.

Eugene Redmond for lines from "Invasion of the Nose" from *River of Bones and Flesh and Blood*, copyright 1971 by Eugene Redmond, and "Inside My Perimeter" from *In a Time of Rain & Desire*, copyright 1973 by Eugene Redmond. Reprinted by permission of Black River Writers Press.

Conrad Kent Rivers for lines from "In Defense of Black Poets" and "The Still Voice of Harlem" and for "Watts" from *The Still Voice of Harlem*, volume 5 in the Heritage Series, published by Paul Bremen Limited, London, 1968. Copyright 1972 by Mrs. Cora McIver Rivers; for lines from "To Richard Wright" from *The Wright Poems*, volume 18 in the Heritage Series, published by Paul Bremen Limited, London, 1972. Copyright 1972 by Mrs. Cora McIver Rivers. Reprinted by permission of Paul Bremen Limited.

Sonia Sanchez for lines from "Malcolm" from *Homecoming*, copyright 1969 by Sonia Sanchez. Reprinted by permission of Broadside Press.

Judy Dothard Simmons for lines from "Schizophrenia" from *Judith's Blues*, copyright 1973 by Judy Dothard Simmons. Reprinted by permission of Broadside Press.

Le Roy Stone for lines from "Flamenco Sketches" from *Burning Spear: An Anthology of Afro-Saxon Poetry*, copyright 1963 by the Dasein

Literary Society. Reprinted by permission of Jupiter Hammon Press of Dasein Literary Society.

Joyce Carol Thomas for lines from "I Know a Lady" from *Crystal Breezes*, copyright 1974 by Joyce Carol Thomas. Reprinted by permission of Firesign Press, Box 402, Berkeley, Calif.

Melvin Tolson for lines from "Rendezvous with America," "Dark Symphony," and "An Ex-Judge at the Bar" from *Rendezvous with America*, copyright 1944 by Melvin Tolson. Reprinted by permission of Dodd, Mead & Company, Inc.; for lines from "Do," "Do" and "Ti" from *Libretto for the Republic of Liberia* by Melvin B. Tolson, copyright 1953 by Twayne Publishers, Inc.; and for lines from "Alpha," "Beta," "Eta," "Gamma," "Lambda," "Xi" and "Zeta" from *Harlem Gallery* by Melvin B. Tolson, copyright 1956 by Twayne Publishers, Inc. Reprinted by permission of Twayne Publishers, a division of G. K. Hall & Company.

Jean Toomer for lines from "Song of the Son" from *Cane*, copyright 1923 by Boni & Liveright; copyright renewed 1951 by Jean Toomer. Reprinted by permission of Liveright Publishing Corporation. Jean Toomer for lines from "Blue Meridian" from *Black Writers of America*, edited by Richard Barksdale and Keneth Kinnamon, copyright 1972 by The Macmillan Company. Copyright 1936 by W. W. Norton & Company, Inc. Copyright renewed 1964 by Lewis Mumford, co-editor with Alfred Kreymborg, of *The New Caravan*. Reprinted by permission of W. W. Norton & Company, Inc.

Mark Traylor for lines from "Cool Black Nights" from *Black Poets Write On: An Anthology of Black Philadelphian Poets*, copyright 1970 by A. Philly Riginalski. Reprinted by permission of the publisher. (Author dead at age twenty-two.)

Quincy Troupe for "White Weekend" from *Embryo*, copyright 1972 by Quincy Troupe. Reprinted by permission of Quincy Troupe.

Alice Walker for lines from "Rage" from *Revolutionary Petunias & Other Poems*, copyright 1973 by Alice Walker. Reprinted by permission of Harcourt, Brace, Jovanovich, Inc.

Romenetha Washington for lines from "Rat Race" from *Sides of the River: A Mini-Anthology of Black Writing*, edited and copyright 1969 by Eugene Redmond. Reprinted by permission of Black River Writers Press.

Lucien B. Watkins for lines from "A Prayer of the Race That God Made Black" from *Negro Poets and Their Poems*, edited by Thomas Kerlin. Copyright 1923, 1935 by The Associated Publishers, Inc. Reprinted by permission of The Associated Publishers, Inc.

Joseph White for lines from "Black Is a Soul" from *Burning Spear: An Anthology of Afro-Saxon Poetry*, copyright 1963 by the Dasein Literary Society. Reprinted by permission of Jupiter Hammon Press of Dasein Literary Society.

Richard Wright for specified lines from "Between the World and Me," copyright 1935 by *The Partisan Review*, and "I Have Seen Black Hands," copyright 1935 by *The Partisan Review*. Reprinted by permission of Paul R. Reynolds, Inc.

CONTENTS

PREFACE

At this perilous juncture in black history, on the eve of America's bicentennial and amid a new wave of Third World humanism, *Drumvoices* comes as a partial rebuttal to those who say poetry's impact on mankind's consciousness has been insignificant. The thesis of *Drumvoices* is simple: that God's trombones have historically blared through or soothed the harsh and stark realities of the Afro-American experience; and that the sources (records) of these blarings and soothsayings, locked in cultural safe-deposit boxes of drums and the intricate acoustics of the folk, remain accessible to anyone desiring to tap them. Such source spirits ("roots") are what the author has tried to conjure up in *Drumvoices*, which owes great debts to a lengthening line of marvelous visionaries, known and unknown.

As a reference work, this text makes a modest attempt to follow in the tradition of Vernon Loggins' *The Negro Author in America*, Benjamin Brawley's *Early Negro American Writers* and *The Negro Genius*, Sterling A. Brown's *Negro Poetry and Drama* and J. Saunders Redding's *To Make a Poet Black*. We have also profited immensely from related works by George Washington Williams, Benjamin E. Mays, W. E. B. Du Bois, John Hope Franklin, Frantz Fanon, Loften Mitchell and Dorothy Porter. Of the literary historians and critics, only Brown is concerned exclusively with poets—though Mrs. Porter's many offerings also include a check list of black poets. Loggins' study views black authors up until 1900; and Redding, Brown and Brawley examine them through the mid 1930s. *Drumvoices* combines all previous ventures in the area of the poetry—giving new interpretations and updating an exciting history which began with Lucy Terry, who wrote a poem 229 years ago.

Initially conceived as a monograph and later enlarged to its present size, *Drumvoices* is aimed at students and teachers of black poetry, literature, history and culture. However, the author hopes that all who read from these pages will benefit. The very general thesis stated above is consistently implied in the book's approach. Unlike some recent works, this one does not present a consciously labored construct or aesthetical matrix, e.g., black nationalism, pan-Africanism, the black aesthetic or alienation, though none of these alternatives has been overlooked whenever and wherever poets or critics have dealt significantly with them. Occasionally chronology is violated, since any time barrier is, by definition, arbitrary. (It was impossible to find birth or death dates for some of the early poets.) Also arbitrary is the author's selection of poets and emphasis on various styles, techniques, themes or periods. Yet the organization of the text is somewhat original since, at the time of this writing, no single work has discussed black poetry from its beginnings into the 1960s and 1970s. As a history, *Drumvoices* includes six chapters: I, Black Poetry: Views, Visions, Conflicts; II, The Black and Unknown Bards; III, African Voice in Eclipse(?): Imitation and Agitation (1746–1865); IV, Jubilees, Jujus, and Justices (1865–1910); V, A Long Ways from Home (1910–1960); VI, Festivals and Funerals: Black Poetry of the 1960s and 1970s. Finally, there is a bibliographical index.

The historical aspect of this two-pronged study (critical and historical) dominates—the rationale being that a text that chronicles the development of the poetry is a prerequisite to sound critical assessment. Also, the author was not unmindful of the fact that most anthologies or studies of recent black poetry are generally "loaded" and top-heavy with household names but none of them has extended its vision to include a representative ("complete" is out of the question) look at the numerous important centers where this poetry is being created. It seemed a worthwhile task, then, simply to suggest the demographic range of the new poetry. Such is the attempt made in Chapter VI, in which the author has purposely decentralized a star-dominated pattern in the new poetry in favor of a more truthful and historical picture of its development. One can pick up a journal or book in practically any library and read glowing praise of the new poetry; hence the author has simply referred readers to these comments instead of rehashing them here.

Unfortunately, significant studies of eighteenth- and nineteenth-century black poetry were not available to the author while chapters on these areas were being written. But Jean Sherman's *Invisible Poets: Afro-Americans of the 19th Century* and M. A. Richmond's *Bid the Vassal Soar: Interpretive Essays on the Life and Poetry of Phillis Wheatley and George Moses Horton*, when finally received, provided additional insight and caused some slight reshuffling of this text. Of great service was *Early Black American Poets*, William Robinson's important anthology (with notes); at this writing, it remains the best such source for the period. The author is also indebted to a number of important works on twentieth-century black poetry: Jean Wagner's *Black Poets of the United States: from Paul Laurence Dunbar to Langston Hughes*, Arthur P. Davis' *From the Dark Tower: Afro-American Writers, 1900–1960*, Donald Gibson's *Modern Black Poets*, Blyden Jackson and Louis Rubin's *Black Poetry in America*, George P. Kent's *Blackness and the Adventure of Western Culture*, and Joy Flasch's *Melvin B. Tolson*.

A book does not *just* happen, and the fuel for this one has been pouring in over a number of years and from a great many sources. Germinating ideas came from various quarters: students, friends, teachers and, most importantly, colleagues at Southern Illinois University's Experiment in Higher Education in East St. Louis. The literally hundreds of poets, writers and thinkers (in Watts, New York, Chicago, New Orleans, Atlanta, Detroit, Cleveland, etc.), with whom the author has met and talked through nights and days, now stand faceless and nameless, but they are as much a part of this book as the author himself. Of special significance were the critical readings of sections of this text by Ted Hornback, friend and former teacher; critic Clyde Taylor, who prompted much rethinking and rewriting, and Charles Rowell, who should have been commissioned to write the chapter on folklore. Likewise, for their patience, assistance and great stores of information, debt is owed to librarians at California State University (Sacramento), the Schomburg Center for Research in Black Culture (New York Public Library), the Moorland-Spingarn Research Center at Howard University, Oberlin College, and Southern University in Baton Rouge.

While a book does not *just* happen in the mind, neither does it miraculously appear on the page. Hours of meticulous and relentless work were invested by my graduate assistant Julie Blattler, who worked on bibliographical and textual problems. My younger assistants in these matters were Keith Jefferson and Ronald Tibbs. However, a lion's share of producing this book was assumed by Marie Collins, supervisor of Sacramento's Oak Park School of Afro-American Thought, who typed and criticized the manuscript and otherwise committed herself to the project. Beverly Williams, CSUS English secretary, also shared a portion of the typing load. Finally, my gracious editor, Marie Dutton Brown, deserves a huge salute for her encouragement, concern and continued support of the writing-research through to the end.

Onward, the POETS!
Eugene B. Redmond
Sacramento, California

CHAPTER I

BLACK POETRY: VIEWS, VISIONS, CONFLICTS

> ". . . the double obligation of being both Negro and American is not so unified as we are often led to believe."
>
> —COUNTEE CULLEN

In recent years, black American poetry has emerged from what appears to have been its assigned position as an illegitimate—sometimes embarrassing—child of American literature into an official flower in the garden of world writing. Everywhere, Afro-American poetry is being vigorously read, listened to and imitated. Disc jockeys on Black-oriented radio stations quip: "Often imitated but never duplicated"—assuring their listeners that the "soul" or "heirloom" of their *tradition* is alive, well, and stored in ancestral vaults. However, a silent reading of the DJ's casually delivered quip belies the charismatic power and verbal dexterousness in *how* it is said. But, in black poetry, the "how" is *always* important and will be one of the cornerstones of the discussions in this book.

To say that black poetry is read or heard all over the world is *not to say* that it is studied in equitable proportion to other poetry. Indeed the recent rash of anthologies and individual collections, and the reissuing of previously published volumes, suggest that a vast literary vacuum has existed. The flood of publications, coupled with the appearance of new black and other-ethnic publishing houses, makes this vacuum glaringly, paradoxically obvious. The absence of black poetry (or black literature) courses from English departments at predominantly white colleges and public schools is ignominiously aided and abetted by the culpable negligence at many predominantly black learning centers—where students are exposed, for example, to Walt Whitman, W. B. Yeats, T. S. Eliot, Robert Frost, Carl Sandburg, Marianne Moore, and Edith Sitwell but receive no instruction in the works of Paul Laurence Dunbar, Jean Toomer, Melvin B. Tolson, Owen Dodson, Robert Hayden, Gwendolyn Brooks, and Margaret Walker. One could go on, of course, reciting the cultural and literary negligence so officially a part of the academic and grants-in-aid patterns. However, the purpose here is to explore the vast richness of black poetical and mythical life.

Black poetry presents many frustrations, challenges, and problems. Instructors preparing to teach the subject must be aware of the many pitfalls, not the least among them the tendency of teacher and student alike to stray from the "study" of the poetry into political and rhetorical catharses. "Black" is a political word, and to study or teach any aspect of the black experience is to become embroiled in controversy and burdened with sociopolitical stresses. That thin line between the ideological implications of a poem and those "trial scenes" in which individuals (particularly in classrooms) find themselves victim is a line walked by all teachers and students of the black experience. In approaching black poetry, then, one must "set" the atmosphere by dealing, from the outset, with substantive background materials: the deepest philosophical, religious, ethical, artistic, and aesthetic tenets of black life and expression. Thus the purpose and intent of this text is to examine the scope and range of black poetry via folk origins, methods of delivery, language, phonology, religiosity, racial character, recurring themes, individual and group identity, and poetic devices as they are developed indigenously or borrowed from other traditions.

Like all other bodies of writing, black literature stems from a folkloristic trunk, making the job of teacher or student twofold: one, to deal with the great and complex storehouse of folk materials and themes; and two, to explore the chronological development of black poetry—from about 1746 to the present. There are minor differences of opinion among scholars about where the study of black written poetry begins. For example, in *The Poetry of the Negro*, Hughes and Bontemps begin with Lucy Terry's "Bars Fight," the account of an Indian massacre in Deerfield, Massachusetts, in 1746. *The Negro Cara-*

van (edited by Brown, Davis and Lee) omits the Terry poem. *Caravan* was first issued in 1941, while *The Poetry of the Negro* was published in 1949. *Caravan's* poetry section begins with Phillis Wheatley, who first published poetry in 1770. Also omitted from *Caravan* is the work of Jupiter Hammon, whose poetry was published in broadside in 1760. In *Cavalcade (Negro American Writing from 1760 to the Present)*, published in 1970 and edited by Davis and Redding, neither Terry nor Hammon appears and the poetry section begins with Phillis Wheatley. *Early Black American Poets* (Robinson) acknowledges Terry, but Johnson's *The Book of American Negro Poetry* opens with Paul Laurence Dunbar. Kerlin's *Negro Poets and their Poems* (1923) makes no mention of either "Bars Fight" or its author, but Dudley Randall's *The Black Poets* (1971) includes the poem. However, this random survey from the dozens of general and specialized anthologies indicates that many teachers of black poetry begin with Phillis Wheatley despite the fact that at least two black poets were writing before her.

One of the main features of this analysis will be the study of related and integral forms of expression such as folk songs, spirituals, blues, jazz, rhythm and blues and what is known today as soul music. However, the black experience is complex and frustrating.[1] At each juncture in the study of the poetry, for example, one reading and teaching it will meet difficulties that may seem insurmountable. Some of these difficulties will be presented in familiar questions: Is a poet considered black if he writes consistently—or temporarily—out of the "white" experience? Can a black poet really record black experiences and feelings in English? Can a white poet write a black poem (like the white musician who has developed a "feel" for black music and has learned to master the technical vocabulary of that music)? Can white people "understand"

---

[1] Most attempts to define the black experience have failed. When one considers the cross-fertilization of folk and literary culture in this country, together with the existence of hybrid cultures all over Latin America and other parts of the world, the term "black experience" does indeed defy neat definition. It is hoped, however, that through a continual return to the *idea* of the black experience (and discussion of black life), the complexity and range of the term can be appreciated (see also bibliography).

black poetry? Should white critics of black poetry be taken
seriously?[2] Is black poetry primarily emotion and lacking
in intellect? Is there a black aesthetic? Can a white professor teach black poetry? How does black language differ
from *white* language or English? And does black poetry
express the universal human condition?

Readers should ask these questions as an indication that
they want more realistic and direct answers to some of the
issues that have consumed black activists, artists, and
academicians, and white scholars of the black experience.
Teachers who are confronting racially mixed classes, all-
black classes or all-white classes will sometimes face a
distressing panorama of anger, rejection, fear, conde-
scension, accusation, anti-intellectualism, intellectual snobbishness, racism, distrust—and any number of other
combinations of the contemporary student personality.
The black poets do not lessen the tensions in this area,
since (like other poets) they, critically and thematically,
are dispersed along a boundless spectrum of opinions, attitudes, creative approaches, ideologies, techniques and literary philosphies. A teacher or student preparing for either a
semester or a year-long course (or for a "black" unit to be
integrated into a humanities course, an American literature course, or a black interdisciplinary project) should
read the literature and lore of the black past in order to
give tentative answers and carry on adequate discussions
when questions such as those above arise. After having
been exposed to black poets of national stature—via television programs such as *Soul* and *Black Journal*, at campus
readings and conferences, black arts festivals and community book parties—many students (especially black students) may be informed, at the popular level, about the
opinions and reading styles of the poets. However, neither
student nor teacher must—and this point has to be
stressed again and again—succumb to the temptation to
"skip all poetry up until 1965."

True, there is great and growing interest in the black poetry produced out of what has been variously called the

---

[2] For a balanced discussion of this and related subjects, see Mphahlele's *Voices in the Whirlwind* (1972).

black consciousness/black power/black nationalist/black arts/neo-pan-African movement. Yet one who goes against the black (or any) tradition will find himself engulfed in a maelstrom of conjecture and ideological hysteria; and the class, whose posture will be *anti-historical*, will be riddled with soap-opera rhetoric about revolution and liberation. Harold Cruse (*The Crisis of the Negro Intellectual*) points out that each generation of black artists and activists suffers from a lack of historical/cultural continuity. That is, the artists fail to study or are unaware of the mistakes and the pitfalls of past struggles and consequently find themselves in predicaments not dissimilar to those of their predecessors. Needless to say, such "cultural amnesia" is not the state from which one approaches the study of black poetry.

As observed earlier, the poets are not in agreement concerning what black poetry is supposed to do, why it is written or whether whites can (or should) write or criticize it.[3] Reasons for the diverse beliefs and positions are numerous: the situation attending the birth and upbringing of the poet (note, for example, the distinctions between Claude McKay and Countee Cullen); his religious affiliation (Robert Hayden is of the Baha'i faith; Askia Muhammad Touré is a Sunni Muslim; El-Muhajir [Marvin X] is a member of the Nation of Islam; K. Curtis Lyle was raised as a Catholic); his political leaning (which, in the case of many writers, is also religious); his preparation for poetry; his associations with other poets (many black poets, for example, associate—and this is historically true —with writers of other races; this author met one black poet in 1970 who had two masters' degrees but had not heard of Melvin Beaunorus Tolson!); his current personal situation (does he live in the inner city? teach? write full time? play a musical instrument? write in other genres?

---

[3] An important point at this juncture of black poetry. For there is growing feeling among some poets and writers (many of whom will not express themselves in public) that there are concerted attempts to muzzle, circumvent or circumscribe some authors because of their personal political viewpoints or their brand of writing. For further allusion to this, see back issues of the *Journal of Black Poetry*, *Black World*, and other periodicals dealing with the contemporary black arts scene.

read primarily black poets?), and his feelings on the question:

> "Are you a poet first and then Black; or are
> you Black first and then a poet?"

Harmless as it may seem, that rhetorical utterance has entrapped scores of black writers in ideological and political prisons—from which some would like to extricate themselves by asking simply: "What difference does it make?"

For many poets, however, it matters a great deal, and they have written profusely on the implications of this question and the several others listed earlier. The teacher or discussion leader must sample opinions of writers and students, sharing the diversity of opinions and reactions to the poetry with the same vigor and thoroughness that is represented in the poetry itself. Such parity allows for a continuous balance in approaching criticism, social undercurrents and the poems themselves. Novelist Ralph Ellison has suggested that he is a writer first and that his racial identity is subordinate to that fact. Poet Robert Hayden has taken a similar stand (see introduction to *Kaleidoscope, Poems by American Negro Poets*, 1967). The same position had been taken several decades earlier by poet Countee Cullen. In his critical-biographical introduction to Cullen's poetry (*The Book of American Negro Poetry*, 1922), James Weldon Johnson observed:

> Some critics have ventured to state that Cullen is not an authentic Negro poet. This statement, of necessity, involves a definition of "a Negro poet" and of "Negro poetry." There might be several definitions framed, but the question raised is pure irrelevance. Also there is in it a faint flare-up of the old taboo which would object to the use of "white" material by the Negro artist, or at least regard it with indulgent condescension. Cullen himself has declared that, in the sense of wishing for consideration or allowances on account of race or of recognizing for himself any limitation to "racial" themes and forms, he has no desire or intention of being a Negro poet. In this he is not only within his right; *he is right*. [italics mine]

Johnson went on to note that because Cullen "revolts against" racial enclosures, the "best of his poetry is motivated by race." One could make a similar comment today about Ellison or Hayden. The works for which both are internationally acclaimed delve into the deepest regions of black psyche and feeling. Meanwhile some younger poets —those who gained exposure in the 1960s—and several poets and critics who straddle both generations lash out, sometimes not so diplomatically, at what they see as compensatory actions and unnecessary self-deprecation by the older poets. Pulitzer prize winner Gwendolyn Brooks said in a preface to *Poems from Prison* that Etheridge Knight was not the "stifled *artiste*." The comment represented an implied rebuttal to black and white "academic" poets. Elsewhere she referred to the "inelegance" of some black poetry as being consistent with the bleak, drab landscape of hopelessness and despair of inner-city dwellers. (Other critics, however, support the position of poet-critic Larry Neal that the black experience should not be defined in terms of "negatives.") During the late sixties, Gwendolyn Brooks became a kind of mother figure to the New Black Poetry Movement (at least in Chicago), ceased publishing with Harper and Row, and began to release her writings through Broadside Press—a Detroit-based black publishing house under the supervision of Dudley Randall. Her new consciousness, she declares, came about as a result of having attended a black writers conference (1967) at Fisk University, where she heard and participated in discussions with poets Imamu Amiri Baraka (LeRoi Jones), Don L. Lee, Nikki Giovanni, novelist John Oliver Killens, and many other writers, activists, and artists. The violent social explosions in the cities, the Vietnam War, which took some black lives and crippled others, the persistent emergence of Africa—all, she said, aided in the development of her new consciousness. She has written that it "frightens" her to think that if she had died before she reached fifty, "I would have died a 'Negro' fraction."

Hayden, disclaiming the Gwendolyn Brooks position, assumes he has been "Black" all along and continues to reject any singular, unarguable position on the black aesthetic or the *poet-first, Black-second / Black-first, poet-second* controversy. Assessing Baraka, Hayden admits that he recognizes the younger poet's power but deplores "his Black nazism." J. Saunders Redding, a dean of the black critical establishment, feels there is no such thing as a "Black Aesthetic"; Poet Paul Vesey (Samuel Allen) calls it "a voyage of discovery—I think it will yield return not as greatly as in music, perhaps, where the black aesthetic dominates an entire cultural area of the west."[4] Other poets and critics, however, ignore questions dealing with aesthetics, the *level* of blackness in their work, their primary audience, and the mood or spirit that influences their writing. At the same time, there are trends, some regional and some national, that can be identified. Identifying and exploring these trends can be immensely rewarding.

Some prerequisites to an understanding of trends and attitudes that stem from the ongoing creative process are: a study of slavery as it was instituted by Europe and refined in the United States, an examination of black social history, and a scrutiny of West African and Afro-American folklore. The thorough student of black poetry will steep himself in the history of Western civilization; he will also develop an appreciation for the complex web of black-white interrelationships in America. All this is necessary in preparing to participate fully and knowledgeably in the often tension-filled readings and discussions stimulated by the works of black poets and writers.

Much of the subject matter of black poetry is unpleasant, since it is pervaded with the weighty memory and impact of slavery. And if slavery is among the less-pleasant items to be discussed, lynching becomes even more repugnant—especially since so much such activity occurred "after" slavery was officially ended. But one soon sees that practically every black poet since the end of the Civil War has written a poem about lynching. The poets who do not deal with actual lynchings, as we have come to know or interpret them, write about half-lynchings, character or cultural defilement and the mental and physical destruction of black humanity. If a discussion of slavery is unpleasant,

---

[4] See *Negro Digest*, January 1968.

then, a consideration of lynching is horrifying. However, skilled discussants will maneuver judiciously through the rough waters of such sessions—keeping emotional deluges to a minimum by admitting facts and clear interpretations. During such occasions, everyone must be on guard lest the classroom become a courtroom. At the same time, a convener who cannot preside over vigorous and thorough discussions of these painful events and details may find himself later trying to bridge even wider gulfs of doubt, frustration, mistrust and alienation. Again, the study of black poetry (or any aspect of black culture) assumes the complexities of the black experience itself. Nevertheless such study is infinitely rewarding, because it is a vehicle that distills the particular insights and perspectives of black Americans into concise and authentic forms: merging the rich rural-biblical-urban idioms with colorfully luscious imagery and (in many cases) peerless technical proficiency in the use of literary English and Western poetic forms. For example, when students are confronted with the various poems on lynchings, study can be underscored by an examination of language, form, posture, poetic toolery and over-all achievement or effectiveness of the poems. In Richard Wright's "Between the World and Me," the poet becomes the persona; the oak tree narrates the lynching in Dunbar's "The Haunted Oak." Countee Cullen speaks as "I" in "Scottsboro, Too, Is Worth Its Song," which remonstrates with white American poets for remaining silent over unjust treatment of black men while they sing

> . . . sharp and pretty
> Tunes for Sacco and Vanzetti. . . .

In Claude McKay's "The Lynching," the killing of the black man is made analogous to the crucifixion; a sonnet, and awesome throughout, the poem descends to its rhyming couplet with a final ghastly irony:

> And little lads, lynchers that were to be,
> Danced round the dreadful thing in fiendish glee.

Certainly in these poems—and the dozens of others that employ the lynching theme—there is much material for further study and discussion. In the four poems mentioned, the poets employ such diverse forms as the sonnet, the ballad (Dunbar) and free verse (Wright). Helpful in this area will be the additional historical inquiry into the development of white hate groups such as the Ku Klux Klan and the history of race riots in America. Riots in at least a dozen American communities in 1919, for example, helped spur McKay to write *If We Must Die*, a poignant sonnet with its even more poignant and popular ending couplet:

> Like men we'll face the murderous, cowardly pack,
> Pressed to the wall, dying, but fighting back!

—a poem that Winston Churchill read before the House of Commons, during World War II, to spark his countrymen in the dim hours. Journalists found the poem scribbled on the wall of a cell during the 1972 prison rebellion in Attica, and the national press attributed it to a prisoner! Of great assistance, too, is a knowledge of the history of slave revolts (many black poets write about them) and the patterns of violence in America. Attuned teachers and students will want to consult sources such as *100 Years of Lynching* (Ginzberg), back issues of black and liberal white news journals and papers and especially past issues of *The Crisis*, the official news and opinion arm of the NAACP. W. E. B. Du Bois, among the first Blacks to receive a Ph.D., edited *The Crisis* for over twenty years, from its beginning in 1910. For further readings, the teacher can refer to the extensive bibliography of this book plus appropriate sections in anthologies, textbooks and other research sources.

The student of black poetry should arm himself to the best of his ability with the tools of criticism and a knowledge of black culture. He must understand the part "duality" plays in the lives of blacks and how such "twoness" is manifested in the poetry; he should recognize the key issues being raised and debated among black artists, scholars and activists, and have some feel for the historical circumstances out of which these issues and debates grew; he ought to understand what Baraka means in his references to some black poets as "integrationists" and "arty poets"; he will have to know what many of the new poets mean when they say they reject Western "forms" and refuse to be judged by *white* standards (Baraka, for example, talks about post-American forms). He will also want to recognize black in-house humor and intracommunal disparagement in such words and phrases as "nigger," "Negro," "Uncle Tom," "oreo," "colored," "the man," "dicty," "bad mouth," "bust a nut," "brother," "crumbcrushers," "main squeeze," and "Mr. Charlie." (For further indication of this dictional and phonological richness and the breath of black language, see *The Dictionary of American Slang*, Major's *Dictionary of Afro-American Slang*, the "Glossary of Selected Terms" in *The Psychology of Black Language* (Haskins and Butts), Abraham's *Deep Down in the Jungle*, Andrews and Owens' *Black Language*, Claerbaut's *Black Jargon in White America*, Twiggs's *Pan-African Language in the Western Hemisphere*, Welmers' *African Language Structures*, Kochman's *Rappin' and Stylin' Out*, and Dillard's *Black English*.

Additionally the reader will want to know the motivations of some of the poets. All poets, for example, do not rate being called "poets" in the traditional (black or white) sense. Redding, in a recent *Muhammad Speaks* (now *Bilalian News*) interview, accused some of the new black writers of lacking "moral and esthetic integrity," calling them "literary hustlers." Observing that Baraka had recently signed a ten-year contract with Random House, Redding said such an act was inconsistent with the poet's nationalistic assertions and positions. In a recent *Black World* article, novelist-poet Ishmael Reed spoke disparagingly of some of the new black critics ("Blackopaths") and poets ("nationtime poets," was the reference). Poet-essayist Haki R. Madhubuti (Don L. Lee) has chided poet Nikki Giovanni for being an "individual" who lacks technical abilities; and in an issue of *Jet* magazine a reader irately asked if Ms. Giovanni deserved respect after accepting a Woman-of-the-Year award from a national white women's organization. Both she and Reed were nominated for National Book Awards in 1973. Hayden, a member of the older group of poets, who was only seventeen years old when the Harlem Renaissance burned out, feels that Madhubuti (praised by Gwendolyn

Brooks, Hoyt Fuller of *Black World*, Randall and Baraka)
has potential as a poet but lacks discipline and seems unable to separate poetic technique from ideological ranting.
On the other hand, Stephen Henderson, author-editor of
Understanding the New Black Poetry, praises the young
poet relentlessly and says his popularity is "tantamount to
stardom." Henderson, who holds a Ph.D., is currently
chairman of the new Humanities Division at Howard
University, where Madhubuti is a writer-in-residence.
Gwendolyn Brooks gives him credit in her "Introduction"
to *The Poetry of Black America* for spawning much of the
contemporary black-consciousness literature.

Any serious discussion of the development of black poetry must consider these intense feelings and positions.
One must also organize orderly discussions or readings
around the divergent views, through which particpants can
develop a complete picture of the vast richness of the poetry, including the political, social and historical tensions
out of which it is generated.

Robert Hayden, for one, understands this confluence of
issues and temperments, as witnessed by his comments on
the new black poetry—with appropriate historical footnotes:

> The emergence of a so-called school of Black Poetry in
> America has been one of the significant literary devel-
> opments of the modern period. Although the Harlem
> Renaissance of the 1920's brought certain Afro-
> American poets into prominence, it was not until the in-
> tensification of the civil rights struggle during the 1960's
> that a separate group of black poets began to take
> shape. Avowedly nationalistic (that is, racially proud)
> and scornful of western aesthetics, these poets contin-
> ued the protest tradition, historically associated with
> Negro writers. But they were more radical in outlook
> than their predecessors. Unlike the Harlem group, they
> rejected entry into the mainstream of American litera-
> ture as a desirable goal. They insisted that their poetry
> could not be judged by white standards, urging its im-
> portance as an expression of black consciousness.

> LeRoi Jones—the most influential of the young acti-
> vist poets—Don L. Lee, Nikki Giovanni, Sonia Sanchez,

Mari Evans, Etheridge Knight, and David Henderson attune their lyres to the "black esthetic." Not yet satisfactorily defined, this term, originating in the sixties, may be interpreted as a sense of the spiritual and artistic values of blackness.

(*The United States in Literature*, Miller, Hayden, O'Neal, 1973).

Hayden's opening comments, then, corroborate the opening sentence to this introduction—that black poetry is one of the most important movements on the literary scene today. Yet, while it is exciting to study this "poetry in process" (if you please), the enthusiast must be on guard not to skip the tradition (the folk precedents) and variations in favor of plunging into a black poem that heaps wrath on Watergate conspirators or urban policemen who shoot rioters and looters.

Many of the "literary hustlers" to whom Redding refers have capitalized on the topical and episodic issues—with little or no training in the black tradition or writing. Hence, the student must not assume that just because a statement is "relevant," it is *poetry!* The black or white researcher will "dig . . . deeper to the gold"—in the words of James David Corrothers—and "establish" a sound tradition against which to measure the black poetry of today. If the black poet in question fails, he fails because he collapses from the weight of the past—instead of being buoyed up by it. In establishing this sound tradition, one must realize first that the black experience is not monolithic—although recurring trends and broad implications do exist in the areas of language, religion, humor, dance, music, and general life style. And odd as it may seem, there is often more consistency in Blacks' knowledge of popular "American" culture than in what they know about themselves.[5] There are several reasons for such a paradoxical imbalance and lack of focus—many of them locked in the enigmatic seesaw of black history. Ellison observed in the 1940s that if black leaders ever unraveled

---

[5] For an exciting recitation and indictment via a "cultural quiz," listen to poet-critic Stanley Crouch's *Ain't No Ambulances for No Nigguhs Tonight* (Flying Dutchman).

the puzzle of the zoot suit and the dark glasses (meaning the secret of black urban "styling" habits), they could, perhaps, take the political and psychological reins of black masses from whites. Ellison's observation was accurate. James Baldwin has written that, in Europe, he looked at the great Renaissance masterpieces and felt ashamed that his race had not produced such work. Baldwin did not know that the great Spanish painter Pablo Picasso had borrowed heavily from African motifs or that LeCorbusier was influenced by African thatched-roof huts. The implications of this part of the discussion are many and far reaching. Ellison's, Crouch's, and Baldwin's observations are timely and important. They suggest that far too many of the students who are in black poetry (black studies) classes do not have a working knowledge of the tradition out of which the poetry grew. Yet it has become popular, in some quarters, to ignore this fact. The importance of a knowledge of the black literary tradition is a point that cannot be stressed too often or too emphatically.

Interestingly, the majority of the persons who want to know something about black poetry are not preoccupied with the *craft* of poetry—the *hows* and *whys* of poetry. Instead, students and casual readers seem to be more interested in the sociological (some say "pathological") aspects of the poetry. The situation varies, of course, from campus to campus, and from black to white to interracial settings. But the enthusiast should keep the pursuit of the work "tight" in terms of the discipline demanded by the poetry itself.

Another problem facing serious readers is how to organize segments when just an "appreciation" of the material is sought. Such an approach could be dictated by one's initial conception of the poetry or by the level of interest and preparation. A casual reader, for example, would not study the same poems with the same intensity as would a senior or graduate literature major. Nevertheless, teachers, students and poetry lovers must bear in mind that they are looking into *black* poetry and not merely some fair-to-middling imitation of traditional Western poetry—even though the two often converge on many points. Moreover, the *differences* are not always easy to identify; but one who assimilates the Afro-American world view into his

study of the poetry will have fewer problems recognizing
the differences than those who read the poetry "cold."
Black and white poets select the same words but for
different reasons. There are many variables, and one has to
be cautious about hard and fast judgments. But we can
say that the Afro-American poet is almost always apt to select a word for its typographical, phonological and political
dimensions. Word selection among European and American poets, on the other hand, is more often made for
allusory and intellectual reasons. This is not to say that
black poets are not intellectual or that Euro-American
poets are not musical. Exceptions to the foregoing groupings are legend. But it is important to identify music
(songified language) as a dominant influence on the Afro-
American poet—not just in an aesthetical or inspirational
sense, but in terms of architectonics, in terms of basic
(original) structures.

Again we are treading on sensitive ground, because in
the context of racial and intellectual mixtures, a curious
melting pot is likely to boil. Example: white students, well
grounded in their own literary tradition but having a skele-
tal knowledge of black culture, may want to speed up the
treatment of the poetry. Failing to recognize that many
students do not know the names and meanings of simple
poetic devices (metaphors, similes, alliteration, onomat-
opoeia), insensitive teachers and aggressive students often
cause premature destruction of group interests. Such situations do occur. Even the best literature teachers sometimes assume students have been drilled in the use of
figurative language. Ironically, most students have been
"drilled" in the figures; but the holes from the drillings
allow information to go in one ear and out the other!
Many students, in the whir of words, will not acknowledge
their ignorance of the language of poetic criticism and
analysis, especially if they happen to be black students and
think the instructor expects them to be "experts" on the
black experience. On the other hand, the intellectual
snobbery often accompanying the student "cliques"
should not be tolerated in a discussion of black poetry.
Luckily, however, the curves, crests and peaks of black poetry keep bringing all aspects of human nature full circle.

Many of the ideas, theses, axioms and broad statements made thus far will be re-examined on a continuing basis throughout the remainder of this book. Within the running history of Afro-American poetry, we will identify the poets' preference for lexical and phonological items: their reliance on major and minor archetypes (as they are derived from the larger as well as the black mythic tablets); their fetish for themes and positions (as these strains become either clustered or occasional); their relationships to each other and the folk and/or literary roots; and their individual and/or group ("school") achievements. Obviously, the folk influences are not as easy to place within the chronology as are the dated literary activities of the poets. So the reader should think of the folk world as one that constantly hovers over the whole of Afro-American literary and cultural life—sometimes calling it to its tasks, other times providing it with just the needed *lift* and *magic*.

CHAPTER II

THE BLACK AND UNKNOWN
BARDS

> O black and unknown bards of long ago,
> How came your lips to touch the sacred fire?
> —JAMES WELDON JOHNSON

ORIGINS OF BLACK EXPRESSION

In this chapter, as in subsequent ones, emphasis will be on
viewing black poetry within the spirit and letter of the
African-American cultural tradition. Unfortunately, many
early scholars either played down or ignored African
influences, though this was certainly not true of all of
them. For while some gloated over the "findings" of
"southern whites"—purporting to prove that the spirituals
were derived solely from English (hymns and Psalms)
sources—Johnson (*The Book of American Negro Spirituals*, 1925, 1926), John Wesley Work (*Folk Song of the
American Negro*, 1915) and others displayed faultless
proof of Africanisms existing in practically all black American folk materials.

This chapter, then, will examine the folk-philosophical
tradition, updating some of the thinking on traditional African views and mannerisms found in black America. Brief
consideration will be given the major trunks of the folk
poetry: spirituals and the seculars (or religious folk poetry
and everyday work-and-play folk poetry). Included is a fair
representation of the original folk poetry. Most
anthologies omit these items, but without a knowledge of
such it is difficult to understand either their development
or the black poet's general use of folk culture (see Dunbar, Johnson, Brown, Hughes, Hayden, Walker, and
others). However, before discussing the origins of black
expression, we should note the role of *griots*—or story
tellers—in preindustrial African societies. The black poet,
as creator and chronicler, evolves from these artisans—
human oral recorders of family and national lore. Trained
to recite—without flaw—the genealogies, eulogies, vic-

tories and calamities of the folk, *griots* (like lead singers
of spirituals) had to spice their narration with drama and
excitement. Few black American youngsters grew up
(even in recent times) without guidance from a sort of
griot (uncle, grandmother, big brother, sister, mother,
hustler, father, preacher, etc.). The job of the *griot* in
ancient African societies was so important that an error
could cost him his life. The *griot* began at a very early
age to master his technique and information. Like the
master drummer, he understudied an elder statesman
of the trade. His training demanded a certain
pyschological adjustment to the significance of his job—
which was to contain (and give advice on) the cultural
"heirlooms" of the community. As years and centuries
passed, this "factual" information was ritualized into a
lore, mythology, cosmology and legend; it became a part
of the vast web of racial consciousness and memory. It became the legacy with which every newborn child entered
the world. Clearly, then, the myth- and legend-building
black poet has a past into which to dip and a future to
project and protect. And any violation of the past, present
or future constitutes a serious crime against one's ancestors
—against one's parents, against one's blood, against one's
god. So it follows that the poet—*griot*—is not some
haphazardly arrived at hipster or slick-talker simply mouth-
ing tired old phrases. To the black American *griot*-
singer-poet the job of unraveling the complex network of
his past and present-future worlds is a painful but rewarding labor of love. We can say, then, that the black experience in the United States continues via the African continuum: a complex of mythical (see Jahn), linguistic (see
Twiggs), gestural (see Emery: *Black Dance*), psychological, sexual, musical, physical and religious forms. This
complex is evidenced in the day-to-day attitudes and activities of Blacks: their sacred and secular (organized and
random) expressions, their physical appearance, their dress
patterns and their family life. Not only in the United
States, but in the Caribbean, in Latin America, in all areas
of the world where Blacks live in substantial numbers—
they exhibit characteristics peculiar to the nature and culture of indigenous Africans. Naturally, general black expression evolves from the myriad components of black

culture; and the artistic (song, poetry) expression—traditional black (African) communities did not separate life from art—is a more sophisticated form refined from basic materials in the general "storehouse."

No one has yet identified exactly the time when the first African sounds or movements were incorporated into "white" or Western frames of reference or vice versa; but we do know that it did happen. Unfortunately, inept reporting on the black experience has muddied the waters so much that one is often shocked by the observations and conclusions of many "researchers." In an unflinchingly brilliant analysis of black African oral literature presented at the First World Festival of Negro Arts (1966) in Dakar, Senegal Basile-Juléat Fouda, noting that "oral literature is as old as creation," coined the phrase "archival literature of gesture." Concluding his important revelations, Fouda said: "Thus in the Black Africa of tradition, literary art is an anonymous art because it is a social art; it is a social art because it is a functional art; and it is functional because it is humanist." Good research is not bounded by color. Black sociologist E. Franklin Frazier (*Black Bourgeoisie*) wrongly held that there was no significant carryovers (cultural transplants) from Africa to the United States. (Slavery, Frazier said, "stripped" the African of his culture and "destroyed" his personality.) White anthropologist Melville Herskovits (*The Myth of the Negro Past*) proved without a doubt that there were African "survivalisms" operating daily in black American culture. (For further research on this see Jahn's *Muntu*, John Work's findings, the memoirs of Katherine Dunham, works of Lorenzo Dow Turner, and *Negro Folk Music of Africa and America* [Folkways Lp].)

Rudimentary black expression and the numerous folk forms it produced (field hollers, vendors' shouts, chants, work songs, spirituals, blues, gospels, jazz, rhythm-and-blues, soul music) form the linguistic and modal bases for most black poetry. The early song and chant forms were almost always accompanied by what we have come to call "dramatic ideograms"—or dances. *Dance* became one of the three basic artistic modes encapsulated by folk expression. The other two are *song* and *drum*. Aside from being the first means of communicating over distances, the drum also played a major role in the social lives of traditional African peoples. The career drummer, like the black American musician today, went through years of grueling practice and preparation—learning not only drumming techniques but the legends, the myths, the meanings and symbols of which the drum was derivative. Dance always accompanied song—Fouda refers to the "acoustical phonetic alphabet"—so that the complex web of oral nuances was vividly and graphically illustrated. Obviously, when teaching or entertaining, the artist/teacher had to present his material in interesting and exciting ways so as not to bore the audience. Thus repetition became a backbone of black expression—a flexible, buoyant repetition that was designed to reinforce and increase group participation. The three essential modes—*drum, song* and *dance*—heightened the immediate experience, which was ecstatic, therapeutic, spiritual, visceral and revelatory. Added to these intricate and varying modal patterns were the colorful costumes, make-up, props and important subject matter. The achievement was not just that of the vicarious experience but one of the act and symbol being actualized together.[1] While such a prospect boggles the mind, a serious study of these forms and the general tradition will prove eye-opening for many a disbeliever. One need only became enmeshed in any aspect of black ritual life to *know* and *understand* this point.

Early black American oral and gestural art forms inherited the qualities described thus far. In language, in dance and, more importantly, in points of view (attitudes) toward *time, life* and *death*, the cosmology of Africa "continued" (with some modifications) in the black culture of the Western Hemisphere. Specifically, information was conveyed by way of aphorisms, riddles, parables, tales, enigmatic dances and sounds (tonal scales), oblique and cryptic utterances, puzzles, jokes and poetry. The pattern remains intact today. One finds the tradition

---

[1] For a brilliant and cogent statement on this aspect of black expression see Samuel Allen's (Paul Vesey's) "The African Heritage," in *Black World* (January 1971). Allen is an acknowledged authority on both African and Afro-American culture. In the article, he identifies African "carryovers" in the black American church (Baldwin), literature (Sterling Brown, Eldridge Cleaver), and secular life.

in black poets, in the sermons of black ministers and in
family and other social gatherings. The scintillating black
poet Melvin Tolson operates in the old, enigmatic (word-
fencing) frame when in "An Ex-Judge at the Bar" he
says:

Bartender, make it straight and make it two—
One for the you in me and one for the me in you.

Tolson (known to carry this black nature into his classroom teaching at Langston University, where he report-
edly gave a student an F to the twentieth power) ends
the poem with an equally enigmatic mock/resolution:

Bartender, make it straight and make it three—
One for the Negro . . . one for you and me.

In the spirituals, one finds similar debts to the African
tradition of *song, dance* and *drum.* So too in the shouts
and hollers, in which actual African words and phrases
were often used.[2] Hence we can say that traditional African phonology and ritual, modified on the anvil of slavery,
were operating and continue to be represented in different
forms of black American expression. The African slave,
forced to acquire functional use of English and to reject
surface aspects of his religion, went "underground," so to
speak, and became bilingual and biphysical. Hence, while
much of the thematic material of the black folk tradition
was taken from the harsh difficulties the slave encountered
in America, the form, spirit and phonology were essentially African. The use of polyrhythms[3] and the introduction of syncopation, the reliance on various rhythmic
instruments (drum-related and sometimes invented), the
adherence to a non-European tonal scale and the employment of the blues tone, the development of a distinct
body of folklore and a rich language to convey the lore—all

---

[2] Raymond Patterson (*26 Ways of Looking at a Black Man*) is currently assembling a book listing several hundred African words that are
used daily in the American vocabulary. See bibliography for more on
this little-known area of scholarship.

[3] Isaac Paggett, a young composer-band director in Sacramento,
California, has said that the word "polyrhythm" (i.e., many rhythms
overlapping each other) should perhaps be replaced by or alternated
with the words "polymeter" or "polymetrics."

represent the African's resourcefulness. Cross-cultural inputs are also evident in the spirituals, which, in many cases, were influenced by the English hymn and the Psalm. Other considerations include the slave's use of and access to European instruments (Imamu Baraka points out, in *Black Music*, that the piano was the last instrument to be mastered by the black musician[4]), black adaptation of songs heard in the "big house," the continual restyling of American fads, and the employment of biblical imagery and language in songs and sermons.

Langston Hughes noted that the blues usually dealt with the theme of the rejected lover and personal depression. Hughes's first volume of poems, in fact, was entitled *The Weary Blues*. However, the blues, like the spirituals, do not simply preach resignation or submissiveness. Rather, as Jahn (*Muntu*) and Howard Thurman (*The Negro Spiritual Speaks of Life and Death*) note, underneath the complaint is a "plaint": *things must get better or change!* For as the slave said:

> Freedom, O Freedom, how I love thee!
> Freedom, O Freedom, how I love thee!
> And before I'll be a slave
> I'll be buried in my grave
> And go home to my Maker and be Free!

BLACK FOLK ROOTS IN AMERICA

"Get it together or leave it alone"
—JACKSON FIVE

Black poets have been writing in the English literary tradition since the middle of the eighteenth century. But it is the folk literature—those productions of the everyday people—that must be examined before a literary or poetic tradition can be viewed in its entirety. There are few persons in the United States who have not been touched or influenced (in one way or another) by the folk expression

---

[4] Eileen Southern, in *The Music of Black Americans*, sets forth a thorough and accurate discussion of these points. She notes with some detail how the Africans (made slaves) had to learn to use the instruments of the New World. Professor Southern also relates how black music influenced whites in the early days of America.

of black America. White Americans began collecting black folk lyrics and stories in the early years of the nineteenth century (see bibliography). In the same century, this aspect of black culture reached wide audiences via at least three major vehicles. The first was the abolitionist movement, which featured black poets (Francis E. W. Harper, James Whitfield, Benjamin Clark, and others), orators and prose writers (David Walker, Frederick Douglass), and journalists (John Russwurm). The second vehicle was the national and European tours (in the 1870s) of student choirs from Hampton Institute and Fisk University (Jubilee Singers). The abolitionist movement popularized anti-slavery and freedom songs, and the college choirs gave wide exposure to the spirituals, considered by most scholars (of black culture) to be the first authentic poetry of black America. The third major vehicle was the publication (in the late-nineteenth century) of Brer Rabbit tales by Joel Chandler Harris. In studies and writings, Harris recognized the mythic worth in black folk tales and exposed readers to such characters as Brer Terrapin, Brer Bear, Brer Fox, Brer Wolf, and others. Many of these tales and characters have African counterparts.

SPIRITUALS

"Tryin' to get home"

Use of the word "spiritual" to describe or identify black religious or church life is, in many ways, a corruption of the modal adaptations of African life in the United States. Learned interpretations, outlined against new information and empirical tenacity, reveal the entire black world as "spiritual": i.e., informed by and responsible to a "higher order"—the order of God or the gods. This spirituality drapes the interdependence and integration of various modes and points of view flowing through and evolving from the community. Such a "feel" or "sense" is witnessed in the exuberance, spontaneity, ecstasy, trance, tongue-talking, racial flavor, and flair in dress (church or night-club), and songified communications systems which are the backbone of Afro-American life. John Work describes this phenomenon as "this difference and this oneness." Robert Hayden employs an understanding of it when, in a

poem to Malcolm X, he proclaims the "blazing oneness"
of Allah. Further proof of this fusion is seen in the emotional abandonment of church folk during picnics, socials
and other events of merriment. Listening to Aretha
Franklin immediately recalls the gospel-blues alternation
in the unity of expression.[5] And it is found, without a
doubt, in the works of the Staple Singers, the Edwin
Hawkins Singers, and in a more vulgarized manner in Flip
Wilson's Rev. Leroy. In the words of one brother, "The
preacher and the pimp style out heavy." Still, it is important that we offer the traditional portrait and breakdown
of black folk expression.

The *spirituals* have been the source of continuing
debate among scholars: Are they completely African in origin? Are they primarily derivative of English (Methodist,
Wesleyan) sources? Or do they represent the conjoining
of African/European themes and religiosity? James Weldon Johnson and his brother, J. Rosamond Johnson, put
together the best-known collection of these songs in *The
Book of American Negro Spirituals* (1925), and *The Second Book of Negro Spirituals* (1926). The spirituals usually deal with physical or figurative contact between the
singer or congregation and God. (Early Afro-Americans
often used the words God, Jesus, Saviour, and Lord inter-
changeably. For a more thorough discussion of this see
Benjamin Mays's *The Negro's God.*) The songs also deal
with a longing for rest and the overcoming of formidable
obstacles or adversaries.

Work's 1915 study was seminal and remains a landmark
reference work on African and black American folk songs.
His work provides many answers to questions and issues
that had been (and continue to be) muddied by the waters of insensitivity and careless research. "Undertaken for
the love of our fathers' songs," the study gives clear connections between African and Afro-American song. His

---

[5] Let us observe that the most brilliant and influential black poets
have intimately understood this aspect of the culture. Almost without
exception (and Kerlin, Brown and others warn young black writers to
follow example), black poets since the Civil War have availed themselves of integral folk rudiments—even when they did not use them in
poetry. It is still a fact that black culture (despite the racist and technological barrages of the West) still remains more consciously "integrated" than most cultural units in the United States.

main interest is in religious songs—although his comments
on form and style are of general value:

> In America we hear it [the song] and see it acted in the
> barn dance, on the stage, in the streets among the chil-
> dren; in fact, many an occasion is enlivened by this spe-
> cies of music, the interest in which is intensified by the
> rhythmical patting of hands and feet. This rhythm is
> most strikingly and accurately brought out in their work
> songs.

Citing the emotionalism and songified intensity of the
black American, Professor Work says, "He worships not so
much because he ought, as because he loves to worship."
This "worship" (or religious sense), of course, is the kind
we alluded to earlier: the integration of sensuality and ecstasy into the sweeping ritual of live and immediate
drama. Such musical activity is "as natural to the American Negro as his breath":

> Indeed, it is a portrayal of his soul, and is as charac-
> teristic as are his physical features. Hear him sing in his
> church, hear him preach, moan, and give "gravery" in
> his sermon, hear the washerwoman singing over her tub,
> hear the laborer singing his accompaniment to his toil,
> hear the child babbling an extemporaneous tune. . . .
> Even those Negroes who have been educated and who
> have been influenced by long study, find it difficult to
> express their musical selves in any other way.

Black song, as is readily observable, possesses both pure-
song (the verse and chorus plan) and chant (use of interjections and expletives) qualities:

> Poor man Laz'rus, poor as I,
> Don't you see?
> Poor man Laz'rus, poor as I,
> Don't you see?
> When he died he found a home on high,
> He had a home in dat rock,
> Don't you see?

Alluding to the deeper, more psychological meaning of
these songs, Professor Work says, "There are closer rela-

tions between the soul and musical expressions than have
been satisfactorily explained. These relations can be felt,
but any accurate description seems beyond the grasp of
man's mind." Nevertheless, this important study goes on
to classify and number these songs of joy, sorrow, sorrow
with note of joy, faith, hope, love, determination, adora-
tion, patience, courage and humility. Like most scholars of
the spirituals, this one points out that there is no hate, resentment or vindictiveness in them. However, Howard
Thurman, theologian and philosopher, has excavated un-
derpinnings of turbulence. In *The Negro Spiritual*, Thurman tells us death was immediate and ever present for the
slave. In such an atmosphere of anxiety and fear, the slave
developed a rather stoic attitude, in which he saw death as
inescapable and as, possibly, the only remaining vehicle
for mediation with the plantation lords. The slave could
take his own life if he wanted to—as he did many times in
preference to slavery or separation from family and/or
loved ones. Thurman's brilliant analysis *must* be read by
any serious student of black thought and culture.

Johnson (who also classified the songs)[6] said a hierarchy
of poets for the spirituals included the song maker
(writer) and the song leader. The leader had to remember
leading lines, pitch tunes true and possess a powerful
voice. Johnson, who (like Professor Work) believes the
earliest black American songs were built on the common
African form, says the spirituals were written by individuals, and set to the moods of groups. Like the blues, their
secular and structural cousins, the spirituals incorporated
antiphony, or call-and-response, which allowed for audience (congregation) participation (either by alternating
or intermingling with the leader):

Leader: Oh, de Ribber of Jordan is deep and
                       wide,
Congregation: One mo' ribber to cross.
Leader: I don't know how to get on de other
                       side,
Congregation: One mo' ribber to cross.

---

[6] Johnson, Brown, Kerlin, and Thurman also give consideration to the
"poetic" content of the spirituals. Johnson and Work discuss the pres-
ervation and promotion of these songs through archival holdings, choir
concert tours and the attention paid to them by composers.

Heavily influenced by Christian imagery and mythology, the creators of the spirituals often chose the most militant of biblical personalities as their heroes. This aspect of these "poems" opens up an entire area of questions and research for the student seeking to compare and contrast biblical themes and characters to the spirituals. Certainly there is need to examine the English hymns and Psalms in the framework of such a study. The spirituals should also be compared and contrasted to the black literary verse of the period during which they were forged—especially the work of Jupiter Hammon, Phillis Wheatley, and George Moses Horton.

FOLK SECULARS

Don wid massa's hollerin';
Don wid massa's hollerin';
Don wid massa's hollerin'
Roll Jordan roll.

We observed that there is a thin line between black religious and secular worlds. This is true for many reasons—some of them stemming from the African tradition of interrelating all aspects of life. As John M'Biti (*African Religions and Philosophies*), Gabriel Bannerman-Richter (Professor at Cal. State U., Sacramento), and others point out, the African takes his religion (his beliefs) with him wherever he goes. They also remind us that most African languages have no words for religion or art. The two are inseparable. Again the ways of African peoples (see Mphahlele's *Whirlwind*) are expressed in "integrated" terms. True, in black America there is some tension between secular and religious communities—but so often (and most Blacks understand this well though they do not always admit it) they are the same: wearing different hats on different occasions. Study, again, the case of a Rev. Jesse Jackson or a Rev. Ike or a Rev. Adam Clayton Powell or a Rev. Martin Luther King!

We have also observed that many motifs and components of black expression are interchangeable. That is, songs and speeches designed for church or other religious activity are often recut (modified) for a secular-social affair. There are numerous examples of this practice. During the civil rights era, we would sing:

"I woke up this mornin' with my mind stayed on *freedom*,"

though we were fully aware that church folk were used to singing it this way:

"I woke up this mornin' with my mind stayed on Jesus. . . ."

Many of recording artist-composer Curtis Mayfield's (and the Impressions') songs rely strongly on the material of songs sung in black churches. Even Mayfield's more recent tunes (see "If There's a Hell Below") carry the black church flavor—with their admonishments, threats of societal destruction, and pleas for love (also such Marvin Gaye pieces as "Save the Children"). Some works by the Temptations ("Runaway Child Running Wild") reflect the historical theme of "searching" found in black religious songs. This same group's "Poppa Was a Rolling Stone" describes Poppa "stealing in the name of the Lord." B. B. King's "Woke Up This Mornin'" is a blues treatment of the idea expressed above in the spiritual "I Woke Up This Mornin'." When we heard the old Supremes singing "Stop in the Name of Love," we wanted to replace "love" with "God." Often the songs contain interchangeable words such as "Lord" and "Mother," "Baby" and "God," "Sweet thing" and "Sweet Jesus," "Captain" and "Maker," and "God" and "Man." The reasons for such usages, as we have stated, are deeply enmeshed in the mythos of Blacks. Richard Wright's "Bright and Morning Star" (in the Bible, a metaphor for Jesus) becomes the son of old Aunt Sue in the short story by that name. The hero of John A. Williams' novel *The Man Who Cried I Am* says, "Thank you, man" to God after a sex act. When we hear a tune like War's "Slipping into Darkness" ("When I heard my mother say"), we must understand the historical significance and function of social (therapeutic) art—just as we must understand the function of the motherlike voice that admonishes Isaac Hayes to "shet yo mouf" in the song "Shaft." When conservative black Christians complained of Duke Ellington's use of religious themes in jazz, he replied, "I'm just an ecumenical cat"—meaning he avoided fine distinctions in where or to whom he played. The church has been the training ground (academy, if you will; see Frazier's *The Negro Church in America*) for the most successful of black popular singers and musicians as well as for orators, race leaders and community businessmen.

Against the previous discussion we can view the folk seculars in their right perspective as a vital part of the rich storehouse of black folklore. Through songs, aphorisms (my own grandmother: "You don't believe fat meat's greasy!" and "If you ain't gon' do nothing, get off the pot!"), fables (see Aesop), jokes (minstrelsy and the black comedy tradition), blues and other enduring forms, Blacks capture severe hardships and tribulations, folk wisdom, joys and tragedies, and longings and hopes during and after slavery. The seculars, more so than the spirituals, give important clues to the inner workings of the common black mind. And a closer look at the total folk tradition will reveal the structure and principles of folk psychology. It is, after all, these folk materials that researchers will have to investigate if they are serious about delineating the feelings, emotions and thought patterns of Blacks. The seculars are surer indexes to the workings of the folk mind, because they are not as limited as the spirituals. Though most Blacks in the United States are aware of and have heard spirituals, an even larger number have had sustained exposure (directly or indirectly) to the secular vocalizations and gestures of black culture. Contemporary black popular music and culture continue to be informed by street and home utterances. An exciting reciprocity allows entertainers to borrow freely from what they hear while the folks "run and tell that" once it's recorded. Some examples of songs, titles and other epithets borrowed directly from the people are: James Brown's "Brand New Bag," "Licking Stick" (see "honey stick" in McKay's story "Truant"), "Give It Up or Turn It Loose," "The Payback" and "It's Hell"; Marvin Gaye's "What's Going On" and "Let's Get It On"; Curtis Mayfield's "Superfly"; the Jackson Five's "Get It Together or Leave It Alone"; Flip Wilson's "What You See Is What You Get" (and the Dramatics' tune by the same name); Aretha Franklin's "Respect" and "Run and Tell That"; and Jean Knight's "Mr. Big Stuff"—to name just a few.

As with the spirituals, whites (primarily abolitionists)

were among the first to collect seculars of whatever type. William Wells Brown, the first published black novelist and playwright, collected "anti-slavery" songs. Thomas Wentworth Higginson, writer and abolitionist who led a black regiment in the Civil War, collected songs he heard among his men around campfires and during marches. Though primarily concerned with religious songs, he also described some of the properties of general black song delivery. One of the most important collections of these seculars was put together by Thomas W. Talley of Fisk University, a colleague of John Work. Talley did pioneering work in the identification and classification of *Negro Folk Rhymes*. The Fisk scholar collected well over three hundred examples. Other important examples and discussions of the artistic products of secular folk life can be found in the works of Hughes and Bontempts, Brewer, Spalding, Dodson, Chapman, Brown (*Negro Poetry*), Abrahams (*Deep Down in the Jungle*), and Bell (*The Folk Roots of Contemporary Afro-American Poetry*). Bell's work is somewhat vague in perspective as a result of an imposed ("foreign") model.

Also valuable to an examination of the seculars are regional works (such as Abrahams') including *Drums and Shadows* (Georgia and South Carolina), Goldstein's *Black Life and Culture in the United States*, Lorenzo Dow Turner's work in the Gullah culture, Dorson's *Negro Folktales in Michigan*, and others (see bibliography). By far the most faithful representation of secular or religious folk materials in the written poetry is in the work of Sterling Brown, (see his *Southern Road*, especially Johnson's introduction, and his critical comments in *Negro Poetry*). Brown takes exception to Johnson's comment that dialect poetry has only two stops—"humor and pathos"—and implies that black poets up until his time had been remiss (or lazy) in not developing broader uses and deepening the meaning of black life through the use of folk materials.

The tradition of "tall" taletelling is, of course, submerged in the American mythos. So the black narrator found a flexible atmosphere into which he could introduce his own manner of storytelling and his own tradition of song. As he had done in the spirituals, he gained a re-

THE BLACK AND UNKNOWN BARDS

sourcefulness in the use of language, acquired instruments
to accompany the song or story, and developed an ability to
seize upon a good or amenable context in which to tell or
sing his story; he also made use of themes and ideas from
the vast ethnic potpourri of America. The seculars grew
up side by side with the spirituals. The spirituals emerged
from the attempt of the slave to web together his
disparate (yet mutual) wounds. Spirituals represent the
slave's perseverance and (in many instances) his hope and
faith in mankind. The seculars, also developing in the
shadows of the "big house," reflect the social life of the
black American on the plantation and later. In songs and
ditties, the black American couched his longings and bit-
ternesses, but voiced his hopes and cynicisms through the
oblique, elliptical and encoded words and seemingly unin-
telligible phonetic symbols.

These African forms (see *Rappin' and Stylin' Out*,
Kochman) have continued up to the present. Few black
youngsters are able to sidestep the rigorous (and sometimes painful) verbal dexterity demanded by playmates
during oral sparring matches that inevitably take place.
The forms of such behavior were intact during slavery—
when a slave might be discussing a master's "moma" or
"old lady" during a rather harmless "rap" (rhapsody? rap-
port?) with his fellow field workers. Frederick Douglass reports in his autobiographical *Narrative* that slave overseers
thought slaves sang because they were happy. We know
that this was not the case (see Du Bois's *Souls of Black
Folk*) and that such refrains as "stealing away" implied a
lot more than wanting to reach the arms of white Jesus on
the cross. Henry Dumas chronicles similar codes in his stories and poems. And Mel Watkins (*Amistad 2*) discussed
an updated version of at least part of this phenomenon in
his article on folk singer-hero James Brown. Though he is
discussing a *secular* character, Watkins' revelations are
similar to Thurman's: that in the absurd context of being
owned by someone else, it is not life or death that looms
so importantly. One lives, Ellison suggests (*Invisible
Man*), the day-to-day absurdity in a sort of comic-tragic
vise. Watkins says:

James Brown's initial acceptance by a black audience is
fixed in this crucial factor. From the moment he slides

onto the stage, whether unconsciously or intentionally, his gestures, his facial expressions and even the sequential arrangement of his materials are external affirmations of a shared acceptance of the absurd or, more ingeniously, of jiving. The impeccably tailored suits, which he brandishes at the outset, become meaningless accoutrements as his act progresses and, sweating and straining, he gets down, literally down on the floor, to wring the last drop of emotion from a song.

Watkins is incorrect about the dress becoming "meaningless" to a black audience, but his general thesis is on target. Elsewhere Watkins, firmly understanding the importance of verbal agility among Blacks, says, "It is common to hear black women discussing a man's 'rap' or 'program' on the same level that they discuss his bank account." Blacks generally withhold their judgment on (or acceptance) of a speaker or entertainer until he exhibits, in his dress-gesture-rap, that he understands the wellspring that produced the "black and unknown bards."

Returning briefly to our historical assessment, we can now see how the folk strain in black written art evolved. From this "song" recorded in the 1850s by Douglass,

Dey gib us de liquor,
And say dat's good enough for nigger,

to the fear of "de Cunjah Man" captured in "Gullah" by Campbell in the latter part of the 1900s,

De Cunjah man, de Cunjah man,
O chillen run, de Cunjah man!

the deceptively "simple" employment of folk expressions has prevailed as an important antidote for the social maladies inherited by Blacks in the Western Hemisphere. "De Cunjah Man" is, of course, equivalent to the "things that go bumping in the night" in Ireland—and thus has ties to general folk superstitions and mythology. But there was also the "buggah-man" (Dunbar's "Little Brown Baby"), the "rag man," "peg-leg," "raw-head and bloody bones" and (in the West Indies) the "obeah man." Most of these supernatural characters are throwbacks to various African religious and ritual practices. Of the new generation of poets, Ishmael Reed (*catechism of a neoamerican hoodoo church*) and Henry Dumas are the innovators in the use of supernatural themes, characters and vocabulary.

The theme of the 2nd Annual John Henry Memorial Authentic Blues and Gospel Jubilee (Cliff Top, West Virginia, 1974) was "Tryin' to Get Home." How steadfastly the folk tradition runs like a vein through black history! In the seculars (and the spirituals) we repeatedly hear something similar to the last stanza of "Rainbow Roun Mah Shoulder":

I'm gonna break right, break right pas that shooter,
I'm goin home, Lawd, I'm goin home.

Again, the use of the word "Lawd" in a "secular" song further bears out the communal *integration* of the folk expression. Blacks regularly interject or exclaim "Lord" and "Lawd" in everyday discussions.

It is next to impossible to list all (or each type) of the seculars. We have mentioned Professor Talley's pioneering efforts at classifying them. But many obstacles lay in the way of recorders of secular folk life. One problem was that of censureship of language. Such censuring marked all types of black creativity, from the slave narratives to religious songs. Hence the more "protesting" aspects of the works were deleted, as were "offensive words." Anyone who has heard "authentic" black folk songs knows that they reflect the convergence of madness, absurdity and hope in the black body. Subsequently what are known as "curse" or "obscene" words are sprinkled throughout much of the "secular" lore. Brown discusses the "realism" in the folk rhymes along with an attempt to classify at least some of them ("fiddle-songs," "corn-songs," "jig-tunes," "upstart crows"): Ballads: Negro Heroes, John Henry (folkified in song), Work Songs, The Blues, Irony and Protest.

Irony and protest, of course, run through black folk and literary poetry from the earliest days (Whitfield, Harper, anti-slavery songs) to the most recent times (Josh White, Leon Thomas, Don L. Lee, Jon Eckels, Johnie Scott). Some observers have pointed to the silliness of many researchers who, white as ever, appeared in person to ask black folk-song writers and singers if they endorsed "protest," then went away satisfied with a "no" answer. Given the nature and history of race relations, one can understand the reluctance on the part of Blacks to tell whites the truth about "anything" let alone about such a sensitive area as "protest." Yet in the dog-eat-dog world of survival, the folk person knows that

"If he dies, I'll eat his co'n;
    An' if he lives, I'll ride 'im on."

In summary we can say that unlike other ethnic immigrant groups (the Afro-American was not a *willing* immigrant!), the black American did not simply transplant his stories—keeping them in their exact same form. He found American or European language counterparts for his themes and vocabularies. But his phonology, style and spirit were informed by the African tradition. The student of black folk poetry will want to compare and contrast the seculars to other ethnic stories and songs. Boasting or "lying," for example, is one ingredient of the "tall" tale. How does the black song or story (e.g., "Shine," "Signifying Monkey," "Dolemite," "Frankie and Johnnie," etc.) fit this motif? How does it conceal deeper meanings on the issues of slavery, inhuman work conditions, or contradictions in Christianity? What are the similarities between the seculars and the spirituals? Between the seculars and the literary poetry? These and other questions (on black heroes, cultural motifs, blues themes, language and endurance) will lead one through exciting corridors of black folk creativity and thought.

FOLK ANTHOLOGY SECTION (SAMPLE)

SPIRITUALS

GO DOWN, MOSES

Go down, Moses,
Way down in Egyptland;
Tell old Pharaoh
To let my people go.

When Israel was in Egyptland,
Let my people go.
Oppressed so hard they could not stand,
Let my people go.

Go down, Moses,
Way down in Egyptland;
Tell old Pharaoh,
"Let my people go."

"Thus saith the Lord," bold Moses said,
"Let my people go:
If not I'll smite your first-born dead,
Let my people go."

"No more shall they in bondage toil,
    Let my people go;
Let them come out with Egypt's spoil,
    Let my people go."

The Lord told Moses what to do,
    Let my people go;
To lead the children of Israel through,
    Let my people go.

Go down, Moses,
    Way down in Egyptland;
Tell old Pharaoh,
    "Let my people go!"

SLAVERY CHAIN

Slavery chain done broke at last, broke at last,
  broke at last,
Slavery chain done broke at last,
Going to praise God till I die.

Way down in-a dat valley,
Praying on my knees;
Told God about my troubles,
And to help me ef-a He please.

I did tell him how I suffer,
In de dungeon and de chain,
And de days I went with head bowed down,
And my broken flesh and pain.

Slavery chain done broke at last, broke at last,
  broke at last,
Slavery chain done broke at last,
Going to praise God till I die.

I did know my Jesus heard me,
'Cause de spirit spoke to me,
And said, "Rise, my child, your chillun
And you too shall be free.

"I done 'p'int one mighty captain
For to marshal all my hosts,
And to bring my bleeding ones to me,
And not one shall be lost."

Slavery chain done broke at last, broke at last,
  broke at last,
Slavery chain done broke at last,
Going to praise God till I die.

NO MORE AUCTION BLOCK

No more auction block for me,
No more, no more,
No more auction block for me,
Many thousand gone.

No more peck of corn for me,
No more, no more,
No more peck of corn for me,
Many thousand gone.

No more pint of salt for me,
No more, no more,
No more pint of salt for me,
Many thousand gone.

No more driver's lash for me,
No more, no more,
No more driver's lash for me,
Many thousand gone.

SHOUT ALONG, CHILLEN

Shout along, chillen!
Shout along, chillen!

Hear the dying Lamb:
Oh! take your nets and follow me
For I died for you upon the tree!
    Shout along, chillen!
    Shout along, chillen!
        Hear the dying Lamb!

SWING LOW, SWEET CHARIOT

Swing low, sweet chariot,
Coming for to carry me home,
Swing low, sweet chariot,
Coming for to carry me home.

I looked over Jordan and what did I see
Coming for to carry me home,
A band of angels, coming after me,
Coming for to carry me home.

If you get there before I do,
Coming for to carry me home,
Tell all my friends I'm coming too,
Coming for to carry me home.

Swing low, sweet chariot,
Coming for to carry me home,
Swing low, sweet chariot,
Coming for to carry me home.

STEAL AWAY

Steal away, steal away, steal away to Jesus,
Steal away, steal away home,
I ain't got long to stay here.

My Lord, He calls me,
He calls me by the thunder,
The trumpet sounds within-a my soul,
I ain't got long to stay here.

Steal away, steal away, steal away to Jesus,
Steal away, steal away home,
I ain't got long to stay here.

Green trees a-bending,
Po' sinner stands a-trembling

The trumpet sounds within-a my soul,
I ain't got long to stay here.

DEEP RIVER

Deep river, my home is over Jordan,
Deep river, Lord; I want to cross over into camp
    ground.
O children, O, don't you want to go to that gospel
    feast,
That promised land, that land, where all is peace?

Deep river, my home is over Jordan,
Deep river, Lord; I want to cross over into camp
    ground.

FOLK SECULARS

HE IS MY HORSE

One day as I wus a-ridin' by,
Said dey: "Ole man, yo' hoss will die."
    "If he dies, he is my loss;
    And if he lives, he is my hoss."

Nex' day w'en I come a'ridin' by,
Dey said: "Ole man, yo' hoss may die."
    "If he dies, I'll tan 'is skin;
    An' if he lives, I'll ride 'im ag'in."

Den ag'in w'en I come a-ridin' by,
Said dey: "Ole man, yo' hoss mought die."
    "If he dies, I'll eat his co'n;
    An' if he lives, I'll ride 'im on."

DID YOU FEED MY COW?

"Did yer feed my cow?" "Yes, Mam!"
"Will yer tell me how?" "Yes, Mam!"
"Oh, w'at did yer give 'er?" "Cawn an hay."
"Oh w'at did yer give 'er?" "Cawn an hay."

"Did yer milk 'er good?" "Yes, Mam!"
"Did yer do lak yer should?" "Yes, Mam!"

"Oh, how did yer milk 'er?" "Swish! Swish!
    Swish!"

"Did dat cow git sick?" "Yes, Mam!"
"Wus she kivered wid tick?" "Yes, Mam!"
"Oh, how wus she sick?" "All bloated up."
"Oh, how wus she sick?" "All bloated up."

SONG
(From FREDERICK DOUGLASS, *My Bondage and My Freedom*, 1853)

We raise de wheat,
Dey gib us de corn:
We bake de bread,
Dey gib us de crust;
We sif de meal,
Dey gib us de huss;
We peel de meat,
Dey gib us de skin;
And dat's de way
Dey take us in;
We skim de pot,
Dey gib us de liquor,
And say dat's good enough for nigger.

MANY A THOUSAND DIE

No more driver call for me,
    No more driver call;
No more driver call for me,
    Many a thousand die!
No more peck of corn for me,
    No more peck of corn;
No more peck of corn for me,
    Many a thousand die!
No more hundred lash for me,
    No more hundred lash;
No more hundred lash for me,
    Many a thousand die!

FREEDOM

Abe Lincoln freed the nigger,
Wid da gun and wid da trigger,

An I ain't gonna git whipped no mo.
Ah got mah ticket
Out of dis heah thicket,
An I'm headin for da golden sho.

O freedom, O freedom,
O freedom after a while,
And before I'd be a slave, I'd be buried in my grave,
And go home to my Lord and be free.

There'll be no more moaning, no more moaning,
No more moaning after a while,
And before I'd be a slave, I'd be buried in my grave,
And go home to my Lord and be free.

No more weeping, no more crying,
No more weeping after a while,
And before I'd be a slave, I'd be buried in my grave,
And go home to my Lord and be free.

There'll be no more kneeling, no more bowing,
No more kneeling after a while,
And before I'd be a slave, I'd be buried in my grave,
And go home to my Lord and be free.

There'll be shouting, there'll be shouting,
There'll be shouting after a while,
And before I'd be a slave, I'd be buried in my grave,
And go home to my Lord and be free.

RAINBOW ROUN MAH SHOULDER

Evahwhuh I, whuh I look dis mawnin,
Looks lak rain, looks lak rain.

I gotta rainbow, tied all roun mah shoulder,
Ain gonna rain, ain gonna rain.

I don walk till, walk till mah feets gone to rollin,
Jes lak a wheel, jes lak a sheel.

Evah mailday, I gets a letter,
"My son come home, my son come home."

Dat ol letter read about dyin,
Mah tears run down, mah tears run down.

I'm gonna break right, break right pas dat shooter,
I'm goin home, Lawd, I'm goin home.

JOHN HENRY HAMMER SONG

Dis is de hammer
Killt John Henry,
Twon't kill me, baby,
Twon't kill me.

Take dis hammer,
Carry it to de captain
Tell him I'm gone, baby,
Tell him I'm gone.

Ef he axe you,
Was I running
Tell him how fast, baby,
Tell him how fast.

Ef he axe you
Any mo' questions,
Tell him you don't know, baby,
You don't know.

Every mail day,
Gits a letter,
"Son, come home, baby,
Son come home."

Been all night long
Backing up timber,
Want to go home, baby,
Want to go home.

Jes' wait till I make
Dese few days I started
I'm going home, baby,
I'm going home.

Everywhere I
Look dis morning
Look lak rain, baby,
Look lak rain.

I got a rainbow
Tied 'round my shoulder,
Ain't gonna rain, baby,
Ain't gonna rain.

Dis ole hammer
Ring lak silver,
Shine like gold.

Take dis hammer
Throw it in de river,
It'll ring right on, baby,
Ring right on.

Captain, did you hear
All yo' men gonna leave you,
Next pay day, baby,
Next pay day?

A BIG FAT MAMA

I'm a big fat mama, got the meat shaking on mah
    bones,
I'm a big fat mama, got the meat shaking on mah
    bones,
And every time I shakes, some skinny girl loses huh
    home.

HOW LONG BLUES

How long, how long, has that evening train bin gone?
How long, how long, baby, how long?

Had a gal lived up on the hill
If she's there, she loves me still
Baby, how long, how long, how long?

Standin at the station, watch my baby go
Feel disgusted, blue, mean an low
How long, how long, baby, how long?

CHAPTER III

AFRICAN VOICE IN ECLIPSE(?): IMITATION AND AGITATION (1746–1865)

> Slaves, though we be enroll'd
> Minds are never to be sold
> —from DAVID RUGGLES' *Appeals*, 1835

OVERVIEW

As we embark on a survey of the chronological development of black written poetry, it is important to remember that any study of such literature concerns that which is "written" and "available." The fact that one writer has made more works accessible to the public than another writer does not make him/her the "greater." In every era, quiet and important writers have been passed over in favor of literature that is more "timely," "flamboyant" and "relevant." So, while this text certainly is not an anthology, representative samplings of poetry are used to reinforce comments on styles, themes, subjects, language and other aspects. These samplings, we feel, are particularly important to an understanding of this early poetry. The poems included, it is hoped, will allow the reader and teacher immediate access to comparisons, contrasts and tentative analyses. There also is no overriding effort to explain the works in a poem-by-poem breakdown. However, each chapter will build on a historical "running" analysis of several poems with emphasis on how the poems can be read silently and aloud. This particular period in black poetry and thought is one of the least understood, but close study shows that subsequent developments owe very much to it.

LITERARY AND SOCIAL LANDSCAPE

Blacks have been in the Western Hemisphere almost as long as whites. After 1501, most of the Spanish expeditions to the New World included black explorers. So, by

the time the twenty slaves-to-be were brought on a Dutch
vessel to Jamestown in 1619, the presence of blacks had
been felt for at least a hundred years (see Bennett,
Franklin).

Crucial to an understanding of early black poetry are
the circumstances surrounding slavery and the political
and religious moods of both England and colonial and revolutionary America. British America did not follow the
Greco-Roman tradition of the well-informed slave. It was
quite unlikely, then, that a "revolutionary" black poet
would emerge from a social and literary landscape so
charged with self-righteousness and neoclassicism (or from
the romanticism of the 1800s). Lucy Terry's "Bars Fight"
(written in 1746 and published in 1895) could hardly be
called "protest"; neither could the work of Phillis
Wheatley, considered the finest black talent of the colonial era, caught between contrivances of the Enlight-
enment and the approaching grip of the romantics. The
neoclassical tradition that reached its height in the poetry
of England's Alexander Pope had already begun to die out
with the death of Pope, in 1744. All over colonial
America, however, white poets were imitating the stiff-
collared conventionality of that period. The moral issues
considered by most poets (black and white)—universal
brotherhood of man, quest for reason and order, the Jeffer-
sonian ideals of freedom, liberty and representative
government—were removed from the everyday brutality of
slavery. Some of the most liberal men of the day (Jefferson, Washington, Hume) implicitly justified slavery by
suggesting that Blacks were in some ways inferior. Despite
Jefferson's pontifications on humanitarianism, he was unable to reconcile the disparity between his public stands
and his failure to manumit his own slaves. Although
Jefferson carried on a written correspondence with black
astronomer and mathematician Benjamin Banneker, he
considered Phillis Wheatley's poetry "beneath criticism."

On the general American scene, the Revolution behind,
a national literature had begun to emerge. Fascinated with
American employment of new technology (Franklin's
lightning experiments, printing presses, etc.) and the prospects of unexplored regions of the New World, writers
started recording travels and observing the mixture of

races and religions. Although religious fervor was still high, political problems dominated. Between 1790 and 1832 the new American Government was being consolidated, and the writings of such men as William Bradford, John Winthrop, Cotton Mather, Thomas Shephard, Roger Williams, Edward Taylor, and Jonathan Edwards were succeeded by the embryonic nationalistic works of Franklin, Jefferson, William Cullen Bryant, Charles Brockden Brown, Washington Irving, William Gilmore Simms, and James Fenimore Cooper. Irving, Cooper, and Bryant were to become the early writers most taught to American school children.

Often called the "New England Renaissance," the early decades of the nineteenth century saw increasing tension between New England puritanism and southern aristocracy over the question of slavery. Debates over slavery continued up to the beginning of the Civil War. The early part of the century also saw the birth of many of white America's greatest writers, along with the development of romanticism and rugged individualism. Mystified by the noble savage (Indians and sometimes Blacks) and challenged by the "new frontier," Americans began to romanticize their situation and especially that of explorers, who became the first original folk heroes. White writers who dominated the period from 1826 to 1865 included Edgar Allan Poe (poet and short-story writer, credited with creating the first detective in American fiction), Nathaniel Hawthorne (considered the first great American novelist —*The Scarlet Letter*), John Greenleaf Whittier, Henry Wadsworth Longfellow, James Russell Lowell, Oliver Wendell Homes, Harriet Beecher Stowe (one of the first white American novelists to feature a black protagonist in fiction—*Uncle Tom's Cabin*), Ralph Waldo Emerson, Henry David Thoreau, Herman Melville (considered to have written one of the handful of "great" American novels—*Moby Dick*), Walt Whitman (termed the "greatest" American poet—*Leaves of Grass*). Other writers, primarily political activists (and some abolitionists), included John C. Calhoun, William Lloyd Garrison, and Abraham Lincoln. Using their own and black material, a number of white composers immortalized the era in songs—many of them nationalistic. It was during this period that Francis Scott Key wrote "The Star Spangled Banner." And Stephen Foster has since been accused of merely setting to music the songs that were sung by slaves.

There was no general encouragement for Blacks to learn to read, but many slaveowners indulged their chattels in writing exercises as personal pastimes and hobbies. So, many of the early black poets grew up in relative security. To be totally free, David Walker observed in his *Appeal* (1829), was to be economically insecure, socially ostracized and psychologically oppressed. Consequently, those slaves privileged to read and write invariably took European literary models. Poets, of course, were not the only ones writing. In addition to abolitionists-essayists, such as Walker and Frederick Douglass, this period of black literary activity was highlighted by exciting slave narratives. The most popular of these, and one of the first recorded, was *The Interesting Narrative of the Life of Olaudah Equiano, or Gustavus Vassa, the African* (1789). Arna Bontemps includes it in his *Great Slave Narratives* (1969). Vassa, who also included some notable verses in his narrative, constructed a story pattern that was to become familiar to readers in early America: that of the escaped, freed or runaway slave who reported his or her hardships and struggles. Vassa describes his life in Africa up until the time of his kidnaping. With vivid memory and detail, he establishes the original bases for what we have come to call the "African continuum" in America. It is not just mere coincidence that this statement (about his own homeland) from 1789 fits most parts of black America of today.

> We are almost a nation of dancers, musicians, and poets. Thus every great event . . . is celebrated in public dances which are accompanied with songs and music suited to the occasions.

Vassa's debut into this literary genre was followed by hundreds of other narratives, many of them fakes. Dorothy Porter, in *Early Negro Writing: 1760–1837* (1971), has discussed the problem of determining authenticity of the narratives. Mrs. Porter is librarian emeritus of the Moorland Foundation at Howard University—which houses an outstanding collection on the black past. Included in her book are constitutions and laws of beneficial societies; speeches before mutual aid and educational societies; the report of the earliest annual convention for the improvement of free people of color; arguments for and against colonization; printed letters, sermons, petitions, orations, lectures, essays, religious and moral treatises, and such creative manifestations as poems, prose narratives, and short essays. Mrs. Porter thus sums up the intellectual and literary output of the first Africans in America. The word "African" was used generously by most writers and speakers of the era. When "African" was not employed, it was replaced by synonyms such as "Coloured," "Black," and "Ethiopian Princess." Placed against the sometimes sophomoric and heretical accusations of some of today's black critics, these early displays of pride in the African heritage make one want to send the many uninformed "experts" back to school!

In addition to the plethora of pamphlets, broadsides, books and news organs that emerged from black individuals and institutions during the period up to the end of the Civil War, there was also much political-social consciousness-raising through oration. In the early years, great religious and political leaders such as Richard Allen, Peter Williams, Absalom Jones, Prince Hall (founder of black Masonry), Paul Cuffee, and Daniel Coker, took up projects of "mutual aid" for Africans. Their work set the stage for missionary, abolitionist, and self-help programs undertaken later by such people as Jarena Lee, Frederick Douglass, R. Martin Delaney, Sojourner Truth, and Alexander Crummell.

The intellectual, religious, and moral work of Blacks in the North was paralleled by the development of folk materials (the songs and stories) of Blacks on southern plantations. In general, few states, North or South, allowed educational or vocational opportunities for Blacks. Thus the energies of early black writers and intellectuals were committed to various "African" societies and free schools, and the promotion of literacy and self-betterment among newly freed slaves.

The Reverend Allen, popular religious crusader and founder of the Bethel African Methodist Episcopal

Church, seems to have been referring to the same black "sensibility" described by Vassa when he said (in 1793) that he

> was confident that there was no religious sect or denomination that would suit the capacity of the colored people as well as the Methodist. . . . Sure I am that reading sermons will never prove so beneficial to the colored people as spiritual or extempore preaching. . . .

Much evidence exists, then, of Blacks banding together for "mutual" concerns in the early days of America. The horrors of slavery, the psychological pressures of northern "freedom," white reprisals in wake of slave revolts (such as those led by Gabriel Prosser in 1800, Denmark Vesey in 1822, and Nat Turner in 1831), made for a most unsettling atmosphere (see Walker's *Appeal*). Reporting on white America's "need" to vent its fears and hatreds on Blacks, Winthrop Jordan (*White over Black*, 1968) noted that whites initially feared three things: loss of identity, lack of self-control and sexual license. In an effort to escape the "animal within himself the white man debased the Negro, surely, but at the same time he debased himself." And a young Frenchman, Alexis de Tocqueville, visiting America in 1831, said racial prejudice was "stronger in the states that have abolished slavery than in those where it still exists."

Needless to say, creative literature of the "arty" sort (though much of it was being done at the time) was not the number one priority for Blacks. Nevertheless, a literary tradition did develop and flourish in black America. The example of the narratives (including those by Marrant, Douglass and Truth) led to publications by the first black novelist and playwright, William Wells Brown. Brown's novel was *Clotel: or the President's Daughter* (1853), and his play was called *Escape: or a Leap to Freedom* (1857). The second novel by a black American was *The Garies and their Friends* (1857) by Frank J. Webb. Delaney published the third novel, *Black, or the Huts of America*, in 1859. The works by Brown and Webb were both published in England. Brown also worked in the cause of abolition and other social-reform programs. His *Anti-Slavery*

Harp (1848) contained songs and poems whose themes are implied in the book's title. The pattern of the black educator, intellectual or artisan carrying on the dual role of creator and activist characterizes the history of black creativity in America. Yet, many critics, black and white, unaware of the stresses and demands on black artists, do not approach their subjects with an understanding of this fact.

Political journalism (see Dann's *The Black Press*, 1827–90), also was a strong vein in the development of black American writing. Beginning with John Russwurm (the second black college graduate and first black newspaper editor—*Freedom's Journal*, 1827–29), and evolving through Ruggles' *Mirror for Liberty* (first black magazine, 1838), *Douglass' Monthly* (1844), and Douglass' *North Star* (1847), to Hamilton's *Anglo-African Magazine* (1859), the tradition of black journalism and research on the African experience was firmly established. Much of the journalistic writing (like the poetry) took pros or cons on the question of immigration, colonization or the elevation of the black man's plight in America.

During the early and middle years of the nineteenth century, white travelers through the South collected and compiled slave songs—seculars and spirituals. These songs later provided the wellspring for much of the black and white writing themes. On the eve of the Civil War, the Dred Scott decision (a blow to slaves and abolitionists) helped to step up the demands for the abolishment of slavery. Brown's *The Black Man* (1863) was a capsule of one era that closed on the blasts of cannon and another that opened on the sound of jubilant shouts.

THE VOICES ON THE TOTEM

"Mean mean mean to be free"
—ROBERT HAYDEN

Against the foregoing background, the poets of colonial-revolutionary-slavery America appear curious, tearful, exciting, paradoxical, frightening and puzzling. Biblical imagery, classical allusions and themes, hatred of slavery and ambiguous praise for slave masters, recollections of Africa, appeals and condemnations—all become enmeshed in the intricate linguistic and psychological webbing of this early poetry.

In 1770, at seventeen years of age, the privileged slave girl Phillis Wheatley became the first black "exception to the rule" in English and American poetry. And for decades, students of American poetry went about their recitations and research as though nothing or no one of importance happened between her time and Dunbar's. It was not until 1893 that Lucy Terry's "Bars Fight"—the account of a 1746 Indian massacre in Deerfield, Massachusetts—came to public light. And readers had yet another twenty-two years to wait before Oscar Wegelin, in 1915, discovered Jupiter Hammon's "An Evening Thought, Salvation by Christ, with Penitential Cries" (1761) in the New-York Historical Society, thus establishing Hammon as the first published African poet in America.

It was mentioned in Chapter I that many anthologies omit "Bars Fight." This is understandable, since Miss Terry (1730–1821) never wrote, or at least presented, any more literary works. America's "first Negro poet," then, is important primarily for being just that—first. Like Phillis Wheatley, Vassa and other New England slaves, Lucy Terry was kidnaped as a child and brought to New England (Rhode Island). She witnessed the Indian raid reported in her twenty-eight-line doggerel, which shows a flair for storytelling. Hence, despite the poem's "obviously weak literary merit," this black writer performed one of the earliest services of the poet—that of a singer of history—in recording actual names and places in her narrative. Since she was sixteen years old and a servant girl, writing was surely not her primary responsibility. Yet "Bars Fight" achieves some success when seen against the oral tradition in poetry:

> Listen my children and you shall hear
> Of the midnight ride of Paul Revere.

or

> Now, children, I'm going to tell you the story
> about raw-head and bloody-bones!

and

There was an old woman who lived in a shoe
She had so many children she didn't know what to do.

Compare the foregoing lines to

August 'twas, the twenty-fifth,
Seventeen hundred forty-six,
The Indians did in ambush lay,
Some very valient men to slay,
The names of whom I'll not leave out:
Samuel Allen like a hero fout,

and the elemental connections will readily be seen. One
has only to read this poem aloud to get both the effects
and Lucy Terry's apparent intentions. When she wrote
"Bars Fight," she worked for an Ebenezer Wells of
Deerfield, Massachusetts; given freedom ten years later,
she married a free black man, Abijah Prince, by whom she
had six children. Prince later became the owner of considerable land and was one of the founders of Sunderland,
Vermont. William Robinson (*Early Black American
Poets*) lists Lucy Terry with the "orator" poets and rightly
so. Other details about her and the Princes can be obtained from George Sheldon's *A History of Deerfield,
Massachusetts*, 1895. See also Eileen Southern's *The
Music of Black Americans*.

Slave   poet   and   intellectual,   Jupiter   Hammon
(1720?–1800?) provides yet another look into the
capabilities, mind sets and limitations of Africans in colonial America. Hammon is generally not regarded as an
"important" black writer—but is distinguished for being
the first African in America to publish his verses. This he
did in 1761 ("An Evening Thought," composed in December of 1760); and later in 1778 ("An Address to Miss
Phillis Wheatley"); in 1782 ("A Poem for Children");
and in the mid 1780s ("An Evening's Improvement").
In "Address to the Negroes of the State of New York"
(written in 1786 and published in 1806), Hammon
joined a tradition that included such pamphleteers as
Quinn, Walker, Ruggles, and others of the period. Hammon's "Address" sought freedom for younger Blacks,
claiming that "for my own part I do not wish to be free."
This statement appears, on the surface, to be the ultimate

in self-debasement and self-denial; but one has to view it in the context of statements by De Tocqueville, Walker, and others, along with the circumstances of the aging and religious Hammon.

That Hammon himself was deeply religious is reflected in his poetry—as with many black poets, e.g. Hayden, today—and he obviously labored under the influence of Methodism and the Wesleyan revival (see *Early Negro Writing*). In the poem to Phillis Wheatley, he notes that it was through "God's tender mercy" that she was kidnaped from Africa and brought to America as a slave. And Hammon seemed, generally, to reflect the prevailing white attitude toward the "dark" continent: one engulfed in ignorance, barbarism and evil. Obviously not as well read as Phillis Wheatley, Hammon was unable to sustain universal and intellectual levels. Born a slave, he belonged to the influential family of Lloyd's Neck on Long Island and was encouraged by his masters to write and publish poetry. There is not a great deal of information available on the life of Hammon; but it is difficult to understand why an intelligent black man, who lived such a long life, mirrored almost complete ignorance of the horrors of slavery—despite the daily local newspaper and verbal accounts and discussions of the "peculiar institution."

Hammon's literary model was the conventional material of hymns of the period. "An Evening Thought," which Dorothy Porter tells us was probably "chanted during the delivery of a sermon," begins:

Salvation comes by Christ alone,
The only Son of God;
Redemption now to every one,
That love his only word.
Dear Jesus we would fly to thee,
And leave off every Sin,
Thy tender Mercy well agree;
Salvation from our king. . . .

Like Lucy Terry, Hammon was not primarily a poet. And hence, unlike approaching Phillis Wheatley, one should not spend too much time or be too harsh in criticizing (or complaining about) him. The basic structure of the English hymn—which merged with the spiritual as Hammon interprets it—is an alternation of iambic tetrameter and iambic trimeter combined with a rather clumsy *a b a b* rhyme scheme. Compared to other hymns, it is no worse and is better than many. Despite the times, pressures and censures, however, it is difficult to accept Hammon's assurance to the slave:

> In Christian faith thou hast a share,
>   Worth all the gold of Spain.

Hammon's works are critically introduced in Robinson's anthology, in Stanley Ransom's *America's First Negro Poet, the Complete Works of Jupiter Hammon of Long Island* (1970), and in Barksdale and Kinnamon's *Black Writers of America* (1972); critical-biographical attention also appears in Vernon Loggins' *The Negro Author* (1931), J. Saunders Redding's *To Make a Poet Black* (1939), and Benjamin Brawley's *The Negro Genius* (1937).

There has been substantial critical-biographical treatment of Miss Wheatley (1753?–84). By far the most gifted and complex poet until Dunbar, Phillis Wheatley was also privileged as a young child and allowed access to the Boston library of John Wheatley, to whom she was sold after being brought from Senegal when she was six or seven years old. By the time she reached her teens she had learned to speak and write English and had acquired a New England education, which put great emphasis on the Bible and the classics. Her poetry also reflects deep interest in and knowledge of religion; but it is also steeped in classical allusions and conventions of the neoclassical writing school. Critical attention to Miss Wheatley (who, like Dunbar, lived a short life) has run the gamut from enthusiastic to unkind. Benjamin Brawley (*The Negro Genius*) reports that Jefferson viewed her as beneath the dignity of criticism. Yet, other great personalities of the day generously praised and received her work. George Washington, so moved by her poetic tribute ("To His Excellency General Washington"), invited the young poet to visit him at his camp at Cambridge, Massachusetts—an invitation which she later accepted; she was treated like royalty.

Phillis Wheatley's earliest verses were penned during

her adolescence. "On the Death of the Rev. George Whitefield: 1770" reflects the elegiac theme of much of her poetry. Manumitted and sent with other members of the Wheatley family to London in 1772, because of frailness and poor health, she was received like a visiting dignitary in London's literary circles and hailed as the "Sable Muse." The next year (1773), while in London, she became (at twenty years old) the first African, and the second woman from America, to publish a book of poems: *Poems on Various Subjects, Religious and Moral, by Phillis Wheatley, Negro Servant to Mr. Wheatley of Boston.* The volume, the only one she ever published, was an immediate success in both England and America and won her an everlasting place in the history of English poetry in both countries. Upon her return to America, her misfortunes seemed to come in such lightning succession that one wonders how she withstood adversity as long as she did. First, there was the death of Mrs. Wheatley, and then, during the 1770s, the deaths of the remaining Wheatleys. The poet then married a John Peters, who "proved to be both ambitious and irresponsible," for whom she bore three children—all of whom died in infancy. Additionally, the Peters family lived in squalor and poverty, like so many New England Blacks. Under these circumstances, Phillis' health, which had been poor for years, failed her finally in 1784, when she was about thirty. Commenting on the circumstances surrounding her death, Barksdale and Kinnamon (*Black Writers of America*) observe with stomach-curdling accuracy:

> Her early death provides a commentary on the desperate marginality of life among Boston's free Blacks at that time. To Phillis Wheatley, at one time a privileged servant who enjoyed an extremely benign master-servant relationship, freedom's uncertainties and insecurities were overwhelming. Certainly, had she been initially free in Boston, she would probably never have had the time, the opportunity, or the peace of mind to write poetry. For the state of freedom for the Black man in the 1780's—even in godly, liberty-loving Boston—was indeed precarious.

The preceding explanation, coupled again with the observations of Walker, De Tocqueville, and others, make Ham-

mon's statement about preferring not "to be free" somewhat more tolerable though not plausible.

We noted that Phillis Wheatley has been praised as
well as condemned. Some critics denounce her for not
being inventive and original enough, claiming that she
simply followed the conventions and themes associated
with neoclassicism: truth, salvation, mercy, and goodness.
Some resent her so-called "pious sentimentality" and ac-
cuse her of calling on Christ when she should be calling
for the abolishment of slavery. Still others, during the current period, have accused her of not being "black
enough." Considered within the literary landscape of the
times, however, she emerges as a genius—with hardly an
equal among black or white contemporaries. James Weldon Johnson, during a comparison of Miss Wheatley's
"Imagination" to Anne Bradstreet's "Contemplation,"
said, "We do not think the black woman suffers by comparison with the white" (*American Negro Poetry*).

During her lifetime, Phillis Wheatley published some
fifty poems, almost half of them elegies, five or six political and patriotic pieces ("General Washington" and
"Liberty and Peace"), and the remainder consumed by religious, and moral subjects—as she states in her title.
Though she never deals with the question of slavery—and
makes only passing reference to her own predicament—
her work sustains a high level of emotional, linguistic, religious and general poetic force. Since her greatest models
were Pope, Dryden, Milton, and the earlier classical
writers, one must examine these sources to uncover some
keys to her techniques and allusions. But one has only to
read (aloud) the following passage from "Rev. George
Whitefield" to *feel* impact:

"Take him, ye wretched, for your only good,
"Take him, ye starving sinners, for your food.
"Ye thrifty, come to this life-giving stream,
"Ye preachers, take him for your joyful theme;
"Take him, my dear Americans, he said,
"Be your complaints on his kind bosom laid;
"Take him, ye Africans, he longs for you,
"Impartial Savior is his title due;
"Washed in the fountain of redeeming blood,
"You shall be sons and kings, and priests to God."

Certainly these lines contain incremental powers that transcend "convention"; and we should state that some of the
previously harsh criticism of Phillis Wheatley has been
tempered in light of increasing feminism and, especially,
efforts by black women writers, scholars, and intellectuals
to re-evaluate her work, most of which is done in heroic
couplets, the dominating form of the period. These pentameter couplets (which would be popularized in the
twentieth century as "unrhymed iambic pentameter" by
Robert Frost) call for end-line rhymes to appear in twos,
with ten syllables per line. Roger Whitlow (*Black American Literature*) complains that Phillis Wheatley "falls
short in what Pope called the 'correctness' of diction and
meter, that near perfect choice of word and measurement
and weighing of syllable." One could agree, *if* her sole aim
were simply to imitate. But there is a great evidence that
she—like many black poets—was trying to achieve an
audibly *readable* poem without losing the essence of the
couplet. After all, as Stephen Henderson (*Understanding
the New Black Poetry*) has suggested, many black poets
have their ears and thought-rhythms attuned to the spiritual and phonological demands of the audience that loves
"extempore" delivery, even when the written lines are
strict and tight.

Also, in placing "Their colour is a diabolic dye" in quo-
tations ("On Being Brought from Africa to America"),
Phillis Wheatley suggests that others deem her color negative but that she may not. This remains a possibility despite her closing couplet:

Remember, Christians, Negroes, black as Cain,
May be refined, and join the angelic train.

Yet there is firm evidence that she was not insensitive, at
least to her own predicament as a slave, without a fundamental and genealogical identity. In "To the Right
Honourable William, Earl of Dartmouth," she says:

Should you, my lord, while you peruse my song,
Wonder from whence my love of Freedom sprung,
Whence flow these wishes for the common good,
By feeling hearts alone best understood,

I, young in life, by seeming cruel fate
Was snatch'd from Afric's fancy'd happy seat:
What pangs excruciating must molest,
What sorrows labour in my parents' breast?
Steel'd was that soul and by no misery mov'd
That from a father seiz'd his babe belov'd:
Such, such my case. And can I then but pray
Others may never feel tyrannic sway?

The capital "F" in "Freedom," the phrase "cruel fate," the sorrow felt for her parents and the reinforcement of the agony via repetition ("such, such"; see Margaret Walker's lines "How Long!"), place her alongside other black voices that searched for answers to the pall of racial insanity that enshrouded them. Phillis Wheatley also experiments with the hymn form. In "A Farewell to America" and "A Hymn to Humanity," one bounces along with her alternating lines and rhythms.

Perhaps the capstone of the critical "shift" in viewing Phillis Wheatley's work was the Phillis Wheatley Poetry Festival, held in November 1973 at Jackson State College, Mississippi, to commemorate the two hundredth anniversary of the publication of *Poems*. At that festival, writer Luci Horton noted that recently there has been more respect for the "slave girl, who under unspeakable circumstances, was able to write poetry or any literature at all." *Ebony* magazine (March 1974) featured a five-page picture essay on the festival, organized and hosted by Margaret Walker, poet-novelist and director of Jackson State's Institute for the Study of the History, Life and Culture of Black People. According to *Ebony*, "eighteen Black women poets converged" on the black college campus to salute Phillis Wheatley, read their own poems, and discuss poetry and life.

Other poets participating in the festival included: Naomi Long Madgett, Margaret C. Burroughs, Marion Alexander, Margaret Esse Danner, Linda Brown Bragg, Mari Evans, Carole Gregory Clemmons, Lucille Clifton, Sarah Webster Fabio, Nikki Giovanni, Audre Lorde, June Jordan, Gloria C. Oden, Paula Giddings, Sonia Sanchez, Alice Walker, Malaika Ayo Wangara (Joyce Whitsitt

Lawrence), and Carolyn M. Rodgers. The festival was also
the subject of a six-page picture essay by Carole Parks in
Black World (February 1974).

Yet, a most revealing comment appeared shortly after
the festival in M. A. Richmond's *Bid the Vassal Soar: Interpretive Essays on the Life and Poetry of Phillis
Wheatley and George Moses Horton* (1974). Reacting to
the adverse criticism of Phillis Wheatley, Richmond
states:

> These poems are vicarious in theme and imitative in
> style. In the circumstances it hardly could have been
> different. She was permitted to cultivate her intelli-
> gence, to develop her feeling for language and her facil-
> ity in its use, but one thing she was not permitted to
> develop: the sense of her own distinct identity as a
> black poet. And without this there could be no personal
> distinction in style or the choice of themes that make
> for great poetry. The barter of her soul, as it were, was
> no conscious contract. Enclosed by a cloying embrace of
> slavery at a tender age, alternatives did not first intrude,
> and later, when she might have chosen one, she was
> drained of the will and perception to do so.

Richmond has provided what appears to be a balanced answer to the protestations of Redding, Brown, Brawley
("no racial value") and others. It remains to be seen
whether current and future generations of black and white
students will keep Phillis Wheatley a "statue in the park"
or bring her to the table and "examine her blood and
heart" (Clyde Taylor). Critical treatment of this first
black woman of letters has been extensive: Julian Mason's
The Poems of Phillis Wheatley (1966); Barksdale and
Kinnamon's critical introduction; Robert C. Kuncio's
"Some Unpublished Poems of Phillis Wheatley" (*New
England Quarterly*, XLIII, June, 1970, 287–97); Loggins'
The Negro Author (1931); Brawley's *The Negro Genius*;
Redding's *To Make a Poet Black*; Shirley Graham's *The
Story of Phillis Wheatley* (1949); and Jerry Ward and
Charles Rowell's article in *Freedomways* (Summer 1974).

Gustavus Vassa (1745–1801), one of the most interesting of the early writers, was born the seventh and youngest

son of an African chieftain (in Essake, now Eastern
Nigeria). Vassa (African name: Olaudah Equiano) was
first sold to a Virginia plantation owner. His journeys later
took him on several Atlantic voyages and then to the
Mediterranean, where he served in the Seven Years' War.
Vassa held technical jobs on ships as a result of his
adeptness at the English language and his mastery of basic
mathematics. He became a tireless worker for the abolition of slavery and worked, briefly, in behalf of efforts to
colonize poor Blacks of England in Sierra Leone. Vassa is
chiefly known for his *Narrative* (1789), which was a best
seller among abolitionists in England and America. Slave
narratives, we have observed, were a part of a branch of
black writing that gave rise to the more sophisticated autobiographies (that stretch from Douglass through Baldwin
and Cleaver), which in turn laid some of the foundation
for American fiction. Vassa was not the first writer of a
slave narrative, as is popularly thought. Briton Hammon
(no relation to Jupiter) published in London *A Narrative
of the Uncommon Sufferings and Surprising Deliverance
of Briton Hammon, a Negro Man* (1760), and John Marrant published (also in London) *A Narrative of the Lord's
Wonderful Dealings with J. Marrant, a Black* (1785).

Vassa, whom we turn to briefly for his efforts in poetry,
included "Miscellaneous Verses" in his *Narrative*. His
verse is interesting because it helps to establish the portrait of a complex and many-sided man; it also provides
further insight into the workings of the African mind
making contact with white culture and especially Christianity. While in his prose and speech-making Vassa was
firm in his attacks on slavery, he proves in the end to be a
believer in some ultimate force of "deliverance." In the
last line of the last stanza of his "Verses" he reminds us,

"Salvation is by Christ alone!"

which is, of course, reminiscent of Hammon's opening
line:

Salvation comes by Christ alone.

Nevertheless Vassa's poetry is less saturated with biblical
terms than Hammon's. And the former, as verse writer,

has a better control of the language. In the "Verses" he applies a driving iambic tetrameter with an *a a b b* rhyme scheme:

> Those who beheld my downcast mien
> Could not guess at my woes unseen:
> They by appearance could not know
> The troubles I have waded through.
>
> Lust, anger, blasphemy, and pride,
> With legions of such ills beside,
> Troubled my thoughts while doubts and fears
> Clouded and darken'd most my years.

In the first stanza Vassa presages the duality and mental pressures that more skilled writers would describe. Implying that the job of the oppressed Black is to keep his head level and up, Vassa says even those who see him in his sorriest state cannot envision the sufferings he has endured. More than a century later, Dunbar says the same thing in a different way in "We Wear the Mask." And Countee Cullen would state it more than 130 years later in yet a different way. This apparent ability of Blacks to "keep cool" and adapt (see Johnson's *The Autobiography of an Ex-Coloured Man*) under the most trying circumstances has been promoted, nurtured and praised by leaders of the race. Vassa, then, is important as an early writer not only because of his skill, but for the insight and understanding he brings to the social and religious pressures, demands and choices around him. There is a releasing therapy in Vassa's work which acts as only one of numerous conduits for black anguish and outrage when the only options were slavery or death. Vassa's *Narrative* is most accessible in Bontemps's *Great Slave Narratives* (1969). In 1967 Paul Edwards published an edition of the *Narrative* including a comprehensive introduction. Edwards also did a two-volume facsimile reprint of the first edition (1969). See also *Africa Remembered: Narratives by West Africans from the Era of the Slave Trade*, edited by Phillip D. Curtin (1967). Loggins assesses the *Narrative* and Robinson provides a handy biographical-critical introduction. More on Vassa can be found in Marion L. Starkey's *Striving to Make It My Home: The Story of Americans from Africa* (1964) and in Whitlow's *Black American Literature*.

The early and middle years of the nineteenth century witnessed the maturation of black autobiography, political journalism and abolitionist activities. George Moses Horton was thirty-four years old when William Lloyd Garrison founded *The Liberator* (1831), the most influential and famous of the abolitionist newspapers. And by 1830 there were more than fifty black antislavery societies in the United States. Blacks in America had been stirred by slave rebellions both in the United States and in places such as Haiti and Trinidad. Especially inspiring to writers and activists during this period was the 1839 revolt of slaves aboard the Spanish schooner *Amistad*. Led by Joseph Cinque, a Mendi-speaking prince, the fifty slaves killed the captain, set the crew adrift and demanded that the shipowners steer the ship to Africa. Apprehended, the Africans were escorted by a United States brig to New Haven, where they faced murder and other charges. Ex-President John Quincy Adams defended the Africans' right to return to their homeland, and in 1842 they sailed to Sierra Leone. Ironically, neither the international press nor most Blacks knew of the connection between the Cinque of the Symbionese Liberation Army, apparently headquartered in northern California during 1973–74, and the Cinque of the *Amistad* revolt.

In light of the growing consciousness among Blacks, it was to be expected that a George Moses Horton (1797–1883) would appear to inveigh against tyranny and slavery. Born a slave near Chapel Hill, North Carolina, Horton is considered to be the first Black to employ protest themes in a volume of verse. His *Hope of Liberty* (1829) ranged over the whole area of general and personal protest. The poet was first owned by a planter named Horton, who later rented him in the service of a janitor to the University of North Carolina. Horton exploited the academic environment by reading the English classics and composing poems. Often called the first professional black writer, Horton hired his poetic skill out to students, who paid him rather handsomely for composing "personal" poems. His second book of poems, *Poetical Works of George M. Horton, the Colored Bard of North Carolina*, was published in 1845. Horton's hopes that he would gain enough money from the sale of his books to secure his freedom were never realized; and he was not freed until

Union soldiers arrived in 1865, when his last volume,
Naked Genius, was published. Horton's themes are not
devoted exclusively to protest, and he has been criticized,
along with Phillis Wheatley, Hammon, and Vassa, for
writing such lines as those that appear in "On Hearing of
the Intention of a Gentleman to Purchase the Poet's Freedom":

When on life's ocean first I spread my sail,
I then implored a mild auspicious gale;
And from the slippery strand I took my flight,
And sought the peaceful heaven of delight.

Hard was the race to reach the distant goal,
The needle oft was shaken from the pole;
In such distress who could forbear to weep?
Toss'd by the headlong billows of the deep!

Horton goes on to say that "Eternal Providence" saved
him when he was on the "dusky verge of deep despair"
and when "the last beam of hope was almost gone." Yet
Horton writes bitterly of slavery as well as lightly of love
and humorously of life in general. Influences on his poetry
are Byron, Wesleyan hymnal stanzas, and other sources in
books he had read. In the poem from which the stanzas
above were taken he pursues a rather monotonous iambic
tetrameter. But in such poems as "Slavery" (published in
The Liberator, March 29, 1834), he varies the hymn pattern in the way that Phillis Wheatley does in her hymn-
inspired works. The effect is almost ballad-like:

When first my bosom glowed with hope,
    I gazed as from a mountain top
On some delightful plain;
But oh! how transient was the scene—
It fled as though it had not been
    And all my hopes were vain.

Is it because my skin is black,
That thou should'st be so dull and slack,
    And scorn to set me free?
Then let me hasten to the grave,
The only refuge for the slave,
    Who mourns for liberty.

Also effective and sustaining in power is "The Slave's Complaint," which features seven 3-line stanzas with a final, indented, one-word refrain, "Forever," which is followed by either question mark, colon or exclamation mark. Horton handles well some of his love poems, and in "The Lover's Farewell" is able to touch base with that broad and painful understanding of what it means to say goodby:

> I leave my parents here behind,
> And all my friends—to love resigned—
> 'Tis grief to go, but death to stay:
> Farewell—I'm gone with love away!

In this and other pieces Horton makes use of dashes—which allow him to develop suspense and render his statements more dramatic. Because of its various uses, the dash has arrived as an important ingredient of modern and contemporary black poetry. Contrary to many of his learned contemporaries and predecessors, Horton apparently consciously thought of, and worked toward, his freedom. This fact is reflected in both his life's work and his poetry. His own position, coupled with his sanguine delivery of folk wit and emphasis, can be seen in the following stanza from "The Slave":

> Because the brood-sow's left-side pigs were black,
> Whose sable tincture was by nature struck,
> Were you by justice bound to pull them back
> And leave the sandy-colored pigs to suck?

For appraisals and selections of Horton's works see Robinson's anthology, Collier Cobb's *An American Man of Letters—George Moses Horton* (1886), comments by Barksdale and Kinnamon, Whitlow's study, Brawley's *Negro Genius*, Loggins' work, Redding's study, Richard Walser's *The Black Poet* (1967), Brown's assessment, Jean Wagner's *Black Poets of the United States* (1973), Richmond's *Bid the Vassal Soar* (1974), and Joan Sherman's *Invisible Poets: Afro-Americans of the Nineteenth Century* (1974).

Horton, of course, trails and precedes a long line of orators and poets, many of whom we know very little about today. In fact, comparatively speaking, there is a wide dis-

parity between the readily available significant information
on white writers of the period and the lack of vital data on
Blacks. We do know that the early decades of the nineteenth century witnessed a developing Christian and political consciousness among Blacks and that most northern
black writers, intellectuals and educators turned their attention to the educational, physical and emotional needs
of free and enslaved Blacks. Of these and other matters,
Dorothy Porter provides ample proof and discussion in
Early Negro Writing.

Occasional verse was also somewhat of a tradition
among many learned Blacks, as was the practice of writing
hymns, Psalms, and other spiritual songs. One such
recorded item is "Spiritual Song" by Rev. Richard Allen,
probably "chanted or sung during the delivery of a sermon." Reverend Allen employs internal rhyme by repeat-
ing similar sounds in the middle and at the end of lines.
Varying his meter and using an irregular end-line rhyme
scheme, he expresses the religious fervor that consumed
many Blacks of the period:

> Our time is a-flying, our moments
>   a-dying,
> We are led to improve them and quickly
>   appear,
> For the bless'd hour when Jesus in
>   power,
> In glory shall come is now drawing
>   near,
> Me thinks there will be shouting, and
>   I'm not doubting,
> But crying and screaming for mercy
>   in vain:
> Therefore my dear Brother, let's
>   now pray together,
> That your precious soul may be
>   fill'd with flame.

Another such example is a "New Year's Anthem" written
by Michael Fortune and "sung in the African Episcopal
Church of St. Thomas" on January 1, 1808. Fortune's anthem is traditional in its use of materials from Methodist

hymns. He tells the congregation to "Lift up your souls to
God on High,"

> Who, with a tender father's eye
> Looked down on Afric's helpless race!

Robert Y. Sidney composed two anthems "For the National Jubilee of the Abolition of the Slave Trade, January
1st, 1809." "Anthem I" begins:

> DRY your tears, ye sons of Afric,
> God has shown his gracious power;
> He has stopt the horrid traffic,
> That your country's bosom tore.
> See through clouds he smiles benignant,
> See your nation's glory rise;
> Though your foes may frown indignant,
> All their wrath you may despise.

This stanza is followed by a "Chorus," "Solo" and "Recitative." In "Anthem II" an abbreviated form is employed
and Sidney drops the solo and recitative—keeping only
the chorus:

> CHORUS.
> Rejoice that you were born to see,
> This glorious day, your jubilee.

Sidney also wrote a hymn that Mrs. Porter includes along
with hymns by religious leaders Peter Williams, Jr., and
William Hamilton. Both men, using the English forms,
celebrate freedom, call for mutual aid among Blacks and
preach the virtues of the Christian God. Williams praises
the "eloquence / Of Wilberforce" after whom a predominantly black university in Ohio was named. For detailed
information on sources for these and similar writings see
Mrs. Porter's Early Negro Writing: 1760–1873. The
collection includes two very touching examples of writings
("On Slavery" and "On Freedom") by twelve-year-old
boys from the New York African Free School established
in 1786.

On reading into the life and works of Daniel A. Payne
(1811–93), one is immediately struck by his dedication to

the task of upgrading Blacks. Educator, university president, missionary and poet, Payne was born in Charleston,
South Carolina, of free parents. He was orphaned at ten
years, and apprenticed to a carpenter and then to a tailor.
Later trained in classical education at the local Minor's
Moralist Society's school, he taught free black students for
a fee and slaves free of charge at night. Payne's travels
took him to various places (New Orleans, Baltimore, Canada and twice to England), where he helped expand the
programs of the African Methodist Church. Trained in
the Lutheran Seminary in Gettysburg, Pennsylvania, he
was ordained in 1839; after preaching for several years, he
was made an A.M.E. bishop in 1852. In the political and
educational spheres, he helped urge Lincoln (on April 14,
1862) to sign the bill to emancipate slaves in the District
of Columbia, and spearheaded the purchase of Wilberforce University—serving as its president for sixteen years.

Payne devoted most of his life to the cause of free and
enslaved Blacks and to writing poetry and religious history.
His *Pleasures and Other Miscellaneous Poems* was published in Baltimore in 1850. He also wrote books on the
history and mission of the A.M.E. Church. Especially val-
ued for its social and intellectual insight into nineteenth-
century Blacks is Payne's *Recollections of Seventy Years*,
published in Nashville in 1888. As a poet, Payne is erudite
and imitative. Robinson observes that a major problem
with the poetry is "the repetition of end-stopped lines,
and his diction, a hybrid of classical and Biblical
vocabularies, can prove distracting to many readers."
Much of this we can forgive, however, when we understand contemporary poet Henry Dumas's remark that "a
black poet is a preacher." Certainly a preacher—in fact or
as poet—knows very well the meaning of and need for
repetition. Yet Payne never fails to convince us of his
seriousness. So hurt was he in the wake of the 1834 South
Carolina law that, effective in 1835, made black literacy il-
legal, Payne wrote "The Mournful Lute of the Preceptor's
Farewell." We find his embossed concern for students in
these lines:

Ye lads, whom I have taught with sacred zeal,
For your hard fate I pangs of sorrow feel;

Oh, who shall now your rising talents guide,
Where virtues reign and sacred truths preside?

Payne is a handler of the language, observing that "two re-
volving moons shall light the shores" after the dread law
"shut the doors" on education for South Carolina Blacks.
Engulfed in the religious and moral fervor of many black
ministers if the period, the poet and orator reflects age-old
concerns about deceit and mistrust in such pieces as "The
Pleasures." He complains:

Men talk of Love! But few do ever feel
The speechless raptures which its joys reveal.

Men "mistake love," Payne notes,

For grovelling lust, that vile, that filthy dame,
Whose bosom ne'er felt the sacred flame.

For insight into Payne's life and works, one could go to
any one of his "considerable number" of writings. Among
others, they include *The Semi-Centenary and the Ret-
rospection of the African Methodist Episcopal Church*
(Baltimore, 1866) and *The History of the A.M.E.
Church* (Nashville, 1866). See also Josephus R. Coam's
1935 (Philadelphia) biography *Daniel Alexander Payne,
Christian Educator,* Robinson's comments, and Brawley's
Negro Genius.

Unfortunately, too little is known of romantic poet
John Boyd, a Bahamian who is often mistaken for an
Afro-American, especially since his work reflects genuine
gifts and talents. Boyd's poetic images are brilliant, sustained, searing and generally accurate even if they are not
always connected in a way that makes them readily accessible. The only record of Boyd is made available by C. R.
Nesbitt, Esq., deputy secretary and registrar of the Government of the Bahamas. Nesbitt must have recognized
the talent and the promise, and he aided Boyd's poetry
through publication in London in 1834. Boyd, it seems,
was self-taught on New Providence Island, where he
remained all his life. His poem "Vanity of Life" was published in the February 16, 1833, issue of the Boston-based
Liberator. His 1834 volume is entitled *The Vision/ and
other/ Poems,/ in Blank Verse/ by John Boyd/ a man of*

Colour/. Practically unedited, the manuscript is what Robinson calls a "publishing scramble." Like most of the poets of the period, Boyd's work owes debt to Milton, the Bible and classical influences. "The Vision/ a Poem in Blank Verse" is immediately reminiscent of Milton's *Paradise Lost*. Boyd skirts a rhyme scheme but employs a fairly regular iambic pentameter. All things considered, his work partially cancels the criticism by Sterling Brown that black poets lag in their stylistic awareness. "Vision" opens brilliantly with:

> Methought the Moon, pale regent of the sky,
> Crested, and filled with lucid radiance,
> Flung her bright gleams across my lowly couch;
> And all of heaven's fair starry firmament
> Delightful shone in hues of glittering light,
> Reflecting, like to fleecy gold, the dewy air.

In his "Vision" Boyd encounters characters of both the heavens and the hells. When the narrator, the "dreamer," joined the train,

> Fervent hosannas struck the astonish'd ear,
> As when in the midhour of calmest night,
> Stillness pervadeth the awakened wave,
> Roused by the secret power that moves the deep,
> It heaves its loud surge on the sounding shore;

The "vision" is also peopled by "grim death and ghastly Sin," who "lay coiled, like snakes in one huge scaly fold," and consider their "inexpiable doom—." Boyd's tones are sacred and surreal and he assembles harmlessly complex subordinate clauses that help build an exciting linguistic crescendo, as in "Ocean":

> When the fiat of the most High,
> Thy fountains burst, and copiously
> Thy secret springs, with ample store,
> Pour'd forth their waves from shore to shore
> Wide as the waters roll, oh, wave.

Boyd's work has yet to be appraised in terms commensurate with its importance. Robinson makes brief but significant comments on his poetry.

Ann Plato, another romantic poet, is also one for whom there exist few important factual data. This second black American female to publish a book almost skirts the racial theme completely. Her *Essays:/ Including/ Biographies and Miscellaneous Pieces,/in/ Prose and Poetry* was published in Hartford in 1841. What little is known of her comes by way of an introduction to her book by Rev. J. W. C. Pennington, pastor of the Colored Congregational Church in Hartford, of which she was a member. Except for her "To the First of August," written in celebration of the 1833 abolition of slavery in the British West Indies, there are only allusions to slavery. Her book also contains essays on religion, moderation, conduct and other conventional themes. These same themes are pretty much paralleled by the twenty poems in her book, which deal with home life, deaths of acquaintances and moral issues. "Reflections, Written on Visiting the Grave of a Venerated Friend," begins:

> Deep in this grave her bones remain,
> She's sleeping on, bereft of pain. . . .

The language and the subject matter are stock, but "Forget Me Not," each stanza of which ends with the title, is well handled and has flashes of the preachment of self-control that Vassa alluded to in his verses:

> When bird does wait thy absence long,
> Nor tend unto its morning song;
> While thou art searching stoic page,
> Or listening to an ancient sage,
> Whose spirit curbs a mournful rage,
>   Forget Me Not.

Her interest in oral literature and the storytelling tradition is apparent in "The Natives of America," in which she asks:

> "Tell me a story, father, please,"
> And then I sat upon his knees.

Again, as in her contemporaries, we find the influences of English writers of a preceding generation or so, the debt to biblical learning and much imitation. For brief critical notes on Miss Plato see Robinson's *Early Black American*

Poets. She is also briefly treated in Sherman's *Invisible Poets.*

Another abolitionist-minister and orator-poet was Elymas Payson Rogers (1814?–61), who, after teaching at public schools in Rochester, New York, took up pastoring in Newark, New Jersey. One of Rogers' students was Jeremiah W. Loguen, who later become an important social-religious leader and a bishop of the A.M.E. church. Fugitive slave Loguen's biography (see *Negro Caravan*) appeared in 1859, in Syracuse, under the title *The Reverend J. W. Loguen, as a Slave and as a Freeman.* Known, as were many of the orator-poets, for reciting his poems orally, Rogers' themes are unashamedly abolition, black betterment and political hypocrisy. Working politically on behalf of Blacks, Rogers apparently designed *The Fugitive Slave Law* (Newark, 1855) and *Repeal of Missouri Compromise Considered* (Newark, 1856) to be read aloud from platforms. Like James W. Whitfield, who came later, Rogers gave up hope in America's ever giving Blacks a fair deal and sailed for Africa, where he died from fever a few days after his arrival. His incisive, no-holds-barred approach to the political climate and conditions of the time is seen in "On the Fugitive Slave Law":

> Law! What is Law? The wise and sage,
> Of every clime and every age,
> In this most cordially unite,
> That 'tis a rule for doing right.

And the ringing cry of the elocutionist can be heard later in the poem, when, discussing the fugitive bill, he asks and answers:

> That Bill a law? the South says so,
> But Northern freemen answer, No!

Anticipating the fiery and torrential Whitfield (and twentieth-century "angry voices"), Rogers continues:

> That bill is law, doughfaces say;
> But black men everywhere cry, "Nay:
> We'll never yield to its control
> While life shall animate one soul.

At times biting and overbearingly harsh as a poet, Rogers resounds in "The Repeal of the Missouri Compromise Considered" with these words:

"I want the land," was Freedom's cry;
  And Slavery answered, "So do I!
  By all that's sacred, I declare
  I'll have my just and lawful share.
  The Northern cheek should glow with shame
  To think to rob me of my claim."

With built-in drama and careful cuts, Rogers assessed the state of the nation during his time. In the works "Law! What is Law?" he purposely begs the question in order to wring the emotional and rhetorical power from the words and to evoke responses from audiences. References to Rogers can also be found in Robinson's *Early Black American Poets* and Sherman's *Invisible Poets*.

Mathematician, poet, educator, and black community worker, Charles L. Reason (1818–98) was born in New York City of Haitian parents. He attended the New York African Free School, where he later returned as a member of the all-black faculty. Seeking the ministry, Reason was, for racial reasons, forbidden full-time attendance at the Theological Seminary of the Protestant Episcopal Church. Eventually, however, he became eligible for a professorship in mathematics and belle-lettres (1849) at the New York Central College in McGrawville, Cortland County. William G. Allen and George B. Vashon were also on the faculty there. He held various educational jobs including a principalship of the Institute for Colored Youth in Philadelphia and grammar school no. 80 in New York City while poet H. Cordelia Ray was a teacher there. Reason was an intellectual and scholar but was not blind to the practical needs of Afro-Americans. He opposed plans to colonize Blacks, claiming instead that they needed to pursue vocational careers here in America. Again, not primarily a poet, Reason is competent as a versifier in "The Spirit Voice," which opens with:

Come! rouse ye brothers, rouse! a peal now breaks
From lowest island to our gallant lakes:

'Tis summoning you, who in bonds have lain,
To stand up manful on the battle plain,

and urges Blacks to fight for freedom and opportunity.
The poem (whose complete title is "The Spirit Voice or,
Liberty Call to the Disfranchised") is indebted to the
rhyming couplet, so famous during the era. It appears
in William Simmons' *Men of Mark* (Cleveland, 1887).
Like that of other orator-poets, Reason's work is designed
to be read aloud in order to stir and move people to action. Therefore he exhorts, reinforces, demands, warns, admonishes and issues veiled threats. His "spirit voice" (see
the idea of African Spirit Force) longs for the time

when freedom's mellow light
Shall break, and usher in the endless day,
That from Orleans to Pass'maquoddy Bay,
Despots no more may earthly homage claim,
No slaves exist, to soil Columbia's name.

The poem was written in 1841 and shows Reason's poetic
abilities etched out under the strain of racism and the
countless chores demanded of an educated Black of the
period. Elsewhere ("Freedom") he gave this familiar cry:

O Freedom! Freedom! Oh, how oft
Thy loving children call on Thee!
In wailings loud and breathings soft,
Beseeching God, thy face to see.

How reminiscent of and "not unlike" the spirituals this
burst is! Certainly the student of this period of black poetry will also want to keep his rhythmic lyres attuned to
the biblical and innovative cadences of those "black and
unknown bards." For assessments of Reason see Robinson,
Brawley, Sherman and Kerlin. More of Reason's work appears in *A Eulogy on the Life and Character of Thomas
Clarkson* (1847) and in *Autographs for Freedom* (1854).

Anticipating the Afro-American poignancy and humor
in this line by Langston Hughes:

America never was America to me

and this one by Lance Jeffers:

to make me more American than America,

James M. Whitfield (1823–78) voiced some of the most powerful and angry protest yet heard in black American poetry when he published *America and Other Poems* in Buffalo in 1853. Barber, worker for black colonization, poet and pioneer journalist, Whitfield had earlier authored various types of writings: *Poems* in 1846; "How Long?" (published in Julia Griffith's *Autographs for Freedom* in Rochester, 1853); "Self-Reliance, Delusive Hope, and Ode for the Fourth of July" (in *The Liberator*, November 18, 1853); "Lines—Addressed to Mr. and Mrs. J. T. Holly, on the Death of Their Two Infant Daughters" (in *Frederick Douglass' Paper*, February 29, 1856); and *Emancipation Oration* (San Francisco, 1867).

Whitfield is known chiefly for *America*, which was received so favorably that he was able to leave his barbershop and devote full time to making speeches for the abolitionist cause, working for colonization programs and general black development. He had personal contact with both Douglass and novelist Martin Delaney, who called the 1854 National Emigration Convention of Colored Men, which Whitfield attended. Douglass apparently respected and admired Whitfield. But the two men differed on the question of colonization and participated in a lively debate. Pursuing his own position with vigor, Whitfield established the *African-American Repository*, in 1858, as a procolonization propaganda organ. Though born in Exeter, New Hampshire, Whitfield spent most of his life in Buffalo, where he barbered and conducted his colonization efforts. He apparently died on his way to look into the possibilities of colonizing black Americans in Central America. Delaney had changed his mind, and the emigration scheme was never realized.

As an orator-poet, Whitfield is writing to be heard, listened to, and read aloud. Consequently much of his poetry (though not lacking in religious fervor) reinforces his ideology and negative views of America. America, the

Sweet land of liberty

becomes for Whitfield "America,"

Thou boasted land of liberty,—

and

To thee I sing

becomes

It is to thee I raise my song,
Thou land of blood, crime, and wrong.

Like Rogers, Whitfield did not believe America was capable of redemption; and, again like his predecessor, he died on a journey to find something better. The idea of "giving up on" America would appear thematically in the poetry of such later writers as Fenton Johnson, Don L. Lee, Baraka, and some of the Muslim poets. It would also be implicit in the work of expatriate writers and artists such as Paul Robeson, Wright, Baldwin, Chester Himes, and Katherine Dunham. In a driving iambic pentameter (in couplets), which has all the openings for spontaneous interjections and expletives, Whitfield, in "America," accuses the United States of killing the black sons who fought for her and of general hypocrisy. Here one can see Whitfield anticipating a current slogan, which Hayden makes use of in "Words in the Mourning Time":

Killing people to save, to free them?

Though more general, Whitfield continues a similar assault (stating that life is hell) in "The Misanthropist," but tones down to a reverent salute in "To Cinque":

All hail! thou truly noble chief,
    Who scorned to live a cowering slave;
Thy name shall stand on history's leaf,
    Amid the mighty and the brave. . . .

Whitfield praises the revolutionary Cinque, who "in freedom's might"

Shall beard the robber in his den;

and

. . . fire anew each freeman's heart.

Since Whitfield's primary goal is to get a political "message" over, his poetry, as art, leaves some things to be desired. Robinson points out that Whitfield "is genuinely angry" (despite the influence of Byron) and that the bitterness and force in his work are not to be mistaken for romantic or linguistic cosmetics. Lastly, we must note that Whitfield expressed concern for global oppression; quite modern in this, he served, more or less, as a chronicler of world turbulence and a harbinger of the direct and emphatic assaults that today's black poets heap upon tyranny. He viewed the "Russian Bear" (reflecting on European despotism of the mid 1800s) in his poem "How Long?":

> I see the "Rugged Russian Bear"
> Lead forth his slavish hordes, to war
> Upon the right of every State
> Its own affairs to regulate;
> To help each despot behind the chain
> Upon the people's rights again,
> And crush beneath his ponderous paw
> All constitutions, rights and law.

Selections of Whitfield's poetry can be found in the Robinson anthology, in *Negro Caravan* (1941), and in the Barksdale and Kinnamon text. Whitlow discusses his poetry and impact, as do Loggins, Brown, Brawley, Wagner, Ruth Miller (*Black American Literature*, 1971), and Sherman.

The most popular black nineteenth-century poet before Dunbar was Frances E. W. Harper (1825–1911), the first black American to publish a short story ("The Two Offers," 1859). Born free in Baltimore as Frances Ellen Watkins, she was educated in Pennsylvania and Ohio, and spent most of her adult life in the cause of antislavery and other types of social reform. She worked in turn for the abolition movement, the Underground Railroad, the A.M.E. Church, and the Woman's Christian Temperance Union. According to Dunn (*The Black Press*), she also contributed to news and propaganda publications. Her reform work was slackened by her marriage to Fenton Harper in Cincinnati in 1860. But after his early death, in 1864, she resumed her efforts, lecturing in all but two southern states and promoting black self-help programs. Her fame rested primarily on her *Poems on Miscellaneous Subjects*, published in 1854 in Philadelphia. A very popular volume, it went through twenty editions by 1874 (see William Still's *Underground Railroad,* 1872). Her literary activity was stepped up after the Civil War and included *Moses, a Story of the Nile,* which went through three editions by 1870; a volume entitled *Poems* came out in 1870, followed by a second edition in 1900; and attempts at prose fiction, including *Southern Sketches* (1872, enlarged in 1896) and a novel, *Iola LeRoy,* published in 1892. Her first work, *Forest Leaves,* has not been located. Critics generally agree that Mrs. Harper's poetry is not original or brilliant. But she is exciting and comes through with powerful flashes of imagery and statement. Her models are Mrs. Hemans, Whittier, and Longfellow, and so we find an overwhelming influence from the ballad. In reading her poetry in public, Mrs. Harper was able to appeal to what Johnson (*God's Trombones*) called a "highly developed sense of sound" in Afro-Americans (see, again, statements by Reverend Allen and Vassa). She apparently knew her limitations, for Robinson tells us that her popularity

> . . . was not due to the conventional notion of poetic excellence, Mrs. Harper was fully aware of her limitations in that kind of poetry, it was due more to the sentimental, emotion-freighted popularity which she had given the lines with her disarmingly dramatic voice and gestures and sighs and tears.

Up until the Civil War, Mrs. Harper's favorite themes were slavery, its harshness, and the hypocrisies of America. She is careful to place graphic details where they will get the greatest result, especially when the poems are read aloud. An example of this is found in "The Slave Mother":

> He is not hers, for cruel hands
>   May rudely tear apart
> The only wreath of household love
>   That binds her breaking heart.

A similar play on the emotions is seen in such poems as "Bury Me in a Free Land," "Songs for the People," "Double Standard" (with its stirrings of feminism), and "The Slave Auction." A woman is not solely responsible for her "fall," she suggests in "A Double Standard," adding:

> And what is wrong in a woman's life
>   In man's cannot be right.

Highly readable and less academic in her use of poetic techniques and vocabularies, Mrs. Harper is nevertheless quite indebted to the Bible for much of her imagery and moral message. And she is able to merge and modify the folk and religious forms in such a poem as "Truth," in which she opens with a debt to the spirituals:

> A rock, for ages, stern and high,
> Stood frowning 'gainst the earth and sky,
> And never bowed his haughty crest
> When angry storms around him prest.
> Morn, springing from the arms of night,
> Had often bathed his brow with light,
> And kissed the shadows from his face
> With tender love and gentle grace.

Several religious songs are suggested here; but she also loves to return to the theme of women, as she does in "A Double Standard" and "The Slave Mother." In the ballad "Vashti" she tells of the heroine who dared to disobey her dictator-husband. The strength and determination of womanhood is expressed in the last two stanzas:

> She heard again the King's command,
>   And left her high estate;
> Strong in her earnest womanhood,
>   She calmly met her fate,
>
> And left the palace of the King
>   Proud of her spotless name—
> A woman who could bend to grief
>   But would not bow to shame.

Certainly a comprehensive biographical-critical study of Mrs. Harper is long overdue. Selections of her work can be found in Kerlin's critical anthology, *Negro Caravan*, Robinson's book, Miller's anthology, Barksdale and Kinnamon, and in numerous other recent anthologies. Her works are critically examined by Loggins, Wagner, Whitlow, Brawley, Brown, and Sherman.

Like other writers, educators and activists of his day, George B. Vashon (1822–78) contributed to the influential *Anglo-African Magazine,* which was published intermittently between 1859 and the end of the Civil War. Vashon had a good, solid education—in classics and history—at Oberlin College, where he received his A.B. in 1844 and M.A. in 1849. He is chiefly known for his "Vincent Ogé," which Sterling Brown tells us "is the first narrative poem of any length by a Negro poet." He also practiced law in Syracuse, taught school in Pittsburgh, served on the faculties of Collège Faustin in Port-au-Prince, Haiti, New York Central College (where he was a colleague of Reason and Allen), and Howard University in Washington, D.C., where he was a law professor.

Much of Vashon's poetry reflects debts to his strong education and the influence of Scott and Byron. All are seen in "Vincent Ogé," inspired by the courageous (but foolish) efforts of Vincent Ogé, a Haitian mulatto who was "entrusted with the message of enfranchisement to the people of mixed blood on the island." The order had come down from the Convention in France, of which Haiti was a colony. Internal disruption in France (due to the revolution, 1789–99) had echoed to its colonies in the Caribbean, where Ogé led a short-lived armed uprising that cost him his life when he was refused asylum in Spanish Santo Domingo and remanded to the French authorities in Haiti. As punishment and a warning to others, the French had Ogé tortured on the wheel, and severed his body into four parts, which were hung up in the four leading cities of the island. Ogé's followers were either put to death or imprisoned and their properties confiscated. Vashon was as moved by Ogé's example as was Whitfield by Cinque's. In the lengthy poem "Vincent Ogé," Vashon immortalizes Ogé in an admixture of classical and biblical language, using a pleasant iambic tetrameter and employing much dissonance in his rhyme scheme, which features an alternating *a b a b/ a a bb.* The style is somewhat reminiscent of Whitfield, who breaks his rhyme scheme (see "America") after each group of eight or nine lines. "Vincent Ogé" and "A Life-Day" were both printed in *Autographs for Freedom* for 1853. For Vashon, the struggle is very much alive:

> And Ogé stands mid this array
>   Of matchless beauty, but his brow
> Is brightened not by pleasure's play;
>   He stands unmoved—nay, saddened not,
> As doth the lorn and mateless bird;

and Ogé, dedicated to struggle, presses on. Vashon carefully weaves the graphic details of his protagonist's execution into the narrative and anticipates the more fire-tipped pens of later black (lynch-theme) poets, such as Johnson, McKay, Hughes, Brown, and Dodson:

> Frowning they stand, and in their cold,
> Silent solemnity, unfold
> The strong one's triumph o'er the weak—
> The awful groan—the anguished shriek—
> The unconscious mutterings of despair—
> The strained eyeball's idiot stare—
> The hopeless clench—the quivering frame—
> The martyr's death—the despot's shame.
> The rack—the tyrant—victim,—all
> Are gathered in that Judgment Hall.
> Draw me a veil, for 'tis a sight
> But fiends can gaze on with delight.

Freighted with emotion and terror like much of the work of Frances Harper, and setting the stage for such awesome poems as Wright's "Between the World and Me," McKay's "The Lynching," Dunbar's "The Haunted Oak" and Dodson's "Lament," Vashon's relentless narrative signals a new and sustaining power in the work of black poets. Compare, for example, the last two lines of the stanza above to McKay's couplet in his sonnet "The Lynching":

> And little lads, lynchers that were to be,
> Danced round the dreadful thing in fiendish glee.

Unlike McKay, however, Vashon cheers up at the end:

> Thy coming fame, Ogé! is sure;
> Thy name with that of L'Ouverture,

And all the noble souls that stood
With both of you, in times of blood,
Will live to be the tyrant's fear. . . .

Compare this ending, if you will, to the ending salute to
"General Washington" by Phillis Wheatley. "A Life-Day"
is a shorter poem, in three parts, and, like "Vincent Ogé,"
is founded on a factual event: the love affair and eventual
marriage of a young white man and a light-skinned Black.
For selections of Vashon's works see *Autographs for Freedom* and Robinson's anthology. For critical discussion see
Brown, Brawley, and Sherman.

As we prepare to move to the next phase in the development of black poetry, it is important that we tarry long
enough to pay brief attention to some of the Creole poets.
We select Pierre Dalcour, Armand Lanusse (1812–67),
Victor Séjour (1817–74), Nelson Debrosses, and Nicol Riquet. Somewhat of an anomaly in Afro-America literature
and poetry, these Creole poets are nevertheless important
if the complete portrait of this many-sided and complex
tradition is to be understood. There is nothing typically
American in their poetry—not even in terms of American
imitators of English forms—and they rarely display any
racial consciousness or concern for slavery and general injustice. Most were fluent in speaking and writing French,
and from that influence their work derives a spicy melody
and an uninhibited treatment of romantic love and revelry.
Much of the work is also imitative and sophisticated in its
use of conventions and materials gained from French edu-
cations. The Creole poets' works appeared as "the first
published anthology of Negro verse in America" in a volume called *Les Cenelles* (THE HOLY BERRIES, New Orleans, 1845). In addition to French, the Creole poets also
wrote in Spanish, Latin and Greek and were generally from
the wealthy, landowner class and owned slaves. Contributors to *Les Cenelles*, included seventeen of these poets,
many of whom had been published in the little magazine
L'Album Littéraire.

About Dalcour little is known except that he was born
of wealthy parents who sent him to France in the early
1800s to receive a good education. Returning to New Orleans after his schooling, he was unable to accept the

racial temper and again took up residency in France. While in New Orleans, however, he wrote a number of poems, one of which was "Verse Written in the Album of Mademoiselle." The poem touchingly relives the "vaulted skies" and "gentle flashes" which, to the poet, are "less lovely" when seen against the lady's eyes

> Beneath their brown lashes.

Lanusse, *Les Cenelles* editor, contributed to New Orleans Creole newspapers *L'Union* and *La Tribune*, served as a conscripted Confederate soldier in the Civil War and spent some time as principal of the Catholic School for Indigent Orphans of Color. He also encouraged literary and other artistic expression among fellow artists and solicited work for *Les Cenelles*. He eulogized his brother, Numa, in the poem "Un Frère/Au Tombeau de Son Frère," recalling that "unfeeling death has cut you down." Elsewhere Lanusse refers to death as "some other hand shutting your eyelids." Somewhat naughtier and more poignant, in "Epigram," Lanusse gives the account of a "woman of evil" who wants to "renounce the devil" but asks,

> Before pure grace takes me in hand,
> Shouldn't I show my daughter how to get a man?

Séjour lived most of his life in France and returned to New Orleans only for brief visits to his mother. Son of a wealthy family, he wrote several plays, twenty-one of which were staged in France and three in New Orleans in the 1850s. Séjour's literary abilities were praised by Napoleon III, and he rubbed shoulders with major French literary personalities of his day. His scope is wider than some of the other Creole poets. "Le Retour de Napoléon" ("The Return of Napoleon") is an elegy and a celebration all in one. Eulogizing Napoleon, Séjour praises both his and France's triumphs and glories. It is a poem of flowing, graphic exaltation. Opening on the scene of a "sea" that "groans under the burning sun," he narrates the growth and collapse of France as a world power:

> And on and on she swept, an unleashed
> tempest wild, and France moved on

ahead. No more. All is over.
. . . Yet, hail, O captain! Hail my
consul of proud bearing.

Admonishing France to "Weep, France, weep," Séjour
reminds the country that "death has lightning struck the
people's giant."

Little is known about the personal life of Debrosses,
which, according to Robinson, "seems in keeping with his
Haitian-gained experience in Voodoo, aspects of which he
practised in New Orleans." In Debrosses' "Le Retour au
Village aux Perles" ("Return to the Village of Pearls"),
he seems to anticipate what Waring Cuney sees through
the "dishwater" in his poem "Images." The Creole poet
returns to the village to find that

Her spirit dances here and there in these
enchanting places

and to locate

—that flower-bosomed grove again, the
witness of our secret passion, and
too, the cherished brook to which my
soul would on this day confide its
happy memory.

A cigar maker by trade, Riquet lived all of his life in
New Orleans, where he pursued a vigorous avocation of
writing light verses. His "Rondeau Redouble/Aux Francs
Amis" ("Double Rondeau/To Candid Friends") leaves
no doubt that Riquet saw himself as at least serious in his
avocation. A rondeau is a French-originated lyrical poem
of thirteen, or sometimes ten, lines. There are two rhymes
throughout the poem, and the opening phrase is repeated
as a refrain. The form is remotely reminiscent of the blues
and spiritual forms of Afro-American poetry. Riquet says
that since his "candid friends are calling for a rondeau!"
he and his "Muse . . . must work a wonder." The duty of
the poet is to "rhyme in an uncommon way" or he will
"earn the name of poetaster—from our candid friends."

Other Creole poets included Michel Saint-Pierre
(18?–66), Camille Thierry (1814–75), Joanni Questi
(18?–69), who compiled an Almanack of Laughter, and

T. A. Desdunes, whom Janheinz Jahn says "is reminiscent of the Senegalese poet Birago Diop."

The Creole poets are examined and represented by selections in E. Maceo Coleman's *Creole Voices* (Washington, D.C., 1945) and in Robinson's anthology. See also Charles Roussève's *The Negro and Louisiana* (Xavier University Press, 1937), and the critical selections by Jahn and Sherman. Lanusse and Dalcour also appear in Hughes and Bontemps's *The Poetry of the Negro* (1949, 1970).

There were also other poets writing and publishing during this same period. Many brought out their works in single editions, and copies of some are no longer extant. Brawley refers to a poet known as "Caesar" who allegedly wrote but whose poetry is not available. Other poets and their collections are Maria and Harriet Falconar, *Poems on Slavery* (London, 1788); James Montgomery, James Graham, and E. Benger, *Poems on the Abolition of the Slave Trade* (London, 1809); Anonymous, *The West Indies and Other Poems* (1811); John Bull, *The Slave and Other Poems* (London, 1824); Rev. Noah C. Cannon, *The Rock of Wisdom . . . To Which Are Added Several Interesting Hymns* (New York, 1833?); Anonymous, "The Commemorative Wreath: in Celebration of the Extinction of Negro Slavery in the British Dominions" (London, 1835), Anonymous, *Anti-Slavery Melodies* (Hingham, Massachusetts, 1834); George Whitfield Clark, compiler, *The Liberty Minstrel* (New York, 1844); William Wells Brown, *Anti-Slavery Harp* (Boston, 1849); "A West Indian," Charleston, South Carolina: *a satiric poem showing that slavery still exists in the country which boasts, above all others, of being the seat of liberty* (London, 1851); Sam ———, *Darkness Brought to light* (Derry, New Hampshire, 1855?); George W. Clark, *The Harp of Freedom* (New York, 1856); and Abel Charles Thomas, *The Gospel of Slavery* (New York, 1864).

In 1860 Blacks represented 14.1 per cent of the United States population and were 4,441,830 strong. The sour tastes left by the worst internal social upheaval (Civil War) until the 1960s and 1970s, the problems of caring for and protecting the soon-to-be released slaves, the need to develop and staff educational facilities for Blacks—all engulfed Afro-Americans in a deluge of horror and hope. Although it is clear that the works of many poets leap the arbitrarily imposed chronological boundaries, the temperaments, themes, dictional preferences and limitations discussed, generally hold for most of the poetry of the period. Despite the surprising successes, and the flashes of brilliance intertwined with mediocrity and comedy, the black poet would labor long to remove "the image of a face" that, in the words of Corrothers, "Lieth, like shadow on the wild sweet flowers."

CHAPTER IV

JUBILEES, JUJUS, AND JUSTICES (1865–1910)

> We have fashioned laughter
> Out of tears and pain,
> But the moment after—
> Pain and tears again.
> —CHARLES BERTRAM JOHNSON

OVERVIEW

This "transitional" period is normally viewed by critics as the gestation of prerevolutionary black writing. We have seen, however, that some of the most politically conscious activists, thinkers, and poets wrote before the Civil War. Frantz Fanon (1924–61), the Martinique-born psychiatrist, established three phases for the literature of oppressed peoples: (1) assimilationist, (2) prerevolutionary and (3) revolutionary. Critics generally agree with Fanon. So, following his reasoning, the period of 1865–1910 (and the previous era) would fall under number one. Number two coincides roughly with the Harlem Renaissance (1920–30). And the 1960s (black arts era) comes under number three. One should exercise caution, however, in placing categories and labels on any artists— especially ones so diverse and complex as black poets. For while it is true that there are general trends in the evolution of the poetry, little said by the so-called "Armageddon" writers of the 1960s and 1970s can be any more "revolutionary" than Walker, Whitefield or Albery Whitman, who favored the murder of black traitors ("Uncle Toms" and "Topsies") to the cause of freedom. On the other hand, as in the past, some contemporary black writers avoid politics like the plague (see Chapter I). Also, the alternatives and options facing Blacks nowadays —resignation, emigration, assimilation, despair, segregation, desecration and so on—have always been there. During the seventeenth and eighteenth centuries, black poets

and activists vigorously pursued these choices, sometimes
participating (Whitfield-Douglass) in fiery debates.

Preceding chapters established a foundation for black
poetry that only recently has become popular and accessible. Therefore, critical comments and background materials will be less extensive from this point on. Certainly, as
Robinson suggests, more careful study of the poets of the
Harlem Renaissance is needed. His observation that
"Afro-American 'Soul' has never received the elaborate
philosophical, poetic, and even political explication that
Négritude has" is also well taken (although there is some
attempt to assess "soul" in *The Militant Black Writer in
Africa and the United States,* by Cook and Henderson).
Understandable, too, is the comment by Sterling Stuckey
(*Ideological Origins of Black Nationalism*): "Had a nationalist of ante-bellum America realized the enormous
importance of Black culture . . . that awareness, articulated into theory, would have been as revolutionary a development as calling for a massive slave-uprising." Of
course we know, looking back at the past hundred years,
that Stuckey's assessment does not take in all the facts.
Early black Americans identified with their cultural roots
more blatantly than do even activist Blacks of today. But
the undermining influences of lynchings and the practice
of stereotyping corroded much initial race pride and self-interest.

Again we note that chronological boundaries are arbitrary and that we could just as well have studied Frances
Harper in the 1865–1910 period (since her *Sketches of
Southern Life* was published in 1873 and her *Poems* ran
through several editions until 1874) just as we could have
placed Benjamin Clark ("What Is a Slave?") and James
Madison Bell in the previous chapter. It is not always easy
to determine where a poet who writes early or late in life
fits in the chronology; but if pursuit of the poetry becomes
a labor of love, boundaries and categories cease to exist.

LITERARY AND SOCIAL LANDSCAPE

Forgive thine erring people, Lord,
Who lynch at home and love abroad
—CHARLES R. DINKINS

Between 1865 and 1910, America played out a drama of contradictions, swelling and receding expectations, continued progress and experimentation in science and the arts, and important beginnings. It was a period of painful adjustment that has continued to echo. On the white literary scene Whitman (the "American poet"), Mark Twain, William Dean Howells, James Russell Lowell, Henry James, Stephen Crane, Jack London, Emily Dickinson, Joel Chandler Harris, and Irwin Russell were the writers of importance. Harris gained popularity for himself and black folklore when he published the Uncle Remus tales in 1879. But while romanticism and local color dominated the last two decades of the nineteenth century, both began to fade with the approach of the new century—whose early years saw experimentation, especially in verse, and the beginnings of naturalistic writings.

On the political and economic fronts, the efforts at solidifying gains, and retrieving losses, were stepped up among Blacks. The NAACP was founded in 1909; but the major vehicles for protest and change were those used during the earlier years: the church, self-help societies, free schools, scholarly research and writing on Blacks, and debates over courses and choices. Important new names in literature, art, science and politics came to the forefront. However, many of the writers, activists and educators from the previous period continued their various programs. Of the new voices, several should be noted: Booker T. Washington (*Up from Slavery*, 1900), W. E. B. Du Bois (*The Suppression of the African Slave Trade*, 1896; *The Philadelphia Negro*, 1899; *The Souls of Black Folk*, 1903), Charles Chestnutt (writer of fiction), Dunbar, James Weldon Johnson, Fenton Johnson, James D. Corrothers, Alain Locke, William Grant Still (*The Underground Railroad*, 1872), Alexander Crummell (founder of the American Negro Academy), Albery Whitman, Benjamin Brawley (*The Negro in Literature and Art in the United States*, 1910), Kelley Miller (*Race Adjustment*, 1909), William Stanley Braithwaite, and Alice Dunbar-Nelson (*Violets and Other Tales*, 1895). Black America witnessed a major step in the development of its stage productions (many designed to destroy "stereotypes" fostered by white minstrels and dialect writers) with Bob Cole's A

Trip to Coontown (1898), the first musical produced and managed by Blacks. Will Marion Cook and Dunbar followed with *Clorindy*, also in 1898; and Cole returned, this time with James Weldon Johnson, to write and play in *The Red Moon* (1908).

The maturation of essays, journalism and autobiography also continued. Elizabeth Keckley, friend to presidents and statesmen, wrote *Behind the Scenes* in 1868; Douglass founded the *New National Era* (1869–72) and published his *Life and Times* in 1881. *Southern Workmen* was established at Hampton Institute in 1872. T. Thomas Fortune founded *The Rumor* in 1879 and edited the New York *Age* in 1887. In the same year, the Washington *Bee* came into being. Others included Penn's *The Afro-American Press* (1891), John H. Murphy's Baltimore *Afro-American* (1892), the Chicago *Defender* (1900), and Monroe Trotter's Boston *Guardian* (1901).

Dunbar, Whitman, Fenton Johnson, Corrothers and Braithwaite are the poets of interest during this period. James Weldon Johnson wrote "Lift Every Voice and Sing" in 1900 but is usually identified with the Harlem Renaissance writers. And Alain Locke, intellectual and scholar, was one of the important chroniclers and interpreters of that era. Du Bois, sociologist and editor, is chiefly known, as a poet, for his "Song of the Smoke" and "Litany at Atlanta," written after the 1906 race riot. Charles Chestnutt was the first important black writer of fiction. Both he and Dunbar were endorsed by William Dean Howells, who presided as a czar over American literary criticism during the last quarter of the nineteenth century. Howells also helped launch the careers of Henry James and Walt Whitman. Generally, with the exception of Braithwaite, Fenton Johnson, Whitman and a few others, black poets followed the dialect tradition of the day. Robinson (*Early Black American Poets*) notes:

> The vogue was established among white southern writers (who failed to appreciate their own amusing dialects) with Irwin Russell (1853–79) whose popular pieces were collected and published posthumously as *Poems by Irwin Russell* (1888) with a loving preface by Joel Chandler Harris, also popular for his Uncle Remus and Brer Rabbit prose tales in Negro dialect.

The major black dialect poets were Dunbar, Daniel
Webster Davis, James Edwin Campbell, Elliot B. Henderson, and J. Mord Allen; but James Weldon Johnson also
wrote in the idiom. Dunbar surpassed all dialect writers—
black and white—including Russell, after whom he patterned his efforts. His ability to empathize with Blacks
rather than simply "report" or parody them, coupled with
his "perfect" ear for the speech, make him more authentic. Dunbar also wrote standard English verse, for which
he wanted to be remembered, but it was his dialect poetry
(which he called "a jingle in a broken tongue") that
gained him notoriety.

The biggest contradiction of the era was that "Reconstruction" occurred in name only. The growth of white
hate and intimidation groups (twenty-five hundred Blacks
were lynched between 1885 and 1900), the development
of a neoslavery, the paradoxical plight of the "freedman"
(see Washington's *Up from Slavery*), the general disappointments in social "paper" programs and the disillusionment on the parts of Blacks who had fought in the
Civil War—all influenced and helped direct the contemporary black mood. Coupled with this was the beginning
of the great migration of southern Blacks to northern
urban centers. While dialect poetry emerged as the most
popular form in poetry and prose, James Weldon Johnson
later observed (*American Negro Poetry*) that it would not
encase the manifold nature of the black experience; white
writers had initiated it and Blacks could only "caricature
the caricatures." Caught up for a while in the potentials
of the Emancipation Proclamation and "Reconstruction,"
many black poets also couched their lines in patriotism
and sentimentality (see Johnson's "Fifty Years").

During this period, the first of a series of black manual-
arts colleges was established. Hampton Institute, Fisk University, Howard University, Morehouse College and Johnson C. Smith College were among the early ones. In 1871,
the year of James Weldon Johnson's birth, the Fisk Jubilee Singers made their first concert tour, with spirituals.
The tour was epoch-making, for it marked the first time a
black indigenous American art form had been given such
worldwide exposure. The period was crucial, too, for all
black folk art, because the burgeoning new black intelligentsia, anxious to remove the bitter taste of slavery,

rushed to divest themselves of all relics of their ante-
bellum past. The spirituals, the rich cadences of folk
speech and the freedom in dance, among other aspects,
were given a back seat in an attempt to Westernize or
"civilize" newly emancipated Blacks.

The Civil War, the Emancipation Proclamation and
the stationing of occupation troops in the South had also
left a bitter taste on the tongues of revenge-bent southern
whites. The attempt to "colonize" the South, as some saw
it, was dramatized by the arrival of "carpetbaggers"—
white Northerners preaching black freedom or exploiting
southern industry. The results were the elaborate and
ruthless rise of white secret societies and the ridicule of
Blacks in newspapers and magazines. Many black poets
unwittingly participated in this ridicule through their own
dialect and sentimental verse. Others went to the extreme
to prove their "goodness" and "Godliness." In the shadows of all these paradoxes, black ministrels and musicians
gained prominence. And "ragtime" heralded an era ultimately to be called the Jazz Age.

Meanwhile more serious debate over the fate of Blacks
was taking place among men such as Douglass, Washington, and Du Bois. In 1895, at the International Atlanta
Exposition, Washington delivered his famous "Compromise" speech, which encouraged Blacks and whites to
work as close as the fingers of the hand in matters needing
mutual concern; but advised that, in all social respects, the
fingers of the hand should be separate. This was seen as a
conciliatory and unprogressive posture by many integra-
tion-minded leaders. Washington, who founded Tuskegee
Institute in 1881, played down civil concerns and integration, and urged Blacks to seek practical skills. Du Bois encouraged Blacks to seek knowledge of the arts and sciences
and predicted that a "Talented Tenth" would emerge to
lead them. In *The Souls of Black Folk*, Du Bois critiqued
Washington's position. The controversy between the two
men is now famous, as is Dudley Randall's poem "Booker
T. and W.E.B." in which the ideologies of both men are
placed against the mood of the times. In an incremental
development of both dialogue and rhyme-refrain, Randall
frames his important statements in iambic tetrameter. The
use of an imaginary conversation between two "opponents"
also allowed the poet to comment on two significant

"poles" in the continuing black push for freedom and self-determination.

The Du Bois-Washington controversy created reverberations that are still being heard around the black world. Du Bois was, ultimately, to rise as the towering and defiant figure of the period (especially among Afro-American intelligentsia), while Washington was reduced to a negative and sometimes obscene symbol. A recent book that deals somewhat indirectly, with these matters is *Booker T's Child* (1974), by poet Roy L. Hill (see Hill's bibliography). See also *Up from Slavery* (Washington, 1901), *From Slave to College President* (Godfrey Pike, 1902), *The Life and Times of Booker T. Washington,* (Benjamin Riley, 1916), and *Booker T. Washington and His Critics* (Hugh Hawkins, ed., 1962). For a recent informative biography of Du Bois see *His Day Is Marching On* (Shirley Graham Du Bois, 1971).

THE VOICES ON THE TOTEM

De Cunjah man, de Cunjah man,
O chillen, run, de Cunjah man!
—JAMES EDWIN CAMPBELL

Although poets of the previous period placed their verses and polemics in various political and news organs, it was during the 1865–1910 era that such a practice reached new levels of importance. Poets had access to numerous regional and national publications, contests, political platforms and educational programs through which they could either read or publish poems. Robert Thomas Kerlin, for example (*Negro Poets and Their Poems*, 1923), collected literally dozens of poems from newspapers, church bulletins, privately printed pamphlets and magazines—many of them no longer available. Some indication of the political nature of both the people and the poetry of the post-Civil War era is seen in this stanza from "The Song of the Black Republicans" (which appeared in *The Black Republican* of New Orleans, April 29, 1865):

I

Now rally, Black Republicans,
   Wherever you may be,

Brave soldiers on the battlefield,
    And sailors on the sea.
Now rally, Black Republicans—
    Aye, rally! we are free!
    We've waited long long
    To sing the song—
    The song of liberty.

Continuing for six stanzas, the poem is obviously aimed at
a public listening and reading audience. It praises "color,"
which comes "from the Lord," and reminds black voters
that Abraham Lincoln ("beneath the Flag of all") "flung
us Freedom through its stars."

Somewhat of a different vein is the work of Benjamin
Cutler Clark (1805?-?) of whom we know very little. A
fugitive slave, he attended the 1835 Annual Convention
of Free People of Color (held in Philadelphia) from his
adopted hometown of York, Pennsylvania, where he had
moved after leaving the slave state in which he was born.
Mostly self-taught, Clark married in York and raised a
large family—writing poetry and prose in his spare moments. He was politically active and opposed colonization
of Blacks, believing that it was "individuals" who
emigrated and "not nations." *The Past, the Present and
the Future* (Toronto, 1867) includes prose reflections on
the state of race relations, and sixty-five poems. He is primarily concerned, in poetry and prose, with the issues of
slavery and racial injustice, although much of his work
deals with domestic life.

In language, sentiment, style, and influence, Clark bears
resemblance to the poets of the period just covered. And
although his work was not published until 1867, he wrote
poems earlier, as indicated, for example, in his "What Is a
Slave" and "Requiescat in Pace," an elegy on the 1857
death of a woman associate. Clark is quite effective as a
poet and, sometimes, even gripping in his ability to make
the poem assume the dimensions of the event it relates.
Like Mrs. Harper, he is graphic in detailing slavery. And,
like Frederick Douglass (see *Narrative*, he is tragicomic in
suggesting that those "at home" (in slavery, that is) may
"miss me." "Do They Miss Me? A Parody" opens each of
its four-lined stanzas with

Do they miss me at home—do they miss me?

and alternates iambic pentameter and tetrameter (with an
a b c b rhyme scheme). Clark describes an unusual kind
of "home":

"Do they miss me at home—do they miss me?"
    By light, as the horn echoes loud,
And the slaves are marched off to the corn field,
    I'm missed from the half-naked crowd.

Using a break (or caesura) reminiscent of the blues, at
the third foot (the blues breaks at the second), Clark
dramatizes slavery and pokes fun at those men who run
the "peculiar institution." He makes similar use of the
dash in "What Is a Slave" in which he achieves incremental power through repetition and syntactical variance:

A slave is—what?
    A thing that's got
Nothing, and that alone!
    His time—his wife—
    And e'en his life,
He dare not call his own.

Employing expletives, spontaneity, and suspense, Clark
shows himself to be a skilled craftsman (all things considered) for his time and training. His rhyme scheme is *a a b
c c b* with an off rhyme in the first couplet of each six-line
stanza. Under the persistent question "What Is a Slave?"
we feel not only the indictment against slaveowners and
racist policies, but some key to the early realizations of
black thinkers that the race was being disrobed both physically and psychologically. As with Vassa, Reason, and
others, the hurt is hidden and defies both definition and
visual contact:

A slave is—what?
    I pray do not
Insist; I cannot know,
    No words impart,
    Or, painter's art,
Describe a slave—ah, no!

Though trapped in the forms of European model builders,
Clark shows his own ingenuity and originality. By varying

his rhyme schemes and meter, and using dashes and expletives, he brings emotional power interlaced with an
ironically detached intellectual assessment of the slave's
plight. He is similarly powerful in "The Seminole," in
which he (continuing a long line of black salutory verse)
praises Osceola, Seminole chief and hero of Seminole wars
in Florida in the early-nineteenth century. In this, he also
anticipates Albery Whitman's work (*Rape of Florida*).
For selections of Clark's works and brief criticism see
Robinson's anthology. See also Joan R. Sherman's *Invisible Poets*.

If Clark's strength lay in his assault against racial injustices, James Madison Bell's (1826–1902) lay in his
"pleas" and "hope." "Fortunate" enough to witness the
Civil War, emancipation, and "Reconstruction," Bell
railed against injustices but primarily expressed hope in his
forty years of observing the black struggle. Bell spent most
of his adult life delivering eloquent and weighty poetic
speeches on freedom, hope, and liberty. He was born in
Gallipolis, Ohio, which he left at age sixteen to pursue the
trade of plasterer and the avocation of orator-poet. A wanderer, Bell played his part in the overthrow of slavery—
soliciting funds and recruiting Blacks for John Brown's
1859 raid at Harpers Ferry. Before the raid, Bell had
moved to Canada, where he continued his friendship with
Brown and fathered a large family. He later traveled to
California, back to Canada, to various cities in Ohio and
Michigan, and, finally, spent time in Toledo. During this
odyssey Bell appeared at concert halls, churches, and various public gatherings to read his poetry at political and
commemorative events. He also took advantage of books
and gained considerable understanding of history and literature. His major themes are devotion, inspiration, love,
unity, collective strength, and political change. Achieving
"something of Byronic power in the roll of his verse"
(Kerlin), Bell's poems are often too long, too tedious, and
lacking in interest. Robinson notes:

> Not to mitigate his obvious technical flaws, it is helpful
> to remember that Bell is best appreciated as something
> of an actor, his poems regarded as scripts.

Unashamedly chronicling his journeys, Bell included the
following as a full title of *Triumph of Liberty* (1870):

A Poem, / Entitled the / Triumph of Liberty. / Delivered April 7, 1870, / Detroit Opera House, / on the Occasion of / the Grand Celebration of the Final Ratification / of the Fifteenth Amendment to the Constitution of the United States. Consisting of 902 lines, the poem erupts through the use of all the "flourishes and vocal modulations at his experienced command." According to Redding (To Make a Poet Black), Bell "unblushingly" claimed the titles of "Bard of Maumee" and "Poet of Hope." Typical of Bell's style is his tribute to his friend John Brown (from Triumph of Liberty):

Although like Samson he was ta'en,
And by the base Philistines slain,
Yet he in death accomplished more
Than e'er he had in life before.
His noble heart, which ne'er had failed,
Proved firm, and e'en in death prevailed;
And many a teardrop dimmed the eye
Of e'en his foes who saw him die—
And none who witnessed that foul act
Will e'er in life forget the fact.

Approaching something of the stature of Vashon's "Vincent Ogé" and Whitfield's "Cinque," Bell's tribute has all the ring of indebtedness to Scott, Byron, Pope, Tennyson, and other English popular masters with whom he was familiar. However imitative and derivative, though, Bell seemed never to be at a loss for exalting, exhortatory poetical flourishes. In "Song for the First of August" he sings a song for "proud Freedom's day":

Of every clime, of every hue,
    Of every tongue, of every race,
'Neath heaven's broad ethereal blue;
Oh! let thy radiant smiles embrace,
Till neither slave nor one oppressed
    Remain throughout creation's span,
By thee unpitied and unblest,
    Of all the progeny of man.

One of Bell's most ambitious works is his "Modern Moses, or 'My Policy' Man" in which—in scalding satire —he assesses the administration of President Andrew

Johnson. Johnson (1805–75), who succeeded the assassinated Lincoln in 1865, was born poor and learned to write and figure from his wife. His presidency reached its height in a showdown between a progressive Republican Congress and Johnson, a reactionary Democrat. Once in office, Johnson began reversing his harsh criticisms of the South, giving former rebels a rather free hand at things and vetoing several bills aimed at giving Blacks a better share of things. Upset by the whole thing, Bell wrote a blistering satire—which often collapses as such—wherein, with couplet-fury, he observes:

> And crowns there are, and not a few,
> And royal robes and sceptres, too,
> That have, in every age and land,
> Been at the option and command
> Of men as much unfit to rule,
> As apes and monkeys are for school.

Following poets like Clark and Whitfield, and anticipating "signifying" poets of the 1960s and '70s (such as Baraka, Crouch, Touré, Eckels: "Western Syphillization," and others) Bell compares Johnson to all manner of evils. Johnson is also contrasted to "good" or liberal whites such as Congressmen Charles Summer and Thaddeus Stevens and abolitionist Wendell Phillips. Cynically calling Johnson "Modern Moses," Bell also uses the derisive "*Mose*" —which appears to be a way of reducing him to the level of the stereotype whites reserve for Blacks (see, for example, such statements as the one by Don L. Lee: "styron / & his momma too"). One must chuckle somewhat at Bell's claim that Johnson cursed in the White House:

> But choose we rather to discant,
> On one whose swaggish boast and rant,
> And vulgar jest, and pot-house slang,
> Has grown the pest of every gang
> Of debauchees wherever found,
> From Baffin's Bay to Puget Sound.

Only recently have we heard echoes of Bell from journalists, congressmen and old ladies astonished at White House tapes showing that ex-President Richard Nixon cursed in the Oval Room. We have observed, then, that

Bell, though a tedious and haranguing poet, is important in a continuing chronicle of the mind and creative development of the Afro-American poet. Bell's works also include *The Day and the War* (1864), dedicated to the memory of Brown; *The Progress of Liberty* (1870), a recollection of the war, praise for Lincoln and black troops, and a jubilant greeting of enfranchisement; and *The Poetical Works of James Madison Bell* (1901), including a preface by his personal friend Bishop B. W. Arnett. Even though Bishop Arnett claimed that Bell's "logic was irresistible, like a legion of cavalry led by Sheridan," the poet recognized his own limitations when he said (*Progress of Liberty*):

> "The poet laments the discord of his harp, and its
> disuse, until answering Freedom's call he again
> essays its harmony."

For other samples and appraisals of Bell's work see Robinson, Brawley, Kerlin, Redding, Brown, Sherman, and Mays (*The Negro's God*, 1938).

Anticipating Melvin B. Tolson of the twentieth century (who wrote a book-length answer (*Harlem Gallery*, 1965) to Gertrude Stein's statement: "The Negro suffers from nothingness," Francis A. Boyd (1844–?) penned his only volume in partial response to Rev. Henry Ward Beecher's concern for "the injured and oppressed sons and daughters of Africa." Boyd's volume, published in 1870, is entitled *Columbiana; / or, / the North Star, / Complete in One Volume*. Boyd explains in the preface that he was born free to Samuel and Nancy Boyd in Lexington, Kentucky, and met hardships trying to acquire an education. *Columbiana*, the author notes in the preface, comes from "I, a scion of that ancient race" who takes "pleasure in dedicating the following lines" to the Reverend Beecher. Made up of five cantos (major breaks in a long poem), *Columbiana* is a poetic narrative on the plight of the black man in slave-founded America. The cantos contain various structural and rhyme schemes—most of which reflect Boyd's knowledge of the classic, neoclassical, and romantic traditions in poetry, and the history of events leading up to the Civil War. In the poem, Freedom (personified) travels, like some classical deity, on a winged chariot from

Egypt, across Israel, Greece, and America. In America, Freedom meets all sorts of evils, like the protagonist in John Boyd's "vision," among them Secessia, the arch-enemy of Blacks and freedom. Secessia, Southerners who seceded from the union, is assessed from all sides during Boyd's iambic tetrametric assault. In "defiance bade to Union laws," the South "Ignored" truth and rightness

> And boldly drew her glitt'ring glaive
> To hamper down the shudd'ring slave.

But the sons and daughters of Africa, who own a part of Secessia, must have a say-so in what happens to her. Freedom (continuing "The Soliloquy" from Canto IV) tells Secessia that

> . . . on thy soil the Ethiop dwells
> In glorious triumph o'er thy foul slave-cells. . . .

Blacks have their eye on the North Star (also the name of Douglass' paper), suggests the narrator in "The Dream" from Canto V, and

> Before we quench the hallowed fire,
> Once more we strike the sacred lyre.
> The North Star lingers in the sky,
> Encircled by a snowy dove.
> Sun, moon and stars confounded lie,
> The North Star outshines all above,
> 'Tis shining here, and shining there,
> Forever ruling everywhere.

The North Star has remained until this very day important in black literature. Robert Hayden is only one con-temporary poet ("Runagate Runagate") making use of it. Confusing both his meter and his rhyme pattern without hints that he is intentional or experimenting, Boyd some-times loses the reader in his labyrinthine deluge. But, con-sidering his station in life and the obstacles he worked against, his work is one more notable step in the develop-ment of Afro-American poetry. For selections from and as-sessments of Boyd, see Robinson.

Henrietta Cordelia Ray (1850–1916) was among the handful of black poets of the nineteenth century (includ-

ing Daniel Payne and Ann Plato) who avoided racial
themes. Miss Ray, however, was one of the first to try
a wide variety of forms. In sonnets such as "To My Father," "Robert G. Shaw," "Milton" and others, she shows
skill at writing this difficult form. And in such works as
"Antigone and Oedipus," "The Dawn of Love," "Noon-
tide" and "The Months" she proves her linguistic dexterity and poetic virtuosity. Even though she avoids outright
racial themes in her poetry, she implicitly commits herself
in "Robert G. Shaw," dedicated to the white Colonel
Shaw (1837–63) of Boston who led the 54th Massachusetts Volunteers (all black) in the Civil War. Killed
leading his troops on an assault on Fort Wagner, South
Carolina, Shaw is eulogized:

> O Friend! O hero! thou who yielded breath
> That others might share Freedom's priceless gains,
> In rev'rent love we guard thy memory.

Dunbar, a younger contemporary of Cordelia Ray's, would
also praise Shaw, who, like Lincoln, became one of the important white heroes to postwar black Americans. Cordelia
Ray, however, was not unaware of the plight of her
brothers and sisters of color in her everyday life. Born one
of two daughters to the Rev. Charles B. Ray (of Fal-
mouth, Massachusetts), distinguished minister and "tireless abolitionist," she was very early made aware of slavery
and racial injustices. After a rather protected upbringing,
which included good traditional training, she went on to
New York University, where she finished in pedagogy, and
to Sauveueur School of Languages to master Greek,
Latin, French, German, and the English classics. For a
while she taught school but, finding it boring, preferred to
attend her invalid sister, Florence (with whom she maintained a lifelong friendship), and travel throughout New
England giving moral support to the antislavery work of
her father. Her poems deal primarily with love, scholarship, intellectual themes, praise of great literary/political
figures and seasons. She loved to do settings, descriptions,
impressions and cycles in her poetry. For example there is
a cycle ("Idyl") which goes through "Sunrise," "Noon-
tide," "Sunset," and "Midnight." Another cycle, "The
Months," consists of twelve poems, five of them in 8-line

stanzas, five in 6-line stanzas and two in 7-line stanzas.
She generally varies her meter and rhyme schemes; but the
ballad form predominates in "The Months," while a 2-
stanza, 6-line form (rhyme scheme: *a a b c c b*) heralds
the four major segments of the day in "Idyl." Cordelia
Ray, as we have noted, is not an original or innovative
poet. But her work does mark a new level of sophistication
—despite her imitation of the models followed by most
black poets of her time. Her published poems included
Poems (New York, 1887), and *Sonnets* (New York,
1893). She also published *Commemoration Ode or Lincoln / written for the occasion of the / unveiling of the
Freedman's monument / in Memory of Abraham Lincoln
/ April 14, 1876.* She coauthored, with her sister, *Sketch
of the Life of the Rev. Charles B. Ray* (New York, 1887).
For selections of her work see Robinson's *Early Black
American Poets* and and Kerlin's *Negro Poets and Their
Poems.* Robinson includes critical comments, as does Sher-
man in *Invisible Poets.*

Declaring, "I was born in bondage,—I was never a
slave,—" Albery Allson Whitman (1851–1902) thus introduced himself and his poetry to the world. A complex and
brilliant poet (Wagner refers to him as a "brilliant" imitator), he must have been anticipated by his contemporary Cordelia Ray in the experiments with various verse
forms. Whitman was born a slave in or near Munfords-
ville, Hart County, Kentucky (in Green River country). A
mulatto, he was orphaned at an early age and received
only bits and pieces of formal training—a glaring irony
against his achievement, the most important in the century until Dunbar. Though it is widely believed that
Whitman wrote the longest poem (over five thousand
lines) by a black American, we now know that at least two
other black poets wrote longer poems: the Reverend
Robert E. Ford's *Brown Chapel, a Story in Verse* (n.d.,
n.p., Preface dated 1903) contained at least 8,600 lines
on 307 pages; Maurice Corbett's *Harp of Ethiopia* (Nashville, 1914) contained over 7,500 lines on 273 pages. Reverend Ford's work is broken up into cantos utilizing
10-line stanzas, while Corbett's epic is divided up into
8-line stanzas.

Whitman utilized a half dozen or so metrical and stanzaic forms and numerous other rhyme schemes. His forms include the *ottava rima*, dialect verse, the Spenserian stanza, blank verse, iambic, trochaic and anapaestic lines in three to five feet (including stressed unrhymed lines), and the various stanzaic and metrical fusions he developed from imitating such writers as Byron, Pope, Whittier, Longfellow, Milton, and Scott. The poet developed his technical facilities while he worked, primarily as a pastor of an African Methodist Episcopal Church in Springfield, Ohio, and financial agent for Wilberforce University (where he had studied under Daniel Payne), to support himself and promote race progress. A fiery speaker, lecturer and reader of his poetry, Whitman was not one to bite his tongue. In declaring that he "was never a slave" he went on to say—at forty years of age—"The time has come when all 'Uncle Toms' and 'Topsies' ought to die."

The title of Whitman's first work, *Not a Man and Yet a Man* (1877) is important both literally and implicitly. For one has only to go a few more steps to place it alongside similar, contemporary titles: *Soul on Ice, Nobody Knows My Name, I Know Why the Caged Bird Sings, Manchild in the Promised Land, Invisible Man,* and scores of other volumes of essays, novels, poems, and autobiographies. The titles are slightly different, but the cry and the passion and aim are the same. *Not a Man and Yet a Man,* for Whitman, ensconces the dilemma of the black man. A mulatto slave, Rodney, saves the life of the daughter of his master during an Indian raid, and afterward falls in love with her. Going against his promise to offer his daughter in marriage to the man who saves her, the master instead sells Rodney to a Deep South planter. In his new habitat, Rodney falls in love with a slave girl, Leona, and after being separated from her for a while, spends a beautiful life with her in Canada. The oversimplified theme of the "tragic mulatto" comes through in much of Whitman's work, which never features the problems or lives of dark-skinned Blacks. Whitman possesses a brilliant gift of descriptive prosaic poetry, as in these lines from *Not a Man:*

The tall forests swim in a crimson sea,
Out of whose bright depths rising silently,

Great golden spires shoot into the skies,
Among the isles of cloudland high, that rise,
Float, scatter, burst, drift off, and slowly fade,
Deep in the twilight, shade succeeding shade.

Somewhat reminiscent of the talented and anonymous
John Boyd, Whitman is competent and relentless when
placed against any other romantics of his day. Elsewhere in
Not a Man, Whitman, echoing Poe and Longfellow, re-
acts to the temporary separation of Rodney and Leona:

A true heroine of the cypress gloom,
Now there to lie, the Creole saw her doom. . . .

In *The Rape of Florida* (St. Louis, 1884), revised and
republished the following year as *Twasinta's Seminoles, or
Rape of Florida*), Whitman engages his readers in another
romantic tale. Under truce, Seminole Indians, who have
fought bravely, are fired on, captured and taken off to
Texas, where they are relocated. Here, in another antici-
pation, we see presages of "relocation" (see Etheridge
Knight's *Belly Song*) that will come in the works of such
modern writers as Baraka, Williams (*The Man Who
Cried I Am*), Baldwin (*Nobody Knows My Name*),
Greenlee (*The Spook Who Sat by the Door*), Crouch
(*Ain't No Ambulances for No Nigguhs Tonite*), the Last
Poets, Gil Scott-Heron (*Free Will, Small Talk at 125th
Street and Lenox*), and numerous others. Whitman, at
any rate, laments the treatment of the Indians, who ex-
tended a brotherly hand to slaves. In a note to the work,
Whitman mentions that he met relatives of one Seminole
chief. *Rape* contains 257 Spenserian stanzas. Atlassa, "an
eminent Seminole chieftain," was "hero-born":

Free as the air within his palmy shade,
The nobler traits that do the man adorn,
In him were native: Not the music made
In Tampa's forests or the everglade
Was fitter than in this young Seminole
Was the proud spirit which did life pervade,
And glow and tremble in his ardent soul—
Which, lit his inmost-self, and spurned
    all mean control.

Whitman's last volume was *An Idyl of the South, An Epic Poem in Two Parts* (New York, 1901). Again ("The Octoroon" and "The Southland's Charm and Freedom's Magnitude") Whitman explores the problems of mulattoes. Here, in chronology and subject matter, he parallels Charles Chestnutt, the black fiction writer who also exploited the theme of the mulatto and "passing." A new edition of *Rape* (1890) also included *Drifted Leaves.* Whitman's *World's Fair Poem: the Freedman's Triumphant Song,* along with "The Veteran" (Atlanta, 1893), were read by himself and Mrs. Whitman respectively at the Chicago World's Fair, attended by Dunbar and the venerable Douglass. Like Dunbar, Whitman became addicted to alcohol, but he managed to maintain his popularity as a hard church worker, freedom fighter and poet. He also published sermons in *Drifted Leaves.* An edition of Whitman's complete works, long overdue, is currently being prepared. For selections of his writings see *Negro Caravan,* Robinson's anthology, Kerlin's book and other anthologies. Sometimes grouped with Phillis Wheatley in the "mocking-bird school of poets," Whitman is assessed by Wagner, Brown, Brawley, Robinson, Kerlin, Jahn (*Neo-African Literature,* 1968), Loggins, and Sherman.

Making only oblique references to racial pressures, George Marion McClellan (1860–1934) is reminiscent of Francis Boyd, and calls to mind Tolson, in his effort to prove Blacks capable of intellectual and literary competence. However, McClellan still does not deserve the abrupt dismissal given him by Sterling Brown (*Negro Poetry*). McClellan writes harmlessly of flowers, trees, birds and love (things Baraka and others have, of late, claimed a black poet should not waste his time on). But he is competent and technically dexterous so as not to bore. Happily, some of the longer pieces are interpolated with shorter ones and this makes McClellan more readable.

After his birth in Belfast, Tennessee, McClellan lived in an economically stable family and later had a good, solid education at Fisk (B.A., 1885, and M.A., 1890) and the Hartford (Connecticut) Theological Seminary (B.D., 1886). Constantly on the go, like Bell, and a fund-raiser, like Whitman, for Fisk University, he spent much of his time on the eastern seaboard executing his important

duties. McClellan pastored and taught in several cities:
Normal (Alabama), Memphis, Louisville (Kentucky), and
Los Angeles, where he finally went in hopes of finding a
cure for his tubercular son. His last years were devoted to
soliciting funds for a tuberculosis sanitorium for Blacks.
Among McClellan's published works are *Poems* (Nashville, 1895), *Book of Poems and Short Stories* (Nashville,
1895), *Old Greenbottom Inn* (1896), *Songs of a Southerner* (Boston, 1896) and *Path of Dreams* (Louisville,
1916). As a poet, McClellan is sharp, crisp and musical in
his use of language and images. "The Color Bane" pulls
us somewhat forward to Fenton Johnson's "The Scarlet
Woman," since the "problem" of having a beautiful but
black face is the theme of both. Even though McClellan's
woman possesses "inexpressible grace."

> For *all* her wealth and gifts of grace
> Could not appease the sham
> Of justice that discriminates
> Against the blood of Ham.

And there is more than a hint in the title of his final volume, *Path of Dreams;* for, as many observers of black writing have noted, the "dream" is a central theme (see
Hughes, Hayden, Nat Turner, Corrothers, Dunbar). Yet,
on the surface, McClellan is delicate and unoffensive. He
writes sonnets, sing-song quasi-ballads, stilted verse reminiscent of Byron, Scott and Milton, and formal ballads
and hymn-inspired praises as in "The Feet of Judas."
Varying meter, stanza and rhyme scheme, McClellan nevertheless refused to write in dialect—the vogue of his day.
Making it analogous to "rag-time," he complained that it
was "considered quite the proper dressing for Negro distinction in the poetic art." For ample selections of
McClellan's writings see Kerlin's critical anthology, Robinson's book and Johnson's *American Negro Poetry.* Robinson, Kerlin, and Brown also give critical views of
McClellan's work. See also Sherman's *Invisible Poets.*

"Rag-picker, tobacco steamer, brickyard hand, whiskey
distiller, teamster and prize-fighter," Joseph Seamon Cotter, Sr. (1861–1949) was also one of the most gifted and
prolific writers of his era. Cotter was born to a black
mother and a white father in Nelson County, Kentucky.

The kinds of work cited above characterized his life when he was forced, at an early age, to interrupt his schooling. Re-entering night school at age twenty-four, he studied to become a teacher and administrator, chores he eventually assumed at the Colored Ward School in Louisville. Cotter also taught English literature and composition and contributed poems, stories and articles to local newspapers including the Louisville *Courier-Journal* (one of America's outstanding newspapers). In his life and work, Cotter looks forward to Blacks like Du Bois, James Weldon Johnson, Mary McLeod Bethune, and Langston Hughes. In his writings, he anticipates the variety and virtuosity of a Dunbar. For, in the words of one critic of the period, "he makes poems and invents and discovers stories, and bardlike, recites them to whatever audience may call for them—in schools, in churches, at firesides" (Kerlin). Brilliant, precocious and enduring, Cotter pursued the complex side of life, daring to examine the often over-simplified phenomenon of race relations in America. Kerlin said of his work: "Some are tragedies and some are comedies and some are tragi-comedies of everyday life among the Negroes."

Cotter (Brown says he has "both point and pith"), it must be said, was among the first black poets to represent, without shame and minstrelsy, authentic black folk life. He wrote in formal—academic, bookish—structures; but he also wrote explicitly in dialect and standard English, of common life and common problems. He achieves "rushing rhythms and ingenious rhymes" when he is at his best; and a quiet, reflective perseverance when he writes introspectively. A disciple of Dunbar, Cotter is able to capture vividly the theme of traveling and weariness that pervades so much black literature and song (see "The Way-Side Well" and repetitions that establish the drudgery and the momentum to carry on). He can be satirical and admonishing in dialect, as in "The Don't-Care Negro":

Neber min' your manhood's risin'
  So you habe a way to stay it.
Neber min' folks' good opinion
  So you have a way to slay it.

In "The Negro Child" Cotter tells the youth to let "lessons of stern yesterdays"

> . . . be your food, your drink, your rest,

and in the same poem he strikes a pose similar to that of Booker T. Washington's when he advises the child to

> Go train your head and hands to do,
> Your head and heart to dare.

Cotter's verses also exalt black and liberal white heroes ("Frederick Douglass," "Emerson," "The Race Welcomes Dr. W. E. B. Du Bois as Its Leader," "Oliver Wendell Holmes") and relish such experiences as reading or listening to Dunbar ("Answer to Dunbar's 'After a Visit' " and "Answer to Dunbar's 'A Choice' ") and Riley ("On Hearing James Whitcomb Riley Read"). He vigorously searches the human heart—and the intangibles of lying, hating, and self denying—in such poems as "Contradiction" and "The Poet." "My Poverty and Wealth" recalls Corrothers' "Compensation," since the richness and strength of commonness, charity and honesty triumph over money and a high social station. A prolific writer, Cotter published several volumes, including: *A Rhyming* (1895); *Links of Friendship* (1898, with a preface by *Courier-Journal* editor Thomas Watkins); *Negro Tales* (1902); a four-act play in blank verse, *Caleb, the Degenerate* (1903); and *A White Song and a Black One* (1909). A good biographical-critical study of Cotter is long overdue. For selections and critical appraisals see Robinson and Kerlin. See also Countee Cullen's *Caroling Dusk* (1927) and Sherman.

Judging from much of the critical reception of Daniel Webster Davis (1862–1913), the prevailing feeling is that he should just disappear. Of all the critics assessing him (Wagner, Brown, Redding, Brawley, Sherman, Johnson and others), only two, Redding and Sherman, seem to feel that Davis has any "sincerity" in his efforts to portray Blacks in dialect. Redding's position is ironic indeed, since in *To Make a Poet Black* he does not discuss the folk tradition in black literature. Davis (who operated on the theory that the most effective writer "is the one in demand") is derivative of the white writers of dialect, as were most of the black dialect writers, and seems only to transcend them in the fact of his being a black man and a preacher—who could deliver the verses with the dramatic impact impossible of Thomas Nelson Page, Irwin Russell, and A. C. Gordon, white dialect writers. Davis was also a serious "scholar of dialect" who wrote from his own firsthand experiences among Blacks. In introductions to his books he draws comparisons and contrasts between black and white southern speech. Redding praises Davis for the same reasons that other critics dismiss him—for his exaggerated depiction of Blacks and his suggestion that plantation "darkies" were content to live out their lives eating "hog meat" and "wadermilluns" and stealing. Redding believes that Davis' poetry "represents the highest imaginative power of the plantation Negro, the prodigal richness of his imagery, and his happy power to resolve all difficulties and mysteries with the reasoning of a child." Redding's comment, not so harsh as it might seem, is nevertheless only partially—if that much—true. For how does one account for the ingenuity of the work songs, the spirituals, the ditties and jingles and the early blues? Did not the same "child" create them also?

Brown, on the other hand, refers to Davis as the "Negro Thomas Nelson Page"—quite a nasty put-down, to use contemporary parlance. And Davis does seem to be making fun of Blacks in giving his poems such titles as: "Hog Meat," "Weh Down Souf," "Bakin an' Greens," "Is Dar Wadermilluns on High?" and "De Bigges' Piece ub Pie." But he is bent on meeting the needs of people who want to be "instructed and entertained." And it will be observed that in some parts of the South *th* is dropped from its ending position in favor of *f* and one certainly finds evidence of Blacks speaking like the characters in Webster's poetry. But another answer might be in a comparison between Flip Wilson (Rev. LeRoy) and Rev. Daniel Webster Davis, who achieved great popularity when he turned his pulpit into a stage from which to unload his own brand of "saving souls" and making the "word" come alive. As Reverend Davis, the dialect poet was not unlike such men as John Jasper, Black Billy Sunday, Brother Easter, and "other Negro preachers" of his day who were so well known. Davis' two collections, primarily in dialect,

are *Idle Moments* (1895) and *Weh Down Souf* (1897).
He also left much unpublished prose. Most of his work
deals with joviality, gluttony, flamboyant sermons, happiness, the "contented" slave and mischievousness—the
stereotypical behavior that white minstrelsy has fostered
on the Blacks. Davis is derivative, as we noticed, to the
point of copying whole lines and phrases, as in "Hog
Meat," in which he takes the words "When the frost is
on the Punkin" from James Whitcomb Riley and changes
them thusly:

> When de fros' is on de pun'kin an' de
>   sno'-flakes in de a'r, . . .

The poem also closely resembles Dunbar's "When de
Co'n Pone's Hot" (although Wagner and other critics
claim that Davis did not borrow from Dunbar but worked
"directly from the models provided by the minstrels and
the southern poets"). Davis acquired first-hand experience
of the black folk predicament, first as a child in North
Carolina and, after the Civil War, in Richmond, Virginia,
where he attended school. Finishing high school with
good marks, he began to teach in the black schools of
Richmond. His popularity was wide among "the less liter-
ate of his own race," according to James Weldon Johnson,
which may be a partial reason for Davis' continual production of his particular brand of "poetry." Known for reading his verses with "comical unctuousness before convulsed audiences," his work, when placed beside Dunbar's,
is unfinished. In style and workmanship, however, it
should be noted that Davis is not unlike some of the
bombastic black poets of today. For when the complete
story is told, many "popular" contemporary poets—speaking and writing a "dialect" and titillating "convulsed"
audiences—may very well meet the fate reserved for
Davis. (Instead of becoming a "prelude to a kiss" they
may end up a footnote to a joke.) In his few standard-
English pieces, Davis also preaches a conciliatory attitude,
as in "Emancipation," in which he claims the African
"roamed the savage wild"

> Untamed his passions; half a man and
>   half a savage child,

until God "saw fit" to teach the black man of "Him and Jesus Christ." It could be that there is more to Davis than has met the eye; at any rate, a complete study of his life and works awaits some serious student of black poetry. For assessments of selections from Davis' writing see Brown, Sherman, Wagner, Robinson, Redding, and Johnson.

Our study makes no claim that every poet briefly considered is any sort of *giant*. In fact, except when such a title or label is obviously warranted, there is an effort to steer clear of such qualitative evaluations. This is true in view of our stated goal: to place into the hands of students and lay persons a handy reference to, and an overview of, black poetry. So Jean Wagner's claim that "it would have required a great deal of indulgence to welcome" the poetry of John Wesley Holloway (1865–1935) into "the literary domain" cannot find credence or reinforcement in this book. Wagner also includes Cotter, Corrothers, and Braithwaite in his list of poets *non grata*.

Holloway, like his contemporaries Davis and Corrothers, was a "preacher-poet." His poetry is in both standard-English form and dialect, which, according to Johnson, is his "best work." In *The Negro's God*, Benjamin Mays classes Holloway with the writers and thinkers who take a conciliatory and compensatory approach to the deity—despite oppression, slavery or whatever. In one poem, Holloway is "Waiting on the Lord"; and even

Though hosts of sin may hedge me round,

he will nevertheless wait "patiently" for help from God. James Baldwin, and other black writers of the twentieth century (getting a first start from Dunbar), call such advice "dishonest." Baldwin, a youthful preacher, saw a contradiction in the preacher's resignation and the rat-infested tenement buildings against whose owners the preachers refused to lead a rent strike. Yet, as a preacher, Holloway exhibits a classic devotion and the ability (see Preface to Johnson's *God's Trombones*) to aid in the welding of the disparate black masses—never an easy task.

A disciple of Dunbar, Holloway was born in Meriwether County, Georgia. His father, one of the first black teachers in the state, had learned to read and write as a slave and sent his son to Clark (Atlanta) and Fisk universities. For a period, young Holloway was a member of the famous Fisk Jubilee Singers. As a poet of dialect, Holloway is both musical and humorous, as in "Miss Merlerlee," who has

> Sof' brown cheek, an' smilin' face

and

> Perly teef, an' shinin' hair
> An' silky arm so plump an' bare!

Reflecting a growing practice of the transitional poets, Holloway makes an honest effort to portray deep black emotions and feelings. His descriptions of black women (especially) and men signal a new and vibrant aspect of black poetry—the merger of the sexual/sensual levels with the racial flavor of postbellum black America. Linguistically, Holloway approaches the sounds and idioms of the Gullah, which will be seen more definitively in James Edwin Campbell. Since the Gullah dialect is spoken in the areas off the shores of Georgia and the Carolinas, it is possible that Holloway picked up accents and expressions as a child. His books include *Bandannas* (n.d.) and *From the Desert* (1919). Especially humorous is his "Calling the Doctor," which is an important cataloguing of folk medicinal remedies, including

> Blue-mass, laud-num, liver pills,
> "Sixty-six, fo' fever an' chills,"
> Ready Relief, an' A. B. C.,
> An' half a bottle of X. Y. Z.

Holloway (as dialect poet) joined Dunbar, Corrothers, J. Mord Allen and Ray Dandridge in being published for the first time (during the first two decades of the twentieth century) in previously "off-limits" white periodicals. For selections from and criticism of Holloway's work see Johnson's *American Negro Poetry* and Mays's *The Negro's God*. See also, for criticism, Brown's *Negro Poetry and Drama*.

Yet another dialect writer, Elliot Baine Henderson, on whom we have little information, was another disciple of Dunbar. A "prolific writer," he published some eight vol-

umes of verse, all in dialect. In much of his writings, as
with Holloway and Campbell, he utilizes the phonetics
and idioms of the Gullah—akin to the West Indian brand
of folk English. Henderson is sometimes concerned with
folk beliefs and the supernatural and black religious
themes and songs ("Git on Board, Chillen"). His dialect
is inconsistent, a problem with most dialect writers (including Dunbar), and while he tries to achieve a phonetic
transcription of what he hears, he spells (in the same
title) "Board" in a standard English way and attempts to
place words like "Git" and "Chillun" in dialect. His volumes include *Plantation Echoes* (Columbus, Ohio,
1904), *Darky Meditations* (Springfield, Ohio, 1910),
Uneddykated Folks (author, 1911) and *Darky Ditties*
(Columbus, 1915).

James Edwin Campbell (1867–95), unlike his contemporary Dunbar, "owes almost nothing to the plantation
poets." Campbell seems to have listened carefully to and
applied the black folk speech around him, whereas Dunbar took his initial cues from the plantation school, chief
proponent of which was Irwin Russell. Born in Pomeroy,
Ohio, Campbell graduated from the Pomeroy Academy
and for a while taught school near Gallipolis. He gained
more teaching and administrative experience at the Langston School in Virginia and the West Virginia Colored
Institute (now West Virginia State College), where oppo-
sition to his administrative policies forced him to leave for
Chicago. There, Campbell was a member of the staff of
the Chicago *Herald and Examiner* for the rest of his life.
Like his contemporaries, Cotter and Dunbar (and others),
Campbell's early verses were published in various newspapers. His first volume of poems (*Driftings and Gleanings*, 1887) contains poems in standard English and two
essays. His second volume, solely poetry, was published in
1895 under the title *Echoes from the Cabin and Elsewhere*.

Campbell is quite competent in both standard English
and dialect; and while some of his sentiments are well
handled in the standard-English poems, it is in the dialect
pieces that he shows his power, complexity and originality.
Among his important themes are interracial love (one of
the first black writers—see Whitman and others—to deal

with this "touchy" subject), the mulatto, satire (see, especially, "Ol' Doc' Hyar"), black pride (though muffled), and realistic presentations of black "social realities, religious formalism, and folk values." (Jean Wagner's *Black Poets of the United States*) It is important to mention his brand of dialect, although a more in-depth study is still to be done. Unlike Dunbar, who seemed to strive for a universal anglicized phonetic, Campbell, (traces are also found in Holloway and Henderson) recorded the speech patterns closely related to Gullah. Such usage is seen in employing the subjective and objective pronouns in the nominative position ("Me see," "Him hab," etc). There is use of the broad *a* as in "Uncle Eph's Banjo Song": "bawnjer" and "dawnce" and the *er* (as in "bawnjer") for the *o*. The verbal copula *to be* is usually omitted (assumed?) and there is a normal lengthening of an *e* or *i* sound in words like "Beeg," "jeeg," "Laigs." The *v* often becomes *b*, and *t* sometimes becomes *k*. There are, of course, other great differences. For more on such linguistic aspects see works by Lorenzo Dow Turner, Herman Blake, Robert D. Twiggs, and others.

Campbell has a more authentic ring than Dunbar, and one gets the impression that he is seriously involved in feeling as well as representing what Hughes called "the pulse of the people." But Campbell and Dunbar are also similar in many ways. In "Negro Serenade" (compare to Dunbar's "A Negro Love Song") Campbell captures a sharp human-social need. In "De Cunjah Man" he achieves a strong musical ring (with the help of a ring-a-round-the-rosy sort of chant) and dabbles in the supernatural—suggesting, as Chestnutt did, that perhaps the black folk tradition holds keys to the "ultimate mysteries of the universe." The recurring refrain of

De Cunjah man, de Cunjah man,
O chillen run, de Cunjah man!

will be ramified and made more dexterous by Hughes, Toomer and Hayden, as they experiment with these exciting oral folk forms. Campbell attempted to capture the cadences and gestural complexities of a contemporary dance, the "buck," in his poem "Mobile Buck." He stated that he sought the "shuffling, jerky rhythm of the famous

Negro dance," which he had seen performed by black longshoremen on the Ohio or the Mississippi. This type of word-movement marriage is not unusual in black poetry. Numerous examples of such pairings abound today. Lastly, we should note that Campbell's near-Gullah dialect would later be revived (in the thirties and forties) by such writers as Ambrose Gonzales and Julia Peterkin. McKay, we have said, employed a similar dialect in his Jamaican poems. Actor-singer Harry Belafonte, son of West Indians, would popularize this same dialect in the 1950s and 1960s ("Daylight come and me wanna go home"). More salient contemporary examples of this idiom (and its cadences) can be found in the lyrics of the West Indian music known as the "reggae")—an island version of Afro-American "soul" music.

One of the first black poets to write in dialect, Campbell deserves much more attention than he has thus far received. At this writing, the most exhaustive studies of him appear in Wagner's *Black Poets* and Sherman's *Invisible Poets*. Though he was a close friend of Dunbar's, his major works in dialect preceded Dunbar's books. In addition to his poetry, he was also a member of a group that edited the *Four O'Clock Magazine*, which was published for several years in Chicago. On one occasion, Campbell is known to have spent time talking to black men, pleading with them to spend their time more wisely than in drinking and gambling. For selections of his work see Johnson, Robinson and *Negro Caravan*. For critical evaluations see Brown, Wagner, Johnson, Redding ("Campbell's ear alone dictated his language"), and Carter G. Woodson's "J. E. Campbell: A Forgotten Man of Letters," *Negro History Bulletin*, November 1938, p. 11.

In 1937 Sterling Brown said, "Eloquent and militant" were the "words most descriptive" of the poetry of William Edward Burghardt Du Bois (1868–1963). Brown, who also termed Du Bois "the leading intellectual influence of his generation," was only two years ahead of a similar accolade from J. Saunders Redding: "They [poems] represent the greatness of Dr. Du Bois as an inspirational force." In the history of black poetry, however, Du Bois does not deserve as large a portion of the limelight as is normally accorded his work as historian, social critic, journalist, novelist, Africanist, organizer of important Pan-African congresses in the 1920s, editor of *The Crisis*, pathfinder-scholar of the black experience, precursor of black militancy and the "new Negro." In 1923, Kerlin (*Negro Poets*) said Du Bois was "celebrated in the Five Continents and the Seven Seas."

As a poet, however, Du Bois is important for his work in the prose-poem form and for asserting a militance, and defiance, and declaiming a hatred of racism and oppression that had not been heard since James Whitfield. Like molten lava, the disgust and anger spill from Du Bois's pen, as in "Hymn of Hate":

> I hate them, Oh!
> I hate them well,
> I hate them, Christ!
> As I hate hell!

Ironically, though, in his hatred Du Bois always managed to re-establish his faith and trust in some higher order—in God. Most of his poems had been published in various periodicals (the *Independent*, *Atlantic Monthly* and *The Crisis*) before several of them were interspersed among the essays in *Darkwater* (1919). Du Bois had, by that time, already gained recognition for his individualized use of poetic prose—which fused biblical language and imagery with his classical education and the expressions from the *Souls of Black Folk* (1903). But in "A Litany of Atlanta," written after the racial holocaust that took several black lives, he assails all fundamentals—including the existence of God. If God does exist, in face of such violence and savagery,

> Surely Thou too art not white, O Lord,
>   a pale, bloodless, heartless thing?

Du Bois also takes the occasion to cite his archenemy (Booker T. Washington):

> They told him: *Work and Rise.*

A seeker after univeral suffrage and brotherhood, Du Bois employed much of his poetry in the service of the political ideologies he espoused. Thus in "A Hymn to the Peoples" he unites socialism and the Christian God under one banner, viewing "the primal meeting of the Sons of Man" as

> Foreshadowing the union of the world!

Other poems in *Darkwater* include "The Riddle of the Sphinx" and "The Prayers of God." His "Song of the Smoke" (written in 1899) makes the American Black the "smoke king." Listing achievements and misuses of Blacks (a favorite habit of black poets), Du Bois at one point asks for acceptance of the black man on equal terms with the white:

> Souls unto me are as mists in the night,
> I whiten my blackmen, I blackon my white,
> What's the hue of a hide to a man in his might!

But Du Bois does not silence his pen without some appeal to God:

> Sweet Christ, pity toiling lands!
> Hail to the smoke king,
> Hail to the black!

For selections from and comment on Du Bois's poetry see Kerlin, Brown, Redding (*Freedomways*, Winter 1965), Johnson (*American Negro Poetry*). For assessments see Jahn, Barksdale and Kinnamon, Wagner, Mays, and Chapman (*Black Voices*, 1968), who rightly calls Du Bois "the intellectual father of modern Negro scholarship, modern Negro militancy and self-consciousness, and modern Negro cultural development." Du Bois's *Selected Poems* was published (1973) by Ghana Universities Press and is available in the United States from Panther House, Ltd.

James David Corrothers (1869–1919) acknowledged his debts to Shelley, Keats ("Dream and the Song") and Dunbar ("Paul Laurence Dunbar"), after whom much of his dialect poetry is modeled. But Corrothers, a minister, displays neither the range (in subject matter) nor the skill of Dunbar. His mother died at his birth in Cass County, Michigan, and his father apparently gave him little care. In Michigan, he worked as a youth in the sawmills and lumber camps, as a sailor on the Great Lakes, and later eked out a living as janitor, coachman and bootblack in a barbershop. Encouraged by associates to continue his education, he studied for the ministry and remained in that profession (pastoring in Methodist, Baptist and Presbyterian churches) all his life. His first publishing opportunity came through *Century* magazine; this brought him a wide reading audience because of the resemblance of his work to that of Dunbar. Corrothers' first volume (*Selected Poems*) was published in 1907, and his second collection (*The Dream and the Song*) came out in 1914. He was in Chicago during the same period that Campbell lived there, and he also worked for various daily newspapers. He met and socialized with Campbell and Dunbar. From newspaper articles and unpublished poems he put together *Black Cat Club* (1907), and his autobiography, *In Spite of Handicap*, was published in 1916.

Corrothers' "At the Closed Gate of Justice" apparently has been misread by a number of critics (Johnson included) as advising resignation and conciliation. But knowledge that Corrothers was a minister should shed more light on his usages and implications. Each one of the four stanzas (except for the fourth, which ends "'Merely a Negro'—in a day like this!") begins and ends with:

To be a Negro in a day like this.

As a sermon, on the surface, the poem appears to tell Blacks to have "patience" and "forgiveness" and so on. But a closer reading will reveal a strong adjective leading into almost every virtue. So the groupings look like this: "rare patience," "strange loyalty" and "utter darkness"— all of which suggest that, in the code of the preacher, it just might be too "rare" or "strange" or "utter." During the delivery of a sermon, or similar verbal activity, Blacks are accustomed to searching for meaning—shifts and levels based on tonal variety and other vocal modulations. So we see yet one more example of a possible "encoding" of messages (see Chapter II) in what "seems" to be, at best, harmless deliveries and, at worst, conciliatory.

"Paul Laurence Dunbar" presages the Harlem Renaissance and the "new Negro" in having the "Dark melodist" venture to the citadels of Western culture—using "Apollo's Fire" and visiting "Helicon," the home of the muses. Even more blatant, however, is Corrothers' brilliant sonnet "The Negro Singer," in which he carries out a major theme of the Harlem Renaissance—reclamation of black cultural values and the black past. The "Singer," tired and frustrated from trying to write (and act) white, finally decides:

But I shall dig me deeper to the gold;

and

Fetch water dripping, over desert miles,

so that at least some of his original virtue and ancestral strength can be exploited in the Western world. Such a course is the only way for the black poet, Corrothers says, the only way for "men" to

. . . know, and remember long,
Nor my dark face dishonor any song.

The same theme (slightly altered) is picked up in "The Road to the Bow," in which the singer again knows

I hold my head as proudly high
As any man.

Tension develops between the black and white men in "In the Matter of Two Men," and "An Indignation Dinner" features a dialect presentation of the popular plantation/minstrelsy theme about Blacks stealing chickens and turkeys. A social lesson occurs in the poem, however, for "old Pappy Simmons ris" and explained to those facing a foodless Christmas that nothing but "wintry wind" (hot air) is "a-sighing th'ough / de street." He tells the persons at the meeting that he has seen plenty food on a "certain gemmun's / fahm" and that

"All we need is a committee foh to tote
the goodies here."

Earlier in the poem, Blacks protest their treatment at the hands of whites; and in a seventeen-part series called "Sweeten 'Tatahs," one annoyed Black complains:

"Evahthaing is 'dulterated
By de white folks, nowadays—
Even chime bones, when you buys 'em
Dey ain't wo'f de cash you pays.

In one poem, Blacks complain of small wages; in another, they protest high prices—familiar stories in the Afro-American communities. They dispel ignorant statements (like Wagner's) that Corrothers is "lacking in personality" and that his works do not belong in "the literary domain." And they cancel, in part, Brown's allegation that Corrothers follows a "typical dialect pattern." For selections of Corrothers' works see Johnson, Hughes and Bontemps, and Robinson. For critical appraisals see Brown, Johnson, and Brawley.

James Weldon Johnson (1871–1938), important in his own right as a poet and for his immense "service to other Negro poets," is looked at in passing here. He will be seen again in Chapter V in connection with the Harlem Renaissance—where he is normally placed even though he was in his fifties when the leading lights of that era—Cullen, Hughes, McKay, Toomer, and others—first started to publish their works. Johnson, considered here as a writer of dialect poetry, was born in Jacksonville, Florida, to middle-class black parents and attended Stanton Central Grammar School (all black), where his mother taught. He entered a preparatory program at Atlanta University, later graduating and returning to assume principalship of Stanton, where, during an eight-year period, he upgraded the school to secondary status. Considered a "Renaissance man" (in the European sense), Johnson founded a local newspaper (*The Daily American*, 1894), studied for the Florida bar (was admitted in 1897), wrote dialect poems (modeled after Dunbar's), and finally made his way to Broadway in New York, where he collaborated with his brother, composer J. Rosamond Johnson, and Bob Cole on light operas. Sterling Brown said Johnson recognized the "triteness" of his early dialect poems (many published in *Fifty Years and Other Poems*, 1917), but several of them—put to music by his brother and Cole—became popular favorites. *The Century* accepted "Sence you Went Away" for publication. And the brothers composed "Lift Every Voice and Sing" (lyrics by James) for the February 12, 1900, anniversary of Lincoln's birth. This poem is generally regarded as the "national anthem" of black America.

Johnson's dialect poems, listed in his book under "Jingles and Croons," leave much to be desired in the area of originality. Perhaps his own experiments in that form are what led him to state so emphatically that dialect has but "two stops": "humor and pathos." Johnson was not totally right, as we shall see later (Brown takes up this issue in *The Negro in Poetry and Drama*). However, Kerlin (who Wagner says shows a "deficiency in critical sense") called Johnson's work "some of the best dialect writing in the whole range of Negro literature. Every quality of excellence is here." Technically, Johnson was quite capable of handling dialect. But his dialect brings nothing new to black poetry (unlike Sterling Brown's or Margaret Walker's) and his themes have been pretty much overworked by the time he reaches print. "My Lady's Lips Am Like de Honey" recalls Dunbar's "A Negro Love Song," Corrothers' "Negro Serenade," and other such pieces. Johnson's poem carries none of the power of Dunbar's "Song." And his subtitle ("Negro Love Song") shows that he is working in the stock trade for the period. The lover finally gets to the point where he

Felt her kinder squeeze mah han',
'Nuff to make me understan'.

"Sence you Went Away" is one of the really touching statements in "Jingles and Croons" and shows Johnson bridging the blues and spiritual styles. It has an authentic (though quietly turbulent) ring in its simplicity—moving and lingering in its spell wrought by seeing the loss of a lover as a cause for disorder in the cosmos. Glimpses of humor come through in a few of the poems, but generally the dialect is used for ridicule—albeit unwittingly—and deals with the "easy" life of the plantation, the stealing of turkeys and

. . . eatin' watermelon, an' a layin' in de shade.

We will meet Johnson again, as critic, maturer poet and user of a different "dialect."

Paul Laurence Dunbar (1872–1906), the towering figure of black American literature until the renaissance of the 1920s, lived a complex, tragic, ambiguous and short life. Born in Dayton, Ohio, to former slaves, Dunbar completed his formal training at that city's only high school—

graduating with good marks and as the only Black in his class. He was sickly at an early age but became the man of the house when he was twelve years old, after his father's death. Completing high school but being financially unable to pursue his interests in law and journalism, Dunbar began work as an elevator boy, maintaining his voracious reading habits. He was fond of Tennyson, Shelley (whom he took as a model for his poems in standard English), James Russell Lowell (whose work, along with Riley, Eugene Field, and Ella Wheeler Wilcox, he found in *The Century*), and others. Much of Dunbar's poetry bears striking resemblance to the works of poets he admired, especially Shelley, Tennyson, and Riley, whose "devices" Dunbar "industriously" set out to "dismantle" and master. Substantial new recognition was accorded the poet when the United States Postal Service issued an official commemorative stamp bearing his picture in 1975.

His volumes of verse include *Oak and Ivy* (1893), privately printed; *Majors and Minors* (1895), also privately printed, with the aid of patrons; *Lyrics of Lowly Life* (1896, with a preface by Howells), which, representing a major breakthrough for a black author, was published by Dodd, Mead, and Company. This third volume included the best poems from the two previous volumes and some that had not been published before. Dunbar, almost instantly famous, continued to write and publish both verse and fiction. His later books of poems included *Lyrics of the Hearthside* (1899), *Lyrics of Love and Laughter* (1903) and *Lyrics of Sunshine and Shadow* (1905), the year before his death. *Complete Poems* was published in 1913. Interspersed among these books of poetry were volumes of short stories and four novels: *The Uncalled* (1898), *The Love of Landry* (1900), *The Fanatics* (1901), and *The Sport of the Gods* (1902). His short stories included "Folks from Dixie" (1898), "The Strength of Gideon" (1900), "In Old Plantation Days" (1903), and "The Heart of Happy Hollow" (1904). Dunbar was prolific almost right up until the time of his death —which he knew was approaching. He had married Alice Ruth Moore, a promising author from New Orleans, in 1898; and his last years were an effort to heal both failing health and a failing marriage.

As poetry, Dunbar's work falls into two divisions: dialect and standard (some say "literary" or "classic") English. We attempt here to present some of his poetic concerns, achievements and themes. But Dunbar's life and works are too far-reaching and complex to be assessed completely in this type of survey. Much has been said about his seeming inability or unwillingness to articulate in verse the mistreatment of his people. Whether this was of his choosing, as a man or as an artist, has yet to be thoroughly ascertained. But much of the answer seems to be locked in his own writings. Dunbar was launched into "curious" fame on June 27, 1896, when literary czar Howells published a favorable full-page review of *Majors and Minors* in *Harper's Weekly*. Some indication of Howells' influence is indicated by Van Wyck Brooks: "Howells was perhaps the only literary critic in the history of American literature who has been able to create reputations by a single review" (Brooks, *The Confident Years*, 1952). But, as Barksdale and Kinnamon note, Howells' review was more of a social commentary (liberal, that is) than literary criticism. Howells singled out the dialect poems for special praise. Dunbar, he said, "was the only man of pure African blood and of American civilization to feel negro life aesthetically and express it lyrically."

Dunbar, later realizing Howells' praise was a curse in disguise, struggled for the rest of his life to remove the dialect stigma. He complained to James Weldon Johnson that the public wanted to read only his dialect pieces. And feeling the pressure to be an intelligent "Sambo," he elsewhere complained of having to play the part of a "black white man." Dunbar's resentment of the "label" of dialect poet when he felt he had more profound and complex things to say is capsuled in this often-quoted stanza from "The Poet":

He sang of love when earth was young,
And love, itself, was in his lays.
But ah, the world, it turned to praise
A jingle in a broken tongue.

Earlier in the poem, Dunbar refers to a "deeper note," which he preferred to sing. But while such poems as

"Sympathy," "The Haunted Oak," "The Debt," and "Ere Sleep Comes Down to Soothe the Weary Eyes" do have deep and complicated meanings, one searches in vain for Dunbar *the man* in them. In the dialect pieces, Dunbar was able to capture the rhythms, phonetics and idioms of black speech. But it is generally agreed that, especially since he used ridicule-directed white models, he saw the black man as a subject for either humor or pity. The South's revenge for the Civil War had come in part through its philosophers and writers, who reflected nostalgically about the "peace and tranquility" of plantation life. This was political chicanery at its worst, but several black poets, Dunbar included, followed the white originators of the minstrel and plantation school of poets. (Whites did not originate minstrelsy—but they did corrupt it; see Loften Mitchell's *Black Drama*.) As a result, Dunbar's treatment of Blacks in his dialect poems is "stock" material for the era: singing, grinning, obsequious, head-scratching, master-loving, watermelon-eating, dancing, banjo-picking darkies. Certainly Dunbar comes through realistically as in "A Negro Love Song" (a written account of a song sung by Blacks he had worked with), "Little Brown Baby," "When de Co'n Pone's Hot" (the good-eating theme), "The Party," "How Lucy Backslid," "The Rivals," and others. He also achieves subtlety and irony elsewhere. "When Malindy Sings" is by all accounts his important linguistic-cultural contribution. Yet Dunbar seemed to reserve the "serious" subjects for standard English—for which black critics will not forgive him—and even in this seriousness he speaks of people behind "masks" or "caged" or "dreaming" or lonely. In these standard pieces, Dunbar treats unrequited love and goes on lofty flights as a knight or wanderer or theologian; or he is resigned, as in "Resignation," in which he invites God to "crush me for Thy use" if need be. Yet accusations that Dunbar was completely torn from the real world of blackness are not true. In "The Haunted Oak," for example, he indicts the judge, the minister and the doctor for the lynching of a black man. He also brooded over his dark skin, feeling that, during a time of preference for light skin and the habit of "passing," his color held him back. But some of his poetry anticipates Gar-

vey's call for "ethnic purity." He praises the brown skin of
Mandy Lou in "Dreamin' Town," and he loves "Dely" for
being

> . . . brown ez brown can be, . . .
> She ain't no mullater;
> She pure cullud,—don't you see . . .
> Dat's de why I love huh so,
> D' ain't no mix about huh, . . .

A similar theme pervades "Song" ("African maid"),
"Dinah Kneading Dough" ("Brown arms buried elbow-
deep") and "A Plantation Portrait" (Browner den de
Frush's Wing"). In his dialect poems, Dunbar reveals a
love for spirit and revelry and good times. But nowhere is
there an indication of the enormous suffering and violence
inherited by postwar Afro-Americans. The lynchings, the
patty-rollers (search squads) swooping down on defense-
less ex-slaves, the night rides of the Ku Klux Klan and
White Citizens Councils, the harsh and debilitating economic situation of Blacks in general—none of these find
their way into Dunbar's poetry. All this, of course, is ironic
against Dunbar's great admiration for such men as Frederick Douglass, Alexander Crummell, Booker T. Washington, and "Black Sampson of Brandywine"—all of
whom he immortalized in poetry. Instead, in his "deeper
note" Dunbar (notwithstanding the examples of Whitfield, Whitman, Du Bois, and others) spoke of heartbreak,
probed his own pessimism and religious doubt and seemed
literally to pine away. (In one dialect poem, however, he
advised Blacks to "Keep Pluggin' Along").

Much of this enigma of Dunbar seems to be explained
in his poem "A Choice" (generally overlooked by critics,
who monotonously quote from "The Poet"), in which he
complains of being tired of problems and stresses:

> But in a poem let me sup,
> Not simples brewed to cure or ease
> Humanity's confessed disease,
> But the spirit-wine of a singing line,
> Or a dew-drop in a honey cup!

On more than one occasion, Dunbar intimated to associates that he was all but fed up with racial agitation—ap-

parently feeling that black-white relations were beyond repair. This could be at least one reason why he "washed his hands" of involvement. There are poets in the middle of the twentieth century who feel the same way. Nevertheless Dunbar's request received a reply from a contemporary, Cotter, who in his "Answer to Dunbar's 'A Choice'" said:

That poets should by swift degrees
    Put back the frail, bring forth the strong,
And wed stern facts to sober song. . . .

Dunbar either did not heed/hear or was not aware of this "answer"; but if he had taken Cotter's advice perhaps the world would know a different poet today. Above all, Dunbar was a skillful reader of his poetry—often bringing audiences to their feet for standing ovations and pleas for encores. His dexterousness in the use of language and style was admired by several generations of black college poets and lay writers who imitated him. In almost every substantial black community there is some public facility named after Dunbar. He wrote in almost every prevailing style—the greatest black exploiter of English poetic techniques between Whitman and Cullen. Sonnet, madrigal, couplet, ballad, spiritual, pre-blues, songs (including use of musical notation in some instances)—Dunbar seems to have tried them all.

Dunbar's poems can be found in *Complete Poems*, the text used for the discussion here. For critical-biographical writing on Dunbar see Wagner's *Black Poets of the United States* (the most ambitious study to date), Brawley's *Paul Laurence Dunbar: Poet of His People*, works by Brown and Redding, Victor Lawson's *Dunbar Critically Examined*, Virginia Cunningham's *Paul Laurence Dunbar and His Song*, and Jean Gould's *That Dunbar Boy: The Story of America's Famous Negro Poet*. Others who have written on Dunbar include Houston Baker, Darwin Turner, Benjamin Mays, James Weldon Johnson, Herbert Martin, Nick Aaron Ford, and Addison Gayle, Jr., who recently published a Dunbar biography (see bibliography).

Junius Mordecai Allen (1875–?), another poet about whom we know very little, is an important figure in this transitional phase of black poetry, which witnessed the

passing of the plantation tradition in poetry and the wilt-
ing of Washington's influence on black thinkers and activists. Allen was born in Montgomery, Alabama, and moved
with his family to Topeka, Kansas, when he was seven
years old. Except for a three-year period during which he
wrote for and traveled with a theatrical group, he spent
most of his life as a boilermaker. His only volume is
Rhymes, Tales and Rhymed Tales (Topeka, 1906).
Mostly dialect, *Rhymes* contains "great felicity of charac-
terization, surprising turns of wit" and "quaint philosophy"
(Kerlin). The book appeared the year of Dunbar's death,
and Kerlin places Allen on a par with Dunbar—somewhat
of an exaggeration. However, Allen is profound in both
his standard-English pieces (he includes two in the book)
and dialect. "Counting Out" is a rather light recollection
of childhood games such as "counting out," "hide-and-
seek," and "I spy." The poem, with its recurring

"Eeny meeny miny mo,"

gives clues to the psychological, linguistic and gestural
development of black youngsters (which is charmingly
sufficient). Allen also knows the consequences of "getting
caught" out at night or in alien territory among vicious,
hate-mongering and lynch-prone whites. The games

Are now with consequences fraught;
There's black disgrace in being caught.

Death as a general reality is also assumed:

For death will soon count down the row,
"Eeny meeny miny mo."

"The Psalm of Uplift" raises questions and doubts,
revealing the pessimistic strain of the poem above (and
that found in Dunbar). He asks if one should strive

Till sunset of eternity

and whether the victories won are worth the struggle.
Here, of course, are echoes of his contemporary Fenton
Johnson, who will also question whether, for the black
man, struggle in America is valid or fruitful. Critics have
noted that Johnson is the first to sound this alarmingly

"foreign" philosophy. But such is not totally true. Allen asks if one should "enter where there is no retreat" simply

> To win one stride from sheer defeat;
> To die—but gain an inch.

His pen remained silent after his first book. And one wonders if Allen, like so many black artists, renounced his artistic inclination (in view of the times) and simply gave up. His dialect poems carry, on the surface, the spirit of the "dialect traditions." But Allen is a biting satirist of middle-class Blacks (Wagner attributes this to an "inferiority complex"), and he pokes fun at whites. Temptation overtakes the preacher who tries to "resist" in "The Devil and Sis Viney," but "Shine On, Mr. Suny" and "The Squeak of the Fiddle" show his close observation of (and take-it-or-leave-it attitude toward) whites. His satire of the black middle class is reminiscent of the impatience suggested in statements by Whitman and anticipates the works, especially, of Frank Marshall Davis and Melvin Tolson.

Allen is also important as a stylistic innovator. In "A Victim of Microbes," he again casts aspersions on whites and spoofs stereotypes of Blacks as field workers and laborers. But he couches his narrative in an exciting new literary form which allows for an alternation between loosely rhymed eight-line stanzas and four-line stanzas of blank verse in which repetition of the sort found in the blues of spirituals occurs:

> I done hyeahed de doctor say it—de
> doctor hisse'f said it—. . . .

Brown was right when he said Allen's work was "unpretentious" and contained "pleasant humor." For selections of Allen's poetry see Kerlin's work; for criticism, see Brown and Wagner.

Primarily important as a writer of prose, journalism and as inspiration to other writers, Alice Dunbar-Nelson (1875–1935) was born and received her public education in New Orleans. Her marriage to Paul Laurence Dunbar came in 1898, after she pursued further study at Cornell and Columbia universities and the University of Pennsylvania. She authored volumes of prose: *Violets and Other Tales* (1894) and *The Goodness of St. Tocque* (1899) and edited *Masterpieces of Negro Eloquence* (1913) and *The Dunbar Speaker* (1920), in which appears some of her poetry. A noted journalist and lecturer, she served for a while as managing editor of *The Advocate* and contributed to numerous magazines. Her poetry has little racial flavor, but she does protest against World War I; her often anthologized "The Sonnet" represents her technical abilities in that form. In "I Sit and Sew" she laments that, as a woman, she can do little else to hasten the end to war. "The Lights at Carney's Point" contains "fine symmetry, highly poetic diction and great allusive meaning" (Kerlin). An easy-flowing poem in four-line stanzas of iambic tetrameter, "Lights" allows the poet (as with many romantic writers) to stream associations from a central theme—the lights. But something was lost when the lights went "gray in the ash of day,"

> And the sun laughed high in the infinite sky,
> And the lights were forgot in the sweet, sane calm.

Studies of Mrs. Dunbar-Nelson's poetry are being written. And her collected poems have yet to be published. "The Sonnet" is printed in several anthologies, and three of her poems appear in Kerlin's book. Kerlin also advances brief criticism.

Although Sterling Brown says that Joshua Henry Jones (1876–?) "gives little besides banal jingling," we mention him briefly as part of our effort to survey the poetic range of the period. (For more listings of lesser-known poets see the end of this chapter.) Jones was born in Orangeburg, South Carolina, and, after completing high school, attended Ohio State University, Yale and Brown. He served on the editorial staffs of several newspapers, was secretary to the mayor of Boston for four years, and published two books of poems (*The Heart of the World and Other Poems*, Boston, 1919, and *Poems of the Four Seas*, Boston, 1921) and a novel (*By Sanction of Law*, Boston, 1924). Jones's poetry treats nature, nostalgia, race struggle (as in "Brothers") and sentimental love ("A Southern Love Song"), themes that Kerlin has compared to John-

son's "Love Song." Though grim, "To a Skull" does show
originality.

Noted more for walking all the way from his home in
the South to Harvard University, where he camped over-
night and was arrested on a charge of vagrancy, Edward
Smyth Jones (18?–?) published *The Sylvan Cabin* in
1911. Called "pompously literary" by Brown, who adds
that his verses are less interesting than his "biography,"
Jones wrote "Harvard Square" while he was in jail. The
poem brought him immediate attention and helped speed
up his release. It is a hodgepodge of imitations of various
European models. He recites the names of Dante, Byron,
Keats, Shelley, Burns, and the like in a bombast of stanzas. "A Song of Thanks," however, shows more sensitivity
and deeper feeling. While it leaves a lot to be desired, one
can certainly feel the power growing through the repetition
(in several dozen lines) of the phrase "For the," which
precedes sun, flowers, rippling streams, and other facets
of nature.

Alex Rogers (1876–1930) is one of the several dozen or
so "minor" writers of dialect during this period. Many
poets published pamphlets themselves, secured places for
their work in newspapers and magazines, and traveled on a
regular reading circuit performing their poems and ditties,
often to the accompaniment of bands or single musical instruments. This practice has continued up until this very
day, when many poets, if not heard live, lose their
significance and dramatic flavor. Such was the case with
Rogers, who James Weldon Johnson notes "wrote lyrics
for most of the songs in the musical comedies in which
Williams and Walker appeared." Rogers was born in
Nashville, Tennessee, educated in the schools of that city,
and finally worked his way North, where he wrote some of
the most popular songs of his day; he made a number of
performers famous, including white entertainers looking
for "Negro stuff." He employs satire, humor and some
slapstick. His titles give some clue to his intentions:
"Why Adam Sinned," "The Rain Song" (a Flip Wilson-
type conversation between "Bro. Wilson" and "Bro. Simmons"), "The Jonah Man," and "Bon Bon Buddy, the
Chocolate Drop." Rogers' significance, however, lies in his
work in the theater and his ground-breaking efforts to

change the popular (minstrel-inspired) image of Blacks. Dunbar had coauthored lyrics for *Clorindy—Origin of the Cake Walk* (1898) and *In Dahomey* (1903). And Rogers was part of a groundswell that brought a new face to black theater. According to Loften Mitchell (*Black Drama*),

> In the latter part of the nineteenth century a group of Negro theatrical pioneers sat down and plotted the deliberate destruction of the minstrel pattern. These men were Sam T. Jack, Bert Williams, George Walker, Jesse Shipp, Alex Rogers, S. H. Dudley, Bob Cole, J. Rosamond Johnson, and John W. Isham. And in destroying the minstrel pattern, these men were to help pave the way for the million-dollar musical pattern which today dominates the American theatre.

Mitchell's observation sheds great light on the importance of many black "poets" who, however dismally they may fare on paper, are of major importance to the aggregate ritual and musical sense/life of ongoing black society. Today we see a similar pattern, with radical variations of course, growing from the work of James Weldon Johnson and others—in Gil Scott-Heron, the Last Poets, the poets who are writing for the ritual theater, and in the efforts of such dramatists as Melvin Van Peebles (*Ain't Supposed to Die a Natural Death*), Paul Carter Harrison (*The Great McDaddy*), Imamu Amiri Baraka (*Slave Ship*), the work of Barbara Teer, Clay Goss (*Andrew* and *Home-Cooking*), Eugene Redmond (*The Face of the Deep, 9 Poets with the Blues* and *The Night John Henry Was Born*), and the experimental productions of Michael Gates (*The Black Coffin, There's a Wiretap in My Soup: or Quit Bugging Me* and *Will I Still Be Here Tomorrow?*). This pattern, practically perfected by Langston Hughes, can also be seen in outstanding performing-cultural centers conducted by Katherine Dunham in East St. Louis and Val Gray Ward in Chicago, and at Elma Lewis' Center for Afro-American Cultural and Performing Arts in Boston.

Sterling Brown's other "minor writers of dialect" include Sterling Means (*The Deserted Cabin and Other Poems*), S. Tutt Whitney, Waverly Turner Carmichael, and just about anybody else who wrote dialect at the time.

Means also wrote in conventional English forms. For evaluations of Rogers and other similar writers see Mitchell's *Black Drama*, Johnson's *American Negro Poetry* and *Black Manhattan*, and Brown.

One of the stream of black "immigrants," George Reginald Margetson (1877–?), was born in St. Kitts (British West Indies) and came to the United States when he was twenty years old. Margetson, a wholly original poet, got a good, solid grounding in literature in his childhood and produced four volumes of poetry: *England in the West Indies* (1906), *Ethiopia's Flight* (1907), *Songs of Life* (1910) and *The Fledgling Bard and the Poetry Society* (1916). His achievement can be seen in the last book, which consists of one 100-page poem. A satire, owing debt to Byron and other English influences, the poem represents one of the most important technical undertakings by a black poet since Whitman's *Rape of Florida*. Margetson uses mostly seven-line stanzas of five-foot meter with the seventh line lengthening to an Alexandrine. His rhyme scheme is *a b a b b c c*, and he exhibits a wacky, uproarious use of both rhyme and humor. The basic stanzaic pattern is interspersed with shifting meters and schemes which appear as four-line stanzas in an *a b a b* movement or an *a a a b* context. The poem begins in a search for the Poetry Society (reminiscent of several European poets) and Margetson assays an old theme: that of poetry being mechanical and one's *success* depending upon school or dress as opposed to talent. During this "quest" Margetson "disgresses" to discuss and explore practically every major current theme in society: social conditions, World War I, politics, religion, literature, the black problem, and he even pokes fun at President Woodrow Wilson:

Come, Woody, quit your honeymooning!

In this important poem, Margetson is scathing, sustained and brilliant. He views the many currents running through the black community and satirically sums up all the confusion:

Some look to Booker Washington to lead them,
Some yell for Trotter, some for Kelly Miller,

Some want Du Bois with fat ideas to feed them,
Some want Jack Johnson, the big white hope killer.
Perhaps some want carranza, some want villa,
I guess they want social equality,
To marry and to mix in white society.

Other, later satirists whom Margetson's work calls to mind
are Tolson (and his incomparable *Harlem Gallery*), Frank
Marshall Davis, Dudley Randall, George S. Schuyler
(*Black No More*), William Melvin Kelley, and Ishmael
Reed. In his other poetry Margetson is strong and competent—he reflects his immense reading background,
"Spenser to Byron"—but none of his earlier work matches
up to *Fledgling Bard*. For samples and criticism of Margetson's writing see Johnson and Kerlin. Brown also makes
a brief critical observation.

In many ways the poetry of William Stanley Braithwaite (1878–1962) has suffered the fate of that of Phillis
Wheatley, Dunbar and others somehow deemed "not
black enough" for inclusion in some Afro-American po-
etic-cultural circles. The Frenchman Jean Wagner said
that a study of Braithwaite does not belong among those
of other "black poets." A mulatto, Braithwaite was born in
Boston to West Indian parents and was mainly self-
educated. He is considered a major influence on "the new
poetry revival" in America and counted among his friends
such white literary figures as Vachel Lindsay, Carl Sandburg, Edgar Lee Masters, Amy Lowell, and Edwin Arlington Robinson.

His career as a poet began with the 1904 publication of
Lyrics of Life and Love, and his second volume (*House of
the Falling Leaves*) was published in 1908. His *Selected
Poems* was published in 1948 by Coward-McCann, Inc.
Best known for his *Anthologies of Magazine Verse,* published from 1913 until 1929, Braithwaite was for many
years a literary critic with the Boston *Transcript*. His other
anthologies include *The Book of Elizabethan Verse*
(1906), *The Book of Georgian Verse* (1908), and *The
Book of Restoration Verse* (1909). For his efforts Braithwaite received the NAACP's coveted Spingarn medal in
1918 for high achievement by an Afro-American. The
same year, he received honorary degrees from two black

universities and later became professor of creative literature at Atlanta University, a position he held until he re-
tired, in 1945. Of Braithwaite's poetry, Sterling Brown
said:

> The result is the usual one: the lines are graceful; at
> their best, exquisite, and not at their best, secondhand;
> but the substance is thin. Even the fugitive poetry of
> some of Braithewaite's masters had greater human sym-
> pathies.

Brown is implying, of course, that some of the white
"models" that Braithwaite used could base their work in a
recognizable reality even if the black poet could not.
Brown is essentially correct: we have tested the thesis in
classrooms, and the best students appear dumfounded
upon confronting Braithwaite after leaving other black
poets. And Braithwaite's problem is not the same sort of
"problem" presented by a, say, Tolson—whose work is
difficult and complex but not unwieldy on repeated readings (Tolson's work is also black-based). Braithwaite
seems to be reaching for a higher science in his words; but
he does not chart his path so we can follow. Brown said
his writing resembled French "poetry of the twilight"—
just as you think you have his meaning, it slips away. This
is especially true of such poems as "Turn Me to My Yellow Leaves" (about a death wish?), "Del Cascar,"
"Ironic: LL.D." (about the wasteland [cf. T. S. Eliot]
and history?), "Scintilla," and "Sic Vita." "Rhapsody" is
one of Braithwaite's most attainable poems, but the message is nebulous. He expresses thanks to the Supreme
Being for "the gift of song" and is replenished in the
knowledge that "world-end things" that dangle on the
"edge of tomorrow" can be obliterated by dreams.

In his critical introduction to Braithwaite, Johnson
(*American Negro Poetry*) apologizes for the poet's lack of
sensitivity to the mistreatment of Blacks and explains his
failure to dip into the black folk-base or express racial
concern:

> This has not been a matter of intention on his part; it is
> simply that race has not impinged upon him as it has
> upon other Negro poets. In fact, his work is so detached
> from race that for many years he had been a figure in

the American literary world before it was known generally that he is a man of color.

Certainly Johnson meant no harm in using the word "color," but it tempts one to punning. Braithwaite, as Brown and others have noted, rejected having his work indiscriminately called "Negro" poetry. This issue continues to raise its head with, first, Cullen and, later, Hayden (including many other, lesser-known poets in between). And there are other poets of the twentieth century who have written (or write) Braithwaite's type of poetry. Some, of course, are experimenting and searching for new forms. See for example some of the work of Cullen, Hayden, Randall (*More to Remember*), Russell Atkins, Bob Kaufman, Tolson, Gwendolyn Brooks, Michael S. Harper (especially *History as Apple Tree*), and others. The debate over how much of (or when) a poet's work is or should be "racial" is a continuing one and is not likely—given the diversity of the poets—to be settled in the very near future.

Interestingly, with the exception of Claude McKay, no other poet has as many (or more) poems as Braithwaite in Johnson's 1922 (1931) anthology. Whether Johnson did this out of debt or respect is not known. Braithwaite, we know, had praised Johnson (*Fifty Years*) for bringing "the first intellectual substance to the content" of Afro-American poetry. But J. Saunders Redding called Braithwaite "the most outstanding example of perverted energy" that was produced in a fourteen-year period of black poetry. At Atlanta University, Braithwaite rubbed shoulders with Du Bois, Mercer Cook, Rayford Logan, and others, which apparently helped him doff some of his Bostonian snobbishness. His poetry in general reflects the influence of Keats and the preromantic British poets. He loves to speak of dreams, trances, impending doom, silence and the prospect of touching other worlds. For selections of his work, see most anthologies of Afro-American literature. He is critically assessed by Brown, Redding and Brawley. Other evaluations are primarily concerned with Braithwaite's work as anthologist and critic. Barksdale and Kinnamon give a good over-all assessment. Braithwaite did include some Black poets in his magazine anthologies, and he stands at an important threshhold of the Afro-American's entry into the era of modern poetry.

Records show that literally hundreds of poets, inspired by the brilliant example of Dunbar and company, took part in this exciting prerenaissance of black American culture and arts. For more on these poets, students should go to such publications as *The Century*, the *Independent*, the Chicago *Defender*, and the numerous other art-and-poetry-conscious publications of the day. Yet it is in some ways appropriate that we approach our close to this chapter with Lucien B. Watkins (1879–1921), first teacher and then soldier, who was called "the poet laureate of the new Negro." Watkins published one volume of poetry, in 1907 (*Voices of Solitude*); his second book (*Whispering Winds*, n.d.) was brought out by friends shortly after his untimely death. Watkins is chiefly noted for his militancy of tone, as typified in his sonnet "The New Negro," which opens with the words

> He thinks in black

and goes on to describe a god with African features. Watkins also wrote his own eulogy, a few weeks before he died. In the hymn-inspired form, he is grippingly aware of his approaching death, as shown in these lines:

> My summer bloomed for winter's frost:
> Alas, I've lived and loved and lost!

"A Message to the Modern Pharaohs" is inspired (introduced) by a passage from John 11:44, in the Bible. The iterations "Loose him!" and "Let him go!" frame each of the six 4-line stanzas. Taking the militant stand characteristic of his work, Watkins tells the pharaohs to let the black man go because he "has his part to play"

> In Life's Great Drama, day by day,—

adding that freeing the Afro-American will "be the saving" of whites' "soul." In many ways a precursor of the Harlem Renaissance, Watkins conducted experiments in verse ("A Prayer of the Race That God Made Black") and expressed pride in his African heritage ("Star of Ethiopia"). He was born in Chesterfield, Virginia, educated at Virginia Normal and Industrial Institute, and was active as a teacher before he served overseas in World War I, which "wrecked his health." Perhaps Watkins' feelings are best expressed in these lines (reminiscent of Margetson's "The white man's heaven is the black man's hell"):

> God! save us in Thy Heaven, where all is well!
> We come slow-struggling up the Hills of Hell!
> ("A Prayer of the Race That God Made Black")

For additional comment on Watkins, see Brawley's *Negro Genius*, Kerlin's study (which includes more selections) and Johnson's *American Negro Poetry* (selections also).

During this very important period of transition, there were countless other black poets writing. We ought to cite T. Thomas Fortune (1856–1928), who wrote journalism and important political studies of Blacks. And although Brawley calls him one of "the most intelligent and versatile Negroes of the era," his collection of poems, *Dreams of Life: Miscellaneous Poems* (1905), shows no marked distinction (though he implies a desire to return to Africa in "The Clime of My Birth"). A preacher-poet, George C. Rowe (1853–1903), published *Thoughts in Verse* (1887) and *Our Heroes* (1890). The first book contains sermons in verse and the second is aimed at "the elevation of the race." Rowe, pastor of the Plymouth Congregational Church of Charleston, South Carolina, also published "A Noble Life," a poem in memory of Joseph C. Price, first president of Livingston College. Known for her now famous *Journal*, Charlotte L. Forten Grimké (1837–1914) is considered to have "possessed sensitivity and creative skills beyond the ordinary" (Sherman) in the few poems she wrote. Uncollected, they are scattered throughout her notes and various periodicals published between the 1850s and the turn of the century. Islay Walden (1847?–84) published *Miscellaneous Poems* in Washington, D.C., in 1873. There is an immaturity in Walden's style, owing, according to Jahn, to the fact that his enrollment at Howard University "destroyed his natural talent." *The Nation's Loss: A Poem on the Life and Death of the Hon. Abraham Lincoln*, by Jacob Rhodes (1835?–?), was published in 1866. In *Lays of Summer*,

John Willis Menard (1838–93), the first elected black congressmen in the United States, makes women his central theme—calling them by name as he praises their hair and lips. For racial reasons, he was denied his "earned" term in the House of Representatives. James Ephraim McGirt (1874–1930) brought out *Avenging the Maine* (Raleigh, North Carolina, 1899), *Some Simple Songs and a Few More Ambitious Attempts* (Philadelphia, 1901), and *For Your Sweet Sake* (Philadelphia, 1906). Charles Douglas Clem published *Rhymes of a Rhymster* (Edmond, Oklahoma, 1896) and *A Little Souvenir* (n.p., 1908).

Sam Lucas (1845?–?) contributed to the postwar transitional shaping with *Careful Man Songster* (Chicago, 1881). One gets the impression that Lucas was a troubador of sorts. Bishop Henry McNeal Turner, well known among his contemporaries, published meditation and exhortatory verse in *The Conflict for Civil Rights* (Washington, D.C., 1881). *Revels of Fancy* (Boston, 1892) reflected the thoughts of William J. Candyne. Prose was included by Frank Barbour Coffin (1870?–1951) in *Coffin's Poems with Ajax' Ordeals* (Little Rock, 1892). James Thomas Franklin published one volume of poetry (*Jessamine / Poems*, Memphis, 1900) and one of prose and poetry (*Mid-Day Gleanings, a Book for Home and Holiday Reading* (Memphis, 1893). *Jessamine* apparently is not extant. *Poems of To-Day* or *Some from the Everglades* (Quincy, Florida, 1893) was published by Cupid Aleyus Whitefield. Joshua McCarter Simpson (1820?–76) released *The Emancipation Car* (Zanesville, Ohio,) in 1874. Simpson included a prose satire called "A Consistent Slaveholder's Sermon." *The Open Door* (1895) was published in Winfield, Kansas, by F. S. Alswell.

Aaron Belford Thompson (1883–1929) was a member of a family that comprised a trio of poets. Thompson and his sisters, Priscilla and Clara, brought out seven volumes of poetry between 1899 and 1926—the middle of the Harlem Renaissance. Priscilla Thompson published *Ethiope Lays* (1900) and *Gleanings of Quiet Hours* (1907). Clara Thompson released *Songs from the Wayside* (1908) and *A Garland of Poems* (Boston,

1926). Aaron Thompson published *Morning Songs* (1899), *Echoes of Spring* (1901), and *Harvest of Thoughts* (1907). *Echoes*, in its second edition of 1907, bore a handwritten, complimentary introduction by James Whitcomb Riley. Their subjects are the conventional ones of the nineteenth century. Charles Henry Shoeman published *A Dream and Other Poems* in Ann Arbor in 1899. *Magnolia Leaves* was published by Mary Weston Fordham in Charleston, South Carolina, in 1897.

Straddling similar fields of expression, as did Alex Rogers, James Weldon Johnson, Nathaniel Dett, and others, George Hannibal Temple (a musician) brought out *The Epic of Columbus' Bell and Other Poems* in 1900. Benjamin Wheeler followed him in 1907 with *Culling from Zion's Poets* (Mobile, Alabama). Several dozen other Afro-Americans wrote poetry during the latter part of the nineteenth and the early twentieth centuries. Among them were Robert Benjamin (1855–?) (*Poetic Gems*, 1883), Lorenzo Dow Blackson (1817–?), Walter Henderson Brooks (1851–1945), John Edward Bruce (1856–1924), Alexander Duman Delaney, Josephine Delphine Heard (1861–19?), Joseph Cephas Holly (1824–54), A. J. Jackson (*A Vision of Life*, 1869), Henry Allen Laine (1870?–?) (*Footprints*), Mary Eliza Lambert (1830–?), Lewis Howard Latimen (1848–1929), Grace Mapps, journalist William H. A. Moore, Gertrude Mossell 1855–?), James Robert Walker (*Poetical Diets*). Other occasional poets who were quite popular among their contemporaries included Solomon G. Brown, William Wells Brown, Katie D. Chapman, W. H. Crogman, Frederick Douglass, Leland M. Fisher, and Virgie Whitsett. Some notable turn-of-the-century poets, a few of whom will be heard from later, were Benjamin Brawley (critic and social historian), Charles Roundtree Dinkins, David Bryant Fulton, Gilmore F. Grant, M. N. Hayson, H. T. Johnson, Jefferson King, J. W. Palsey, Otis M. Shackleford, Walter E. Todd, Richard E. S. Toomey, Irvine W. Underhill, Julius C. Wright, and others. For more on these poets, including delightful pictures of some, see Brawley's *The Negro Genius* (and other works), Sherman's *Invisible Poets*, and Kerlin's *Negro Poets and Their Poems*.

Kelly Miller's *Race Adjustment* appeared in 1909 as a

partial answer to some of the evils and ills plaguing Blacks. But against the holocaustal "panorama of violence" (to borrow from poet Larry Neal) and bloodshed, the title of Miller's book seemed almost hollow. The NAACP was born in 1909, and a year later Du Bois was put at the helm of its publicity department and made editor of *The Crisis*. Echoes from the 1906 Atlanta riots, in which thirty Blacks were "butchered," could still be heard reverberating in speeches and fear-seized black hearts. (For more on this senseless and sadistic murder of Blacks, see John Hope Franklin's *From Slavery to Freedom* and Ralph Ginzberg's *100 Years of Lynching*.) On the lecture-circuit rampage, Du Bois heatedly criticized President Theodore Roosevelt, who had declared, "Rape is the greatest cause of lynching." The nation was trying to turn back the clock, as evidenced by the nostalgic minstrelsy, and was conducting a good "sabotage" of Reconstruction. And Blacks were feverously mobilizing to keep from being sold "back into a new form of slavery."

CHAPTER V

A LONG WAYS FROM HOME
(1910–1960)

> Sometimes I feel like a motherless child,
> A long ways from home;
> A long ways from home.
> —*Afro-American spiritual*

OVERVIEW

The disruption of chronology will be readily evident in this chapter because poets of the same age do not always achieve recognition at the same time. We have looked at James Weldon Johnson, for example, but we mention him again. In fact—for reasons to be shown—Johnson overshadows almost the whole of black poetry in America. Melvin B. Tolson, born before Hughes and Cullen, will be viewed after them in the so-called postrenaissance period. And since the primary aim of this study is to cite the most significant names and events in the development of the poetry, criticism will remain minimal.

From this point (early-twentieth century) on, black poets—and Blacks on the larger artistic spectrum—begin being viewed by American critics alongside all other artists. And appraisals of Afro-American poetry become a bit more difficult, since up until the second decade of the twentieth century, black poets were viewed as somewhat of a novelty. They were the subjects for "curious" whites or for a few dedicated Blacks and possessed very little armament with which to fight critical or literary "lynchings." Their models were essentially white (some contemporary black poets continue this practice), and so were their critics. In the 1920s they provided one of many "exotic" diversions for some of the bored and thrill-seeking whites. In the postrenaissance, their skills were often directed toward integration and various other social programs.

The most incisive and perpetual blow to black poets is a disrespect and rejection that parallel the general treatment

of Blacks. Criticism of black poetry is invariably political
and racial—just as most of the poetry is forced to be.
Some poets lament and protest against this because it
implies that protest and anger are reserved for them. It
also says that the whole range of human behavior is somehow placed off limits to the Afro-American poet, criticized
by whites for not being "universal" and by his own people for not being "black" enough. Needless to say, it is a
dilemma of some magnitude, and no amount of words or
lamentations will answer or solve it here. We do comment
on these matters, though, because they begin to appear as
serious—unavoidable—plagues to the black poet from this
period on in our study.

Many poets (Mari Evans, Lance Jeffers, James
Emanuel, Ray Durem, Dudley Randall, Zack Gilbert, Bob
Kaufman, Frank Horne, and others) were publishing in
periodicals before 1960 but did not bring out volumes
until the decade opened. Poets who had been publishing
books during the years before 1960 (Hayden, Gwendolyn
Brooks, Conrad Kent Rivers, Hughes, and others) brought
out new works sometimes reflecting different themes and
attitudes. Poets who had been publishing substantially in
periodicals or anthologies before 1960 will be noted in
passing. There will be no attempt to give individual attention to the scores of black poets writing and publishing in
the 1960s and '70s.

LITERARY AND SOCIAL LANDSCAPE

Night is a curious child, wandering. . . .
                    —FRANK MARSHALL DAVIS

TO 1930

In 1910 the population of black America was almost 10
million. Langston Hughes was a boy of ten and the
NAACP was one year old. By 1930, however, the black
population had increased to 11,891,143 (or 9.7 per cent);
a major migration of Blacks to northern industrial centers
had taken place; race riots had scorched more than half a
dozen American cities; the country had engaged in and

ended its first global war, and lynchings continued to be among the most fearful prospects for black men.

Booker T. Washington had chronicled the hardships and bitter disappointments of Blacks in his *Up from Slavery*. The new "freedom" was short-lived and illusive, Washington observed, because the ex-slave had no skill, no land and no place to go. "Emancipated" Blacks were not faring much better than their foreparents. Du Bois had begun to raise some of the broader, global issues of black oppression and place the black experience in its proper perspective in *The Souls of Black Folk*. During the second and third decades of the twentieth century, black scholars, activists and writers continued to record the black experience with telling accuracy and drama.

Additionally, a number of changes and developments in black communities set off a chain reaction of cross-examinations, intense debates, calls for changes and the charting of new directions. Accordingly, the student of black poetry must understand the mood of the times in terms of:

1. The decline of Dunbar's influence among poets.
2. Failing support of Booker T. Washington's "accommodationist" philosophy.
3. The continued disillusionment of survivors and heirs of Reconstruction.
4. The development of white hate and intimidation groups (Ku Klux Klan, etc.).
5. The presentation of "stereotypes" of Blacks in the mass media and creative literature of the period.
6. The "Jim Crow" laws of the South, and job discrimination and general segregation in the North.
7. The splits and confusion in the black community due to the "new middle class: the appearance of West Indians in the United States and class alignment according to color stratification (i.e., light skin, dark skin, near white, etc.). Much of the literature of the period deals with the theme of "passing" or of miscegenation.
8. Race riots in various parts of the country between 1905 and 1917.

In America, science and industry were developing rapidly. Indications of this were radio, technological warfare and the automobile. The "new psychology" was taking hold, and the *realism* of the previous literature was bowing out to *naturalism*. This new mode is seen in the works of such writers as Theodore Dreiser and William Faulkner. Interest in local color and dialect, which had dominated the latter portion of the nineteenth century, was also dying, and the black American was "rediscovered" by white writers as a subject for realistic fiction, drama and poetry. White writers who published popular accounts of back life included DuBose Heyward, Sherwood Anderson, and Carl Van Vechten. Revolts in interests and manners characterized American society Black critic James A. Emanuel points out that during the 1920s, many whites went to Harlem to "forget the war and engage their new Freudian awareness by escaping into exotic black cabaret life" (*Negro Digest*, August 1969). Hughes records this exotic indulgence in his autobiography, *The Big Sea* (1940). Such "diversion" is also noted by Claude McKay in *A Long Ways from Home* and by Johnson in *Along This Way* and *The Autobiography of an Ex-Coloured Man* (novel).

Drama of the period was dominated by Eugene O'Neill, who won Pulitzer and Nobel prizes. Two of O'Neill's plays (*The Emperor Jones* and *The Hairy Ape*) symbolically dealt with the psychological involvement of Blacks and whites and suggested a transracial mixture of fear, hatred and admiration. Black actor Charles Gilpin starred in *The Emperor Jones*; reviews of Gilpin's performances ("naked body . . . dark lyric of the flesh") typified preoccupation with the exotic savage—a trend that had continued from Jack London (*The Call of the Wild*, *The Sea-Wolf*) and the white writers of local color: Page, Harris, Cable. However, many writers, like O'Neill and Dreiser, had begun to shake off the mystique of the American Dream and deal instead with the "illusion." Such was Dreiser's theme in his novel *An American Tragedy* (1925).

The founding of *Poetry: a Magazine of Verse*, by Harriet Monroe (1912) signaled the birth of the new poetry movement in America. In 1915, the anthology *Some*

Imagist Poets appeared to challenge dissident factions that wanted to dispense with traditional forms. Imagism was influenced by Ezra Pound's theories and French Symbolism as well as oriental and ancient Greek poetry. Chief spokesman for the Imagist poets was Amy Lowell, who was joined by John Gould Fletcher and Hilda Doolittle, among others. During the next two decades, the group waged a successful battle against the dissidents, but they also reworked traditional forms and cornered a new reading market for poetry in America and England. Poet Vachel Lindsay, an advocate of using rhythm and the reading aloud of poetry, is credited with having "discovered" Langston Hughes. Black poets who participated in this "revival" of American poetry were the innovator Fenton Johnson and the anthologist William Stanley Braithwaite.

The most significant development of the period, however, was the black cultural flowering, principally in Harlem, that has become known as the Harlem Renaissance, the Negro Awakening and the Negro Renaissance. Central to the "renaissance" (critics differ over whether it should be called such) was the migration of southern Blacks to northern urban centers. With the working-class Blacks also came (and grew) the black intelligentsia, artists and activists. Current black creativity or scholarship cannot be understood unless the Harlem Renaissance is placed in proper perspective, because the Harlem period is the most important bridge existing between slavery and the modern and/or contemporary era. Hence, it is necessary that we sketch out the important political and artistic developments that led up to (or happened during) the Harlem Renaissance. A partial listing of these developments must include:

Founding of the Boston *Guardian* by Monroe Trotter (1901)

Founding of the National Association for the Advancement of Colored People (1909) and establishment of *The Crisis*.

Founding of the Urban League (1911).

Founding of the Association for the Study of Negro Life and History by Carter G. Woodson (1915).

Establishment of *The Journal of Negro History* by
  Woodson (1916).

Black troops' involvement in World War I.

Great migration of Blacks to northern urban centers,
  1916–19; the trend continued through the middle of
  the century.

The recording of black achievements in all areas; black
  scholarship is brilliant and sustained throughout the
  entire period.

The writings, especially, of W. E. B. Du Bois, Charles
  S. Johnson, Alain Locke, and James Weldon Johnson.

The high point in the influence of Marcus Garvey's
  Universal Negro Improvement Association (Garvey,
  who came to the United States from Jamaica in 1916,
  preached a back-to-Africa movement. He was imprisoned in 1925 for mail fraud).

Founding of *Opportunity, A Journal of Negro Life*
  (1923). *Opportunity* and *The Crisis* published much
  of the new work of the Harlem Renaissance writers
  and offered annual prizes.

The flourishing of black music and musical dramas
  (Noble Sissle and Eubie Blake do *Shuffle Along*,
  1921; Louis Armstrong, with his own band, opens at
  the Sunset Club, Chicago, 1927; Duke Ellington
  opens at the Cotton Club, Harlem, the same year).

The postwar Pan-African congresses (Paris, 1919; London, 1921, 1923; New York, 1927; Du Bois was primary organizer).

James Weldon Johnson edited the first twentieth-cen-
tury American anthology of black poetry, *The Book of
American Negro Poetry*, in 1922. Johnson's work was fol-
lowed in quick succession by five other poetry anthologies:
Negro Poets and Their Poems (Robert Thomas Kerlin,
1923); *An Anthology of American Negro Verse* (Newman
Ivey White and Walter Clinton Jackson, 1924); *Negro
Songs: an Anthology* (Clement Wood, 1924); *Caroling
Dusk* (Countee Cullen, 1927); *Four Negro Poets* (Alain
Locke, 1927).

Of note also was F. F. Calverton's *An Anthology of
American Negro Literature* (1929), which contained sixty
pages of poetry. Cullen and Locke were two major figures

of the renaissance, along with McKay, Johnson, Hughes, and Jean Toomer. Locke edited the anthology that heralded and chronicled the new black mood and achievements: *The New Negro: an Interpretation* (1925); it remains a classic today. He also produced the equally important *A Decade of Negro Self-Expression* (1928). A Rhodes scholar from Pennsylvania, Locke received a Ph.D. in 1918 from Harvard and is still considered a foremost interpreter of black creativity of the Harlem Renaissance. Cullen published *Color*, his first book of poetry, when he was twenty-two, and was instantly recognized as one of the best young poets in America. McKay and Cullen adhered to the strict tradition of English poetry. Considered the best "formal" writer of the renaissance period, Cullen was meticulous and careful in his poetic workmanship, and he joined those who climbed "The Dark Tower" to brood over being called "Negro" poets.

In addition to Cullen, other key poets of the Harlem Awakening published important volumes or anthologies and added to the creative and critical interest. Johnson and his brother, J. Rosamond, edited *The Book of American Negro Spirituals* (1925) and *The Second Book of Negro Spirituals* (1926). McKay published poetry in both England and America. Johnson said McKay belonged "to the post-war group and was its most powerful voice. He was pre-eminently the poet of rebellion." Hughes and Cullen won national recognition (and poetry awards) at about the same time. There, however, the comparison ends. Hughes was one of the most widely traveled of all the renaissance writers. He was also the most prodigious and multitalented, writing successfully in all genres. Hughes, who when he died in 1967 was the most widely translated American author, is known as the international poet laureate of black people.

Johnson recorded much of this creative outpouring in various ways. As a scholar, he is known for his anthologies and his seminal interpretations of black culture—the spirituals in particular. Of great importance was his 1922 anthology, in which, in an illuminating preface, he cited the four major black artistic contributions to America:

1. The Uncle Remus stories, collected by Joel Chandler Harris.

2. The spirituals ("to which the Fisk Jubilee Singers made the public and the musicians of both the United States and Europe listen").
3. The Cakewalk (a dance that Paris called the "poetry of motion").
4. Ragtime ("American music," for which the United States is known all over the world).

Johnson is also noted for his work with the U.S. diplomatic corps, his pioneering efforts with the NAACP and his brilliant employment of black idioms and psychology in his poetry and discussions.

One of the most unique voices of the Harlem Renaissance was Jean Toomer, who along with Hughes, Cullen and McKay make up Locke's *Four Negro Poets*. A complex of personalities, talents and racial mixtures, Toomer was a constant enigma to critics and fellow writers. Although he admitted that he was of seven racial strands, he acknowledged, "My growing need for artistic expression has pulled me deeper and deeper into the Negro group." In 1924, Toomer's *Cane* was published. Set primarily in the Deep South—in Georgia—it also deals with the urban impact on migrating Blacks. Love, racial conflict, sex, violence, religion, nature, and agrarian themes are all explored directly and allegorically.

Racial pride, the lower side of black life, and a romantic engagement with Africa were the main thrusts of the renaissance literature. So too with the painters, musicians, scholars and activists. Garvey had set up a regal court reminiscent of ancient African kingdoms and had infused his followers with visions of returning to the "homeland." His "court" was resplendent with hierarchical titles and lavish regalia for parades. Black Star Line was the name of his fleet of ships. The prevailing spirit of the day was one of black indulgence, and many whites sought for, and got their share of, it. But the Negro Awakening was not the exclusive property of Harlem. For, as Kerlin points out (Preface, *Negro Poets and Their Poems*), the mood of change spread to other sections of the country. Among anthologies published were *The Quill* in Boston, *Black Opals* in Philadelphia and *The Stylus* in Washington,

D.C. Important, too, were the collections and studies of folk songs. Noteworthy collections for the period included:

Negro Folk Rhymes (Thomas W. Talley, 1922)
The Negro and His Songs (Howard W. Odum, 1925)
Negro Workday Songs (Howard W. Odum, 1926)
Rainbow Round My Shoulder (Howard W. Odum, 1928)
Wings on My Feet (Howard W. Odum, 1929)
American Negro Folk Songs (Newman Ivey White, 1929).

Other brilliant and exciting poets and writers shared the renaissance scene—though they are normally overshadowed by Hughes, Toomer, McKay, Johnson, and Cullen. Some of these writers—most of whom did not publish volumes until a later period—were: Arna Bontemps, Georgia Douglas Johnson, Waring Cuney, Robert Hayden, Gwendolyn Bennett, Sterling Brown, Owen Dodson, and Melvin Tolson. Prose writers of the period included Eric Walrond and Rudolph Fisher as well as Hughes and Toomer. Bontemps, anthologist, critic, librarian, poet, and novelist, published in leading magazines of the period and won numerous awards for poetry. Brown pursued the folk tradition while cultivating an ear and technique that rivaled some of the best modern poetry. His debt to folk idioms and characters is obvious in such poems as "Odyssey of Bib Boy," "Southern Road," "Memphis Blues," and "Long Gone." Brown contributed to periodicals of the time, wrote a regular column for *Opportunity*, and later published important critical studies. Dodson wrote verse plays and collaborated with Cullen on at least one writing project. He, too, won numerous awards for his plays and poetry. Hayden and Tolson, both significant modern poets, were to be heard from in succeeding decades as critics and outstanding teachers as well as poets.

FROM 1930 TO 1960

When the stock market crashed in 1929, white patronization of black artists ended. Black creativity and scholarship, however, had grown up during the first three decades of the century, and important writing and musical development continued.[1] Migration of Blacks to northern urban centers was stepped up before and after World War II—with many Blacks being attracted by shipbuilding and other war-manufacturing industries. Afro-Americans have participated in every U.S. military conflict since colonial days. During World War II and Korea, however, they were used almost exclusively as fighting troops (between 1943 and 1945, Jim Crow was abolished in the armed forces). Nevertheless, black soldiers, returning home from European and Pacific war theaters, still faced unemployment and lynching; and in some southern cities they were forbidden to appear on the streets in military uniforms. Baldwin is one of many perceptive American writers to note that the black man, seeking the fruits and realization of the American Dream, tried throughout history to adjust and "fit" into American society. So, in face of official American contempt for his humanity and his welfare, the black soldier marched also with an "equality" of death into the Korean War.[2]

James Weldon Johnson had opened the dismal period of the Depression with *Black Manhattan,* a social history of Harlem. *Black Manhattan* was one of the dozens of studies on urban black communities that had been begun by works such as Du Bois's *Philadelphia Negro: a Social Study* (1899). Like Johnson, many of the poets and artists turned their writing skills toward the recording of black social problems and artistic achievements (Johnson's *Negro Americans, What Now?,* 1934, and Charles S. Johnson's *The Shadow of the Plantation,* 1934). Some of the writers were subsidized by WPA grants, while others managed to obtain jobs as teachers and journalists. Still others, like the common folk, stood in soup lines. It was also during the period of 1930 to 1960 that white schools

---

[1] The writing of poetry continued, but publishing was slowed down. James O. Young, in *Black Writers of the Thirties* (1973), notes, "Black writers produced less than one volume of poetry per year between 1929 and 1942."

[2] This turned out to be not so true in the Vietnam War when a dead black veteran was refused burial in a white cemetery near his home in Georgia.

of higher learning started accepting more Blacks, as students and teachers.

Generally, the United States witnessed rapid advancements in science and industry. Radio drama became a cultural mainstay, and the motion picture industry provided a new and exciting diversion. Baseball continued as the "national pastime" (for Blacks, it was the era of Jackie Robinson). Jack Johnson had already (in the previous era) dazzled America with his pugilistic skills. But it was the prize fighter Joe Louis (the "Brown Bomber"), however, who captured sports-minded America with one of the greatest records in boxing history. Louis' defeat of German Max Schmeling (1938) came at a crucial time in U.S. history—just before America's rising might among the world of nations would be challenged *on the battlefield* by Hitler. Two years earlier, a racist Hitler had refused to acknowledge the feats of America's black Olympic track star Jesse Owens.

In prose and drama, white American writers continued to straddle a thematic path between realism and the American Dream. A distinctly "postwar" group of writers emerged. Dominating the period were Dreiser, Anderson, Sinclair Lewis, Willa Cather, Thomas Wolfe, O'Neill, Faulkner, Ernest Hemingway, Tennessee Williams, John Dos Passos, Katherine Anne Porter, Erskine Caldwell, and Carson McCullers. Using symbolism and allegory to attack war, decadence and the atomic bomb, American writers often took as models such Russian writers as Chekhov, Dostoevski and Tolstoi. Many employed the *stream of consciousness* technique—a style influenced by the "new psychology" and Irish writer James Joyce—which allowed for uninterrupted explorations on the thoughts of characters who "streamed" their references. A similar mood prevailed in the poetry—much of which dealt with social decadence, war and the mechanization of man. E. E. Cummings, known for his typographical trickery and general linguistic and syntactical experiments, was one of the most relentless critics of bureaucracy and war. Such themes had also concerned T. S. Eliot, considered one of the greatest modern poets, in such poems as "The Love Song of J. Alfred Prufrock" and *The Waste Land*.

The Imagist poets pursued their development via such voices as "H.D.," Ezra Pound, and Marianne Moore.

Historically, black music had been marked by white imitation and exploitation. There always existed the need to create a "white" musical face that could be palatable to Americans at large. From the minstrelsy of plantation days to the sophisticated operettas and musicals of the twenties, this pattern ran unbroken. During the modern period, bebop became the musical heir to ragtime, early jazz and Tin Pan Alley. While the big-band leaders and composers—Basie, Ellington, Fletcher Henderson, W. C. Handy, Eubie Blake, Noble Sissle, etc.—continued their important work, different kinds of experiments were going on among other musicians. From these new formations and probings came some of the giants of modern black music: Miles Davis, Charlie "Yard Bird" Parker, Lester "Prez" Young, Sonny Rollins, Gene Ammons, Art Blakey (who studied drums in Africa), Ornette Coleman (see *Four Lives in the Bebop Business*), Chano Pozo (Afro-Cuban), Dizzy Gillespie, and Babs Gonzales (bop poet and singer: *I Paid My Dues*, 1967). From the musicians and their supporters emerged an underground, "hip" language. This tradition, of talking in metaphors and encoded cultural neologisms, had begun during the renaissance. Often, too, black vocalists were featured with the musicians: Ella Fitzgerald, Sarah Vaughn, Billie Holiday, and Bessie Smith—who died in 1937. The migration to cities also saw the continued rise of urban or big-city blues. By 1960, however, the blues had gone through several important periods of development. Some names associated with the modern period were Louis Armstrong, Fats Waller, Cab Calloway, Bill Broonzy, Pops Foster, Eddie "Son" House, Robert Johnson, Johnny Temple, Roosevelt Sykes, Elmo James, B. B. King, Leadbelly, Jimmy Reed, Muddy Waters, Josh White, Sonny Boy Williams, Howlin' Wolf, John Lee Hooker, Lightnin' Hopkins, and Big Joe Turner. These men were the keepers of the flame ignited by Leroy Carr, Blind Lemon Jefferson, and W. C. Handy.

Several notable black literary explosions occurred during the period between 1930 and 1960. Important were the publication of *Native Son* (Richard Wright, 1940); the publication of *For My People* (Margaret Walker, 1942); the appearance of *Invisible Man* (Ralph Ellison, 1952) and Gwendolyn Brooks's winning of the Pulitzer prize for poetry (*Annie Allen*, 1950). *Native Son*, a novel, featured a black protagonist named Bigger Thomas, who symbolized (and in many ways contained) the anger, rage and pressures felt by urban Blacks. The book was the first by a black author to make the best-seller lists and was also a Book of the Month Club choice. During the same period, Wright, who died an expatriate in France in 1960, published several other novels, short stories, books of essays and miscellaneous prose. In 1945, *Black Boy*, his autobiography, appeared. Wright is significant for many reasons, foremost among them being that he was the first black writer to deal accurately and on a par with the best fiction writers of the day, with the philosophical and psychological complexity of the black urbanite. In doing this, he opened a new range of possibilities and helped free black fiction in many ways. There were other excellent fiction writers during this period: Rudolph Fisher, Zora Neale Hurston, McKay, Hughes, Bontemps, Ann Petry, Du Bois, Frank Yerby, Eric Walrond, Chester Himes, William Demby, and Sterling Brown. Wright, however, was the first to forge and sustain a *major* black art piece out of mythical and racial materials. James Baldwin, whose reign succeeded Wright's, made his entry in 1953 with the publication of *Go Tell It on the Mountain*. His other important work includes *Notes of a Native Son* (1955) and *Giovanni's Room* (1956).

Margaret Walker, who teaches literature at Jackson State College, was twenty-two years old when she wrote "For My People"—one of the most famous black poems. Her book by the same name won the Yale Series of Younger Poets award in 1942. Rich in cultural folk references, black phonology, and social history, the slim book brilliantly illuminates the hope, humor, pathos, rage, stamina, and iron dignity of the race.

The winning of the Pulitzer prize by Gwendolyn Brooks (and Ellison's accolade) told the world that black writers had mastered the "ultimate" English literary crafts of poetry and fiction to a degree that no longer called their abilities into question. Many black critics feel, however, that there were excellent volumes before *Annie Allen* that should have received the Pulitzer prize. These critics say black artists, like the black experience, come periodically into fashion (e.g., Harlem Renaissance)—to be tolerated at the whims of white literary bastions, despite their proven abilities. The citation of Gwendolyn Brooks (who published A Street in Bronzeville, 1945) was a citation of the black experience, however—despite the fact that the prize was not a major piece of news in the black community. Blacks, caught up in the postwar mood, job-searching and questing for social equality, were not reading much poetry.

Ellison, who has not published a novel since Invisible Man (1952) remains one of the most controversial figures in American literature, much of the controversy arising from what he says outside of fiction (see Introduction). Communist-oriented papers generally condemned Invisible Man when it first appeared. They held that it was a "dirt-throwing" ritual for Ellison—who combines naturalism and complex symbolism in the book. Black novelist John Oliver Killens also gave it a negative review. Generally, however, the work is considered, by black and white critics, to be a great novel—perhaps the greatest American novel. It won the National Book Award in 1952 and, in a subsequent poll of two hundred journalists and critics, it was judged the most distinguished single work of fiction since World War II.

Inflamed by the spirit and example of the Harlem Renaissance, black poets of the prewar, war and postwar years continued their exciting experiments. Gwendolyn Brooks recalls that a brief encouragement from the "great" James Weldon Johnson when she was a child spurred her on her way. Some of the poets of the renaissance, however, quit writing altogether or began writing in other genres. Johnson reported in 1931 that Fenton Johnson had been "silent" for ten years. Poet Bontemps also wrote novels—the most famous of them being Black Thunder (1939), an adaptation of the 1831 Nat Turner-led slave revolt. He edited and wrote, and sometimes collaborated with others on anthologies and biographies for young readers. With Hughes, he edited The Poetry of the Negro: 1764–1949, considered a breakthrough in modern black literary activity. One of the handful of renaissance black writers to survive into the seventies, Bontemps died in 1973. Some have called the period between 1930 and 1954 the age of Langston Hughes in black letters. Indeed, Hughes remained prominent and productive throughout the three periods—the renaissance, 1930–54, and the contemporary era. During the prewar, war and postwar periods, Hughes continued to turn out everything from newspaper fiction columns (Jesse B. Semple) to juvenilia to plays. Hughes in poetry, like Wright, Ellison, and Baldwin in prose, faithfully recorded the black mood; with the others, he also predicted the social violence of the sixties. Poets and other volumes of the period included: Sterling Brown, *Southern Road* (1932); Cullen, *The Medea and Some Poems* (1935); Hayden, *Heart-Shape in the Dust* (1940); Naomi Long Madgett, *Songs to a Phantom Nightingale* (1941); H. Binga Dismond, *We Who Would Die* (1943); Tolson, *Rendezvous with America* (1944); Dodson, *Powerful Long Ladder* (1946); Cullen, *On These I Stand* (post-humously, 1947); Hayden, with Myron O' Higgins, *The Lion and the Archer* (1948); Tolson, *Libretto for the Republic of Liberia* (1953); *Selected Poems of Claude McKay* (posthumously, 1953); Ariel W. Holloway, *Shape Them into Dreams* (1955); John C. Morris, *Cleopatra and Other Poems* (1955); Alfred Q. Jarette, *Black Man Speaks* (1956); Beatrice Wright, *Color Scheme* (1957); May Miller, *Into the Clearing* (1959); Percy E. Johnston, *Concerto for Girl and Convertible* (1960); Oliver Pitcher, *Dust of Silence* (1960); and Gwendolyn Brooks, *The Bean Eater* (1960). Also writing and/or translating during this period were Dudley Randall, Samuel Allen (Paul Vesey), Margaret Danner, Richard Wright (who also wrote poetry), and Frank Marshall Davis.

Black and white poets exchanged ideas and socialized, and many of the former were introduced to publishers and the reading public by well-known white poets or critics. Such a practice was to come under fire, during the late 1960s and 1970s, by some black poets and critics, who felt that whites could not judge black writing. Reviews of the period were generally favorable to black writers who showed great finish in their work. Hayden, Walker, Brooks, Tolson, and Dodson were among the poets who received high praise for their technical virtuosity. Stephen Vincent Benét wrote the foreword to *For My People* and Allen Tate to *Libretto for the Republic of Liberia*, and Hayden won Hopwood awards twice. Tolson received accolades from *Poetry: A Magazine of Verse*—regarded as the white American olympus of poetry.

One of the most important anthologies of the post-renaissance period was *The Negro Caravan* (1941), edited by Brown, Arthur P. Davis, and Ulysses Lee. The best inclusive anthology of black literature, it remains today an outstanding textbook. Brown also published two important works of criticism, *The Negro in American Fiction* and *Negro Poetry and Drama*, both in 1937. And J. Saunders Redding published his critical work *To Make a Poet Black* in 1939. In 1940 *Phylon* was established, with the venerable W. E. B. Du Bois as editor.

In 1954, as American soldiers prepared to return from Korea and television glared to consume the world, the Supreme Court decision of May 15 closed the book on one era of black American history and opened up Pandora's box on another. Wright's *Black Power* (1954), a commentary on his experiences in Africa's Gold Coast, may have been more than just a hint of what was to come. He would witness some, but not all, of the ingredients of Pandora's box, for when a black woman in Montgomery refused to give up her seat on a public bus to a white man, a new era of black struggle was born. A successful boycott of buses was led by Martin Luther King, Jr., founder (in 1957) of the Southern Christian Leadership Conference. Like flames of flesh, hordes of young Blacks (and some whites) began sit-ins and various other "ins" as the "Freedom" cry reached a new pitch. This was the gestation period for the Congress of Racial Equality and the Student Nonviolent Co-ordinating Committee. And all the while, white youth took to television and swayed to the rhythms of Chubby Checker, the Chantels, and the Five Satins. But as America "twisted the night away," another and different mood, expressed through a different voice, was hugging the rim of the "dream." And we were not yet "Beyond the Blues."

THE VOICES ON THE TOTEM

> Good mornin', blues,
> blues, how do you do?
> —LEADBELLY

THE COMING CADENCE: PRERENAISSANCE VOICES

As the twentieth century continued to open its bewildered
(some say "shocked") eyes, many changes were occurring
—not the least among them in black poetry and the arts.
With the increase in the number of publications accepting
their work (due to the pioneering efforts of Dunbar, Corrothers, Campbell, Cotter, and others), black poets could
at least anticipate having their manuscripts read by white
editors. Many of the poets writing in the first and second
decades of the century would never be heard from again,
but few would become "minor" lights of the Harlem
Renaissance. The poets ranged over a surprising diversity
of styles, linguistic bents, themes, temperaments and age
categories, and came from practically every corner of the
United States, the West Indies and Latin America.

Among the early poets were Kelly Miller (1863–1939),
Leslie Pinckney Hill (1880–1960), Charles Bertram John-
son (1880–?), Benjamin Brawley (1882–1939), Raymond
Garfield Dandridge (1882–1930), Otto Leland Bohanan,
James Edward McCall (1880–?), Angelina Weld Grimké
(1880–1958), Jessie Redmond Fauset (1882–1961),
Walter Everette Hawkins (1883–?), Mrs. Sarah Lee
(Brown) Fleming, Leon R. Harris (1886–?), Effie
Lee Newsome (1885–?), Walter Adolphe Roberts
(1886–1965), Eva Alberta Jessye (1897–   ), Georgia
Douglas Johnson (1886–1966), Theodore Henry Shackel-
ford (1888–1923), Roscoe C. Jamison (1886–1918),
Charles Wilson (1885–?), Mrs. Mae Smith Johnson
(1890–?), Andrea Razafkeriefo (1895–?), Benjamin
Ebenezer Burrell (1892–?), William Edgar Bailey, Joseph
Seamon Cotter, Jr. (1895–1919), Clarissa Scott Delany
(1901–27), and scores more.

Major poetic contributions were made by James Weldon Johnson, Fenton Johnson, Cotter, Jr. (cut down before he could develop his promise), and a few others; yet it is important that we at least mention some of the lesser lights of this period. Brown and Redding feel that nothing of importance, beyond the Johnsons, occurred in the first two decades. But, for purposes of our study and continuity, we must note that this was not a period of inactivity among poets. Technically, there was some experimentation. However, most of the poets either helped phase out the dialect vogue or wrote harmless pieces on nature, love, gardens, death, and human sorrow. Others wrote harshly and bitterly of the war.

Miller, mathematician and sociologist, was a leading black spokesman of the day and only occasionally wrote poetry. His prose poem "I See and Am Satisfied" provided fuel for further discussion of contemporary racial issues. Consisting of twenty-five stanzas, it is reminiscent of Fenton Johnson ("Tired") and Margaret Walker ("For My People").

Leslie Pinckney Hill produced many good students while he was principal at Cheyney Training School for Teachers (later Cheyney State College). He attended Harvard and taught at Tuskegee; his literary influences were Longfellow, Wordsworth, Milton, and Burns. His published works are *The Wings of Oppression* (1922) and *Toussaint L'Ouverture—A Dramatic History* (1928). Roy L. Hill, poet and educator, is a protégé of the senior Hill who feels that the rugged Afro-American "constrained oppression to give him wings"; his poetry has a strength laced with Washington-type feelings about race relations. He tells us that he will "mourn the travail of my race." Most grippingly memorable, however, is his "So Quietly," a poetic distillation of an actual lynching.

Charles Johnson published *Wild Whisperings* (a pamphlet, 1900), *The Mantle of Dunbar and Other Poems* (a pamphlet, 1918) and *Songs of My People* (1918). Johnson was an educator and preacher in Missouri, and his poetry is both light and serious. He lures the reader into what appears to be a path of ease, then takes some ironic twist or turn. For him, "life" is a "pulsed song" ("Soul and Star").

An occasional poet, Brawley attended Morehouse, Har-

vard and the University of Chicago, and for years taught
in English departments at southern black colleges. He is
primarily known for his pioneering work in literature and
social history. He published *A Short History of the American Negro* (1918), *A Short History of English Drama*
(1921), *A New Survey of English Literature* (1925),
Early Negro American Writers (1935), *The Negro Genius* (1937), and *Negro Builders and Heroes* (1937). It is
to Brawley's studies that we must go for vital information
on the development of black American poetry.

Dandridge's poetry is rich and sometimes racial in concerns. "Time to Die" advises "Black" brothers to give
their life "for something." Apparently embittered by the
aborted Reconstruction and contemporary violence against
Blacks, he asks:

Or can it be you fear the grave
Enough to live and die a slave?

"Zalka Peetruza" recalls McKay's "Harlem Dancer" in
that every part of the woman is dancing "—save her
face." A native of Cincinnati, Dandridge suffered a stroke
when he was thirty years old, which left his legs and right
arm paralyzed. Thereafter writing most of his poetry from
his bed, he published *The Poet and Other Poems* (1920)
and *Zalka Peetruza and Other Poems* (1928). Dandridge
also wrote competent poetry in dialect and was a disciple
of Dunbar.

Bohanan and McCall contributed poetry to various
magazines. A teacher from Washington, D.C., Bohanan
did not publish a volume. Neither did McCall, who became an editor of the *Independent* after suffering blindness due to typhoid. Angelina Grimké published a three-act
play (*Rachel*) in 1921, but her poetry remains uncollected. Born in Boston, she was educated in various schools
in several states, and later taught English for many years
at Dunbar High School in Washington, D.C. More than
slightly presaging Gwendolyn Brooks, her work contains
some of the most distilled language in modern American poetry. Scintillating, precise, and poignant, she
writes of love, seasons, darkness, and high spirits during
her maturing years—the things typified in the phrase "the
new Negro." Although she had been publishing poetry in

periodicals, her first big break came when she was included in Cullen's anthology *Caroling Dusk* (1927). Not
until the sixties, however, would such lines as the following take on their full political/cultural significance:

> Why, beautiful still finger, are you black?
> And why are you pointing upwards?

In "The Want of You," even the moon and clouds join in
"the crying want of you." Long overdue is a detailed study
of Angelina Grimké. But she is included in the best
anthologies of Afro-American poetry and literature. Critical comments on her work can be found in the work of
Kerlin, Barksdale, Kinnamon, and Brown, who characterized her work as "irony and quiet despair."

An exceptional student in college and for several years
literary editor of the famous magazine *The Crisis*, Jessie
Fauset also served as an interpreter for the Du Bois-
inspired Second Pan-African Congress, in London. A native of New Jersey, she attended Cornell (Phi Beta
Kappa) and the University of Pennsylvania, and published
four novels: *There Is Confusion* (1924), *Plum Bun*
(1929), *The Chinaberry Tree* (1931), and *Comedy,
American Style* (1933). Her poetry appeared in numerous
periodicals during the twenties and thirties. Her skill is evident in "Oriflamme," her most famous poem. Inspired by
a quotation from Sojourner Truth, the poem views the
black mother "seared with slavery's mortal scars" but vows
that her sons are

> Still visioning the stars!

Black poets apparently spent time reflecting during the period between the beginning of the century and the
Harlem Renaissance. So much of the poetry takes us into
their private lives—sometimes via racial tones and sometimes not. Some of Jessie Fauset's verse, for example, mirrors her knowledge of French (she taught the language and
translated into English several West Indian French-speaking poets). This is seen in the titles of some of the poems
and in other places where she interpolates French words
into the texts. Generally her tone is quiet and her poetry
is neat and well written.

Hawkins (a native of North Carolina) graduated from

Kitrell College in 1901 and worked for many years in the railway mail service. In "Credo" he announced:

I am an Iconoclast.

With obvious irony, Hawkins goes on to claim he is "an Anarchist," (see Brown) and "an Agnostic." Additional irony and cynicism is seen in such poems as "A Spade Is Just a Spade" and "The Death of Justice." In his rush of language and boldness of subject matter, Hawkins anticipates Tolson. His *Chords and Discords* was published in 1909, and his work appears in *The Poetry of Black America* (Adoff, 1973) and Kerlin's anthology, which includes critical notes. Brown also comments on Hawkins (a "foreshadow" of new "Negro Poetry").

Harris, Mrs. Fleming, Mrs. Newsome, Roberts, Eva Jessye, Shackelford, Jamison, Wilson, Mrs. Johnson, Razafkeriefo, Burrell, and Bailey were among other poets contributing to various periodicals of the day. Harris brought out *The Steel Makers and Other War Poems* in pamphlet form in 1918. He served as editor of the Richmond (Indiana) *Blade* and published short stories in *The Century*. "The Steel Makers" is emotionally and technically akin to some of the work of Walt Whitman and Carl Sandburg. It praises the steelworkers—among whom Harris himself numbered at one time. In another place Harris asks the white man to accept him, since, despite color and feature differences,

The Negro's the same as the rest.

Harris' work can be found in Kerlin's book.

Mrs. Fleming published *Clouds and Sunshine* (1920) in Boston at the inception of the renaissance. Mrs. Newsome, who writes primarily for children, did not publish a volume of poems until 1940 (*Gladiola Garden*). Among the "earliest Negroes to employ free verse with artistic effectiveness" were Razafkeriefo and Will Sexton. During the 1920s and 1930s Sexton contributed to various periodicals, as did Razafkeriefo, whose work appeared in *The Crusader* and *The Negro World*. Carrying through the theme of the day, Sexton announced:

I am the New Negro.

Taken from "The New Negro," this line will be seen again in various places and temperaments, including Tolson's "Dark Symphony." In "The Bomb Thrower" Sexton plays the role of "America's evil genius" and sardonically proposes a reversal of the ideals of democracy. Razafkeriefo, born in Washington, D.C., to Afro-American and Madagascaran parents, had only an elementary education. He asks, in "The Negro Church," for "manly, thinking preachers"

> And not shouting money-makers,

after declaring (in the manner of a Stokely Carmichael, Malcolm X, or Rap Brown) that the church has great "power." Preachers, he warns, should work to "fit the Negro"

> For this world as well as heaven.

In addition to anger and impatience, this poet also expresses race pride and praises "The Negro Woman." If it were left up to him to pick a woman for "queen of the hall of fame," he would "select the wonderful Negro woman."

Burrell, who contributed poetry to magazines, echoes Razafkeriefo in "To a Negro Mother." In four 8-line stanzas (using iambic octameter) Burrell celebrates the "grace and fortitude" of the black mother. Recalling the greatness of black history, he asks the Negro mother to

> Create anew the captains of the past;
> Build in your soul the Ethiopian power, . . .

The two preceding poems call to mind Hughes's "The Negro Mother," Watkins' "Ebon Maid and Girl of Mine," Mrs. Johnson's "To My Grandmother," Dodson's "Black Mother Praying," and other moving tributes to the Afro-American woman.

Wilson's "Somebody's Child" is not good poetry but its subject is. He worked as a printer and theatrical performer and served time in the Missouri State Penitentiary, where he put together a small book of his verses. Shackelford was a native of Canada who studied at an industrial training school and the Philadelphia Art Museum. His book *My Country and Other Poems* was published in Philadelphia in 1918. Jamison published *Negro Soldiers and Other*

Poems in South St. Joseph, Missouri, in 1918. Jamison writes about "Castles in the Air," love, "Hopelessness" and "The Negro Soldiers." The latter poem has something of the flavor of Dunbar's "Colored Soldiers" and salutes the bravery and courage of black troops whose "souls grandly rise." These troops, Jamison points out, fought for America instead of seeking "vengeance for their wrongs."

A native of Missouri, Bailey's only volume of poems (*The Firstling*) was released in 1914. "The Slump" makes a baseball game (via Christian symbolism) analogous to the hardships of black life:

Well, we're all at the bat—

and warns that the "ball may be hurled" as a plea. "Mr. Self" is at the bat but

There's the Beggar and Gate—

and a whispering voice from above calls "Strike three."

Eva Jessye wrote moving poetry but is much better known for her work in developing and leading professional choruses. Born in Kansas, she received musical training at Western University in Kansas and Langston University in Oklahoma. Moving to New York City in the twenties, she worked with such figures as Will Marion Cook, J. Rosamond Johnson, Hall Johnson, and others. In her famous concerts around the world she has used work from *Porgy and Bess*, John Work's compositions and those of the men listed above. Her published collections include *My Spirituals* (1927), *The Life of Christ in Negro Spirituals* (1931), *Paradise Lost and Regained* (Milton's work adapted to black songs, 1934), and *The Chronicle of Job* (a folk drama, 1936). Important for the same reasons noted in our discussion of Alex Rogers, Eva Jessye successfully combined the poetic and the musical language (though they are so similar to start with!). Her poem "The Singer" recalls the work of Corrothers, Dunbar, (James) Johnson, and numerous other poets who have bridged the gap between the two art forms. One is reminded of Johnson's "O Black and Unknown Bards" in Eva Jessye's statement that the singer's "speech was blunt and manner plain." Like the "unknown bards," his *unlettered* song was "but the essence of the heart." Her poems, published in newspapers during the twenties, show lightheartedness but sincerity and a sense of conviction. She writes about "spring" and the "Rosebud," and while she is not singularly distinguished as a poet, her life's work is an indispensable float in the grand parade of Afro-American creativity in the arts. In choral work, she is especially noted for her direction of the Original Dixie Jubilee Singers, later named the Eva Jessye Choir. For a thorough discussion of her life and works (along with those of her contemporaries), see Eileen Southern's *The Music of Black Americans*. For poetry selections, see Kerlin.

During the period of the Harlem Renaissance, poets such as Georgia Johnson, Jessie Fauset, Anne Spencer, Alice Dunbar-Nelson, Hill, McKay, James Weldon Johnson, Dandridge, and Cotter, Jr. (who had achieved recognition before 1923), continued their output either through magazines or book publication. Much of this work is recorded in Johnson's *The Book of American Negro Poetry* (1922, 1931), Kerlin's *Negro Poets and Their Poems* (1923, 1935) and *Contemporary Poetry of the Negro* (1921), Cullen's *Caroling Dusk* (1927), and in other such compilations and periodicals.

Anne Spencer was born in West Virginia and studied at the Virginia Seminary in Lynchburg, where she has spent most of her life. For a long time she was librarian at Dunbar High School in Lynchburg. The poet's work hardly ever reflects racial or political concerns, but she is one of the most technically sure of all black poets. She writes about women, love, carnivals, and the workings of the mind. In its brevity and conciseness, her poetry anticipates the work of Gwendolyn Brooks and is loosely akin to Angelina Grimké's (though the latter's work is racially flavored). Her poetry also bears some kinship to the "Imagist" school of poets writing in the early years of the century. Elements of this particular technique and style can also be seen in Hayden ("The Diver," "Night-Blooming Cereus") and others. In Anne Spencer's "At The Carnival" we smell sausage and garlic that

Sent unholy incense skyward

and are told (in an echo of the romantics) that

Whatever is good is God.

"Dunbar" laments "how poets sing and die!" and places the eulogized black poet in the same class as Chatterton, Shelley, and Keats. Her most moving poem, it seems, is "Translation," wherein two lovers never speak.

But each knew all the other said.

Calling her the "most original of all Negro women poets," Brown advised, in 1937, that her "sensitive, and keenly observant," work should be "collected for a wider audience." But as of this writing, no one had undertaken Brown's suggestion. Considering her span of years, Anne Spencer (somewhat like Hayden) has not been prolific. Her work can be found in several anthologies and periodicals of the twenties. Critical assessments are given by Kerlin, Brown and Johnson.

James Weldon Johnson, we noted earlier, published *Fifty Years and Other Poems* in 1917. It included dialect as well as conventional, standard-English commemorative pieces. Not highly original, the work was one more step in the long and fruitful development of perhaps the most important figure in the history of black poetry. It seems Johnson was involved in as many things as could have been humanly possible. After his involvement on Broadway (with light operas), he worked for the re-election of Theodore Roosevelt, served as United States Consul (a reward for his political work) in Nicaragua and Venezuela, published (anonymously) *The Autobiography of an Ex-Colored Man* in 1912, wrote editorials (for more than ten years) for the New York *Age* and became the NAACP's first secretary-general—working in that post for fourteen years. A deeply psychological work, *Autobiography* dealt with such an explosive contemporary topic—the theme of *passing*—that Johnson would not affix his own name to it until it was reissued during the renaissance (1927) with an introduction by Carl Van Vechten.

The conventional poetry of *Fifty Years* shows Johnson to be politically at the threshold of the "awakening." Brown stated, incorrectly, that Johnson's "Brothers" was the most "vigorous poem of protest from any Negro poet up to his time." We know that Whitfield, Whitman, Du Bois, Hawkins, and others were just as strong and forceful. *Fifty Years* was highly praised by Braithwaite ("intellectual substance"), Brander Matthews ("should be grouped with the noblest American commemorative poems"), and other influential critics. This first book shows a strength, virility, and robustness that would mark Johnson's future writings—especially *God's Trombones* (1927). The poems are patriotic ("Fifty Years," which commemorates the fiftieth anniversary of the Emancipation Proclamation), nostalgic ("O Southland!"), descriptively amorous ("The Glory of the Day Was in Her Face"), strong and virile ("The Young Warrior"), race-proud (angry) and didactic (see "Brothers"), and fundamental and religious ("O Black and Unknown Bards"). The last poem, more important for what it records than for how it is assembled, is an artistic tribute to the makers of the spirituals. Using actual words and names from spirituals, Johnson weaves in the strength and artistry characteristic of the songs he loved—and to which he devoted so much research and listening time. Great art, he says, is produced by

These simple children of the sun and soil.

Johnson knew, too, that these makers would not be

O black slave singers, gone, forgot, unfamed,

if work of the sort he was doing continued in the hands of those to whom he passed the torch. Although *Fifty Years* is strong, solid work, it is later that Johnson comes into his own as experimentalist and pace setter.

Georgia Johnson also wrote race-conscious lyrics. Her themes are suggested in her titles: *The Heart of a Woman* (1918), *Bronze* (1922) and *An Autumn Love Cycle* (1928). "Skillful and fluent," her poetry deals primarily with loneliness, sorrow, seasons and unrequited love, and is intellectually based. The first black woman after Frances Harper to achieve wide recognition as a poet, she is explicitly racial in *Bronze*, although allusions to blackness sometimes appear in her other work. Yet she seems to know something about the heart of all women (and men) when she says the singer's songs

Are tones that repeat
The cry of the heart
    Till it ceases to beat.

"The Octoroon" deals with a woman who is tainted because she is the victim of

> One drop of midnight in the dawn of
> life's pulsating stream

but who finds hospitality in the "humble fold"—presumably the black community. This poem recalls Cotter, Sr.'s, "The Mulatto to His Critics," which depicts the multiracial predicament of one (probably Cotter himself) made up

> Of Red Man, Black Man, Briton, Celt,
> and Scot,

but who loves the dark-skinned, curly-haired race that "puts sweet music in my soul." Georgia Johnson develops a similar tension in "To My Son" where she is caught between advising her son that "dusky pall or shadows screen the highway of sky" and encouraging him to "storm the sullen fortress" founded on racism. In addition to writing such powerful and lasting poetry, she was of service to young writers for several decades. A female counterpart to Langston Hughes, she hosted regular and spontaneous writers' meetings in her home in Washington, D.C., where she moved after receiving academic and musical training at Atlanta University and Oberlin College. A native of Georgia, she was employed in government service most of her adult life. For critically introduced selections of her work, see Barksdale and Kinnamon, Johnson, and Kerlin. Brown also supplies a good assessment.

We should note, in passing and by way of introduction to Fenton Johnson, H. Binga Dismond (1891–1956), who did not publish a volume of poetry until 1943 (*We Who Would Die*). Dismond, like Johnson and Frank Marshall Davis, was one of the many writers of the period who was not physically present in Harlem during the renaissance. Dismond was born in Virginia and, a track star (as was Frank Horne), studied physical therapy at Rush Medical College after attending Howard University Academy and the University of Chicago. (The Midwest's participation in the renaissance has not been given adequate attention.) Dismond, who wrote some crisp and poignant poetry of love and protest, is more important to us during this period for his journalistic work. With Johnson,

he edited *The Champion Magazine* (starting in 1916) for
several years. They also coedited *The Favorite Magazine*
("The World's Greatest Monthly"), which published
their poems and articles.

Johnson had several of his plays performed in Chicago's
Pekin Theatre when he was nineteen and is generally seen
as one of the most creative links between the poets of
Dunbar's era and the Harlem Renaissance. Born in
Chicago in an economically sound family, he attended the
city's namesake university and taught school for a year in
the South. He privately published three volumes of poetry,
one (*A Little Dreaming*, 1917) in Chicago, and two (*Visions of the Dusk*, 1915; and *Songs of the Soil*, 1916) in
New York, where he lived for a short time. Harriet
Monroe and "The New Poetry" group had established *Poetry* (1912) in his home town, and Johnson made contact
with her. In 1920, he published *Tales of Darkest America*
—short stories. A participant in the "poetry revival" in
America, Johnson had his work accepted for *Poetry* and
the anthologies *Others* (1916, 1917, 1920), *The New Poetry* and *An Anthology of American Poetry: Lyric
America, 1630–1930*.

In saying Fenton Johnson was ultimately the poet of
"despair" and that he was the only poet writing in such a
vein (as Brown, Redding, Johnson, Wagner, and others
have done), critics presented only part of the man. He did
borrow from Masters, Lindsay and Sandburg; this allowed
him to voice something *relatively* new in black poetry
while he provided an avenue of experimental exchange between his black and white contemporaries. But in poems
such as "Tired," "The Banjo Player," "The Scarlet
Woman" and "Rulers" he displays much more than "despair." Reflecting, as Brown noted, the "two extremes of
Negro poetry after 1914," Johnson can deal with either
the brawling urban blues or the down-home, "we shall
overcome" motifs. Because his work does not contain a
consistent spirit of hope, James Weldon Johnson said his
message mirrored ideas "foreign to any philosophy of life
the Negro in America had ever preached or practiced."
Johnson thought this was "startling" despite the "birth,"
about the same time as Fenton Johnson's work, of the
blues era—and the work of W. C. Handy (1873–1958),
who is sometimes called its "father." Fenton Johnson is

"Tired" of a civilization that has given him "too many" children and no chance for them to share in the American dream. He proposes to his wife that they

> Throw the children into the river:

and observes that

> . . . It is better to die than it is to
> grow up and find out that you are
> colored.

Johnson writes about roustabouts, prostitutes, vagrants, laborers, and strong will, and is, as Jay Wright said (during the late 1960s) of Henry Dumas, "the poet of the dispossessed." He is also the poet of the blues. In breaking away from traditional black poetic diction and form, Johnson not only received influence from the white experimenters of free verse but he borrowed heavily from the blues and, at this level, must share some of the accolades usually reserved almost solely for Hughes.

It is now widely accepted that the blues do not simply preach resignation. To the contrary, the blues, telling about heartache and personal failures, carry hope in the singing and the going on. Margaret Walker is only one of the many poets whose work seems to reflect the influence of Johnson. And do we really believe that Johnson meant for the children to be thrown in the river, any more than we take the blues singer literally when he promises to "lay my head down on some railroad track?" Johnson's "note of despair" is one more brilliant distillation of the strange psychological web that produced the sorrow songs, the spirituals, the ditties, jokes, rhymes, and blues. At the time Johnson wrote his poetry, Handy was composing some of his most famous blues songs ("St. Louis Blues," "The Memphis Blues," "Yellow Dog Blues") and arranging such traditional blues pieces as "Train's A-Comin'," "Let Us Cheer the Weary Traveler," "Come on, Eph," and "Juba." And in this list alone are locked partial answers to much of the work of several Afro-American writers: Hughes, Walker, Tolson, Wright, Brown, Jayne Cortez, Gil Scott-Heron, and numberless others. It is possible that critics looking at Johnson were unprepared for his irony and poetic assimilation of themes and feelings previously glossed over by Christianity and other anesthetics. In

"Rulers," Johnson discusses a "monarch" on "Lombard Street in Philadelphia," who "was seated on a throne of flour bags." Near the "monarch," two young boys with guitars played "ragtime tunes of the day." Clearly this "monarch" (a black laborer in reality) is being serenaded and saluted just as any other ruler would be. He presides as a prince of the blues ("Ragtime"). Johnson's work is in most anthologies of Afro-American poetry, and critical assessments of him have already been noted. For more thorough discussions of the poetry-blues concept, see Stephen Henderson's *Understanding the New Black Poetry* and the bibliography in this book.

At the dawn of the Harlem Renaissance, there appeared a slim volume of poetry by Seamon Cotter, Jr., the precocious son of the Cotter already discussed. Young Cotter died an early death, which cut short the work of one of the most promising figures in Afro-American poetry. Born in Kentucky and frail from childhood like Dunbar, Cotter had to end his college career at Fisk University when he developed tuberculosis. An innovator, as was his father, Cotter shows a sharp awareness (in *The Band of Gideon*, 1918) of the plight of Blacks and an even sharper ability to express that plight along with other sentiments and feelings. He echoes much of black poetry's concerns in "And What Shall I Say," and "Rain Music" anticipates many of Hughes's pieces—experiments in *The Weary Blues*, "Jazzonia," and so on—when he recalls the "dusty earth-drum" which hammers falling rain:

> Now a whispered murmur,
> Now a louder strain.

Bearing the import of much of the "exotic" black literature of the renaissance, Cotter nevertheless sees in the beat of the

> Slender, silvery drumsticks

a rejuvenation of life as ordered by God, "the Great Musician." Cotter began writing poems as a teen-ager. His technique, like Fenton Johnson's, combines the best of traditional Western poetry with the new wave of free verse. His poems are about love, "Negro Soldiers," religion, blackness, justice and his own illness. "Is It Because

I Am Black?" seems to have been looking forward to a 1960s "soul" song of a similar title wherein the singer says

> Something is holding me back!
> Lawd, is it because I'm Black?

In his poem Cotter asks why whites are so amazed that he can "stand" in their important meetings, look them straight in the face, and "speak their tongue"? Cotter's work appears in *The Book of American Negro Poetry*, *Negro Caravan*, Kerlin's study ("The stamp of the African mind is upon" Cotter), and *The Poetry of Black America*. Although Kerlin submits brief critical comments, a study of this young poet's work is sorely needed. He also left several plays and unpublished sonnets.

POETS AS PROPHETS: THE HARLEM RENAISSANCE

> A wave of longing through
>   my body swept. . . .
>   —CLAUDE MCKAY

The Harlem Renaissance is normally seen as a decade-length (1920–30) outpouring of cultural and artistic activity in what James Weldon Johnson called the Negro cultural capital. There is harmless disagreement as to when the renaissance actually began and how long it lasted. Some say it started in 1925 and ran until 1935. Others give the first time span, mentioned above. Still others (including Wagner, *Black Poets of the United States*) designate the period between the two world wars (1918–39).

Poets of the Harlem Renaissance—which included dance, painting, sculpture, music, theater, literature, political activism, science, and scholarship—knew and read each other's works. Ironically, however, only one of the leading figures is said to have been born in New York City: Countee Cullen (1903–46), and he was raised in the "conservative atmosphere of a Methodist parsonage," the adopted son of a minister. Langston Hughes (1902–67) spent much of the decade of the twenties traveling; so did Claude McKay (1890–1948), who wandered over "Europe and North Africa"—in many instances literally "a long ways from home." Jean Toomer (1894–1967), disturbed and haunted by his complex ethnic background, was a mysterious figure who died the same year as Hughes in the anonymity of a Quaker commune in Philadelphia (obscure after having given up writing several years before). Often called "minor" writers of the Harlem Renaissance, neither Sterling Brown (1901–) nor Arna Bontemps (1902–73) was born in New York. And neither published books during the twenties, but they did have poems accepted by such magazines as *The Crisis* and *Opportunity*.

McKay, labeled the renaissance's poet of anger and rebellion, is chiefly known for his famous sonnet "If We Must Die," which winds down (up?) to the following couplet:

> Like men we'll face the murderous, cowardly pack,
> Pressed to the wall, dying, but fighting back!

McKay wrote the poem in 1919 shortly after a series of race riots that took hundreds of black lives. Many critics use that year as the beginning of the renaissance. But McKay had made his entry into the Harlem world of letters two years earlier (1917) with the publication of two poems ("Harlem Dancer" and "Invocation") in *Seven Arts Magazine*. He came to the United States in 1912 from his native Jamaica, where he had devoured much European literature and philosophy, to study agriculture. Enrolling first at Tuskegee and later at Kansas State College, he finally went on to Harlem, where he worked as a porter, waiter and restaurant proprietor. Before leaving Jamaica, McKay had established his reputation as a poet of dialect poetry with his *Songs of Jamaica* (1912) and *Constab Ballads* (1912), the latter work reflecting his onetime employment as a policeman on the island.

In New York, he gained quick entrance into literary and political circles, establishing a lifelong friendship with Max Eastman (who wrote a biographical note for *Selected Poems* [1953]). McKay counted among his friends some of the most influential literary and political figures of the day: John Reed, Floyd Dell (*The Masses*), Waldo Frank, Frank Harris (*Pearson's Magazine*), Marcus Garvey (*Negro World*), and others. Fiery and forceful, McKay was the subject of much attention and discussion. Although he never joined the Communist Party, he defended its stand in most of the publications for which he wrote. "If We Must Die" was read into the United States *Congressional Record* as an example of black unrest and resentment. In the fury, McKay left the United States in 1919, returned for a brief period the following year, and left again to travel all over Europe and North Africa for fifteen years. He returned to America in 1934 and remained until his death in 1948.

McKay's other volumes of poetry include *Spring in New Hampshire* (1920, with a preface by the famous critic I. A. Richards); *Harlem Shadows* (1922) and *The Dialect Poetry of Claude* McKay (1972). *Songs of Jamaica* was reissued in 1969, and a new volume of prose and poetry (*The Passion of Claude McKay*) was published in 1973. It contains published and unpublished writings, 1912–48. McKay died obscure and poor in Chicago, where he had gone to teach in Catholic schools. His life, like those of so many black artists (Dunbar, Charlie "Yardbird" Parker, Lester "Prez" Young, Sam Cooke, Leroy Carr, Blind Lemon Jefferson), was lived with consummate speed, fear, contradiction, and tragedy. Though he lashed out at whites, his closest friends were white; while he wrote defiant, angry and militant verse, he denied that it was inspired by the Blacks' predicament. There are other contradictions and enigmas in his life. But we make no attempt to unravel them here. Keys to much of McKay's complexity, however, can be gained by reading his autobiography (*A Long Ways from Home*, 1937, 1970), his novels (*Home to Harlem* [1928], *Banjo* [1929] and *Banana Bottom* [1933]), and his many articles and short stories (*Gingertown* [1932]). He also wrote a study entitled *Harlem: Negro Metropolis* (1940). The best source for McKay's poetry is his *Selected Poems*.

In many ways it is ironic that McKay is called the poet of anger (Nathan Huggins, *Harlem Renaissance*, calls him the "black Prometheus"), since most of his poems deal with quiet topics such as motherhood, nature, nostalgia, loneliness, mental reflection, religion, world travel, and descriptions of city life. Of the literally dozens of poems he published, only about ten can be called "angry." Of course, there is often seething unrest ("America"),

And I am sharp as steel with discontent, . . .

in much of the poetry that is not overtly violent. Such is
true of everyday black life. And in this sense most black
Americans could be labeled "militant" or "violent"—har-
boring, as it were, polarizing tensions ("Baptism") that
make one defy all:

> I will come out back to your world of tears,
> A stronger soul within a finer frame.

Though one of the greatest influences on black thought
and art of his day, McKay perhaps did not know that his
writings inspired various spokesmen for African nationalism: Léopold Sédar Senghor, Ousmane Soce, and Aimé
Césaire. And he is today seen as the major link between
the Harlem Renaissance and the militant writings of the
1960s. Just as his dialect poems (such as "Two-an'-Six")
had charmed and entertained his fellow Jamaicans, the
disciplined anger of his popular American poems incited
and inspired Blacks, and titillated and fascinated whites.
For during this period, whites around the world were in-
dicating a new interest in Blacks; and Blacks, inspired by
the growing nationalist feelings in some European countries, found ready fuel and propaganda in their brothers of
color returning home from the war.

Yet, for all the anger, McKay never swerved from his
use of conventional English verse. With Cullen—though
not so religiously—he avoided experimentation. The folk
materials of American Blacks, the examples of Fenton
Johnson and others—none of these seems to have had
much influence on McKay. But his English is designed to
cage fury and passion in "sonnet-tragedies," as James Weldon Johnson called them. Above all, he is a poet of passion, distrust, anger and hatred. We have seen some
hatred before in black poetry (Du Bois, Gwendolyn Bennett) but not quite as we see it in McKay, whom Wagner
says "is *par excellence* the poet of hate." This feeling is
expressed in such poems as "The White City," "Mulatto," "One Year After," "Of Work I Love to Sing," and
"Polarity." But McKay is not always the hater. He examines hate in the hands of whites—or as a product of Western sickness and decadence, vented albeit on the Blacks.
The nobility of the black soul is to stand above this emotion and not to be destroyed by it.

Other themes in the work and of McKay are the importance of the earth (and the countryside), disillusionment (see Dumas) with city life, race pride (celebrations of the black past and virtues ["Harlem Dancer"]), primitivism and romantic treatment of Africa, Harlem as a Pan-African crossroad, and spiritualism and religion. While McKay was not an experimentalist, he did make previously unnoticed modifications in the sonnet form. As the first black poet to make sustained use of the sonnet as a political/racial weapon, he must be given credit (instead of being disparaged—c.f. Huggins) for turning this "white" form into a vehicle of protest, love and race pride. We observed that Lucian B. Watkins opened his sonnet to "The New Negro" with

He thinks in black.

But in no other quarter, before or since McKay, does a black poet persist—infusing blues and tragic irony—with the sonnet. Gwendolyn Brooks will later invent her memorable "sonnet-ballad." And Cullen's sonnets certainly must be taken into account. McKay, however, endures with an ironic inconclusiveness that verges on the "despair" critics seem to see in Fenton Johnson.

For McKay the sonnet is a form of therapy—allowing him to loose controlled anger. His is the anger of a native Jamaican ("home boy") caught up in the straitjacket of white literary amenities. He wants to be freed. And freedom comes through poetry—principally the sonnet. This open-endedness can be seen in "The Negro's Tragedy," "The Negro's friend," "In Bondage," and "The Lynching." As a correct and carefully nurtured darling of Western poetry, the sonnet had been in the annals of English and Italian literature for centuries when McKay began using it. Containing fourteen lines (in either of two standard stanzaic patterns and various rhyme schemes), it is designed to pose a problem, squirm in it for a while, and close in a neat answer which usually begins with line nine, the first line of the sestet. Presto! Just like solving a problem in mathematics. "Solving" the "race problem," however, is not quite so easy. Hence McKay, in employing the Italian strand of the sonnet, finds that it cannot "solve" a lynching. But he places it in the most awesome, gruesome

contexts by equating the lynching with the crucifixion of
Christ (see Cullen's *The Black Christ* and "Colors"), and
by failing to resolve the white man's moral and religious
crises. The blue-eyed women come to view the body, but
show no sorrow,

> And little lads, lynchers that were to be,
> Danced round the dreadful thing in fiendish glee.

Clearly this is not how Petrarch, Shakespeare, Spenser,
Milton, Wordsworth, Arnold, or Santayana would have
wanted the problem "solved" or "restated." There was no
answer—except for Blacks' "fighting back" here and there
—so McKay modified the concept of at least one type of
sonnet in order to deal with a real "problem."

Most critics of black literature and culture have
discussed McKay's work. His *Selected Poems* is available
and he is now being represented even in white "prestige"
anthologies (e.g., *Norton Anthology* by Brooks, Lewis and
Warren, *The United States in Literature* and others). The
most ambitious study of McKay to date is by Jean
Wagner (*Black Poets*). Another recent study (which includes prose writings) is Arthur P. Davis' *From the Dark
Tower: Afro-American Writers, 1900 to 1960* (1974).
Also see appendixes to most anthologies, the bibliography
section of this work, and especially the listings in *Black
Writers of America* (Barksdale and Kinnamon).

Unlike that of the "pure-blooded" McKay, Jean
Toomer's body housed seven racial strains and he looked
white. Evidence to support the fact that Toomer rejected
his black blood and "passed" cannot be found in his
major work: *Cane* (1923). Neither is it in "The Blue Meridian," written in 1936 and sadly overlooked, in which he
tries to unite the disparate elements of the American personality into one person. Apparently unhappy in childhood, Toomer never knew his father, who abandoned the
boy's mother, shortly after he was born, in Washington,
D.C. Toomer's possible claim to name and money had
been thwarted earlier when his mother, the daughter of P.
B. S. Pinchback, an important Louisiana Reconstruction
politician, had to reduce her social status and relocate in

the upper-class black area of Washington. It was there
that Toomer found spirit and robustness: "more emotion,
more rhythm, more color, more gaiety" (Barksdale and
Kinnamon). After attending local public schools (including Dunbar High), he enrolled in one college after another, never becoming a serious degree candidate. From
this latter type of life, he went through a series of jobs,
finally getting into serious writing and putting poems and
stories in several avant-garde little magazines. Toomer also
formed close associations with New York intellectuals:
Hart Crane, Waldo Frank (to whom he dedicated a section of *Cane*), Gorham P. Munson, Alfred Stieglitz, Paul
Rosenfeld, Kenneth Burke, and others. Later, while working as superintendent (for four months) of a small black
school in Sparta, Georgia, he gained much of the material
for the first and third sections of *Cane*. After publication
of *Cane*, Toomer's life returned to "psychological disar-
ray" and he turned to other sources in search of a self-
unifying methodology. With other intellectuals/associates,
he delved into the philosophies of F. Matthias Alexander,
P. D. Ouspensky, and, most importantly, George J. Gurdjieff—whose disciple he later became. Gurdjieff, a Russian,
assimilated aspects of Yoga, religious mysticism, and
Freud to produce what he called Unitism. Toomer later
espoused the theory and won over converts. For a short
while he also lived in a heterosexual experimental commune. In quick succession, Toomer married two white
women. After his second marriage, in the thirties, he
quipped: "I do not know whether colored blood flows
through my veins." Earlier, however, he had noted in a
biographical sketch accompanying work he submitted to
The Liberator,

I have lived equally among the two race groups. Now
white, now colored. From my own point of view I am
naturally an American. I have strived for a spiritual fusion analogous to the fact of racial intermingling. Without denying a single element in me, with no desire to
subdue one to the other, I have sought to let them live
in harmony. Within the last two or three years, however, my growing need for artistic expression has pulled

me deeper and deeper into the Negro group. And as
powers of receptivity increased, I found myself loving it
in a way that I could never love the other.

Although James Weldon Johnson complained that
Toomer refused (allegedly out of contempt for racial cat-
egorizing) to be included in the second edition of *The
Book of American Negro Poetry*, it was later brought out
(conversation between Sterling Brown and Jean Wagner)
that ill feelings existed between the two men. At any rate,
Toomer's poetry and prose appear in practically every subsequent anthology of Afro-American literature.

Toomer exerted more influence on the black intellectuals of the era than any other Harlem Renaissance
figure. No other writer experimented with literature or
depicted Blacks quite the way he did. Reciprocal influence
seems to have occurred between him and Hart Crane. And
Robert Bone (*Negro Novel in America*) places *Cane* on a
par with the writings of some of the best American contemporaries: Hemingway, Stein, Pound, Eliot. This is
surprising, since *Cane*, when originally published sold
fewer than five hundred copies. As a work of art, however,
it reflects Toomer's efforts to achieve unity of both self
and purpose. Called variously a novel, a collection of short
stories/vignettes, a poetic drama, *Cane* defies labels. In
classrooms, we often refer to it as a blues epic—concep-
tually similar to the great nationalistic sagas of the world:
Beowulf, Siegfried, The Song of Roland, Chaka, and
others, but welded by black spirituality and the rhythms
of Afro-American ritual. *Cane* has three basic movements
—Toomer had been interested in both music composition
and painting—which involve (1) Georgia and the South,
(2) Chicago, Washington, D.C., and the North, and (3)
Georgia again, where Toomer waxes autobiographical. In
the first part of *Cane*, there are numerous pictures of
women, any of whom, such as Karintha, will be ripened
"too soon." In the second section, Toomer views northern
urban decadence and corruption and their influence on
Blacks. In the third movement, a naïve northern black educator goes South (Georgia) to find his African roots. He
rather clumsily passes through a series of rites during
which Toomer uses startling symbolism to heighten the
man's fear and confusion. Many of the stories are intro-

duced by and interspersed with poetic sketches. The third, and final, section, "Kabnis," is similar to a play.

Karintha's skin "is like dusk on the eastern" horizon, and immediately, at the opening of *Cane*, we find significant symbols in the words "dusk" and "eastern." Throughout the book, Toomer assays the plight and joys of Blacks through tight and sometimes enigmatic poetry. Word meanings are given double, triple, and even more levels, as in the "Reapers" sharpening their scythes for farm chores but also, perhaps, for a massacre. Black beauty is sometimes surprising in the context of white barrenness and brutality ("November Cotton Flower"). "Face" is an old, tired black woman in Georgia. "Cotton Song" celebrates the worksong, unity among field workers, and encodes revolutionary messages:

"We aint agwine t wait until the Judgment Day!"

The "Beehive" is a metaphor for the ghetto, compressed, cordoned off, impoverished. The narrator wishes he could rest "forever" in a flower on some farm (again rural versus city life). In the poetry, Toomer writes about sun and evening "songs," "Conversion" and "Portrait in Georgia," the electricity of a woman's lips, "Harvest Song," and the cane scents and pine needles. From the pen of the poet spill the lives—broken, mended, some barely begun—of the severely damaged men and women who, "with vestiges of pomp," carry their

Race memories of king and caravan

and go singing through the "Georgia Dusk." Original, awesome and sustained in craftsmanship, *Cane* as poetry is a classic of Afro-American literature. In the most important poem in the book, "Song of the Son," Toomer encases both his superior techniques and the concept for *Cane*. The son sings:

Pour O pour that parting soul in song,

because he knows the tradition is intact. Just "pour" the song, he asks,

And let the valley carry it along.
And let the valley carry it along.

The songs of "slavery" will be transformed into powerful
dirges, compositions and epics (like *Cane*). And Toomer's
was a fitting observation in the years following the blues
(Handy and others) and preceding the birth of big black
jazz bands (Basie, Ellington). The plaintive soul will soon
be gone, but it will leave

> An everlasting son, a singing tree. . . .

Likened by some to a series of artistic sketches, by others
to a symphonic composition, by still others to the syncopation and vocal blendings of Afro-American folk music,
Cane—according to one critic—was at least two decades
ahead of the era in which it was written.

Less impressive as black material but brilliant as a general work of art is "Blue Meridian." Heavily influenced by
the modernist school of poetry (Pound, Crane, Eliot,
etc.), "Meridian" was overlooked for years and is finally
being anthologized (see *Black Writers of America*). More
than seven hundred lines, the poem makes use of various rhyme schemes, stress formulas, linguistic and stylistic
marriages. It owes a lot to Walt Whitman in its sweep
and intent. And there are muted shades of Sandburg.
"Meridian" seems to be Toomer's near-final effort to per-
suade the different elements of himself to "live in harmony." Eliot had knelled the doom of Western civilization in 1922 (*The Waste Land*), and other poets had
echoed him. Fenton Johnson, of course, had preceded
Eliot with this proclamation. Toomer had intimated the
same thing in *Cane* ("November Cotton Flower"). But it
is in "Meridian" that he warns of the impending downfall
of the West—noting that such fate might not be un-
deserved. The world is full of "crying men and hard
women" and

> We're all niggers now—get me?
> Black niggers, white niggers,—take your choice.

These omens of doom come in the first section of the
poem. But the second section heralds the coming of the
new man (for Toomer, perhaps, an admixture of races and
colors), who is spiritually and psychically elevated above
race and other immaterial problems. The new man is a
"blue" man, possibly a cross between a black and a white

man, and even sexual crosses are suggested. For we know all these things troubled Toomer. He was concerned as a teen-ager about his "nascent sexuality." And he declared that he was above both sex and race if ever they meant obstacles or defeat.

It is a challenge to the curious student, however, to unravel the life and works of one of the most complex geniuses in American letters. Whatever the outcome, Toomer's is an achievement to be reckoned with. His work can be found in most anthologies of Afro-American literature. He also published *Essentials*—"definitions and aphorisms"—in 1931. Toomer wrote more things, but most are uncollected and remain at Fisk University. An unpublished segment of his autobiography, *Earth-Being*, appeared in the January 1971 issue of *The Black Scholar*. While Wagner's treatment of *Toomer* does not equal his discussion of other poets of the Harlem Renaissance, it is good. Brown, Redding, and numerous other critics discuss Toomer's work in various places. Of special aid is John M. Reilly's "Jean Toomer: An Annotated Checklist of Criticism," *Resources for American Literary Study*, Vol. IV, No. 1 (1974). See also Toomer listings in Barksdale and Kinnamon.

Countee Cullen, another brilliant tragic figure in black poetry, spent most of his life trying to bridge the gap between a "Christian upbringing" and a "pagan urge." How can the *educated* Afro-American, Cullen seems to ask, remain true to his native instincts and feelings while he wears the mantle of European "respectability?" This particular aspect of Cullen's life and work is often taken too lightly by critics who view his highly stylized poetry as simply intellectual (and hence not real) journeys into the awesome world of death, religion and color. Yet Cullen knew, as he said it in "The Shroud of Color," that being black in white America requires "courage more than angels have." History, of course, shows that so far Cullen's name has withstood heat from the furnace of "Baptism" just as many others before and after. And such figures as Gwendolyn Brooks, Carl Van Vechten, and Eleanor Roosevelt have lauded his passionately searching and skillful effort to avoid being devoured by the dragon of racism he tried to slay. However, Cullen did not consciously seek

after the unity so desperately thirsted after by Toomer.
On the one hand, Toomer felt free to explore all facets of
the religious and mystical world; on the other, he was
committed to an intellectual and spiritual search of his African origins. Cullen embraced Christianity and developed
the first major black tragedy figure by reincarnating Christ
into a black man. The "pure" and noble Black becomes
the new "only-begotten Son" on a several-hundred-year
march up Calvary. Here, of course, Cullen was close to
McKay; but in sustaining such efforts, and in making
them allegorical, he surpassed McKay.

Cullen's already complicated personal situations were
aggravated by his reluctance to deal truthfully with the details of his early life. It is still unclear as to whether he
was born in Baltimore, Maryland, or Louisville, Kentucky,
though he makes references to both ("Incident" and
"The Ballad of a Brown Girl"); or if he was raised by his
mother or his grandmother (up until the time of his adop-
tion by the Rev. Frederick Asbury Cullen). Johnson (*The
Book of American Negro Poetry*) says Cullen was born in
New York City (as do the editors of *The Negro Caravan*)
—probably because this is what Cullen wanted readers to
think. Possibly, Wagner notes, he was an illegitimate child
and, out of fear of embarrassment, purposely confused the
issues. This mystery, coupled with Cullen's troubled sexual life and his desire to assume the persona of an English
romantic poet, haunted the precocious bard throughout
his life.

Cullen's initiation into poetics came, as with Dunbar
and Hughes, in high school, where he won poetry contests
and published pieces in a student publication he helped
edit. By the time he had finished New York University
(Phi Beta Kappa), he had won several awards (including
the Witter Bynner award for excellence) for his poetry
and received a contract from Harper and Brothers for publication of his first book (*Color*, 1925). This marked the
first time since Dunbar's death that a major publisher had
brought out the work of a black poet. It also marked the
first time in almost twenty years that such a book had
been published for a live black poet. The most skillful
black user of English verse forms, Cullen achieved almost
instant success. *Color* sold over two thousand copies during the first two years of publication. He received his M.A.

from Howard during the same period. He generally sided with McKay in not breaking away from traditional English poetry. He especially admired the poetry of Keats and Shelley. Johnson, noting that "he might be called a younger brother of Housman," said some critics argued that Cullen was not an "authentic Negro poet." And Cullen, reminiscent of Toomer's position, straddled the fence on the question of inspiration and themes for black poets. On one occasion, he acknowledged his debt to the black tradition, but, on another, complained that the black poet ought to be able to "chant" poetry "in which no spiritual or blues appears." His aesthetics were stated more concisely in 1927, however, in the foreword to *Caroling Dusk* (1927), an anthology of Afro-American poetry which he compiled. His comment was startling, especially at the height of the Harlem Renaissance and coming, as it were, from a "new Negro":

> As heretical as it may sound, there is the probability that Negro poets, dependent as they are on the English language, may have more to gain from the rich background of English and American poetry than from any nebulous atavistic yearnings towards an African inheritance.

Consequently, Cullen called *Caroling Dusk* an anthology of "verse by Negro poets rather than an anthology of Negro verse." But Cullen could not always subscribe to this particular aesthetic, for much of his own poetry can be labeled "atavistic yearnings towards an African inheritance." Examination will show that such poetry is found in his early volume (*Color*) as well as in his later works: *Copper Sun* (1927), *The Ballad of the Brown Girl; an Old Ballad Retold* (1927), *The Black Christ and Other Poems* (1929), *The Medea and Some Poems* (1935) and his selected poems *On These I Stand* (1947). Cullen also wrote books for children: *The Lost Zoo* (1940) and *My Lives and How I Lost Them* (1942). He translated Greek literature (*The Medea*), wrote numerous lyrics for music and worked on a dramatic adaptation ("Saint Louis Woman") of an Arna Bontemps novel: *God Sends Sunday*. In 1932, seeking to renew his diminishing creative powers, he published his only novel, *One Way to Heaven*. Most of Cullen's poetry represents the vast influence of

Christianity. He wrestles with the Lord or asks God why this event or that event occurs. Especially is this seen in his poetry of racial conflict, in which the contradictions of white Christianity are exposed over and over. "For a Lady I Know" depicts a white woman in heaven who thinks "black cherubs" (or servants) will do her "celestial chores." "Scottsboro, Too, Is Worth Its Song" chides "American poets," outraged by the plight of Sacco and Vanzetti, for not defending black boys kangarooed for "rape" in an Alabama court. Their cause, Cullen says, is also "divinely spun." In "Colors" the "swart" (i.e., black) man is hanged on a "newer Calvary." Cullen's longest poem and treatment of this theme is *The Black Christ* (published in France). It deals allegorically with a lynching. A black man, Jim, attacks and kills a white man who insults a white woman. Jim is lynched, as southern law requires. His statements leading up to the lynching, and the action of the poem, suggest the crucifixion. Redding called the poem "the childish mysticism of a bad dream." But, despite the poem's evasiveness and "mysticism," lynching is much worse than a "bad dream." Finally (though the theme continues in countless other poems), there is the famous "Yet Do I Marvel." Here Cullen applies the sonnet to the riddle of the Afro-American poet, concluding, after high and mixed praise of God:

> Yet do I marvel at this curious thing:
> To make a poet black, and bid him sing!

Curious, indeed, was the black poet—curious both for Cullen and the whites who lavished praise and gifts upon these New and Unusual Negroes. And Cullen's fame (recalling Dunbar's) was also "curious." Here was a poet making waves with old, outdated forms of English verse. Johnson said he gave them "fresh beauty." This is true, but Cullen's white audience seems to have gotten special pleasures out of his ability to handle black anger, black grief and black pathos in such amusingly antiquated poetic clothing.

Prevalent themes in Cullen's poetry, then, are race pride, endurance, lynchings, cynicism and pessimism ("can death be worse?"), a primitive or romantic view of Africa ("Heritage" and many others), religious and psychological conflict, love and death, spiritual freedom, personal or racial inferiority, doubt and fear, the tensions created by being black among whites, and Christ as a symbol of conflict and contradiction. Cullen saw the plight of the Afro-Americans as true tragedy in a Christian land. This comes through in many of his poems, but poignantly in "Heritage":

> Father, Son, and Holy-Ghost,
> So I make an idle boast;
> Jesus of the twice-turned cheek,
> Lamb of God, although I speak
> With my mouth thus, in my heart
> Do I play a double part.

For the black American, trapped in Christian attire but longing deep inside for what Zack Gilbert calls "that all-Black Saturday night," it is indeed a tragedy. Cullen, as we noted earlier, tried all his life to reconcile a "Christian" education with a "pagan urge." Toomer wanted to "unite" his several parts. And McKay tried to find a "home" in the desolate and sometimes contemptuous place Elijah Muhammad calls "the wilderness of North America." McKay went all the way to Europe and North Africa. Cullen made annual treks to France for several years. Black literature abounds with the tragedies incurred when black "intellectuals" relinquished their "dance" for a "book." Earlier in "Heritage," Cullen admits this deep need, felt by Blacks caught in white worlds everywhere to "Strip!" and

> Doff this new exuberance.
> Come and do the Lover's dance!

McKay's "Lynching" remains unsolved by the sonnet, and Cullen is unable to make his "heart and head" know that

> They and I are civilized,

despite the "unremittent beat" of his impressive iambic tetrameters. A classic statement on the inner workings of the mind of a black genius who must "twist and squirm" in an alien world. "Heritage" has yet to be seen on the many psychological dimensions on which it operates.

Though it is a "romantic" excursion into Africa, it is also a devastating surgical exploration of the black psyche.

This and related themes also pervade other poems by Cullen. "From the Dark Tower" is inspired by his column of a similar name in *Opportunity*. Although black artists and thinkers "were not made eternally to weep," they must either face destruction of their potential or wear the mask and "tend our agonizing seeds." Cullen also writes about timid lovers and black prostitutes, about many, many "brown" girls (another favorite theme) and the ache of the human heart. He writes in the shadow of Keats and Shelley and pens epitaphs to them. His employment of traditional English verse forms is not as startling as McKay's. But he does bring a black force and intellectual veracity to these devices and techniques which had long housed "white" hopes and feelings. He took the best of Keats and Edna St. Vincent Millay and made it work with an admirable technical ability. Brown identifies his "gifts" as "fluency and brilliant imagery." But he is likened by many critics to the standard-English work of Braithwaite and Dunbar.

Cullen consciously developed misery—apparently in an effort to "suffer" like the romantics, so he could know what real inner strife was all about. He had not seen the underside of black life in the way that McKay (*Banjo, Banana Bottom*), Hughes (*The Weary Blues*), Fenton Johnson, and others had come to know and understand it. He subdued his anger and violence into a pristine verse. Most critics allude to the womanlike, or "prissy," nature of Cullen's work. Redding complained that he viewed "life through the eye of a woman who is at once shrinking and bold, sweet and bitter." In Cullen's "atavistic" or "primitive" piece, one feels that he is not really there himself—much as one feels in reading white poet Vachel Lindsay's poems on Africa and the "Congo." But Cullen remains one of the searing meteorites of black poetry. His passion has yet to be surpassed even among contemporary Afro-American poets. Though he does not convince the reader that he would actually "Strip!" and do the "Lover's dance!" he does distill an intellectual fury that chronicles the death-during-life vortex (Davis calls it "alien-and-exile") that so many Africans in America struggle against.

Wagner's *Black Poets* contains the most up-to-date and incisive critical assessment of Cullen. See also criticism by Redding, Brown, Johnson, Huggins (*Harlem Renaissance*), Bontemps (including *Harlem Renaissance Remembered*), the listings in the Cullen section of *Black Writers of America* and the bibliography of this book. Many of Cullen's unpublished works are deposited in the library at Atlanta University.

James Weldon Johnson, whom we have cause to mention again, ranks today as one of the most distinguished men of black American letters. His *Autobiography* was reissued in 1927 carrying Johnson's own name, the earlier pseudonym dropped. During the twenties, Johnson continued to combine his keen social observations of black America with his poetic development and output. *The Book of American Negro Poetry* (1922, 1931) was one of the high points of the Harlem Renaissance. Important for more than just the poets included, the anthology represented the first sustained effort of a black critic to identify "Negro" elements in poetry written since Dunbar. It was also the first anthology of Afro-American poetry to be published in the twentieth century and the first ever to be published in English. One can safely say that any serious study of black criticism has to begin with James Weldon Johnson. His subtitle (*with an Essay on the Negro's Creative Genius*) suggested the huge dimensions of Johnson's concern in the anthology. He identified the various influences on the poets, noted distinctions between different kinds of dialects, and gave assessments of the poetry. Discussing the problem of dialect, Johnson declared that it possessed only two emotions: humor and pathos. (Brown, reacting fifteen years later, implied such a statement was a copout.) Johnson also issued the following challenge to black poets:

What the colored poet in the United States needs to do is something like what Synge did for the Irish; he needs to find a form that will express the racial spirit by symbols from within rather than by symbols from without, such as the mere mutilation of English spelling and pronunciation. He needs a form that is freer and larger than dialect, but which will still hold the racial flavor; a

form expressing the imagery, the idioms, the peculiar
turns of thought, and the distinctive humor and pathos,
too, of the Negro, but which will also be capable of
voicing the deepest and highest emotions and aspirations, and allow the widest range of subjects and the
widest scope of treatment.

It was a gigantic challenge. Did any black poet rise to
meet it? Has any succeeded? We shall see.

With his brother, J. Rosamond, Johnson also coedited
The Book of American Negro Spirituals (1925) and *The
Second Book of Negro Spirituals* (1926). Both volumes
carried musical arrangements by J. Rosamond. Johnson
tried to meet his own challenge with *God's Trombones:
Seven Negro Sermons in Verse* (1927), a rendering of the
works of the old-time black preachers. His pamphlet *Native African Races and Culture* was published in 1927. A
study of Harlem, *Black Manhattan*, came out in 1930. His
autobiography *Along This Way* appeared in 1933. And a
social/political commentary, *Negro Americans, What
Now?* was published the same year. His selected poems
(*St. Peter Relates an Incident of the Resurrection Day*)
came out in 1930. Johnson had established himself as a
prolific and exemplary man, a combination of formidable
talents, by the time he was killed in an automobile acci-
dent in 1938.

Aside from their literary and social value, the sermons in
God's Trombones have, in the years since their publication, brought delight and instruction to many through the
various ways in which they have been read or otherwise
dramatically presented. In our classes, we assign one sermon per student and, allowing days for research and preparation, stage the works for a larger, campus or community, audience. Just how much of his own challenge (see
above) was attempted in *God's Trombones* is indicated
by Johnson's Preface, in which he briefly gives the history
of black preachers and explains why he chose the trombone as the central symbol in the work:

> He [the preacher] strode the pulpit up and down in
> what was actually a very rhythmic dance, and he
> brought into play the full gamut of his wonderful voice,
> a voice—what shall I say?—not of an organ or a trum-

pet, but rather of a trombone, the instrument possessing above all others the power to express the wide and varied range of emotions encompassed by the human voice—and with greater amplitude. He intoned, he moaned, he pleaded—he blared, he crashed, he thundered. I sat fascinated; and more, I was, perhaps against my will, deeply moved; the emotional effect upon me was irresistible.

This scene occurred at a church Johnson attended in Kansas City. While the preacher was strutting and delivering, Johnson recalled that he jotted down notes for "The Creation." *God's Trombones* contains seven sermons and one prayer, "Listen, Lord." The sermons, each taken from a text in the Bible, include "The Creation," "The Prodigal Son," "Go Down Death—a Funeral Sermon," "Noah Built the Ark," "The Crucifixion," "Let My People Go," and "The Judgment Day."

Coming as it did at the high point of the Harlem Renaissance—1927—*God's Trombones* was rather odd in that a less than ostensibly religious verse was being written by other poets. There were religious themes in much of the poetry—but none of the poets dipped into the same reservoir in the same manner as did Johnson. Johnson was, however, able to fuse some of the jazz and blues patterns of the day into his work—though they are not that noticeable. The sermons are not in black dialect, since Johnson said that the Afro-American poet must transcend that form. The language is generally that of any white American or Englishman. What Johnson does is instill racial feeling and dramatic (ethnic) touches through spontaneity, repetition, and various free-verse forms. Margaret Walker, Hughes, and Brown later placed all those elements in a more secular context—although Brown interpolated religious expletives and exclamations in much of his work. The double negative, which Johnson makes great use of, is not an exclusively black product. But we do find him interspersing black sayings, usages, and other idiomatic spices into the texts of the sermons. It was the first time that a black poet had undertaken such a task solely for literary reasons. So this alone makes the work important—not to mention its anthropological and sociological value.

The overriding achievement of the sermons is their graphic, full-blown images and their inferential "blackening" of God (see Cullen, Toomer and others). This analogy is more obvious in "The Creation," in which God,

> Like a mammy bending over her baby,
> Kneeled down in the dust
> Toiling over a lump of clay
> Till He shaped it in His own image;

It seems only natural that Johnson would pay this tribute to the black mother—most black poets writing since, say, 1880, had done so. And he had earlier complained of John Wesley Holloway's "Black Mammies" in dialect, saying: "The black mammy is material for better poetry than this." From Johnson's "milk-white horse," through phrases like "O—Mary's Baby—," "sinners in their headlong plunge," and "Blacker than a hundred midnights," the power of the dramatic black sermon can be seen. There are threats and warnings, admonishments and pleas, fire and brimstone, force and, even worse, fury. "The Prodigal Son" is warned:

> Young man—
> Young man—
> Your arm's too short to box with God.

The incremental lines, the spontaneity, the witty turns of phrases, the colorful and sometimes bombastic language—all give *God's Trombones* authenticity. Johnson does use symbols that express from "within," rather than from "without," the black experience. For, as he noted in his Preface, "The Negro today is, perhaps, the most priest-governed group in the country." The old-time preachers knew the "secrets" of ancestral oral and gestural power, Johnson says; they knew the "secret of oratory, that at bottom of it is a progression of rhythmic words." The preachers had inherited the "innate grandiloquence of their old African tongues." Once in the pulpit, the minister fused these "tongues" with biblical language, because this "gratified a highly developed sense of sound and rhythm in himself and his hearers." These were the concepts and ideas under which Johnson labored in *God's*

Trombones. Doubtlessly, the volume is one of the most precious in the annals of Afro-American writing. There is hardly a person who cannot "feel" these sermons—and yet their power and their intuitive embracing of a world of emotions and temperaments make them lasting as classical literature of whatever definition and hue.

Johnson's *Saint Peter,* following a tradition of Dunbar's "The Haunted Oak," Hughes's "Song for a Dark Girl," McKay's "The Lynching," and Cullen's *The Black Christ* and "Scottsboro, Too, Is Worth Its Song," attempts to place the desecration of black humanity within its proper contradictory Christian context. In each of the poems, the lynching is connected to a higher order—usually the Christian God. Using a "visionary type of imagination," Johnson applies satire to the segregation of black and white gold-star mothers. Sending the parents to visit their sons' graves, the War Department puts black mothers on a foul, crowded boat (reminiscent of a slave ship) and white mothers on a modern liner. Johnson, in the poems, imagines that the Unknown Soldier arrives in heaven and is discovered to be black. Various patriotic and terrorist organizations (the G.A.R., the D.A.R., the Legion, the Klan and others) want him buried again. For more criticism of Johnson, see Davis, Wagner, Bontemps (including note in *American Negro Poetry*), Brown, Redding, Huggins, and others.

Langston Hughes was at the opposite end of the poetic spectrum from Cullen when he wrote, in "Mother to Son,"

> Well, son I'll tell you:
> Life for me ain't been no crystal stair.

For while both men achieved recognition about the same time, Hughes was a folk troubador with his finger on the "pulse of the people." He was also free from the restraints of conventional English verse that dominated practically all of Cullen's poetry.

Born in Joplin, Missouri, Hughes had published more than a dozen books of poetry and several volumes of prose and plays, and had seen his own dramas staged all over the country, by the time of his death. Of the quartet of first-line Harlem Renaissance poets, Hughes would be the only

one to remain active until the Black Arts Movement of
the 1960s. McKay and Cullen succumbed to high blood
pressure in the forties, and Toomer, as we noted, died in
the obscurity of a Quaker community. Hughes, whose ma-
ternal grandmother had been married to one of the five
Blacks who participated in John Brown's raid on Harpers
Ferry, moved first to Lawrence, Kansas, and, later, to
Cleveland, where he finished high school and was elected
class poet. Upon completion of high school, he went for a
while to live with his father in Mexico, returning to the
United States fifteen months later and enrolling in Columbia University. Spending most of his time haunting
jazz spots and hanging out in Greenwich Village, and dis-
satisfied with Columbia, Hughes finally quit school and
worked odd jobs before signing on as a member of the
crew of a freight steamer. This allowed him to visit the
Canary Islands, the Azores and the West Coast of Africa.
Returning for a while to New York, he left the country on
his twenty-second birthday and went to Paris, again working odd jobs, on to Italy and Genoa, and after a number
of varied experiences (see *The Big Sea* and *I Wonder as I
Wander*), returned to America. He then spent time in
Washington, D.C. (where his mother had moved), working in the office of Dr. Carter G. Woodson, editor of the
Journal of Negro History, and later serving as a bus boy
(see "Brass Spittoons") at the Wardman Park Hotel. At
the latter, he had a chance to show some of his poems to
Vachel Lindsay—thus "launching" his "career" through
the newspapers.

His volumes of poetry include *The Weary Blues*
(1926), *Fine Clothes to the Jew* (1927), *Dear Lovely
Death* (1931), *A Negro Mother and Other Dramatic Rec-
itations* (1931), *Scottsboro Limited* (1932), *The Dream
Keeper and Other Poems* (1932), *A New Song* (1938),
Shakespeare in Harlem (1942), *Freedom's Plow* (a long
poem, 1943), *Jim Crow's Last Stand* (1943), *Fields of
Wonder* (1947), *One-Way Ticket* (1949), *Montage of a
Dream Deferred* (1951), *Ask Your Mama: 12 Moods for
Jazz* (1961), and *The Panther and the Lash: Poems of
Our Times* (1967). Hughes also wrote short stories and
novels (including collected stories from the Jesse B. Sem-
ple series, which he originated). Prose works are *Not
Without Laughter* (1930), *The Ways of White Folks*

(1934), *Simple Speaks his Mind* (1950), *Laughing to Keep from Crying* (1952), *Simple Takes a Wife* (1953), *Simple Stakes a Claim* (1957), *Tambourines to Glory* (1958), *Something in Common* (1963), and *Simple's Uncle Sam* (1965). *Five Plays by Langston Hughes* was published in 1963. Hughes also either wrote (or collaborated on with others, usually Bontemps) many books for young readers as well as works of general and specific interest on black culture.

In his early years, Hughes was influenced by Walt Whitman and Dunbar. In high school, a teacher introduced him to the poetry of Amy Lowell, Lindsay, Masters, and Sandburg. He was especially indebted to Sandburg, of whom he would speak, in *The Big Sea*, as his "guiding star." Fenton Johnson had been the only poet up until Hughes to sustain such an energetic poetry of black folk life. Hughes improved on what Johnson began, adding fresh portraits—though not the ridicule sometimes appearing in Dunbar—and actually using music to inspire his writing or accompany his live readings. He made recordings with Charlie Mingus, among other jazz greats. And he is given credit for originating the practice of reading poetry to jazz. Interestingly enough, this interweaving of music and poetry (discussed in Chapter IV) becomes a virtual backbone of black architectonics. Baldwin, for example, speaks of listening repeatedly to the records of Bessie Smith to gain rhythm in his prose. Certainly the same fusion of style and spirit can be found in Ellison, Wright, Tolson, Baraka, and Crouch. Novelist-poet Greenlee stated in a biographical note to his own *Blues for an African Princess* (poems),

> My chief literary influences are Charlie Parker, Lester Young, Miles Davis, and Billie Holiday. As a writer, I consider myself a jazz musician whose instrument is a typewriter.

Michael S. Harper, a black poet who came to maturity in the sixties, also attributes much of his style and poetic philosophy to jazz musicians, who helped him understand "pain" and make it "archetypal." Part of Hughes's impact on this area of black poetry is documented by Bernard Bell in *The Folk Roots of Contemporary Afro-American Poetry*. Basically, Hughes's poetry falls into three stylistic categories: dialect (primarily of an urban sort), blues and traditional free verse. His use of dialect is seen in practically every book he published. His blues and free-verse forms are especially evident in *The Weary Blues*. One of his most famous free-verse poems is "The Negro Speaks of Rivers," written right after he finished high school and published in *The Crisis* in 1921. This form according to Redding, is much more effective a vehicle for Hughes than dialect or blues. Hughes comes through, Redding feels, in the "purer verse forms." In "Rivers," Hughes reaches into the deep, deep well of black history and struggle, uniting in spirit the global African:

> I've known rivers:
> I've known rivers ancient as the world and
> older than the flow of human blood in
>   human veins.
> My soul has grown deep like the rivers.
>
> I've known rivers:
> Ancient, dusky rivers.
> My soul has grown deep like the rivers.

The use of words like "soul" and "rivers"—which run like spines through black folklore and literature, allows Hughes to touch the deepest longings and spiritual wellsprings of his people. In "veins," "deep," "flow," "dusky," "ancient" and the cataloguing of actual place names important to Blacks, he establishes the longevity of life and struggle. Similar strength and longevity are put into "Poem," "The Negro," and numerous others.

Hughes's dialect and blues-oriented poems were not sweet to the ears of some Harlem black intellectuals of the twenties. Just as many of them had sought to censure Cullen for not writing more blatantly about black struggle (in black idioms), they criticized Hughes for dealing with the "lower strata," or underside, of black life. But the hidden and robust ("taboo") aspects of black life were beginning to come to the fore in the works of black (McKay) and white (Van Vechten) writers. And Hughes joined this growing tendency in speaking frankly about "Suicide," "Po' Boy Blues," "Mulatto" ("A little yellow/bastard boy."), "Hard Daddy," "Ruby Brown," and more such experiences and subjects. The blues form calls for three-line stanzas: the second line repeats the first, and the third rhymes with the two preceding ones. During his lifetime, Hughes worked this medium for much of what it was worth. These various forms also helped establish Hughes's themes and subjects. Linguistic freedom allowed him to treat a theme with cynicism, irony, pity, humor, tragedy, violence or compassion. In many of his poems, Hughes is able to develop a dialogue between the black underdog and the white ruler. This occurs in "Brass Spittons," in which the bus boy interlaces a portrait of a common black worker with dazzling rhythms of church, white men's orders, black party and night life and the shiny spittoons Blacks must keep polished. We see it technically, though not racially, in "Jazzonia" in the call-and-response pattern coupled with carefully rearranged chordal structures:

Oh, silver tree!
Oh, shining rivers of the soul!

Three stanzas later, the same idea appears in this form:

Oh, singing tree!
Oh, shining rivers of the soul!

And five stanzas later, it appears thusly:

Oh, shining tree!
Oh, silver rivers of the soul!

This brilliant use of the same intricate pattern of dialogue and call-and-response continues in "Mulatto." The "bastard boy" is rejected first by the white father and later by the white brother, both representing (through the interjection of dialogue) different types and generations of white men—one objecting to the existence of an "illegitimate" son and the other (the former's offspring) refusing to extend a hand of brotherly concern. Hughes's themes, which remained with him through most of his life, are: racism, protest, racial unity, race pride (but not the "atavistic yearnings" of Cullen or McKay), black women (beauty and strengths), jazz, blues, religious music, violence against Blacks, and integration. Hughes was especially the spokesman of the black masses. And he often

relished the common profundity of Blacks at dance, play,
worship or work. In "Negro Dancers," he recalls J. Mord
Allen's "The Squeak of the Fiddle" and James Edwin
Campbell's "Mobile Buck." Allen hints that whites cannot dance. And Campbell reproduces in poetry the
rhythms of a contemporary dance known as the "buck."
Hughes, showing off black improvisation, claims that he
and his baby have

Two mo' ways to do de Charleston!

—a popular contemporary dance. Even if whites "laugh"
and "pray," Blacks can take satisfaction in the knowledge
that they can tap their own reservoir of spontaneity and
creativity when they want to side-step or annoy the mechanical, white world. But Hughes also wrote poetry about
being "alone" at "night" and afraid. There are cynicism
and sarcasm and tragedy in this poet who observed his
people through a deep and creative affection.

Hughes's personal life, of course, was just as fascinating
as his poetry. He won numerous awards and writing
grants, but was often introduced to audiences as "the poet
laureate of Harlem." In his autobiographies (*The Big Sea*
and *I Wonder as I Wander*), he writes about many
things, including how he filled a car trunk with books and
traveled throughout the South reading his poems and
speaking at black churches and colleges. He rubbed shoulders with the ranking writers and intellectuals of his day
but remained in contact with the black masses. The tradition of senior black writers aiding younger ones has also
been traced to Hughes. Poet Léon Damas, of French
Guiana, credits him with establishing Pan-African literary
and artistic ties. Hughes was one of the elder statesmen of
black culture at the First World Festival of Negro Arts,
held in Dakar, Senegal, in 1966. He also edited
anthologies of African prose and poetry. His play *Mulatto*
ran longer on Broadway than any other black production,
and his plays were staged successfully in other parts of the
country. In an article in *The Nation* in 1926, Hughes
delivered a manifesto as important as Johnson's challenge.
He declared that the "younger Negro artists" would express their "individual dark-skinned selves." If either
Blacks or whites approved or disapproved, it did not matter: "The tom-tom cries and the tom-tom laughs."

In the thirties, Hughes received high praise from new
black critics Brown and Redding, although Redding said
he was not of the intellectual stature of other Harlem
Renaissance writers. Speaking of Hughes's "experiments"
in verse, Redding said, "He feels in them, but he does not
think. And this is the source of his naïveté." It is true that
Hughes maintained a low literary profile and did not
aspire to lofty intellectual heights, but to say he "does not
think" is untrue. Though not always successful in his free
verse, he has a brain-dance intellect: a gymnastic intelligence—and a furious power with words. And his poetry proved to be irresistible and inspiring to almost a
half century of contemporaries. The nexus of Hughes's poetry
seems to be about a "Dream Deferred." The dream again,
as in so much black poetry. And he was never more prophetic than in that particular poem, in which he asked,
without answering, the question:

What happens to a dream deferred?

In the poem, which gave Lorraine Hansberry the name for
her famous play *Raisin in the Sun*, Hughes also displays
his mastery of technique. He uses five highly effective
similes in an aggregate analogy that lengthens to:

Or does it explode?

And he lived to see the explosion in Watts, Newark, Detroit and other places.

His writings are in all twentieth-century anthologies of
Afro-American literature. Detailed critical studies of his
work appear in Wagner's *Black Poets* and Davis' *From
the Dark Tower*. He is also assessed in words by Brown,
Kerlin, Redding and Johnson, and in numerous other
studies and compilations. James Emanuel's biography of
him (*Langston Hughes*) was published in 1967. Other
important source items on Hughes are François Dodat's
Langston Hughes (Paris, 1964), Raymond Quinot's *Langston Hughes* (Brussels, 1964), Milton Meltzer's *Langston
Hughes: a Biography* (1968), Elizabeth P. Meyers'
Langston Hughes: Poet of His People (1970) and
Charlemae Rollins' *Black Troubador: Langston Hughes*
(1970). Of the plethora of material steadily pouring out
on Hughes, a most valuable book is *Langston Hughes:
Black Genius: a Critical Evaluation* (1971), edited by

Therman B. O'Daniel. O'Daniel includes a selected
classified bibliography detailing Hughes's lengthy career as
creative writer in all genres, as anthologist and as critic.
Hughes inspired generations of black Africans and Americans and also edited the following anthologies: *An African
Treasury: Articles, Essays, Stories, Poems by Black Africans* (1960); *Poems from Black Africa* (1963); *New
Negro Poets: U.S.A.* (1964); and *Voices: A Quarterly of
Poetry* (Negro poets issue, winter 1950).

MINOR, OR SECOND-ECHELON, POETS OF THE RENAISSANCE

Dozens of poets helped to make up the variegated atmosphere of the New Negro Movement. And just as the "new
black poetry" of the 1960s cannot be characterized in
terms of four or five individuals, so the Harlem Renaissance cannot be understood unless the complete poetry
scene is examined. Many of the so-called minor, or second-
echelon, poets writing during the peak of the renaissance
had already established reputations before 1923. Principal
among these were Arna Bontemps, Angelina Grimké,
Gwendolyn Bennett (1902–   ), Anne Spencer, Clarissa-
Scott Delany, Frank Horne (1899–1974), Georgia Douglas
Johnson, George Leonard Allen (1905–35), Donald
Jeffrey Hayes (1904–   ), Jonathan Henderson Brooks
(1904–45), Helene Johnson (1907–   ), Waring Cuney
(1906–   ), Lewis Alexander (1900–45), and Lucy Ariel
Williams Holloway (1905–   ). Other poets, to be mentioned at the end of this unit, can be distributed rather
widely along a spectrum of relative significance. Many of
them won prizes and places for their poems among the
pages of *The Crisis* and *Opportunity* and then disap-
peared from the scene. Others met untimely deaths—
while yet others chose different careers or leaped into the
freedom fight. Cullen's *Caroling Dusk* (1927) contains
the best representation of Afro-American poetry written
between 1910 and 1925. Johnson's *The Book of American
Negro Poetry* (1922) presents poets between Dunbar and
the time of its last edition (1931). Major and minor poets
are also to be found in Kerlin's *Negro Poets and Their
Poems* (1923, 1935). Hughes and Bontemps made many

of these lyricists available in *The Poetry of the Negro* (1949, 1970). At least half a dozen of the lesser known poets are included in Alain Locke's *The New Negro* (1925). Randall (*The Black Poets*, 1971) displays work by Horne and Bontemps, but only Bontemps is included in Randall's *Black Poetry* (1969). Henderson does not list one of these transitional figures in *Understanding the New Black Poetry* (1973). And only Cuney and Bontemps are included in Rosey Pool's *Beyond the Blues* (1962). But we are randomly sampling the anthologies for content. See the bibliography for more-detailed listings.

The best contemporary anthology of twentieth-century black poetry is Arnold Adoff's *The Poetry of Black America* (1973), which lists more than 140 poets and practically all of the minor ones of the Harlem Renaissance, although the omission of Cuney and Edward Silvera is appalling. Unfortunately, no black anthology of the magnitude of the Norton series has appeared. *The Negro Caravan* (Sterling Brown, et al.), a comprehensive anthology published in 1941 and reissued (unrevised) in 1970, contains nearly a dozen of the minor voices. In "Frank Horne and the Second Echelon Poets of the Harlem Renaissance" (*The Harlem Renaissance Remembered*, Bontemps, 1972), Ronald Primeau launches an impressive and important discussion of these lesser known figures. While Wagner (*Black Poets of the United States*, 1973) makes a partial effort to discuss these poets, he seems generally to dismiss them as cliquish seekers after an African past. So, at this writing, Brown's "Contemporary Negro Poetry (1914–1936)," in his *Negro Poetry and Drama* (1937), remains the best critical overview of these poets.

Bontemps is one of three important renaissance figures (along with Hughes and Brown) to survive physically and creatively up until the 1960s. Wagner calls Bontemps "one of the most brilliant minor poets of the Harlem Renaissance," and Brown also has high praise for his poetry and fiction. Davis (*From the Dark Tower*) sees an "alien-and-exile" theme continuing from the major trunk of renaissance poetry into the work of Bontemps. With the notable exception of Georgia Douglas Johnson, the important minor renaissance figures did not publish books of poetry until the 1960s. This fact alone tells us much about Bontemps's seeming poetic obscurity between 1930 and 1960. But more important, for the record, is the fact that Bontemps's efforts were directed toward fiction, drama, children's literature, history, chronicling the development of other black poets, and ground-breaking library work. Born in Alexandria, Louisiana, Bontemps moved to California when he was still a child. He attended Pacific Union College and the University of Chicago.

His diverse writing output, almost as prodigious as Hughes's, includes numerous books, pamphlets and articles. His novels are *God Sends Sunday* (1931; dramatized as *St. Louis Woman*, 1946), *Black Thunder* (1936, about the Nat Turner revolt) and *Drums at Dusk* (1939). Bontemps also coedited, with Hughes, the very influential anthology *The Poetry of the Negro* (1949, 1970), and he brought out *American Negro Poetry* in 1963. Other anthologies are *Golden Slippers: an Anthology of Negro Poetry for Young Readers* (1941), *The Book of Negro Folklore* (with Hughes, 1958), *Great Slave Narratives* (1969), *Hold Fast to Dreams: Poems Old and New* (1969) and *The Harlem Renaissance Remembered* (1972, a collection of articles). Additionally Bontemps published twenty-odd works of bibliography (usually on black heroes), juvenilia, culture and history. He served as university librarian at Fisk for more than twenty years and was a member of the faculties of the University of Illinois and Yale—where he was in charge of Afro-American studies at the time of his death. Between 1924 and 1931 Bontemps's poems were published widely in various magazines and periodicals and he won poetry prizes from both *The Crisis* and *Opportunity*. His only published volume of poetry, *Personals*, did not come out until 1964 (Paul Breman).

Personals is a personal statement that sums up much of Bontemps's poetry. For throughout the book there is the use of "I" or "we" or "us." His poetry is personal, like Robert Hayden's, Countee Cullen's and Frank Horne's. A comfortableness also attends Bontemps's poetry—not a smug comfort, but the comfort of stability and careful workmanship. He was among those poets who, unlike Dunbar, had the security of college degrees and access to books unlimited. Consequently there is little of the yearning for instant recognition or the overanxiety that the anticipation of fame creates. Bontemps writes of love ("love's brown arms"), the African past ("The Return" and "Nocturne at Bethesda"), the South ("Southern Mansion"), defiance and strength ("Close Your Eyes"). Reminiscent of Toomer's "Reapers," "A Black Man Talks of Reaping" surveys the sturdy, dependable tradition of black labor and concludes that the laborers' children "feed on bitter fruit." Billie Holiday would later reflect on a hanging in the South and write "Strange Fruit." And we recall that since James Whitfield, black poets have pointed to the contradictions in American Christianity and the barren-versus-bearing theme.

Bontemps also followed the Harlem Renaissance pattern of romanticizing a pagan Afro-American or African. With the taste of slavery and the dialect tradition still bitter on their tongues, these poets leaped backward over slavery to another place and another clime. Bontemps does just this in "The Return," which closely resembles Cullen's "Heritage" and some of the atavistic pieces of Hughes and McKay. Bontemps speaks of "remembered rain," "the friendly ghost," "lost nights," "dance of rain," "jungle sky," "muffled drums," and then suggests:

Let us go back into the dusk again. . . .

Dusk, ebony, jet, night, evenings, purple, blue, raven, and other such synonyms for Blacks are frequently employed to great effect and power by Afro-American poets. Likewise symbols or images of invisibility and blindness are also prevalent in black writing. Bontemps employs and implies such states in several poems in which he achieves a surreal quality—a dreamlike longing for another time and another place (again, a pattern in the poetry of the period). If you "Close Your Eyes," Bontemps says, you can go back to what you were, and maybe the song, as with Toomer, will "in time return to thee." Closing the eyes will also allow one to "walk bravely enough." Away from the daily limelight and without the constant pressure (cf. Cullen) to succeed and hold up the light of the race, Bontemps developed strong statements using conventional poetic patterns with occasional free-verse experimentation.

Personal and powerful, Bontemps's poetry looks ahead to
a similar stamina (this time in a new dialect) exhibited by
Sterling Brown in *Southern Road*. For even though Bontemps tells us, in "Golgotha Is a Mountain,"

> One day I will crumble,

we know that the dust will fossilize and "make a mountain":

> I think it will be Golgotha.

There has been very little critical assessment of Bontemps's poetry. But brief reactions to his work can be
found in *The Harlem Renaissance Remembered* (which
he edited), Brown's study, Barksdale and Kinnamon's anthology, Robert Kerlin's critical anthology, Davis' *From
the Dark Tower*, and *The Negro Caravan*. For a nearly
complete listing of Bontemps's published works, see *Black
World*, XX (September 1971), pp. 78–79.

Along with Angelina Grimké, Lewis Alexander, Anne
Spencer, Bontemps, Georgia Douglas Johnson, and
Helene Johnson, Gwendolyn Bennett helped to fill out
the list of lesser known Harlem Renaissance poets who appeared in *The New Negro* (see 1968 edition, with a preface by Robert Hayden). Unfortunately, however,
Gwendolyn Bennett's best foot was not put forward in the
"Song," which Alain Locke accepted for publication in
the above-named anthology. "Song" is not representative
of her generally high craftsmanship; it is flawed by imbalance and an attempt to say too many things in one poem.
Characteristic of the poetry of the period, "Song" reaches
back to "forgotten banjo songs" and

> Clinking chains and minstrelsy,

but her interpolation of dialect lines does not come off
with the ease and power of Brown's similar efforts. On the
other hand, her sharp, crisp and precise imagery employed
in poems that appeared in magazines and other
anthologies show her as a poet with many gifts and resources.

Gwendolyn Bennett was born in Giddings, Texas, to
professional parents. After graduation from the Girls'
High School in Brooklyn, New York, she attended

Teachers College, Columbia University, for two years and studied in the Fine Arts Department—thereafter establishing a dual career as poet and artist. She later attended Pratt Institute, taught in the Fine Arts Department at Howard University, and then received the thousand-dollar Foreign Scholarship of the Delta Sigma Theta sorority, which enabled her to go to Europe, where she studied for a year in Paris at the Académie Julian and the École Panthéon. She returned to New York at the height of the Harlem Renaissance and for a while was a member of the editorial staff of *Opportunity*, in which several of her poems appeared. In reading her finest poems, one recalls the depth of black womanhood revealed in the poetry of Frances Harper, Georgia Johnson and Angelina Grimké. "To A Dark Girl" is a meditation on the sisterhood that retains aspects of "old forgotten queens." We recall the word "forgotten" from "Song"; but it abounds in the poetry of this period. Her "brown girl" (Cullen!) is "sorrow's mate," but if she forgets her slave background she can still "laugh at Fate!" "Nocturne" distills "distant laughter," and "Sonnet—2" recalls "Negroes humming melodies." "Heritage" is almost identical, in theme and tone, to Countee Cullen's poem of the same name. Just as Cullen laments the disparity between his "heart and head," this poet sees the same duality in her "sad people's soul"

Hidden by a minstrel-smile.

Finally, "Hatred" is sharp and stinging

Like a dart of singing steel,

and we are reminded of the poems of the same theme: Du Bois's "The Riddle of the Sphinx" and McKay's "To the White Fiends" and "The White House."

For Clarissa Scott Delany, "Joy" seems to contain the emotional intensity that "Hatred" holds for Gwendolyn Bennett. The daughter of Emmett J. Scott, the "distinguished secretary to Booker T. Washington," Mrs. Delany lived a tragically short life and died at the peak of the renaissance. "Joy" is what she vows to "abandon" herself to in an effort to avoid the troubling "maze" of life. Her poetry is quietly powerful and seems to complement that of

Bontemps, since it is deep and flows from tradition, stamina and endurance. Born at Tuskegee Institute, Alabama, she attended Bradford Academy in New England and then Wellesley College, after which she taught three years at the famous Dunbar High School in Washington, D.C. According to Kerlin, Clarissa Delany also "studied delinquency and neglect among Negro children in New York City." Her poetry reflects a perceptive and analytical mind. Initially, she appears detached and metallic—deceptively so, like Gwendolyn Brooks, but the poem usually winds down to a gripping message on pretense, loneliness, joy or despair. The night in "Interim" is a "gracious cloak" used to conceal the defeat of the soul. "The Mask" immediately brings to mind Dunbar's "We Wear the Mask." Except for the differences in persona and dramatic affects, the two poems are quite similar. Rereading "The Mask," one is reminded of Smokey Bill Robinson's recently popular song "The Tears of a Clown," which carries the theme of duality and schizophrenia so often found in black thought and writing. While all black artists do not display this "twoness" with the intensity of a Cullen or an Ellison, it is almost always present in their works. Especially is this true of the black American writer, forced to use the communication tools of the overseers to speak about that which is closest to him. This particular aspect of black poetry gives rise to much speculation, since poems devoid of racial or ethnic flavor take on added significance when we know their authors are black. Such is the case with Gwendolyn Bennett's "Hatred" (in which "you" could be whites) and W. E. B. Du Bois's "The Riddle of the Sphinx" (in which "them" probably means whites).

Frank Horne, who won a poetry contest in *The Crisis* in 1925 but did not publish a book until 1963 (*Haverstraw*), fits into this context. Horne was born in New York City, where he attended public schools. As a student at the College of the City of New York, he won varsity letters in track and wrote poetry. He later graduated from the Northern Illinois College of Ophthalmology with the degree of Doctor of Optometry. Horne worked in Chicago and New York, taught in Fort Valley, Georgia, and was for some time employed by the United States Housing Authority. He died in September of 1974.

Horne "possesses the authentic gift of poetry," according to James Weldon Johnson; and Brown mentions his "intellectual irony." Indeed Horne is cynical, skeptical, reserved and almost bare in his short lines and economical language. The corpus of his early poetry revolves around "Letters found near a suicide," for which he won a *Crisis* award. Most of the poems are addressed to individually named persons and recall some point of contact (contention?) between the alleged suicide victim and the person addressed. As noted earlier, many of the poems have to be placed in the context of black poetry if they are to have specific racial meaning. Dominant themes are the shortness of life, contradictions in Christianity, betrayal, endurance, love, hatred, survival of the spirit over physical death, music, scientific inquiry adapted to the poet's questioning, racial injustice, and victory as fact or idea. Horne's verse is sanguine but, for the most part, avoids the romantic treatment of Africa found in other Harlem Renaissance poets. His "Nigger (a Chant for Children)" catalogues black heroes: Hannibal, Othello, Crispus Attucks, Toussaint L'Ouverture, and adds *Jesus* near the end. A choral iteration, anticipating Brown and complementing Hughes, it includes:

"Nigger . . . nigger . . . nigger. . . ."

"To the Poets" recalls Cullen's "Scottsboro, Too, Is Worth Its Song"; both poems chide other poets for singing songs over wrong causes. Horne "yelled hosannas" into the emptiness, but yelling got him nowhere. (Neither did yelling move mountains for Baldwin, who, as a boy preacher, quickly saw the contradiction in singing, "You can have all dis world but give me Jesus.") Horne's knowledge of science is put to good use in such poems as "To Henry" and "Q.E.D." And his skepticism continually surfaces as in "To You," in which he examines the road to salvation, which is through "Your" (Christ's) body. But later he is involved in a worldly experience with "her," and when he returns to the altar to eat and drink of "Your" splendors he can think "only of her."

Much of Horne's poetry employs the symbolism and vocabulary of athletic contests—principally football and track. He also uses language associated with the playing of music or singing. "To Caroline" and "To Catalina" merge

melody, harmonies, pain and ecstasy. "Caroline" plays
"skin" as well as the piano. "Catalina" is warned that the
piano will give (and take) joy and hurt. "To Chick" recalls the days of the "Terrible Two" on the football field.
The signal called in football is analogous to the "signal"
called in real life. In both instances the poet crosses the
victory line "fighting and squirming." "To one who called
me 'nigger'" is a comment on the white man's ability to
do everything but face America's race problems. Continuing his theme of skepticism, Horne presents a "Toast" to
eyes, lips, heart, and body, even though the person addressed has an "unborn" soul. His poetry is solely in free
verse and, though spare, his language invariably operates
on multiple levels. "To a Persistent Phantom" is an excellent example of Horne "complicating" the meaning of
words through the use of repetition, ellipses, and the
strategic use of the words "tears," "tangled," "deeper,"
"charms," and "buried."

If the language and action of athletic competition
influenced Horne, it was melody that captured North
Carolinian George Leonard Allen, a poet who lived only
thirty years. Showing much book learning in his poetry,
Allen achieved wide recognition before his death; "To
Melody" won first prize in a 1927 state-wide poetry contest sponsored by the North Carolina Chapter of the
United Daughters of the Confederacy. His poems also appeared in *Opportunity, American Life, The Southern
Christian Advocate, The Lyric West,* and *Caroling Dusk.*
"Pilate in Modern America" employs what is, by Allen's
time, a traditional theme in black poetry: equating black
suffering to the crucifixion of Christ. The "Pilate" of
America pleads with God for redemption, claiming that
"one man's voice" (of dissent) could not be heard in the
din of the lynch mob. But God's voice (the white man's
conscience) tells "Pilate" that his guilt is as great as the
crowd's. "To Melody" has no racial import. It simply
praises song and is imitative, in language and theme, of
early-nineteenth-century English poetry. As a sonnet, it
only remotely suggests the work of McKay and Cullen.
"Pilate" is well handled in iambic pentameter.

A certain formalism also marks the work of Donald
Jeffrey Hayes. Hayes was born in Raleigh, North Carolina;

his education, which was quite extensive, was gained primarily through private study, in which he pursued his interests in singing, directing and writing. During the twenties and thirties, Hayes appeared in several Broadway productions as a member of a singing chorus. His poetry, much of which reflects his interest in music, was published in *Harper's Bazaar*, *Good Housekeeping*, and *This Week*. "Appoggiatura"—a musical term—draws sustained comparisons between a woman's movements and sounds of water. It is a towering poem full of surreal images, mysticism and watery-like flow. Ultimately the woman seems to become a mermaid. He hears the "indistinguishable sound of water silence," and then the woman disappears:

"Sea-Woman—slim-figured-water-thing . . ."

This theme of having lost something or someone pervades Hayes's poetry. And while he never mentions Africa or the lost black purity lamented by other renaissance poets, it is possible that he had those in mind. "Benediction" is for the departed rather than a prayer to end a religious service. "Poet" pursues Horne's theme of life's briefness. A eulogy, the poem notes that the poet's "kiss was sweet." "Prescience" depicts the poet trying to stall for time before death. His concern is not for his own physical and emotional well-being, but for the "you" addressed in the poem. The speaker cannot bear the thought of his loved one being alone after his death. Except for "Haven," death haunts all of Hayes's anthologized poetry. He writes in free verse and conventional forms. "Poet" and "Prescience" make the most of careful meter and rhyming couplets.

Another poet, Jonathan Henderson Brooks, writes with allegorical eloquence. His work is deeply religious; but it is not a canned religiousness. He takes Christian symbolism and makes it work for the black cause. He also equates black suffering to the sufferings of Christ. And like Phillis Wheatley, he ensconces his deep and troubled feelings in religious fervor. "The Resurrection" is a poetic narrative—employing dialogue in which racial concerns can only be inferred. But "My Angel" leaves little doubt as to its intent. Freighted with both hope and doubt, with "Despair and my disgrace," the poem depicts "my angel" attempting to lift the burden from the shoulders of black Americans. But the angel who struggled "All night," is unable to lift

The heaviest load since Lucifer. . . .

Carefully and startlingly, Brooks weaves in the relatively new black poetic theme of indifference toward (and distrust of) Christianity. On behalf of "black necessity," the angel intervenes; but after the all-night struggle, he wearily flies off

"To angels' resting place,

thus leaving the narrator with his despair and disgrace. It is a chilling poem, one that blatantly carries a doubt more subdued in other of Brooks's pieces. Alternating between iambic tetrameter and trimeter, and using six-line stanzas, he presents an exciting technical achievement with an *a b c b d b* rhyme scheme.

Brooks was born in Mississippi, on a farm "twelve miles southwest of Lexington." After his parents separated, he stayed with his mother until he was fourteen; later he went to Jackson College for four months on money his mother had saved. At Jackson he won a prize for a short story and later completed his high schooling at Jefferson City, Missouri. He then resumed college at Tougaloo, Mississippi, later doing graduate study at Columbia University. Though religion is the outstanding influence on his poetry, he is nevertheless unconventional in his use of it, and his poetry is always well crafted. His overriding achievement appears to be "She Said, . . ." a poem dedicated to the memory of the first black soldier from Alcorn County, Mississippi, to be "killed in action in the invasion of Normandy." Again using Christian symbolism and terms, he imagines the response of the soldier's mother, who wonders if her son screamed when he was shot, if "unhurrying Death" was called, and if he died in sunshine, rain, or night. The mother finally equates herself to "Mary of Galilee" and notes that the two women must have felt the same emotion. This is an irresistible idea and theme in black poetry. The searching, skillful contemporary poet Raymond Patterson presented a similar situation in his elegy on the death of Mrs. Martin Luther King, Sr. ("All Things Abide," *Black World*, September

1974). Patterson echoes concerns of Wheatley, Du Bois, McKay, Hughes, Cullen, and Dunbar when he asks who among us can really say how Jesus' mother died:

—Jesus, crucified?

The question mark aids in calling up all the gore and grief and passion and terror that engulf and interlace black existence as it is infused by Christianity, Africanisms and the American experience of slavery. Skepticism and cynicism are there again. Was Jesus really crucified? In his poem, Brooks achieves a haunting yet immediate requiem by tying the soldier's death to the cosmos—anticipating Dodson's "Lament"—and relating place names of importance. He establishes other associations: the stars and stripes (of the flag) are connected to the "sun's shining," the sunlight and moonglow are associated with the "stars forever," bullet and death and days and hours and sunshine and night and rain and battleground—all set the stage for Mary and the "Garden" and the suggestion of a rising. Lastly, the sections of the narration that occur in the mind are italicized. Brooks is certainly worth much more study.

Helene Johnson's small output should be collected and published in book form, because she is an important minor poet. Born in Boston, where she attended local public schools and Boston University, she arrived in New York in 1926 to do additional study at the Extension Division of Columbia University and to become one of the important "younger" figures of the renaissance. Her poems were published in *Opportunity*, *Vanity Fair* and several other periodicals and anthologies. Her poetry is terse, emphatic and diverse in form, style and language. She is at home with the sonnet, free verse, conventional rhyme pieces, and with what James Weldon Johnson calls "colloquial style—a style which numberless poets of this new age [1910–1930] have assumed to be easy." (Johnson sounds as if he is anticipating some of the poets of the current "new age," 1960–!). And Johnson is right about Helene Johnson when he says that she is aware that a poem written in dialect, colloquial or street language "demands as much work and workmanship as a well-wrought sonnet."

Helene Johnson's dominant themes are cultural reclamation (the African heritage), the ludicrous (sometimes peacockish) dress and mannerisms of black men, black beauty and love. Almost always she expresses longing, either for personal love or a return to preslavery Africa. In "Summer Matures," "Fulfillment" and "Magalu" she invites lovers both literally and metaphorically. "Magalu," like "Sonnet to a Negro in Harlem," "The Road," "Poem" and "Bottled," suggests that the black American is better than he thinks he is, that examination of his African past and his innate rhythmic richness will allow him to maintain both his past glory and his present sanity. The hint that whites are crass, immobile and inhibited (a theme recurring in black thought and writing) also creeps through these poems. "Magalu" is told to ignore the teachings of the man in a "white collar" who carries a Bible. Poetry, or ancestral and cultural worship, is better than Christianity, the poet says. Here, of course, she advances an answer to the riddle of Cullen, who appears to have wanted to "dance" but could not throw off the cloak of Western education, sentimentality and respectability. Helene Johnson asks Magalu:

> Would you sell the colors of your sunset
> and the fragrance
> Of your flowers, and the passionate wonder
> of your forest
> For a creed that will not let you dance?

Continuing this theme in "Sonnet to a Negro in Harlem" (and recalling McKay's "Harlem Dancer" and other poems), she depicts the Harlem Black as being psychologically and religiously detached from the environment in which he or she lives. Somehow, the black American has remained untainted by crass, Western ways and inflexible thought. All this is embodied symbolically in the Harlem Black, who, in his divine barbarism, stylistic richness and refusal to imitate those "whom you despise," is "too splendid for this city street." Helene Johnson seems to direct her poetry at Cullen and others who are unable to resolve the clash of "Christian" training and "pagan urge." Nor is the answer an easy one. For despite all the renaissance proposals calling for spiritual or physical return to the essences of the African self, the writers had no concrete suggestions to offer. Except for Du Bois, Garvey and

a few others, they simply exhibited romantic declarations
and yearnings. This mood is evident also in Helene Johnson's "Poem," in which the "Slim, dark, big-eyed" boy becomes a prince like the "monarch" laborer in Fenton
Johnson's "Rulers." Yet there is important immediate social commentary in a poem of the same type, "Bottled,"
which ridicules a Superfly-type character of the 1920s. Her
"Negro dressed fit to kill" refuses to dance the Charleston
or the Black Bottom since he is too "dignified." Instead of
a cane, she says, he should be "carrying a spear with a
sharp fine point." The tip of the spear should be dipped
in poison. And the rest, of course, is obvious. Finally, the
poem laments the apparent internal turmoil of a black
man who is "all glass" ("plastic," in today's language).
"Bottled" is typical of much of the thematic focus of
black writing in all genres of the period. And it anticipated the continuing satire that would be found in the
writings of Frank Marshall Davis, George Schuyler,
Hughes, and others. A young contemporary woman poet,
Barbara McHone (*Black World*, August 1974) assesses a
character similar to Helene Johnson's in "A Sea of Brown
Boys." She chides the boys for wearing high-heel shoes,
carrying purses, and patterning their lives after Shaft,
Superfly and Sweetback. After stating the urgent needs of
the times and implying that black masculinity is being un-
dermined, she asks:

where did our love go?

Helene Johnson seems to make her most cogent statement, however, in "The Road," in which she links into a
theme long associated with black struggle: "Keep on moving." "The Road" encourages Blacks to see their beauty as
well as their fight. "Trodden beauty" is "trodden pride."
Reminiscent of James Weldon Johnson's "Lift Every
Voice and Sing" and Fenton Johnson's "Children of the
Sun," she advises her people to

Rise to one brimming golden, spilling
    cry!

Perhaps not coincidentally, Helene Johnson's work is
similar, in language and theme, to the poetry of Waring
Cuney, who (along with Hughes, William Allyn Hill and

Edward Silvera) belongs to the group sometimes called
the Lincoln University poets.[3] Cuney was born a twin in
Washington, D.C., where he attended public schools and,
after Howard and Lincoln Universities, studied music at
the Boston Conservatory of Music and in Rome. The
twins had similar interests: Waring's being singing and his
brother's the piano. After his poem "No Images" won an
Opportunity prize, James Weldon Johnson stated that
Cuney's work held "exceptional promise." However,
Cuney never became a prolific writer of literary poetry. Instead he divided his time between writing lyrics for songs
and his other numerous chores. His protest lyrics were set
to music and sung by Josh White on the album *Southern
Exposure.* And his poetry was not published in book form
until 1960, when the Bibliophile Society in the Netherlands brought out *Puzzles.* He usually writes in free
verse and maintains "great economy of phrase." His poetry surveys the whole of the human experience, but most
of it carries either a racial or a folksy note. There is also
cynicism and skepticism of the sort found in Fenton Johnson, McKay, Cullen, and Horne. Heavily influenced by
Hughes, Cuney's early work depicts frank pictures of black
and general life and often uses plain, direct folk speech as
a major vehicle. This trend is seen in such poems as
"Hard Times Blues," "Crucifixion," "Troubled Jesus,"
and "Burial of the Young Love." Though his poems were
published in several magazines and anthologies of the era,
his "No Images" ties in with a general poetic theme of
the Harlem Renaissance: that black beauty and creativity
are too good to flourish in the decadence of Western civilization. The black woman in Cuney's poem is similar to
the Harlem Negro of Helene Johnson's poem, the dancer
of McKay's "Harlem Dancer," the ravished and tormented
narrator in Cullen's "Heritage," and the split personality
in Toomer's "Kabnis" (*Cane*)—they all seek to be whole

---

[3] See *Four Lincoln University Poets* (Hughes, 1931) and *Lincoln University Poets* (Cuney, Hughes, and Bruce McM. Wright, 1954). Hughes
called Lincoln University (Pennsylvania) "a place of beauty and the
ideal college for a poet." His assessment seems to have been correct.
Raymond Patterson, Larry Neal and Gil Scott-Heron are only three of
the newer poetic talents nurtured at Lincoln. Tolson also attended Lincoln.

in a world that denies and caricatures their humanity. Cuney's woman figure

    . . . thinks her brown body
    Has no glory.

But if she had an opportunity to dance as her natural self —"naked," perhaps—in her natural habitat—Africa—where her "image" would be reflected by the river, *then* she would "know" how beautiful she is. But civilization destroys the trees and the naturalness and, consequently, deprives Blacks of their own beauty and their healthy self-image:

    And dishwater gives back no images.

Dishwater is a kind of death—a spiritual and moral death —for Cuney, whose work shows him to be preoccupied with death. Several of his poems ("Threnody," "The Death Bed," "Crucifixion," "Burial of the Young," "Finis" and "Dust") react to, anticipate or contemplate death. For Cuney, who seems to place a strong trust in the folkways, there is an irony in the fact that the God who protects the oppressors is also expected to protect the oppressed. This particular brand of black cynicism makes its dramatic debut with Dunbar and remains a dominant theme in black poetry up until this very day. In "The Death Bed" the dying man sends all the praying "kinfolk" away from his bed. The praying ones, of course, think this is strange and continue praying against his will in a room across the hall. Failing in an attempt to sing a final song, the dying man relapses and, knowing death is imminent, wonders

    What it was they could be saying.

"Hard Times Blues" is a protest song-poem that talks about drought, hunger, depression and general bad times in the South. The refrain contains this paradoxical plea-assertion:

    Great-God-Amighty
    Folks feeling bad,
    Lost all they ever had.

The indirect association of God with the misery, coupled with an oblique prayer for help, is different indeed—though its antecedents can clearly be seen in the coded spirituals, blues, jokes, and oral epics of the folk. A similar paradox and irony is contained in "My Lord, What a Morning," in which the speaker is ecstatic over "black" Jack Johnson's defeat of "white" Jim Jeffries. Admitting to the "Lord" that "Fighting is wrong," the speaker nevertheless exclaims:

> But what an uppercut.

Making God a colloquial person—black, that is—in several of his poems, Cuney recalls Johnson's feat in *God's Trombones* in which God is likened to a "mammy." Another important later achievement of Cuney's is "Charles Parker, 1925–1955." The legendary jazz musician is given credit for reshaping the blues idiom in music—and hence revitalizing the black aesthetic. The poem is made up of lines of one to three words and includes phonetic renderings of saxophone sounds. And throughout the piece, the reader is advised to "listen."

Lewis Alexander apparently also wants us to "listen" to his "Enchantment," which embodies, again, the theme of the exotic and beautiful African. This time the "body smiling with black beauty" is wearing "African moonlight." Alexander divides his poem into two sections: "Part I," which is "*Night*," and "Part II," the "*Medicine Dance*." Part one gives the setting, moonlight in Africa, juice gushing from overripe fruit, palm trees, silence. In part two the medicine dancer is placed in relief against the "grotesque hyena-faced monster" who (seeming to represent whites) is driven back into the "wilderness" by his own fear and the spell cast on him by the medicine dancer. The poem is in free verse and features several exclamation marks and single-word lines. Typographically, the poem works well, with its depiction of dancing, mystery, suspense, fright, and anticipation. There is a quickening here, a stalking there, finally a resolution, and the black body now dances with "delight" as

> Terror reigns like a new crowned queen.

Alexander was born in Washington, D.C., educated in public schools including the celebrated Dunbar High, and

Howard University. His interests somewhat paralleled those of Cuney and Donald Jeffrey Hayes, and he acted in the Ethiopian Art Theatre Company; for a while he was a member of the Playwriters' Circle and the Ira Aldridge Players. Many of the major themes and experimental techniques of the Harlem Renaissance can be found in Alexander's poetry, from an examination of the Black anatomy to nature. Hughes says the faces, eyes and souls of "my people" are beautiful, like the night, stars and sun. Alexander finds, on the other hand, that the heavy-hanging sky, the curved scars of the moon, the twinkling of stars, and the trembling earth all parallel the burdensome hair, wrinkled brow, flowing tears ("an aging hurt") quivering eyelids and cupping tears ("Negro woman"). For Hughes, nature is a partner to black beauty; for Alexander, it is a companion to agony, suffering and historical pain. Alexander also probes the possibilities of color and shade symbolism. "Dream Song" advises one to "dream when night falls black." In "Nocturne Varial" shadow (Blacks) becomes light (beautiful, aware) and the deeper the blackness gets (spreads its influence) the more changes (the greater the impact) will occur among whites. In the deepest core of the night, "Each note is a star" but the light emitted from that darkness is not blinding. Then, after this searching contrast and overlay of what painters call chiaroscuro, we are told:

I came as a shadow,
To dazzle your night.

The idea of transfiguration and change weighs heavily upon Alexander's poetry. Significant changes occur in "Negro Woman," "Enchantment," "Nocturne Varial," and "Transformation." After having arrived as a "shadow" in "Nocturne Varial" the poet (or the persona "I") decides to "return" a bitterness that has gone through the wash of tears. The bitterness becomes "loveliness" that has been "Garnished through the years." Announcing that the bitterness has been worn from the taste of the past, Alexander implies here, as he does in other poems, that he is a forgiving person. Indeed he may be saying that Blacks will hold no hatred (for whites) or desire for retribution. Alexander's poetry is concise and neat, mostly in free verse and conventional language.

Neat also is the only anthologized poem by Lucy Ariel Williams Holloway. Found in *Caroling Dusk* (Cullen), *The Poetry of the Negro* (Hughes and Bontemps), and Johnson's *The Book of American Negro Poetry*, "Northboun'" garnered the coveted *Opportunity* poetry prize in 1926. We mention it because it shows great talent and *feel* in the employment of black southern speech and it embodies not only periodic but historical concerns of Blacks. The world is neither flat nor round, the poet tells us:

> H'it's one long strip
> Hangin' up an' down—

and there's only "Souf an' Norf." The foregoing is part of the chorus in this song-poem which comically predicts how people "all 'ud fall" if the world "wuz jes' a ball."

Those who brag about the city seen by Saint John, Lucy Holloway challenges them to see Saginaw. Opportunities for Blacks are good in Saginaw (heaven), and pretty women are plentiful. The poem restates the belief (developed during slavery and abolition efforts) that the North is heaven compared to the South (hell). Lucy Holloway emotionally chronicles the feelings, anticipations and oral narratives connected with "moving north." Such a preoccupation can be seen throughout the literature of the period, in the stories, the poems, the plays, the novels, the articles and the songs. Finally, she tells us what we have since heard Hughes, Ellison, Baldwin, Claude Brown, and Sterling Plumpp refute:

> Since Norf is up,
> An' Souf is down,
> An' Hebben is up,
> I'm upward boun'.

Lucy Holloway's poem is interesting for another reason: coming, as it did, at the thrust of the renaissance, it represented a throwback to the dialect and minstrel traditions that most of the New Negro writers were trying to escape. And although James Weldon Johnson and Langston Hughes worked in dialect, their major efforts were decidedly different from those of the Dunbar school.

Reading Lucy Holloway's poem, however, one is immediately reminded of Dunbar, Campbell, Corrothers, and Davis.

Yet a final reason for using the example of Lucy Holloway is to lead into at least a partial listing of the poets who published in magazines, regional anthologies and newspapers during the Harlem Renaissance and afterward. From among the dozens of lesser and unknown poets, we mention the following: Gladys May Casely Hayford (born in West Africa), Allison Davis, Esther Popel Shaw, J. Mason Brewer (*Negrito*, 1933), Kenneth W. Porter, Harvey M. Williamson, Eleanor Graham Nichols, Corrinne E. Lewis, Mary Effie Lee, Edward Garnett Riley, Albert Rice (a member of Georgia Douglas Johnson's writing workshop), Carrie W. Clifford (*The Widening Light*, 1922), Marcus B. Christian, Winston Allen, Mae V. Cowdery, Tilford Jones, Adeline Carter Watson, Will Sexton, and Edward Silvera. Some of these occasional and newspaper poets made temporary "splashes" and moved on. Mae V. Cowdery won a *Crisis* poetry prize in 1927 and published a volume of her poetry in the thirties. Of this group of poets, however, Christian and Silvera are the most important. Christian (1900–) was born in Houma, Louisiana, and was primarily self-educated. For a while, he served as supervisor of the Dillard University Negro History Unit of the Federal Writers' Project. He later received a Julius Rosenwald Fellowship to complete a historical study begun on the project before going to work in the Dillard Library. His poems appeared in various anthologies and magazines. And his available work has both general and racial flavor and shows him to be a skilled word handler. "The Craftsman" is about artistic excellence. The artist—presumably the poet—must work with "consummate care" and be "free of flaws." This is so because art is above everything else. The poet knows that if he writes well, he "lives" forever. Christian employs a form—the sonnet—that is consistent with his high calling. Another sonnet, "McDonogh Day in New Orleans," is a celebration of the beauty of blackness. Detailing the difficulty a poor black girl has in trying to get the kind of clothes she needs, Christian finally has her at-

tired "Like some dark princess" wearing "blue larkspur"
coupled with "yellow marigold." True, she looks good
going to school,

> But few would know—or even guess this fact:
> How dear comes beauty when a skin is black.

Silvera (1906-37) lived a productive, if tragically short,
life. He was born in Jacksonville, Florida, attended local
public schools and was graduated from Orange High; he
then went to Lincoln University in Pennsylvania, where
he participated in sports and wrote poetry, some of which
was included in *Four Lincoln Poets*. His poetry also appeared in magazines and anthologies. Much of Silvera's poetry is quiet and spare—reminiscent of Cuney, his friend
Horne, and many of the introspective poets of the period.
But his work does carry the prevailing themes of Harlem
Renaissance poetry. "Jungle Taste," for example, celebrates the Africa of old—Africa before the appearance of
the "civilization" Fenton Johnson condemns. The
"Coarseness" in the "songs of black men" does not sound
"strange" to Silvera. Neither does the "beauty" in the
"faces of black women" seem unusual. Yet black men
alone can "see" this "dark hidden beauty." In "Forgotten
Dreams" only a "heap" of entangled thread now lies
where once a beautiful dream had been spun. Here, Silvera seems to be lamenting the loss of something—maybe
viewing his approaching death. Likewise, in another poem,
"On the Death of a Child," he again uses the "spun"
image. The child comes without a "voice" to announce its
arrival. The lark sings, but "shadows" have already "fore-
told" that death is near. The "shroud" had been "spun"
and the end comes. Silvera's and Christian's works appear
in the Hughes and Bontemps anthologies. Silvera's poetry
also appears in Kerlin's *Negro Poets and Their Poems*.

The dominant themes in poetry of the Harlem Renaissance—cultural reclamation, stylistic experimentation, romantic engagement with Africa, a presentation of the
rawness of black life—can also be found in the fiction,
drama, painting, music, criticism, and belles-lettres of the
period. The best documentation of these items is Locke's
The New Negro. Some of the major names in prose
(fiction and non-fiction) also wrote poetry: Jean Toomer,

Eric Walrond, Jessie Redmond Fauset, Rudolph Fisher,
Nella Larson, Zora Neale Hurston, McKay, Hughes,
Cullen, Walter White, Du Bois, Charles S. Johnson,
Carter G. Woodson, Bruce Nugent, John Matheus, Cecil
Blue, Montgomery Gregory, Arthur Huff Fauset, James
Weldon Johnson, E. Franklin Frazier, and Arthur A.
Schomburg.

RENAISSANCE FALLOUT: NÉGRITUDE POETS AND PAN-AFRICAN WRITING

Claude McKay's influence, as a novelist (*Banjo*), on
leaders of African nationalism has already been noted. But
McKay's impact was not the first of its kind, nor the last.
During the eighteenth and nineteenth centuries, Africans
in the Western Hemisphere had exchanged ideas and
made pacts with each other and with their fellows of color
in Africa. In Chapter III we noted this pervasive influence
as seen in documents, the establishment of African societies and the African Methodist Episcopal Church, the
founding of Liberia, and the daring and courageous example of the West African Cinque. We also noted the arrival in the United States of a number of West Indian,
and Latin American Blacks—a flow that has remained
unabated up until this very day. We call immediately to
mind such names as Russwurm, Garvey, McKay, and
Stokely Carmichael. The poet John Boyd, discussed in
Chapter III, was a Bahamian.

It was during the 1920s, however, that the Pan-African
flavor was most dramatically and thoroughly demon-
strated. Garvey's Universal Negro Improvement Association, which claimed thousands of followers and members,
was in full swing by the time of the Harlem Renaissance.
Du Bois was the driving force behind four Pan-African
congresses, which met successively between 1919 and 1927
(in Paris, London and New York). And the predominant
themes in renaissance literature were reclamation of the
African heritage and celebration of the beauties and
talents of African peoples.

Consistent with our study, however, is a consideration
of one of the most important spin-offs from the renaissance: the *négritude* school of poets from such areas as

Martinique, Capetown, Paris, Dakar, and Algiers. As natives of French-colonized areas, these young black students and intellectuals were trained in French schools and held dual citizenship. (This practice represents a throwback to the Creole poets, many of whom were educated in France.) But we only summarize the négritude poets' activities here. Chief among them are Aimé Césaire (1913–) of Martinique, Léon Damas (1912–) of French Guiana, and Léopold Sédar Senghor (1906–) of Senegal. More information, including examples of *négritude* poetry, can be found in Jean-Paul Sartre's "Orphée Noir" ("Black Orpheus"), which prefaced Léopold Sédar Senghor's anthology of African and West Indian poets *Anthologie de la nouvelle poésie nègre et malgache de la langue française* (Paris, 1948). Although the important preface has appeared in various hard-to-get translations, it appeared in book form for the first time in C. W. E. Bigsby's *The Black American Writer, Volume II: Poetry and Drama* (1971). For further study see the works of Frantz Fanon, writings of Senghor (see also, *Léopold Sédar Senghor and The Politics of Négritude*, Irving L. Markovitz, 1969), and the numerous anthologies of African poetry by Langston Hughes, Marie Collins, Keorapetse Kgositsile, Ellen C. Kennedy, William Robinson, Wilfred Cartey, Quincy Troupe and Rainer Schulte, and Mercer Cook and Stephen Henderson's *The Militant Black Writer in Africa and the United States* (1969). This list is not exhaustive.

Négritude has been eloquently and illustratively defined by Sartre, Senghor, Cook, Paul Vesey (Samuel Allen), and others. The term (roughly corresponding to black American *soul*) refers to the mystique of blackness that pervades the thought, actions, creativity, and general lifestyle of some Africans. Senghor calls it a philosophy of humanism; Vesey finds elements of it in the Afro-American church and in the works of artists such as Baldwin and Ellison; Sartre notes: "From Haiti to Cayenne, there is a single idea, *reveal* the black soul. Black poetry is evangelic, it announces good news: Blackness has been rediscovered." The first creative work to emerge from this French-speaking sector of Harlem Renaissance influence was Léon Damas's *Pigments* (1937). Like the works that followed, *Pigments* extolled black beauty and lamented black suffer-

ing. The influence of Hughes is more evident in Damas
than in other *négritude* poets. Damas freely admits in conversation that he (and his compatriots) owes much to
Hughes, who offered prizes to African writers and helped
expose African literature to the world. *Pigments* heralded
the arrival of *négritude*. Its style, reminiscent of Hughes,
is "sharp, slangy, tense and fast-moving" and was revolutionary to French poetry when it appeared.

Césaire published *Cahier d'un retour au pays natal*
(*Return to My Native Land*) in 1938. Senghor has published *Chants d'ombres* (*Songs of Shadows*, 1949), *Hos-
ties Noires* (*Black Victims*, 1948), *Chants pour Naett*
(*Songs for Naett*, 1949), *Éthiopiques* (1959), and *Noc-
turnes* (1961). Both Césaire and Senghor have been
heavily influenced by jazz, blues and the poetry of the
Harlem Renaissance. Exposed to these forms in the salons
of Mademoiselle Nardal between 1929 and 1934, they
found Afro-American expression liberating and "fertiliz-
ing." (The salons of René Maran afforded them similar
exposure after 1935.) Also contributing to this convergence were the efforts of Mercer Cook, who, as statesman
and scholar, played an important part in bringing the
works of black Americans to their African and Caribbean
contemporaries.

Senghor's great poem about New York has immediate
ties to both the renaissance and the impact of Harlem on
him. As in many of his poems, Senghor designates the in-
strument(s) to accompany the piece. For "New York" he
chooses "*Jazz Orchestra: solo trumpet.*" New York's
beauty at first "confused" Senghor, but after a couple of
weeks in that city one grows accustomed to buying
"artificial hearts." He is ecstatic about

Harlem Harlem! I have seen Harlem Harlem! . . .

Senghor writes of the African landscape, warriors, love and
his admiration for black women. As president of Senegal,
he presided over the First World Festival of Negro Arts,
held in Dakar in 1966.

Damas deals with problems of color and class in his poetry and defines *négritude* in a series of rolling, vigorous
stanzas in free verse. His other collections of poems include *Poèmes nègres sur des airs africains* (1948), *Graffiti*

(1952), *Black-Label* (1956), and *Nevralgies* (1965?).
(Many critics seem to feel that the Africans and Caribbean poets surpassed their American brothers and sisters.)
Damas's cynicism and irony can be detected in the following titles: "Enough," "S.O.S.," "Position," "Good Breeding," and "Almost White." He satirizes the black middle
class and the black habit of straightening hair and using
bleaching creams.

Similar themes can be found in the poetry of Césaire,
who also employs free verse and makes great use of irony.
Return to My Native Land catalogues all the scientific
things that Blacks have not invented, but later gives them
credit for being the backbone of the human race. Césaire
has served as mayor of Fort de France and as a deputy to
the French National Assembly, representing the independent revolutionary party of Martinique. He quit the
French Communist Party in the 1950s and has since been
active in African nationalism. His other collections of poetry are *Les Armes miraculeuses* (1946), *Soleil cou coupé*
(1948), *Corps perdu* (1950), and *Ferrements* (1960).
Césaire, Damas and Senghor have also written drama
(mostly about black historical figures) and essays on *négritude* and Pan-African liberation. Damas is currently living
in Washington, D.C., where he teaches literature at Howard University and Federal City College. The *négritude*
movement in poetry—best recorded in Sartre's articles and
in Norman R. Shapiro's *Négritude: Black Poetry from Africa and the Caribbean* (1970)—encompassed several
other important black areas and figures: Ernest Alima
(Cameroon), Joseph Miezan Bognini and Bernard Dadié
(Ivory Coast), Jean-Fernand Brierre and René Depestre
(Haiti), Siriman Cissoko (Mali), David Diop, a great
poet, killed in an airplane crash in 1956 (Senegal),
Camara Laye (Guinea), and Émile-Désiré Ologoudou
(Dahomey), to name just a few. In some black French-
speaking territories, the *négritude* concept took hold under
different names. In Haiti it was called *Indigènisme*.

The Harlem Renaissance and the subsequent concept of
négritude influenced these poets in various ways and to
greater or lesser degrees. But the influence *is* there. However, the poets bear greater resemblance to their Afro-

American counterparts in themes, emotions and politics than in styles and techniques. This interchange among writers and thinkers of the black world has swollen to its current rich and important tide (more on this in Chapter VI).

THE EXTENDED RENAISSANCE: '30S, '40S, '50S

Some critics view the Harlem Renaissance as simply the peak of a nearly century-long Afro-American push in art, belles-lettres and consciousness-raising. And, as observed earlier, there is also divergent opinion over whether an actual renaissance occurred. But, arguments aside, the stock market crash of 1929 is generally seen as the official end of the period designated as the Harlem Renaissance—since white patronage ended and the black writers had not developed followings among the grass roots. Important here also are positions taken by two critics of the era, Sterling Brown and J. Saunders Redding, both of whom feel the awakening was primarily a fad; Brown called Harlem a "show-window" and Redding claimed the writers mistook Harlem for real black life:

> First of all, Negro writers, both poets and novelists, centered their attentions so exclusively upon life in the great urban centers that the city, especially Harlem, became an obsession with them. Now Harlem life is far from typical of Negro life; indeed, life there is lived on a theatrical plane that is as far from true of Negro life elsewhere as life in the Latin Quarter is from the truth of life in Picardy. The Negro writers' mistake lay in the assumption that what they saw was Negro life, when in reality it was just Harlem life. (*To Make a Poet Black*)

By way of parallel, it is instructive to note that a leading contemporary black critic, Addison Gayle, Jr., accuses black writers of the 1960s and 1970s of being similarly remiss. In the September 1974 issue of *Black World*, Gayle discussed "The Black Aesthetic: 10 Years Later" and attempted to lay out a blueprint for "Reclaiming the Southern Experience." His claim that hardly any of the new black literature is rooted in the South shows him to be less familiar with recent black writing than he should be. (See, for example, the works of Dumas, Alice Walker, Pinkie Lane, Arthenia Bates, Alvin Aubert, and others.) But, generally, his thesis, derived from John Oliver Killens' statement "We are a southern people" is solid and well taken. Gayle's and Redding's comments ought to be measured against Donald Gibson's view[4] of the "New" poetry as an "urban" product.

The works of black poets in the three decades following the 1920s borrowed from a rich cross section of technical and thematic reservoirs. The Great Depression was felt world-wide by Blacks and whites, poor and rich. The droughts, referred to in Cuney's "Hard Time Blues," the ravages of the boll weevil, the plight of the sharecroppers, the workers' push for unionization, and the attraction of the Communist Party (with its credo of racial unity and equality), all inspired and informed Afro-American poetry of the thirties, forties and fifties. So did lynching, unemployment, black history, cultural reclamation and protest; but the tendency, in general, was to seek the deliverance of "all men." McKay, Hughes and others (in the twenties and thirties) flirted with communism. Desperately seeking to fight racism, Afro-American artists, intellectuals, and writers not only became Communists, but expatriates, integrationists, Pan-Africanists, relentless seekers of the American Dream, civil servants, or model citizens. Few of the writers, however, followed the example of Richard Wright and W. E. B. Du Bois, who joined the Party. Such, then, were the stances cast against the Depression in the thirties, World War II in the forties, and Korea and McCarthyism in the fifties.

Compared to the first three decades of the century, relatively little black poetry was published in book form between 1930 and 1960. In a 1935 article in *Opportunity* Alain Locke lamented the low quality and quantity of post-renaissance poetry. With the exception of Hughes and Cullen, most of the older pens were silent during the thirties. Several new poets, however, made their debuts. Frank Marshall Davis (1905–   ) and Sterling A. Brown (1901–   ) made major impacts, but Davis went to Hawaii in the late forties and Brown was not heard from

---

4 See his *Modern Black Poets* ("Introduction").

again. Robert Hayden (1913–), Melvin B. Tolson (1900–66) and Margaret Walker (1915–) also made first appearances in the thirties, but they sustained lengthy and productive careers. Fiction writer Richard Wright (1908–60) was an infrequent poet who joined the thirties group. A second wave of poets, some part-time and all "transitional," appeared in the forties, fifties and early sixties: Owen Dodson (1914–), Dudley Randall (1914–), Gwendolyn Brooks (1917–), Margaret Danner (1915–), Pauli Murray (1910–), Bruce McM. Wright (1918–), Myron O'Higgins (1918–), Samuel Allen (Paul Vesey, 1917–), Ray Durem (1915–63), M. Carl Holman (1919–), Gloria C. Oden (1923–), Naomi Long Madgett (1923–), May Miller, Helen Johnson Collins (1918–), Lance Jeffers (1919–), Russell Atkins (1926–), Raymond Patterson (1929–), James C. Morriss (1920–), Oliver Pitcher (1923–) and Sarah E. Wright (1929–).

Most members of this transitional group did not get a real hearing until the sixties; they will be looked at as a group in Chapter VI. Dozens of others published or wrote occasionally. Brown separates the poets writing in the thirties into "new realists" and "romantics." The word "romantic" seems to be analogous to "library" or "literary," and both are used to speak somewhat disparagingly of poets thus categorized. The "realists" and writers of protest included Welborn Victor Jenkins (*Trumpet in the New Moon*, 1934), Frank Marshall Davis and Wright. Among those concerned with "romantic escapes" were Alpheus Butler (*Make Way for Happiness*, 1932), J. Harvey L. Baxter (*That Which Concerneth Me*, 1934; *Sonnets for the Ethiopians and Other Poems*, 1936), Eve Lynn (*No Alabaster Box*, 1936), Marion Cuthbert (*April Grasses*, 1936) and Mae Cowdery (*We Lift Our Voices*, 1936). The romantics wrote about nature, delicacy, love and quaintness, and their work reflects more book learning than anything else. Brown said that Jenkins' work deserved "an original place in Negro poetry," but *Trumpet in the New Moon* is out of print and Jenkins' poetry is absent from every anthology of Afro-American poetry. His poetic sketches of the black life encompass practically every important facet. Though owing much to Whitman

and Sandburg, Jenkins' work is still important enough to
be reissued as well as anthologized.

Wright, often called the father of the modern black
novel, was a poet in his own right. No other American
writer's personal odyssey has been so bleak and difficult.
From poverty, orphanhood, educational deprivation and
racism, he emerged as one of the most influential and
dominant forces in American literature. Not only did a so-
called "Wright school" of black writers result from his
efforts, but countless white writers also imitated him. His
most discussed novel, *Native Son* (1940), summed up the
emotional and psychological history of black urban
America over the preceding twenty years. His other writings chronicle the hopes (and disillusionments) of Blacks
"Northboun'" to seek the Promised Land.

As a poet, Wright deserves more than passing interest.
He joined the Communist Party in the thirties and
remained a member until 1944. His poetry, protest
coupled with calls for unity between Blacks and whites,
was published in various journals and news organs of the
period: *International Literature, New Masses, Anvil, Mid-
land* and *Left*. Much of it is quoted in Dan McCall's *The
Example of Richard Wright* (1969), and his poems appear in *The Norton Anthology of Modern Poetry* (Ellmann and O'Clair), *The Negro Caravan, The Poetry of
Black America, American Negro Poetry,* and other anthologies. Born near Natchez, Mississippi, and experiencing an
erratic education and home life, Wright finally settled in
Chicago, where he worked with the Federal Writers' Project during the Depression (becoming a friend to Davis,
Margaret Walker and others). He died in 1960 in Paris,
where he had settled (at the suggestion of Gertrude
Stein) and joined the Existentialist group of writers, led
by Jean-Paul Sartre and Simone de Beauvoir. His poetry is
in free verse and the Japanese haiku form—which he discovered late in his life. His haikus are harmless elliptical
statements, as haikus often are. They are rarely racial in
flavor. But his protest poetry of the thirties shows him to
be a poet of unmistakable talent and sensitivity. "I Have
Seen Black Hands" owes debts to the American school of
poetry developed by Whitman, Fenton Johnson, Masters,
Sandburg, Hughes, and others. In the poem, Wright

catalogues the services rendered and corresponding disservices received by Blacks. He announces,

> I am black and I have seen black hands, millions
>   and millions of them—

and that these "hands" have reached naïvely, creatively, harmlessly, softly and with strength, out to each other and to do the white man's bidding. Despite their stamina, vigilance and dependability, these same hands are the last put to work and the first idled. They held the "dreaded lay-off slip." They suffered from "unemployment and starvation."

> And they grew nervous and sweaty, and opened and
>   shut in anguish and doubt and hesitation
>   and irresolution. . . .

Wright continues, as in his prose works, to develop a psychological portrait of the abused and dehumanized Blacks. There is a drive and an incremental swell reminiscent of Margaret Walker's "For My People" as he recalls having seen "black hands" grip prison bars, knotted and clawlike under the lynch rope, or "beat fearfully at tall flames." But black hands and white hands will someday merge as "fists of revolt" and create a new "horizon." Here Wright urges Blacks and whites to become Communists. "Between the World and Me," however, sustains a different angle of the theme begun in "I Have Seen Black Hands": A black man has been lured into a wooded area and seduced by a white prostitute; the narrator becomes the lynched body whose remains are

> . . . dry bones . . . and a stony skull staring in
>   yellow surprise at the sun. . . .

Making use of awesome, horrifying images and clashing, brilliant colors and sounds, the poem recounts the most insignificant details of the lynching:

> And the sooty details of the scent rose, thrusting
>   themselves between the world and me. . . .
> There was a design of white bones slumbering
>   forgottenly upon a cushion of ashes.
> There was a charred stump of sapling pointing a
>   blunt finger accusingly at the sky.

There were torn tree limbs, tiny veins of burnt
  leaves, and scorched coil of greasy hemp;
And upon the trampled grass were buttons, dead
  matches, butt-ends of cigars and cigarettes,
  peanut shells, a drained gin-flask, and a whore's
  lipstick;
Scattered traces of tar, restless arrays of feathers,
  and the lingering smell of gasoline.

The poem continues, as the narrator, who "stumbled suddenly upon the thing," becomes one with the victim. It is
a fascinating and highly appropriate poetic technique.
Owing much to the psychological school of writing, but
indicting the cosmos (as Dunbar does in "The Haunted
Oak"), "Between the World and Me" states that the
lynch victim is every Black. And the world (through the
recitation of usually passive components of the natural
landscape) shares in the guilt, the revulsion and the horror
of the act. Before God and the world, the victim

. . . clutched childlike, clutched to the hot sides
  of death.

In *Black on White* (1966), David Littlejohn calls
Wright's poem and Robert Hayden's "Middle Passage"
"the two finest poems by Negroes."
  Sterling Brown's poetry also falls into the category of realism though not in the political sense in which it is applied to other writers of the era. Like Cuney, Wright,
Davis, Hughes, and others, Brown in *Southern Road*
(1932) depicts the harshness and starkness of black
misery, but his poetry is "chiefly an attempt at folk por-
traiture of southern characters." A highly respected critic
and scholar of black folk literature, Brown approached his
"portraits" as a student of the linguistic and thematic materials with which he worked. He was born and reared in
Washington, D.C. At Williams College, he was elected
to Phi Beta Kappa in 1921 and in 1923 received an M.A.
from Harvard. Since that time, Brown, the son of educator parents, has had a long and distinguished career as
writer, editor, teacher, and professor of English at Howard
University. He has also taught at New York University,
Vassar College, and Atlanta University. From 1926 to

1939, he was Editor of Negro Affairs for the Federal Writers' Project, and in 1939 he was a staff member of the famous Carnegie-Myrdal Study of the Negro. The recipient of numerous awards, Brown is the author of *The Negro in American Fiction* (1937) and *Negro Poetry and Drama* (1937). In 1941, he served as senior editor (with Arthur P. Davis and Ulysses P. Lee) of *The Negro Caravan*, probably the most influential and definitive anthology of Afro-American literature ever published. In the twenties, Brown began his ceaseless pattern of publishing articles, reviews and criticism in various journals, newspapers and periodicals.

Perceptive, relentless and seemingly always in focus, Brown performed important surgery on black folk culture and its manifestations in the poetry, music and language. His findings were published in *Negro Poetry and Drama*, where he also concluded that the New Negro Movement (1914–36) produced the following five "major concerns" among the poets:

1. a rediscovery of Africa as a source for race pride;
2. a use of Negro heroes and heroic episodes from American history;
3. propaganda of protest;
4. a treatment of the Negro masses (frequently of the folk, less often of the workers) with more understanding and less apology;
5. and franker and deeper self-revelation.

Brown's own poetry revived interest in black dialect from a vigorously different angle from what had gone before. Cullen (*Caroling Dusk*) and Johnson (*The Book of American Negro Poetry*) had forecast the doom of dialect poetry. Cullen said its day was over and Johnson reduced it to "two stops": humor and pathos. (Interestingly, Arthur P. Davis, in *From the Dark Tower*, 1974, repeated Johnson's position!) However, Brown took the stand that dialect has limitless possibilities if poets and writers only have the courage and the ingenuity to work with it. Of the debate and conflict over dialect poetry, he said:

Dialect, or the speech of the people, is capable of expressing whatever the people are. And the folk Negro is

a great deal more than a buffoon or a plaintive minstrel.
Poets more intent upon learning the ways of the folk,
their speech, and their character, that is to say better
poets, could have smashed the mold. But first they
would have had to believe in what they were doing. And
this was difficult in a period of conciliation and middle-
class striving for recognition and respectability.

Brown himself used his knowledge of folk culture to interpret the people through poetry. And he considered this
approach "one of the important tasks of Negro poetry."
Some observers see a contradiction in Brown's dazzling academic achievements and his poetic work in the folk materials. But today's young scholars and poets could learn
much from his example.
Wagner (*Black Poets of the United States*) points to
the irony and humor in Brown's asking Johnson to write
the Introduction to *Southern Road*. For, in doing so,
Johnson was literally forced to take back much of his own
criticism of dialect poetry. Indeed Johnson had to admit
to Brown's formidable achievement with the folk forms.
Before *Southern Road*, in *The Book of American Negro
Poetry*, the elder poet and critic acknowledged that Brown
was "one of the outstanding poets of the younger group";
for the "best work," Brown "dug his raw material from
the great mine of Negro folk poetry," thus expressing the
folk idiom with "artistry and magnified power." Kerlin
(*Negro Poets and Their Poems*) ranked *Southern Road* as
a first volume with Cullen's *Color* and Hughes's *The
Weary Blues*. Even from Senegal, Africa, praise has come
to Brown in the form of Senghor's assertion that Hughes
and Brown are "the most Negro" of black American
poets. There is always the temptation to compare the two
poets but, as Wagner suggests, Brown is the "antithesis of
Langston Hughes," since Hughes is the poet of the city
and Brown the bard of the soil. In his closeness to the soil
and his serious studies of black folk culture, Brown has
been compared to Johnson and Zora Neale Hurston (see
Jonah's Gourd Vine and *Mules and Men*).
The folk idiom, coupled with drama and word portraits,
provides the meat of Brown's work; though it must be
mentioned that he also writes in conventional English

with marked success. His poetic universe is generally drab
—with occasional flashes of wry humor. His is the poetry
of hard times and suffering. He expresses skepticism in
face of religion and God; and ironically there is no reference to Africa as in (almost thematically) most poetry of
the period. Brown seems to be saying the fight is here in
America, not in an Africa of mind or fact, and that the
black man is pitted against forces of nature that alternately work for and against him. Writing during the
Depression years, Brown was concerned with the deadly
cholera, the boll weevil, the ravages of the flooding Missouri River, the plight of the sharecropper and tenant
farmer, and white racism. It is clear that, for Brown, the
hope (if it is there) for the black man lies in his own
stamina, his own historical endurance and strengths. Consequently the poet infuses these strengths and defiances
with folk rhythms—especially the dramatic narrative and
the contrapuntal pattern that incorporates italics for emphasis and the various sounds of men at work, play,
prayer, dance or battle. "Strong Men" is perhaps the best
example of Brown's style. Using a line from Sandburg—
"The strong men keep coming on"—he actually borrows
exact phrasings, aphorisms, bits of parables, and parts of
secular and religious songs from the folk culture. The formal English narrative is set in dramatic and musical relief
through the use of the technique described above. Steeped
in a tradition that spans Whitman, Fenton Johnson,
Masters, and Eliot, Brown catalogues the numerous injustices Blacks have suffered; he interjects "The strong men
keep a-comin' on" or "keep a-inchin' along" or "Walk
togedder chillen." Even though Blacks were "dragged"
from their native land and degraded in every possible way,
they kept "Gittin' stronger."

The same message is in "Strange Legacies," "After
Winter," "Southern Road" (a near paraphrase of a work
song), "Ma Rainey," and the six-part sequence "When de
Saints Go Ma'ching Home." What Du Bois called
"dogged strength" is what Brown gives his characters. As
Margaret Walker suggests, there is room to "stagger" but
none to halt! Reminiscent of "The Weary Blues," "When
de Saints" depicts the "Trouble, Trouble" deep down in
the "soul" of a black singer. But that trouble, like the

"weariness" of Hughes, is a collective trouble—the weight, the fatigue, the burden of the folk. We hear it everywhere in black expression, from Bessie Smith to Marian Anderson, from Paul Laurence Dunbar to Paul Robeson, from Fenton Johnson to Marvin Gaye (*Trouble Man*), from the "sad" and "sorrow" songs of the slaves to the blues singers of the river towns and depression years. After the singer in Brown's poem had played his various sad and sin songs, he always played one in which he stepped out of the role of "entertainer." He would then give forth his "chant of saints." Anticipating his arrival in heaven and others who would be there, he would carefully describe what each of the entrants would be wearing. It is a gala affair—initiation into heaven—and most of the arrivals come in the clothes they wore in life on earth. The sinners, of course, are not allowed in heaven. They include Sportin' Legs, Lucky Sam, Smitty, Hambone, Hardrock Gene, and others.

Brown also wrote in the ballad form ("He Was a Man"), conventional verse ("Effie" and "Salutamus"—a sonnet) and the blues form popularized by Hughes in *The Weary Blues*. His black men are on the run (from a mob or police), in trouble with whites as a result of an arrogant act or response, getting killed, trying to figure out how to feed the household, or being assaulted by natural disasters. In a large number of these poems there are sorrow, devastation, catastrophe, violence, death, tragedy, social disruption, chaos, ruin, need, pain, skepticism, and the paranoia inherent in black life. "He Was a Man" depicts how a black man beat a white man (who drew first) to the draw but was lynched in the tradition of handling Blacks. Despite the fact that "strong men" keep coming "Strong Men" is a poem replete with negatives. "Sister Lou" is a longing for heaven as a respite from the hardships and racial injustices suffered here on earth. "After Winter" is the portrait of a black man "ragged" as "an old scarecrow," whose "swift thoughts" are about the food, drink and space he must obtain for his family. "Ma Rainey" ("Mother of the Blues") is therapeutic in her words and her delivery. But she resembles Fenton Johnson's "monarch," who presides over sacks of merchandise. The people come to Ma Rainey to "keep us strong." But they cry and feel sad when she sings. And on goes the *Southern Road* with the exception of the Slim Greer story-poems and the lover-man themes, which nevertheless feature men who must either love quick and run or those reminiscing about their loves while they swing the hammer on the chain gang. Slim Greer finds himself in various predicaments. Most memorable are his visits to heaven and hell ("Slim in Hell"), his absurd effort to pass for white though he is dark "as midnight" ("Slim Greer") and his bout with the Atlanta law that requires Blacks to laugh only in a "telefoam booth" ("Slim in Atlanta"). Brown's really great achievement, however, is seen in the brilliant "Memphis Blues." Here the poet asks what difference is it to Blacks whether Memphis is destroyed by "Flood or Flame." Memphis, Babylon, and Nineveh are all the same:

> De win' sing sperrichals
> Through deir dus'.

Forecasts of doom can be seen in much American literature, but black writers have used this theme to carve out a special place for themselves. This allows them to place their racial predicament in relief against Christianity or Christianization. We have observed that such concern runs like a spine through black poetry: Dunbar, Fenton Johnson, Cullen, McKay, Hughes, and certainly Brown, for whom God is alternately black and white. And here, of course, is the contradiction, because the God of the whites (the oppressors) cannot be trusted; and the black God seems somewhat helpless against a white power structure, of which Brown says, in "Old Lem":

> *They don't come by ones*
> *They don't come by twos*
> *But they come by tens.*

Having published only one book, which has just been reissued (1974, with a new Introduction, by Sterling Stuckey), places Brown in a rather difficult and sometimes inaccessible position. But there have been good, if few, appraisals of his work. Jean Wagner takes a long look at him (*Black Poets of the United States*). Brown takes a short, but helpful, look at himself in *Negro Poetry*. So does Redding in *To Make a Poet Black*. Also helpful is Stephen Henderson's "A Strong Man Called Sterling Brown," *Black World*, XIX (September 1970) 5–12. Benjamin Brawley (*The Negro Genius*) assesses Brown as poet and critic, as does Blyden Jackson in *Black Poetry in America*. Charles Rowell, a young critic-teacher at Southern University, Baton Rouge, has prepared a yet unpublished criticism of Brown's poetry. See also *Black Writers of America* (Barksdale and Kinnamon). Brown's work appears in most anthologies of black literature and poetry. We were pleased to learn during the final stages of preparation for this book that Broadside Press published *The Last Ride of Wild Bill* (including the Slim Greer series) in 1975 with a preface by Dudley Randall.

One characteristic of black poetry of the thirties was a cry for unionization of Blacks and whites. Brown's "When de Saints Go Ma'ching Home" allows room in heaven for a handful of whites who befriended Blacks. According to the Marxist/Communist-influenced thinking of the times, downtrodden peoples—of whatever color—were in the same boat. Their struggles were the same. One finds this feeling in Frank Marshall Davis' "Snapshots of the Cotton South," which paints a rather pathetic and depressing picture of voteless Blacks who "lack the guts" and "po'" whites who "have not the brains" to fight the rich plantation owners and the police. The poems also reek with irony and satire—a Davis trademark. Even though racial "intermingling" is "unthinkable," syphilis is passed from the "shiftless son" of a plantation owner (a lynch-mob leader) to a washerwoman, who gives it to the chief of police, who gives it to a young mulatto cook, who gives it to the mayor of "Mobtown," who gives it to his wife.

Currently living in Hawaii, where he is a salesman, Davis was born in Arkansas City, Kansas, attended local public schools and studied journalism at Kansas State College, where he was the first recipient of the Sigma Delta Chi Perpetual Scholarship. He later left school for Chicago to do newspaper work. In 1931 Davis went to Atlanta to help establish the Atlanta *Daily World*. Returning to Chicago, he worked with the Associated Negro Press until the late 1940s, when he moved to Hawaii. In 1937 he received a Julius Rosenwald Fellowship to write poetry. He has published four volumes of poetry: *Black Man's Verse* (1935), *I Am the American Negro* (1937), *Through Sepia Eyes* (1938), and *47th Street* (1948). Davis established himself early as a social-minded poet who combined his journalistic training with an innovative free-verse form to create interesting lyrics. (Gwendolyn Brooks later developed a form known as verse journalism.) Stephen Henderson (*Understanding the New Black Poetry*) notes the similarities between Davis' poetry and that currently being written by Chicago-area poets. The influence of Masters and Sandburg can be seen in much of Davis' work, but his poetry is highly flavored with black themes and (sometimes) idioms. Like Hughes, he is the poet of the city. But he renders believable pictures of black "society" and the hard times of southern living. In "Snapshots" he warns whites that death and the boll weevil do not nibble only on "nigger cotton." Ironically placing the "Democracy" of death and natural disasters alongside a hollow American "Democracy," Davis is able to turn the poem into a piercing sword of social criticism. Ironies also spine such poems as "Robert Whitmore," "Arthur Ridgewood, M.D.," and "Giles Johnson, Ph.D." —bourgeois Blacks destroyed by status-climbing. Whitmore, having reached the peak of social and business success, dies when he is mistaken for a waiter. Dr. Ridgewood, forced to choose between the life of a poet and a doctor, dies from a nerve disruption caused by worry over rejection slips and money problems. Dr. Johnson will not teach and cannot do labor; he dies of starvation. The great tragedy, in this stream of poetic ideas, is the story of the poet "Roosevelt Smith." Smith could be Davis himself or possibly Countee Cullen or Melvin Tolson—or one of any number of black poets who wrote as they were directed only to end up having "contributed" nothing to their "nation's literature." Smith's first book is attacked by white critics for imitating Sandburg, Masters and Lindsay. His second book, written after he had done firsthand study in the South, is criticized by Blacks for being too sordid. Critics dismiss his third book, an experimental effort, as not being consistent with the depth and breadth of the philosophical material treated by Stein and Eliot. A black man has no business imitating the "classic" works of Keats, Browning and Shakespeare, they say of his fourth book.

He ought to use his rich African background. Of his fifth book, critics are suspicious: since it contains no traces of anything done previously by a white poet, then it must be "just a new kind of prose." The poet then becomes a mail carrier, and has time to read in the papers that black writers have contributed so "little" to American literature.

Davis also wrote free verse utilizing themes of love, night, and the stark life of Blacks in Southside Chicago. His poems about love are quiet and well sculptured. They are placed in the category of "mystic escapist" by Brown. In his first volume, Davis strikes vivid pictures in such pieces as "Chicago's Congo," "Jazz Band," "Mojo Mike's Beer Garden," "Cabaret," "Lynched," and "Georgia's Atlanta." In "Jazz Band" he anticipates the work of literally dozens of poets of the sixties (Neal, Crouch, Cortez, Lee, Baraka, Harper, the Last Poets, Carolyn Rodgers). And certainly one recalls Hughes's "Jazzonia" and "Jazz Band in a Parisian Cabaret" when one hears

Play that thing you jazz mad fools!

and the steady hammering of

Plink plank plunk a plunk. . . .

Everybody and every place has the blues since Blacks brought the sound to town: Chopin, Wagner, London, Moscow, Paris, Hongkong, Cairo, Dios, Jehovah, Gott, Allah, Buddha, and so on. Everyone can partake of the happy-sad sound being played by the "black boy." Unfortunately, a close study of Davis' work has yet to be done. He had many things in mind for his work: one poem is designed to be read aloud by eight voices. There is a brief, but good, assessment of him in Wagner's book; Sterling Brown sets forth crisp and poignant criticism. Benjamin Brawley discusses Davis' poetry (*Negro Genius*). But he appears all too infrequently in anthologies. For a current look at Davis see Dudley Randall's interview with him in *Black World*, XXIV (January 1974), 37–48.

Robert Hayden has one of the longest poetry-writing (and publishing) records of any living American poet. His poems have appeared in numerous anthologies, newspapers, periodicals, books, and pamphlets since 1940. Born in Detroit, Michigan, Hayden attended local schools and Wayne State University, and in 1936 "graduated to the

Federal Writers' Project," heading research into local
Afro-American history and folklore. He resumed his training in 1938, when he enrolled at the University of Michigan, where he received a teaching assistantship and did advanced work in play production, creative writing and
English. Hayden received an M.A. and taught English at
Michigan for two years. He garnered the Hopwood award
for poetry in 1938 and 1942 and in the meantime had an
opportunity to study with W. H. Auden, whose poetry his
own sometimes reflects. In 1940, his first book of poetry,
Heart-Shape in the Dust, was published. And he joined
the faculty of Fisk University in 1946. During the sixties
he became involved in a series of "meaningful encounters
with proponents of a black literary aesthetic" (Barksdale
and Kinnamon), which resulted in his leaving Fisk and
joining the faculty of the University of Michigan (1969).
Hayden has received Rosenwald and Ford grants, and in
1966 his *Ballad of Remembrance* (Paul Bremen 1962)
was awarded the Grand Prize in the English poetry category at the First World Festival of Negro Arts in Dakar,
Senegal. In presenting Hayden with the award, the festival
committee cited him as

> . . . a remarkable craftsman, an outstanding singer of
> words, a striking thinker, a *poète pur-sang.* He gives
> glory and dignity to America through deep attachment
> to the past, present and future of his race. Africa is in
> his soul, the world at large in his mind and heart.

In 1948 Hayden collaborated with Myron O'Higgins in
publication of *The Lion and the Archer.* His *Figure of
Time: Poems* appeared in 1955, and *Selected Poems* was
published in 1966. *Words in the Mourning Time,* with its
portraits of violence and destruction, came out in 1970; it
was nominated for a National Book Award (1972). *The
Night-Blooming Cereus,* showing Hayden as a reflective
lover of nature and deeply religious poet, was published in
1972 by Bremen.[5] He has also written and produced plays

---

[5] During 1975–76, several long-overdue honors came to Hayden:
Angle of Ascent: New and Selected Poems was published; he was
elected to the American Academy of Poets (Fellow) for "distinguished
poetic achievement," and appointed Consultant for Poetry to the Library of Congress, replacing Stanley Kunitz.

(*Go Down Moses*), and during the forties he was drama and music critic for the Michigan *Chronicle*. Hayden's work appears in practically every anthology of Afro-American literature or poetry published since *The Negro Caravan*. His editorship of anthologies includes *Kaleidoscope: Poems by American Negro Poets* (1967), *Afro-American Literature: an Introduction* (1971, with Burroughs and Lapides), and *The United States in Literature* (1973, with Miller and O'Neal). The latter work contains many of Hayden's seminal ideas as well as brilliant crystallizations of black and general poetry movements in the United States. His individual poems have appeared in *Opportunity*, *Poetry* and *Atlantic Monthly*. Currently, he is poetry editor of the Baha'i magazine *World Order*.

Although, as a poet, Hayden has maintained a steady balance between racial concerns and the modern poetic tradition, he is what Sterling Brown would call a library poet. Classical allusions, obscurantism, surrealism, and complicated syntax go hand in hand with experimental blues poetry and muted anger. Bontemps said that the term "Negro poet" was particularly "displeasing" to Countee Cullen; and Hayden (a Cullen admirer), in *Kaleidoscope* rejected being judged "by standards different from those applied to work of other poets." The black poet should not be limited to a racial utterance, Hayden believes. (Ironically, a poll of black poets today might easily show that a great many of them feel the same way—even though such is not suggested by the "popular" image of the contemporary black poet.)

Speaking of his "influences" in O'Brien's *Interviews with Black Writers*, Hayden noted:

When I was in college I loved Countee Cullen, Jean Toomer, Elinor Wylie, Edna St. Vincent Millay, Sara Teasdale, Langston Hughes, Carl Sandburg, Hart Crane. I read all the poetry I could get a hold of, and I read without discrimination. Cullen became a favorite. I felt an affinity and wanted to write in his style. I remember that I wrote a longish poem about Africa, imitating his "Heritage." All through my undergraduate years I was pretty imitative. As I discovered poets new to me, I studied their work and tried to write as they

did. I suppose all young poets do this. It's certainly one
method of learning something about poetry. I reached
the point, inevitably, where I didn't want to be
influenced by anyone else. I tried to find my own voice,
my own way of seeing. I studied with W. H. Auden in
graduate school, a strategic experience in my life. I
think he showed me my strengths and weaknesses as a
poet in ways no one else before had done.

Hayden thus establishes himself as a poet of the book as
opposed to the raw experience—vis à vis Brown, Hughes,
Davis, Margaret Walker, and numerous others, although
such a division is *not* absolute and must consider many
variables. (See, for examples, Hayden's excellent poems on
the black folk character and revolutionary.)

According to Davis, in *From the Dark Tower*, Hayden
has repudiated his early poetry—some of it blatant protest
and influenced by folk materials. This poetry shows
Hayden as an imitator of the older Harlem Renaissance
poets and under the influence of the Communist-Socialist
thought of the 1930s and 1940s. In "Prophecy" he depicts
destruction and the people returning to the "ruined city"
to rebuild a new society. "Gabriel" recalls the final moments in the life of revolt leader Gabriel Prosser. "Black
Gabriel" is hanged for leading slaves

From forgotten graves. . . .

Interweaving italics and colloquialisms (like Sterling
Brown), Hayden re-creates the terror and drama of
Gabriel's death. Black and golden in the air, Gabriel dan-
gles from a noose above black men who

Never, never rest. . . .

"Speech" is just that—a harangue calling black and white
"brothers" to fight the common oppressor, presumably to-
talitarianism, fascism and greedy overseers. "Obituary" is a
sensitive and pained reflection of a "father" who lived

Prepared for wings.

Among these early pieces (found in *Caravan* and
Hayden's first volumes) "Bacchanal" is especially interesting—for it collects the new dialect into the kind of social

statement Brown had perfected. There is irony in using
"bacchanal" to describe a black factory worker getting

> High's a Georgia pine

to forget that the factory closed "this mawnin." The black
man, who in "Gabriel" can never rest, is seeking real
"joy" on earth. But, minus money and woman, his
"bacchanal" becomes a weighty blues statement—not the
revelry of ancient Greek or Roman party life.

One finds none of these pieces in *Selected Poems*. Instead there is the polished Hayden of "The Diver," "A
Ballad of Remembrance," "Sub Specie Aeternitatis,"
"Middle Passage" and "Runagate Runagate." Neither
does one find them in *Words in the Mourning Time*.
Hayden has obviously elevated his protest themes. To be
sure, he does make his social comment, as does Cullen.
But his "Zeus over Redeye" (*Mourning*) carries none of
the urgency of Hughes's "Dream Deferred" or "Ask Your
Moma." And "Runagate" and "Middle Passage" address
with subtlety and allusion the concerns of Dodson ("Lament"), Margaret Walker ("Since 1619") and Frank
Marshall Davis ("Snapshots of the Cotton South"). Yet
Hayden brings a fine and intense intellect to his poetry—
regardless of subject matter. His output has been relatively
small, considering his long career, but *Words in the
Mourning Time* proves that his intensity has not lessened.
And he must be admired for sticking to his aesthetic con-
victions and his unswerving devotion to poetic craftsmanship, which have gone hand in hand with his enduring
interest in history, racial and general. His manuscript of
poems dealing with slavery and the Civil War, *The Black
Spear*, won him his second Hopwood award. The idea for
a book-length series of narrative poems on black history—
"from the black man's point of view"—came to Hayden
after he read Stephen Vincent Benét's long narrative
poem *John Brown's Body* (1927). *The Black Spear* never
emerged as a book, but remnants of it can be found in
section five of *Selected Poems*. Using black history, Hayden champions such heroes and heroines as Nat Turner,
Frederick Douglass, Harriet Tubman, Cinque, Martin
Luther King, and Malcolm X. He also includes whites
who shared the burden of the black struggle: William

Lloyd Garrison, Ralph Waldo Emerson, Henry David
Thoreau, John Brown, John and Robert Kennedy, and
others.

Hayden's history poems, however, reflect the complexity
and disturbances inherent in man's continuing struggle. In
a non-racial poem such as "The Diver" there can be floating, plunging, piercing, blurring, disillusionment, wreck-
age, drunken tilting, "numbing / kisses," and other suggestions of dramatic tension between the real and
assumed, between the shadow and the substance. But the
same "feeling" comes through in poems of racial flavor.
"Middle Passage" certainly bears this out, as Blyden Jackson notes in "From One 'New Negro' to Another" (in
Jackson and Rubin, *Black Poetry in America*, Baton
Rouge, La., 1974). Situated, as it were, "in the rocking
loom of history," Middle Passage" is at once Hayden's
and black America's achievement. Opening with the
names of slave ships—*Jesús, Estrella, Esperanza, Mercy*—
the poem crisscrosses the vast geographical, chronological
and spiritual web of racial horror since slavery. The names
of the ships are simultaneously contradictory and reminiscent of the expletive "Jesus, have mercy" (and similar
phrases) heard daily in black communities. But *this* Jesus
will have no Mercy—and serves as the albatross around
the neck of Christian slavers.

Any middle passage is exciting as well as dangerous—
since it represents the peak and the unfinished quest.
Hence Hayden's middle passage suggests both the horrible
and brutalizing experience of slaves aboard ships crossing
the Atlantic and the incompleted "adventure" of Blacks
in America. The poem also satisfies many of the demands
of modernist poetry. "Middle Passage" in fact is related
stylistically to such poems as Eliot's *The Waste Land*,
Pound's *Cantos*, Crane's *The Bridge* and Williams' *Paterson*. Especially is it akin to *The Waste Land* in its use of
allusion, fragments of obscure information (old documents, letters, conversation, etc.), typographical variation
and the stream of associations.

Hayden's poem, after its sharp and arresting opening,
weaves together objective narration, notes from a slave
ship's log, sections from a ship's officer's diary, testimony
at a court of inquiry (into a revolt aboard the Cuban

slaver *Amistad* 1839), the tale of an old sailor whose
bones "fever melted" down, paraphrasings of a Shake-
spearean text and familiar expressions from the Bible
and live religious services. The poem depicts every imagi-
nable disaster and conflict: storms, rebellions, suicides, a
plague that causes blindness ("ophthalmia"), the lusty
crew members' sexual exploitation of female slaves, the
"nigger kings" who sold the Africans into slavery, descriptions of the smells and sounds of dying, and the ha-
tred/respect the slave ship's surviving spokesman has for
rebellion leader Cinque. (Almost one hundred years before "Middle Passage," James M. Whitfield had honored
this same revolutionary in "To Cinque.")

The idea of the remade man, a "voyage" that takes one
"through death" into "life," recurs in Hayden's poem:
here, again, the sense of one meandering through a
"wasteland" in search of the right society, the sane environment. Indeed in much black American writing, mirror-
ing sometimes the literature of larger America, there is the
assertion that the new man arrives only after paying the
dues of being brutalized and oppressed. Even in everyday
life, Blacks are often intolerant of others who have not
"gone through" the fire and brimstone of depravity and alienation. Thus, for Hayden, the "middle passage" is both
spiritually and physically a "voyage" through death in
order to achieve life. In the middle passage the slaves are
halfway between their African homeland and America.
They will not be returning to Africa, and yet they know
nothing of the life "upon these shores." Too, the middle
passage symbolizes the initiation of every man into the
awesome awareness and responsibility of adulthood—and
his own mortality. The middle passage is where we all triumph or perish, just as in the wasteland one must create a
new world or drift with the debris. However, the care-
takers of slave ships crossing the middle passage are as
acutely aware of their mission as are the reflective slaves
(and poets). They are also bringing life through death.
They bear

   black gold, black ivory, black seed.

All this occurs against the pervasive irony of the ship
names *Jesús* and *Mercy* and the double irony of the

slaver's spokesman who renounces Cinque for rebelling against the crew:

> . . . true Christians all. . . .

While the "Middle Passage" places Blacks somewhere in the middle of things, "Runagate Runagate" continues the irony and ambiguity of moving through death to life. There is little to be envied in the "life" of the runaway slave depicted in this poem. The hound dogs, the slave trackers, the auction blocks, the WANTED signs, the brandings on the cheeks, the driver's lash—all relive the terror, the nightmarish nature of black life after the middle passage. For Blacks, then, the initiation continues beyond the first death (the enslavement). The anxiety and "never, never rest" life of the slave is dramatically captured by Hayden, who employs a rich tapestry of language, syntax, color, imagery, narration, and biblical phrases alongside the symbolism and linguistic "sweep" seen in modern poetry; added to this is the dramatic use of italics. The poem celebrates the courage and endurance of escaping slaves and honors black and white abolitionist leaders. Hayden allows the reader to relive the experience of the runaway slave and the accompanying tension-filled hide-and-seek drama. We hear and see the runaway in the opening line. By avoiding the use of punctuational breaks, Hayden achieves a rush of language very similar to the relentless drive of black oral expression and to the "never, never rest" feeling he established in "Gabriel." The runaway

> Runs falls rises stumbles on from darkness into
> darkness

and the hunt is on, as the escapee reflects on the "many thousands" already channeled through the Underground Railroad. We see and hear the mixed jubilance and fear of the slave, who vows that he will never return to the auction block and the driver's lash:

> And before I'll be a slave
> I'll be buried in my grave. . . .

Keeping with the trend of modern poetry, Hayden introduces incidental notices and data: an announcement describing runaways (including age, dress, brandings, and a suspicion that they can turn themselves into quicksand, whirlpools or scorpions), WANTED posters, and names of prominent abolitionists of the day. Typographically and syntactically, the poem is designed to be read without significant pauses, so that the non-stop hurtle of the slave toward freedom actually occurs in the text; it is, Blyden Jackson suggests (though of "Middle Passage"), "as if it repeats history." Especially notable is Hayden's treatment of Harriet Tubman, the greatest of Underground Railroad leaders, who was wanted "Dead or Alive" and who was known to level a pistol at a doubting runaway:

> Dead folks can't jaybird-talk, she says;
> You keep on going now or die, she says. . . .

"Middle Passage" and "Runagate Runagate" are only two of Hayden's magnificent poems. Other poems in the historical vein are "Frederick Douglass" (an experimental sonnet without rhyme), "The Ballad of Nat Turner" ("The fearful splendor of that warring"), "O Daedalus, Fly Away Home" ("Night is juba, night is conjo"), and "A Ballad of Remembrance" (a surrealistic, complex and erudite poem). Hayden poems (prior to *Words*) capture supernaturalism ("Witch Doctor"), folk life ("Homage to the Empress of the Blues," "The Burly Fading One," "Incense of the Lucky Virgin," and "Mourning Poem for the Queen of Sunday"), and folk reminiscences ("Summertime and the living . . . ," "The Whipping," "Those Winter Days").

Words in the Mourning Time, which we will return to briefly in Chapter VI, reflects Hayden's general and specific concerns as a poet. Again he judiciously handles the spectrum of themes, subjects and styles that assures him a place in the world of Western as well as Afro-American poetry. Such poems as " 'Mystery Boy' Looks for Kin in Nashville," "Soledad," "Aunt Jemima of the Ocean Waves," and "El-Hajj Malik El-Shabazz," show Hayden is in touch with the times and willing to share his poetic vision with revolutionaries, pacifists, cultural nationalists and black-pride advocates. On the other hand, he is at home with poems such as "Locus," "Zeus over Redeye," and "Lear Is Gay"—which mirror his reading, travels, broad concerns, and personal friendships. Hayden

admits that the battle over aesthetics in the 1960s jolted
him. And while it is clear that the fight took place more
outside of poetry than in (see Chapter VI), Hayden has
not recanted in his position that the black poet must not
be limited to racial utterance. Hayden, of course, has his
right to his own opinion. But, like John Ciardi, Richard
Wilbur, Robert Lowell, and other poets of the academy,
his trek has not been easy or devoid of controversy. And
despite statements Hayden makes outside his poetry, such
poems as "Middle Passage" and "Runagate Runagate"
stamp him as a gifted handler of *black* themes and materials. Since he is an Afro-American poet, it is not likely
that he will be known for work that lies drastically outside
the passage, pace or plight of black Americans.

Much-needed critical attention is just beginning to
come to Hayden. He is treated in Davis' *From the Dark
Tower*, Gibson's *Modern Black Poets* (Charles T. Davis,
"Robert Hayden's Use of History"), Jackson and Rubin's
Black Poetry in America, O'Brien's *Interview with Black
Writers*, Barksdale and Kinnamon's *Black Writers of
America*, and *How I Write/I*, (Hayden, Judson Phillips,
Lawson Carter, 1972). See also Rosey Pool's "Robert
Hayden, Poet Laureate," *Negro Digest* (*Black World*),
XV (June 1966), 39–43; D. Galler's "Three Recent Vol-
umes," *Poetry*, CX (1967), 268, and Julius Lester's re-
view of *Words in the Mourning Time* in the New York
Times Book Review, January 24, 1971, p. 4. Dudley Ran-
dall displays good insights into Hayden in "The Black
Aesthetic in the Thirties, Forties, and Fifties" (*Modern
Black Poets*); there is also a sensitive treatment of the
poet in James O. Young's *Black Writers of the Thirties*.
Finally Michael Harper reviews *Angle of Ascent* in the
New York *Times Book Review*, February 22, 1976, pp.
34–35.

Having helped make the Harlem Renaissance, Langston
Hughes continued his vast and imaginative poetic output
into the thirties, forties, fifties, and sixties. He published
four books of poetry in the 1930s, three in the 1940s, two
in the 1950s, and two in the 1960s, in addition to dozens
of short stories, essays, novels, plays, and autobiographical
writings. These things he accomplished along with his
travels and his dedicated work on behalf of Blacks. But it
would be "much too casual," notes Hughes's friend Bontemps, simply to dismiss him as "prolific." For Hughes

was a "minstrel and a troubador in the classic sense."
(Donald C. Dickinson, *A Bio-bibliography of Langston
Hughes, 1902–1967*, Hamden, Conn., 1972) Hughes
worked rapidly, turning out prodigious amounts of writing, a fact, Blyden Jackson reminds us, that caused some
to deny him a place alongside such "serious" black writers
as Ellison, Wright and Baldwin.

Hughes always involved himself in "contemporary
affairs"—even during the renaissance, when Cullen,
McKay, and others roamed the Elysian fields of Africa and
France or pined away in the "dark tower." This tendency
was part of the reason why Redding (*To Make a Poet
Black*) complained that Hughes employed rhythms in his
poetry but little intellect. True, his early work is experimental and not uniformly good; but it opened important
new roads. And the thirties and forties—with their step-up
in radical activities—placed Hughes in the position of having to forge even newer protest weapons from his "weary
blues." James O. Young noted: "His poetry was popular
because it could be read easily by people of all ages and
backgrounds." In the sixties, similar comments would be
made of the new black poets: Haki R. Madhubuti (Don
L. Lee), Sonia Sanchez, Niki Giovanni, David Nelson,
Arthur Pfister. These writers and others, questions of
aesthetics aside, contributed immensely, like Hughes before them, to the popularizing of black poetry.

In his early years, however, Hughes's poetry was considered "decadent" and "unacceptable" to Communist critics, who wanted him to shift from strict racial themes
and champion the fights of proletarians everywhere.
Hughes made the switch-over, and works like *Scottsboro
Limited* (1932) show the impact that Communist
thought had on him. The pamphlet was dedicated to
black youths on trial for allegedly raping two white prostitutes in Scottsboro, Alabama. Hughes places the boys
alongside such revolutionary saints as John Brown, Lenin
and Nat Turner. The effect—resembling aborted efforts
of some martyr-making poets of the 1960s—was to make
the boys, "ignorant pawns" though they were, "militant
proletarian heroes." The poem-play "Scottsboro Limited"
shows "Red Voices" convincing black youths that the
Communists are on the side of

Not just black—but black and white.

Hughes published widely during the thirties in Party presses. In *Good Morning Revolution* (1973, foreword by Saunders Redding), Faith Berry has compiled his "uncollected writings of social protest." They give many clues to Hughes's social concerns during the three decades following the Harlem Renaissance. He called for a union of "workers" in Germany, China, Africa, Poland, Italy, and America—through the pages of *New Masses, The Negro Worker, The Crisis, Opportunity, International Literature, Contempo, Africa South, The Workers Monthly, New Theatre,* and *American Spectator*. In "Good Morning Revolution," he tells personified revolution:

We gonna pal around together from now on.

Section titles of *Good Morning Revolution* show Hughes to be acutely attuned to the problems and needs of oppressed peoples—long before Frantz Fanon, Stokely Carmichael, and Eldridge Cleaver—and in sympathy with Third World struggle: Section 1, Revolution; Section 2, Memo to Non-White Peoples; Section 3, The Rich and the Poor; Section 4, War and Peace; Section 5, Goodbye Christ; Section 6, The Sailor and the Steward; Section 7, The Meaning of Scottsboro; Section 8, Cowards from the Colleagues; Section 9, Portrait Against Background; Section 10, Darkness in Spain; Section 11, *China*; Section 12, The American Writers Congress, and Section 13, Retrospective (including "My Adventures as a Social Poet"). Iconoclastic and sacrilegious, Hughes incurred the wrath of many black leaders with his poem "Goodbye Christ," published in the Baltimore *Afro-American* in 1932. Addressing Christ, Hughes noted:

You did alright in your day, I reckon—
But that day's gone now.

And "Christ Jesus Lord God Jehovah" is told to "make way" for a new deity, who has no religion, and whose name is

Marx Communist Lenin Peasant Stalin, Worker,
    ME. . . .

Religious leaders especially condemned Hughes's "blatant atheism." But Melvin Tolson, coming to Hughes's aid, said that the young poet was simply showing that the Christian offering of a better life after death had little meaning for the world's suffering millions.

Hughes was never a member of the Communist Party, but his works showed heavy proletarian influences, like those of many other black writers of his era: Tolson, Wright, Hayden, Frank Marshall Davis, Margaret Walker, Ellison. While his poetry and other writings of Communist-oriented social protest were appearing in radical publications, Hughes continued, like Sterling Brown, developing and experimenting with black folk materials. He painstakingly pointed up the contradictions in the promises and realities of American democracy, assailed social inequality, lamented black and white poverty, railed against double standards, attacked racial segregation, satirized the black bourgeoisie, and immortalized the beauty of everyday Blacks. Much of Hughes's fight is condensed into "Let America Be America Again," first published in 1936 in *Esquire* and included in *A New Song* (1938). It is immediately reminiscent of Walt Whitman—in its sweep —and recites, in the manner of Hayden's "Speech" and Tolson's "Rendezvous with America," the multiple ills and ingredients of America. Throughout the poem, as he catalogues the various ethnic stocks and contributions, he interpolates the haunt-refrain: "America never was America to me."

By the late forties Hughes's interest in black music and folk materials was being worked more artfully into his poetry. He carried his interest in blues to his work in jazz (later recording his poetry with Charlie Mingus and others), and the bebop era is strongly reflected in his poetry and his writings (see the Simple stories). Especially is music evident in *Montage of a Dream Deferred* (1951), in which, according to Wagner, "jazz has strongly influenced the tone and structure of these poems." The most famous poem in the volume is "Harlem," in which the black American is likened to a "dream deferred." Hughes draws explicit comparisons between raisins, sores, rotten meat, syrupy sweets, heavy loads, and the ever-present "dream." Perhaps, Hughes notes at the end, the dream will "explode."

Hughes was not "perfect"; he remained an experimenter throughout his writing career. *Ask Your Mama—Twelve Moods for Jazz* (1961) was published after forty years of experimentation in verse forms. It is indeed the attempt at the synthesis we referred to earlier: that of jazz, blues and related folk idioms and themes. Contemporary white poets E. E. Cummings and Kenneth Rexroth had chosen to place all letters in lower case; Hughes did just the opposite, capitalizing everything. Dedicated to Louis Armstrong—"the greatest horn blower of them all"—the volume is an extension of ideas attempted in *The Weary Blues, Shakespeare in Harlem,* and *Montage of a Dream Deferred.* The driving social protest is there, but the indignation is muted, as in his early work. A recession in larger America

IS COLORED FOLKS' DEPRESSION.

The work is punctuated by the line "IN THE QUARTER OF THE NEGROES," and Hughes continues the black poet's concern with history: honoring black heroes and race leaders, displaying the beauty of blackness and recalling the rites of passage. *Ask Your Mama* also includes extensive notes on staging and musical accompaniment for the poems.

Politician, organizer of sharecroppers, poet, dramatist, teacher and raconteur, Melvin Beaunorus Tolson was born in Moberly, Missouri to the Reverend Mr. and Mrs. Alonzo Tolson. Tolson lived his young life in various Missouri towns, publishing his first poem at the age of twelve in the "Poet's Corner" of the Oskaloosa newspaper. He graduated from Kansas City's Lincoln High School (1918) where he had been class poet, director and actor in the Greek Club's Little Theater and captain of the football team. Throughout his adult life, Tolson maintained an active interest in sports, dramatics and debating clubs. He attended Fisk and Lincoln universities—graduating from Lincoln with honors and winning awards in speech, debating, dramatics, and classical literatures. He also captained the football team at Lincoln.

In 1924 Tolson, commencing a rich and varied career, began teaching English and speech at Wiley College, in Marshall, Texas. There he wrote prose and poetry and directed a drama group and a debating group that established a ten-year winning streak. Tolson interrupted his work at Wiley to pursue an M.A. in English and comparative literature at Columbia University, where he met V. F. Calverton, editor of *The Modern Quarterly*. Later, in 1935, at Wiley, Tolson's career as a debating coach peaked when his team defeated the national champions, University of Southern California, before eleven hundred people. And in 1947, the same year Tolson was appointed poet laureate of Liberia by President V. S. Tubman, he became English and drama professor at Langston University, Langston, Oklahoma, of which city he served as mayor for four terms. At Langston he directed the Dust Bowl Players and dramatized novels by Walter White and George Schuyler. A revered and feared teacher and organizer, Tolson became a legend in his own time. Hardly a student at any Deep South black college had not heard of Tolson's work as poet, dramatist, debating coach and educator. His column "Cabbages and Caviar" was a regular in the Washington *Tribune* during the thirties.

Tolson published three volumes of poetry: *Rendezvous with America* (1944), *Libretto for the Republic of Liberia* (1953), and *Harlem Gallery, Book I: The Curator* (1965), and wrote a number of unpublished novels and plays. His work appeared in *The Modern Quarterly, Atlantic Monthly, Common Ground, Poetry*, and other periodicals. He won numerous awards and citations, among them first place (1939) in the National Poetry Contest sponsored by the American Negro Exposition in Chicago (for "Dark Symphony"); the Omega Psi Phi Award for Creative Literature (1945); *Poetry* magazine's Bess Hokim Award for the long psychological poem "E. & O.E." (1947); honorary doctorate in letters, Lincoln University (1954); permanent Bread Loaf Fellow in poetry and drama (1954); District of Columbia Citation and Award for Cultural Achievement in Fine Arts (1955); first appointment to the Avalon Chair in Humanities at Tuskegee Institute (1965); and the annual poetry award of the American Academy of Arts and Letters, including a grant of twenty-five hundred dollars (1966), the same year he died following three operations for abdominal cancer.

As a black poet and intellectual in the mid-twentieth

century, Tolson assumed the multi-leveled stance of his eighteenth- and nineteenth-century predecessors (Prince Hall, Benjamin Banneker, James Whitfield, Alexander Crummell, Frances E. W. Harper, and others) who served as teachers, abolitionists, revolutionists, defenders of what they believed to be decent in the promise of America, and character models for black communities. Tolson's predecessors fought for the right to be called humans; he fought the battle of integration. As Tolson lay dying, other, younger poets were fighting the battle of self-determination—albeit using the same tools employed by poets and intellectuals of the previous two centuries. So it is indeed ironic (and sad!) when a young writer like Haki R. Madhubuti (Don L. Lee) complains that Tolson is not accessible to the everyday reader (see review of *Kaleidoscope*, *Negro Digest*, January 1968). But Joy Flasch points out (*Melvin B. Tolson*, 1972) that Tolson was aware that he was not writing for the "average" reader but for the "vertical" audience. In "Omega" of *Harlem Gallery*, Tolson asks if a serious artist should "skim the milk of culture" and give those demanding immediacy and relevancy

a popular latex brand?

Tolson did not live, as did Hayden, Brown, Redding, and others, to make close contact with proponents of the "black aesthetic" of the 1960s. But some *opponents* have continued to rake him over the coals of *responsibility*. Black poet Sarah Webster Fabio (*Negro Digest*, December 1966), challenged Karl Shapiro's statement (Introduction to *Harlem Gallery*) that Tolson "writes in Negro." His poetic language is "most certainly not 'Negro,'" she averred, noting that it is "a bizarre, pseudoliterary diction" taken from stilted "American mainstream" poetry, "where it rightfully and wrongmindedly belonged." White critics and writers joining in the assault on Tolson included Laurence Lieberman and Englishman Paul Bremen (of the Heritage Series). Lieberman takes exception to Shapiro's statement, saying that he teaches black students from all over the world who are steeped in black language but do not understand Tolson (review of *Harlem Gallery*, *The Hudson Review*, Autumn 1965). Yet Tolson's publishers had high hopes that he might get

the Pulitzer Prize for *Libretto*; and Gwendolyn Brooks,
who sided in the late 1960s with proponents of the black
aesthetic, said she thought *Harlem Gallery* should have received the award.

Rewriting and rethinking his poetry over a period of
decades, Tolson became more difficult as he made adjust-
ments to fit modernist trends in poetry. The stars of English poetry were Eliot, Pound, Yeats, Crane, and Stevens,
and Tolson admired and patterned his work after them.
Yet throughout his poetic life, he maintained an "enormous love for people," which was reflected in his everyday
work as well as in his poetry. The title *Rendezvous with
America* indicates Tolson's commitment to love and do
battle with America. America has cancer and promise, and
Tolson performed operations while he feasted on his nation's delights. His title poem, "Rendezvous with
America," reflects the Whitman influence and Tolson's
awesome word skills, technical virtuosity and musical ear.
He enumerates the races and types of people who also
must rendezvous with America. He sees how

Time unhinged the gates

to allow the beginning of America, noting such landmarks
as Plymouth Rock, Jamestown, and Ellis Island, which he
juxtaposes with such ancient sites as Sodom, Gomorrah,
Cathay, Cipango, and El Dorado. The "searchers" came
to America, which is

. . . the Black Man's country,
The Red Man's, the Yellow Man's,
The Brown Man's, the White Man's.

America flows, Tolson believes, as

An international river with a legion of tributaries!
A magnificent cosmorama with myriad patterns of
    colors!
A giant forest with loin-roots in a hundred lands!
A cosmopolitan orchestra with a thousand instruments
    playing
                        America!

His manipulation of traditional form, coupled with what
he called the Three S's—"biology, psychology . . . sociol-

ogy," or the synchronizing of *sight* and *sound* and *sense* in a poem—yielded much poetic fruit in his long years of writing and rewriting his poetry. *Rendezvous with America* is not a great first book, but it marked him as an able handler of unique verse forms. His major themes (history, black presence in the world, religion, hatred for class structures, and the plight of the underdog) are stated in a variety of forms: sonnets, rhymed quatrains, ballads, free-verse forms, and special two-syllable lines. Known as an iconoclast, Tolson used his poetry to de-stool pomposity and those who manipulated everyman's sufferings from behind a cloak of high office.

Music and art inform much of his poetry—another reason why his allusory writing has been criticized—as in "Rendezvous" and "Dark Symphony," the most popular poem in his first book. In "Rendezvous," in addition to his musical structures, he lists America's melodies by associating factories, express trains, power dams, river boats, coal mines, and lumber camps with musical terminology: "allegro," "blues rhapsody," "bass crescendo," "diatonic picks," and "belting harmonics." "Dark Symphony," immediately musical and radical in its title, is separated into parts along musical lines and terminology: Part I: Allegro Moderato; Part II, Lento Grave; Part III, Andante Sostenuto; Part IV, Tempo Primo; and Part V, Larghetto. "*Rendezvous*" and "*Dark Symphony*" are patterned after the ode from (which Tolson would expand on in *Libretto* and *Harlem Gallery*). "Dark Symphony" carries the same theme as "Rendezvous"—people pitted against their injustices—but the latter poem is more racial in flavor and subject matter. Located, temporally and spiritually, between the concerns of Whitman (the "yawp") and John Steinbeck (*Grapes of Wrath*), "Dark Symphony" opens by reminding Americans that "Black Crispus Attucks" (Boston Massacre) died for them

Before white Patrick Henry's bugle breath

asked for liberty over death. A strongly masculine poem (as is so much of Tolson's work), it moves robustly to recite the deeds of "Men black and strong." Part II tells of the "slaves singing" in the "torture tombs" of ships in the middle passage, the swamps, the "cabins of death," and "canebreaks." In the remaining parts, the black American, speaking through the collective "we," vows not to "forget" that "Golgotha" has been trod or that "The Bill of Rights is burned." The new Negro wears "seven-league" boots and springs from a tradition that produced Nat Turner, Joseph Cinque ("Black Moses of the Amistad Mutiny"), Frederick Douglass, Sojourner Truth, and Harriet Tubman ("Saint Bernard of the Underground Railroad"). *Grapes of Wrath* and *Native Son* are invoked as indexes to the suffering and the breeding of slums. And, finally, the historical concerns of the black poet:

> Out of abysses of Illiteracy,
> Through labyrinths of Lies,
> Across waste lands of Disease . . .
> We advance!

Brilliant, esoteric, complex, innovative, and able to span the world of black folk idiom and academic intellectualism, Tolson always punctuates his undaunted lyricism with ribald humor and thigh-slapping uproariousness. However, Paul Bremen disparagingly referred to Tolson as posturing "for a white audience . . . with an ill-conceived grin and a wicked sense of humor . . . an entertaining darky using almost comically big words as the best wasp tradition demands of its educated house-niggers." (Maybe, one might suggest, Tolson was "even" too deep for the Englishman Bremen.) Nevertheless, the poets of the academy apparently loved Tolson, and more than one of them tried to get him deserved recognition before he died. William Carlos Williams saluted Tolson in his fourth book of *Paterson*; Allen Tate wrote a now famous preface to *Libretto*; Shapiro introduced *Harlem Gallery*, launching Tolson into the same *curious* fame that Howells brought to Dunbar seventy years before; Robert Frost, Stanley Edgar Hyman, Seldom Rodman, John Ciardi, and Theodore Roethke all tried to "bring Tolson to the general literary consciousness, but with little success" (Shapiro).

Tolson's severest critics usually have in mind *Libretto* or *Harlem Gallery*. *Rendezvous* has been out of print for several years and many of the younger black poets and scholars have not read it. But any casual look at Tolson's work will confirm reports that he is not digestible in a single reading. Even before the erudition of *Libretto* and *Harlem Gallery*, Tolson accustomed himself to the allusion. Indeed, his strongest weapon is the literary or historical reference—the mark of the library poet, the learned person. In "An Ex-Judge at the Bar" Tolson is at his finest as he juxtaposes humor, allusion, and irony with philosophy and social commentary. This ex-judge is at a "drinking" bar. And rich in oral power, like most of Tolson's poetry, the poem surveys the history of a white man who, after serving in the war and returning home to become a judge, is shown guilt-ridden in a tavern, where he discusses his life with the bartender. The opening couplet:

> Bartender, make it straight and make it two—
> One for the you in me and one for the me in you . . .

reflects the black American's dexterousness with oral language and Tolson's rich background as storyteller and debating coach. The couplet contains the kind of musical, seemingly nonsensical statement that black men love to exchange during fierce verbal sparring matches—even though the judge is presumably white. Drunk, the judge relives his war experiences and, in a vision, sees the "Goddess Justice," whom someone "blindfolds"; meanwhile the lawyers railroad defendants before him. But Justice "unbandaged" her eyes and accused the judge of lynching a black man to "gain the judge's seat," even though, ironically, he fought in the last war to "make the world safe for Democracy." The judge, seeking consolation and implying that no one is perfect, is finally moved to self-evaluation, repents and orders another round of drinks:

> Bartender, make it straight and make it three—
> One for the Negro . . one for you and me.

"An Ex-Judge at the Bar"—with its ironies and *double-entendres* in the very title—is a poem that slips away from the reader. One thinks, though one is never sure, that one has the meaning under control. The poem refers to Caesar, Pontius Pilate, the Koran, the Sahara, "September Morn" (a painting by American Paul Chabas), French words, Flanders field, and Macduff in Shakespeare's *Mac-*

beth. Certainly these are not the ideal ingredients for a poem directed to the "people." On the other hand, for the reader ready to do battle with history and world knowledge, Tolson proves quite rewarding. Dudley Randall ("The Black Aesthetic in the Thirties, Forties, and Fifties," in *Modern Black Poets*) states, with a strained air of seriousness: "If the reader has a well-stored mind, or is willing to use dictionaries, encylopedias, atlases, and other reference books," Tolson's work "should present no great difficulty."

Randall had in mind, specifically, *Libretto*, a section of which appeared in *Poetry* along with the book's preface. In this long poem—constructed loosely around an ode form—Tolson celebrates Liberia's centennial. According to Randall, "Tolson used all the devices dear to the New Criticism: recondite allusions, scraps of foreign languages, African proverbs, symbolism, objective correlatives. Many parts of the poem are obscure, not through some private symbolism of the author, but because of the unusual words, foreign phrases, and learned allusions." Randall goes on to point out that reading *Libretto* is like reading other "learned poets, such as Milton and T. S. Eliot."

However, reading Tolson is not *exactly* like reading other learned poets, for he places black information in front of the reader. He bends the ode into an Afro-American musical structure and celebrates the black past. Continuing a pattern set in such poems as "Rendezvous with America" and "Dark Symphony," Tolson separates *Libretto* along the lines of the Western musical scale: Do, Re, Mi, Fa, Sol, La, Ti, Do. Specifically, *Libretto* acknowledges the one hundredth birthday of Liberia, founded in 1847 by the American Colonization Society for free men of color. "Rooted in the Liberian mentality as fact and symbol," *Libretto* traverses the kaleidoscopic range of African history: the magnificent ancient and medieval kingdoms, European exploitation, various theories as to the reason for the question-mark shape of Africa, the origins of black stereotypes, Africa's contributions to the world, the impact of Christianity, Islam and other religions. All this Tolson does with what Allen Tate calls "a great gift of language, a profound historical sense, a first-rate intelligence." Tate also pondered, as did Emanuel and Gross (*Dark Symphony*, 1968), "what influence this work will have upon Negro poetry in the United States." More than slightly recalling Howells in his endorsement of Dunbar, Tate says: "For the first time, it seems to me, a Negro poet has assimilated completely the full poetic language of his time and, by implication, the language of the Anglo-American tradition."

Relentlessly posing the one-word question "Liberia?" and reinforcing the nation's existence in "fact and symbol," Tolson opens *Libretto* with lofty erudition and color. The fifth stanza of Do, after the initial "Liberia?" and accompanying recitation of what the nation is *not*, addresses its citizens thusly:

> You are
> Black Lazarus risen from the White Man's grave,
>   Without a road to Downing Street,
> Without a hemidemisemiquaver in an Oxford stave!

Later, in section, Re, Tolson excerpts a chant from "The Good Gray Bard of Timbuktu":

> *"Wanawake wanazaa ovyo! Kazi Yenu Wanzungu!"*

Hayden has been called one of the most skilled craftsmen since Countee Cullen, but Tolson without a doubt has sustained the more powerful poetry which adheres rigorously to the tenets of the modernists. His *Libretto* is the drama of *"The Desert Fox"* and the German "goose-step" across Africa (Mi); of the snake, "eyeless, yet with eyes" (Fa); of "White Pilgrims" and "Black Pilgrims" who sing "O Christ" that the worst will "pass"! (Sol); of "Leopard, elephant, ape" and "A white man spined with dreams" (La); of a "Calendar of the Country" to "red-letter the Republic's birth!" (Ti); and of "a professor of metaphysicotheologicocosmonigology" who is also

> a tooth puller a pataphysicist in a cloaca of error
> a belly's wolf a skull's tabernacle a ♯13 with stars
>   a muses' darling a busie bee *de sac et de corde*
>   a neighbor's bed-shaker a walking hospital on
>   the walk. . . . (Second Do)

The symbols, the syntax, the grammar and the language
tumble on placing

Quai d'Orsay,
White House,
  Kremlin,
Downing Street . . .

in the catalogue while

Again black Aethiop reaches at the sun, O Greek (Ti).

The history of world wars, the gossip in high circles ("Il
Duce's Whore"), the concoction of innumerable languages, and book-buried erudition, reveal Tolson as a complex and difficult modern poet. The tragedy, Randall and
others have pointed out, is that as Tolson wrote *Libretto*
and *Harlem Gallery*, white scions of the modern verse
were turning their backs on erudition for a more common,
everyday language in poetry. Trapped in the middle (he
held on to *Harlem Gallery* for more than thirty years),
Tolson continued to labor in the best tradition of the
modern poetry to the disbelief of contemporaries—who,
like Cummings, Rexroth, and Hughes, were influenced by
bebop and a freer language structure. Tolson's sustained
scholarship and complex allusions are reinforced by the
addition of scores of footnotes, which cite the works of
such as Dryden, Shakespeare, Emerson, Tennyson,
Lorenzo Dow Turner (*Africanisms in the Gullah Dialects*), J. A. Rogers (*Sex and Race*), Firdousi, Gunnar
Myrdal, Aeschylus, Boccaccio, Baudelaire, and hundreds of
others. The work ends (Do) in a use of mystical and technological symbols that examine "Futurafrique" and "tomorrow . . . O . . . Tomorrow."

Tolson's career is a terrifying example of the confusion
that can occur in the black literary artist. When he first
sent the manuscript of *Libretto* to Tate (who had been
across town at Vanderbilt with the "Fugitive" poets while
Tolson was at Fisk), the white poet rejected it, saying he
was not interested in "propanganda from a Negro poet."
(Flasch). Tolson then diligently rewrote the manuscript
to subscribe to the bizarre intellectual, technical, and
scholarly demands of the modern poets (Tate, John
Crowe Ransom, Eliot, Pound, Robert Penn Warren,

Donald Davidson, and others). He sent the manuscript back to Tate, who agreed to endorse it. In 1920, Tolson had stumbled upon a copy of Sandburg's "Chicago" but was warned by a professor to "leave that stuff alone" (Flasch). His maturation as a poet, then, was stunted—causing him to spend thirty years searching for his own voice.

Harlem Gallery (the first of a planned five-volume epic) provides another example of the chaos in Tolson's poetic life. In 1932, he completed a 340-page manuscript called "A Gallery of Harlem Portraits," which was turned down by publishers. When the derivative ode *Harlem Gallery* was finally brought out in 1966, Tolson had published two newer manuscripts: *Rendezvous* and *Libretto*. *Harlem Gallery* had been placed in the poet's "trunk" for twenty years—a period during which he switched from the Romantics and Victorians (and Masters, after whose *Spoon River Anthology* "Portraits" was modeled) to the Moderns. Tolson said he then "read and absorbed the techniques of Eliot, Pound, Yeats, Baudelaire, Pasternak and, I believe, all the great moderns. God only knows how many "little magazines" I studied, and how much textual analysis (sic) of the New Critics."

A staggering poem, *Harlem Gallery* "is a work of art, a sociological commentary, an intellectual triple somersault." (Flasch). It meets the vigorous intellectual, scholarly, and stylistic whims of modern poetry, but at the same time is "impossible to describe." Yet it is Tolson's crowning achievement in more ways than one. First it continues his fascination with black and general history. Second, it pursues his intense interest in the psychodynamics of both the Afro-American character and the artist; he is particularly concerned with the plight of the twentieth-century black artist (hence *Book I, The Curator*). Third, it provides one of the most powerful and authentic links between the Harlem Renaissance and the Black Arts Movement of the 1960s and 1970s. The very title of *Harlem Gallery* gives it a black setting; and the fact of its being conceived and initially drafted during the renaissance indicates that Tolson labored over the years (from the standpoint of memory, technique, and subject matter) in the afterglow of the literary flowering watered by

McKay, Cullen, Toomer, Hughes, Fisher, Johnson, and Locke. Finally, the characters in *Harlem Gallery* are black: the Curator, Doctor Nkomo (Bantu expatriate and Africanist), Mr. Guy Delaporte (president of Bola Bola Enterprises), Black Orchid (blues singer and mistress to Delaporte), the half-blind Harlem artist John Laugart, Black Diamond (ghetto promoter of the Lenox Avenue policy racket), and Hideho Heights (the light-skinned poet of Lenox Avenue).

The Curator of the Harlem Gallery is an admixture (continuing concerns begun in *Rendezvous*) of races ("Afroirishjewish"), an octoroon who passes for black in New York and white in Mississippi. He is a digestion of the humor and pathos Blacks see in those of their race who attempt to "pass." Tolson noted that since thousands of light-skinned Blacks passed over, there is a standing joke among Blacks that asks, "What white man is white?" *Harlem Gallery*, then, is designed to parade the black "types" (ultimately Everyman types) through the gallery of life as it is shaped by the view of the literary genius: Tolson. Specifically, the book is a huge answer to Gertrude Stein's charge that the "Negro suffers from nothingness." All of his poetic life, Tolson worked to reconstruct black history. Now, in *Harlem Gallery*, he was coming with speed and poetic precision from his corner of the syntactic and semantic ring to do battle with Miss Stein's charge. In the Introduction to *Harlem Gallery*, Shapiro explains in part the reason why Gertrude Stein would herself be so ignorant. Whites do not get a chance to read about black achievement, since "Poetry as we know it remains the most lily-white of the arts." *Libretto* may have pulled "the rug out from under the poetry of the Academy," but "*Harlem Gallery* pulls the house down around their ears." Assailing Eliot and others for "purifying the language," Shapiro praised Tolson for "complicating it, giving it the gift of tongues."

Tolson certainly gave *Harlem Gallery* the "gift of tongues." He uses tidbits from the range of world languages; but his work is more sustained and coherent than in *Libretto*. Both story line and language are more accessible in *Gallery*—with its interpolation of rich black speech and musical terminology into stilted academic language and form. Set up musically, with each section bearing the

A LONG WAYS FROM HOME

name of a letter of the Greek alphabet, *Gallery* shows Tolson again displaying his amazing technical virtuosity and his merger of an ode form with related black orally derived structures: blues, jazz, spirituals, folk epics, and oral narratives ("Satchmo" in Lambda, "The Birth of John Henry" in Xi). The verse pattern in *Gallery* owes some debt to Do in *Libretto*, with its tapered typography and irregular line organization which forces the reader to either speed up or slow down to catch the rhyme. Alpha opens describing the spice of Harlem as "an Afric pepper bird," before the Curator tells us:

> I travel, from oasis to oasis, man's Saharic
> up-and-down.

The grand sweep and intellectual storage of Tolson are gathered from line to line, between lines, in the margins, around and throughout the poem. Recalling the verbal jousting in "An Ex-Judge at the Bar," the Curator assesses his "I-ness," his "humanness" and his "Negroness," and this recipe

> mixes with the pepper bird's reveille in my brain
> where the plain is twilled and twilled is plain.

The academic stilts are shortened for the sake of understanding (Beta):

> one needs the clarity
> the comma gives the eye,
> not the head of the hawk
> swollen with rye.

Like Hayden's "Middle Passage," *Gallery* views the physical and spiritual predicament of the black man: what has he gone through, how much more can/will he take, how long? How long? The answer is that man may have to endure suffering forever—but if he is doomed to suffer, he is likewise "doomed" to survive. The Curator is told that others have suffered and survived. The Afro-American and the artist create in their suffering. So the "Afroirishjewish Grandpa" of the Curator (Gamma) tells him:

> "Between the dead sea Hitherto
> and the promised land Hence
> looms the wilderness Now:

> although his confidence
> is often a boar bailed up
> on a ridge, *somehow,*
> the Attic salt in man survives the blow
> of Attila, Croesus, Iscariot,
> and the Witches Sabbath in the Catacombs of Bosio."

Certainly this survival theme is close to the heart of the
Afro-American and the artist. Artists are often among the
first to plead for clemency, for free expression, for truth.
The spirituals and the vast body of folk expression reaffirm
the Afro-American's faith in man and the quest for survival. Acknowledging this aspect of black expression and
strength, Tolson (and Hayden: "Mean mean mean to be
free.") incorporates the rich blast of folk materials. In
heaven (Lambda), Gabriel announces:

> *"I'd be the greatest trumpeter in the Universe,*
> *if old Satchmo had never been born!"*

And the birth of John Henry is an epic birth—akin to
that of Jesus, Buddha, Muhammad, and others.

> *The night John Henry is born an ax*
> *of lightning splits the sky,*
> *and a hammer of thunder pounds the earth,*
> *and the eagles and panthers cry!*

Reciting a soul-food menu at birth, John Henry

> *Says: "I want some ham hocks, ribs, and jowls,*
> *a pot of cabbage and greens;*
> *some hoecakes, jam, and butter milk,*
> *a platter of pork and beans!"* (Xi)

Tolson remains at home in synchronizing the Afro-
American and Western heritages. In *Gallery* his forte is
still the literary allusion juxtaposed with history or religion
(as in *Libretto*), but he loves to ascend the stuffy mountain of academia and then suddenly drop into the midst of
ghetto fury. He moves (Zeta) from thoughts that tilt like
"long Nepalese eyes" to a "catacomb Harlem flat"

> (grotesquely vivisected like microscoped maggots)

to the "Elite Chitterling Shop" (Eta), which contains the
"variegated dinoceras of a jukebox" (singing the "ambiva-

lence of classical blues"). Meanwhile, Doctor Obi Nkomo, "the alter ego" of the gallery, speaks

Across an alp of chitterlings, pungent as epigrams. . . .

The doctor returns to the theme of survival and free expression:

> "The lie of the artist is the only lie
>   for which a mortal or a god should die."

Tolson's ever-present need to synthesize (and yet separate) the three ingredients of man (biology, sociology and psychology—extending into the three S's: *sight, sound* and *sense*) recurs in the poem (Eta) as the artists paint

> the seven panels of man's tridimensionality
>   in variforms and varicolors
>   since virtue has no Kelvin scale
>   since a mother breeds
>   no twins alike, . . .

and since no man who is

> judged by his biosocial identity
>   in toto
>   can be
>   a Kiefekil or a Tartufe,
>   an Iscariot or an Iago."

Hence Tolson extends, sometimes in camouflage, his ideas about man's similarities and differences. To be sure, he *is* saying that black men and white men *are* different— but that the differences are not significant enough to keep them from working together for the mutual good. This particular stand, which laces the work of Hayden, Tolson, Hughes, and early Gwendolyn Brooks, is not one that will remain popular among poets who subscribe to the black aesthetic of the 1960s. Nevertheless, Tolson dug underneath the hysteria and the ideological neatness to probe the time-honored questions about man. Psi (a much-anthologized section of *Gallery*) finds him doing battle with anthropologists, the D.A.R., the F.F.V. (First Families of Virginia), Uncle Tom, the Jim Crow sign, the Great White World, and Kant, in an attempt to answer the questions "Who is a Negro?" and "Who is a White?"

Tolson's work contains great satire—and great wisdom in the satire. To be misled by his incredible and dazzling wordplay is to miss the essential Tolson, who warned the coming generation that, although Uncle Tom was "dead," they should beware of his son: "Dr. Thomas." Suspicious of fame and wealth and desiring to see no man placed over another (in privilege), Tolson remarked after John Laugart's murder (Zeta) that among those things remaining were a bottle of gin

and infamy,
the Siamese twin
of fame.

Are we privileged, here, to see a sneak (thirty-year) preview of Watergate?

We do not know what would have been Tolson's fate as a poet had he come to his own comfortable style as a young man in the Harlem Renaissance. He was nearly fifty when he sent Tate the manuscript for *Libretto*. And fifty is quite an old age for a poet to be still at odds with his craft—or to have it overseen by a patronizing critic. Nevertheless Tolson, not admitted (as Shapiro noted of black poets) to the "polite company of the anthology," had to get his voice "together" without the immediate financial and emotional aid available to the "Fugitives" or those in other molding centers of the modern poetry. Few black poets at the time were attempting Tolson's feat—Blacks' interest in poetry declined during the forties and fifties—and there is much evidence that Tolson generally intimidated other black scholars and intellectuals with his vast knowledge and great talents. Like poets of other generations, he was a part-time poet, expending much of his energies on students and school-related work. Randall has pointed out that unless black poets imitate Tolson—and thus keep him apparent and interesting—he will not exert a major influence on Afro-American poetry. But, as Barksdale and Kinnamon note, a poet of Tolson's range and power cannot go unnoticed for long.

Criticism of Tolson is sparse. Joy Flasch's *Melvin B. Tolson*, in the Twayne United States Authors Series, offers good insights into Tolson's techniques. Barksdale and Kinnamon give brief criticism in *Black Writers of*

America. Randall appraises him in the article on black poets of three decades following the Harlem Renaissance and in his "Portrait of the Poet as Raconteur," *Negro Digest,* XV, 3 (January 1966), 54–57. See also "A Poet's Odyssey," an interview with Tolson (conducted by M. W. King) in *Anger, and Beyond* (1966) and reviews by Lieberman, Fabio and Lee.

Margaret Walker's poetry and life provide a rich and rewarding change in the writing activity of this period: *For My People* (1942) was the first book of poetry by a black woman since Georgia Douglas Johnson's volumes of the twenties; the poetry departed in theme and technique from the prevailing mood of poetry by black women; and she had the rare opportunity to fraternize, during her most impressionable years, with such Chicago-based writers as Wright, Davis, Fenton Johnson, and Hughes. Her experiences included the Depression, World War II, and McCarthyism—along with various racial and politically radical perspectives on contemporary life.

Margaret Walker was born in Birmingham, Alabama, the daughter of a Methodist-minister father and a schoolteacher mother, both university graduates. She attended church schools in Mississippi, Alabama, and Louisiana, and received her B.A. from Northwestern University in 1935. During the next four years, she worked as a typist, newspaper reporter, editor of a short-lived magazine, and with the Federal Writers' Project (like Hayden and Wright) in Chicago. In 1939 she entered the University of Iowa (after short stints as a social worker in Chicago and New Orleans), where she received an M.A. in 1940, her thesis being a collection of poems. She obtained a Ph.D. in creative writing from Iowa in 1965 after submitting *Jubilee,* a novel, in lieu of a dissertation. *Jubilee* received the Houghton Mifflin Literary Award in 1966 and has been translated into several languages. Between 1940 and 1965, Margaret Walker (Mrs. Firnist James Alexander and the mother of four children) was a professor of English at Livingston College in North Carolina, received the Yale Younger Poets Award in 1942 (*For My People*), was awarded a Rosenwald Fellowship for Creative Writing (1944), served as visiting professor at Northwestern University, and became a member of the English faculty at Jackson State College, where she is currently director of the Institute for the Study of History, Life, and Culture of Black People (since 1969). Arthur P. Davis says, "Miss Walker is a better poet than she is a novelist," and one can hardly quarrel with him.

In addition to *For My People*, she has sustained a high quality of poetry in *Prophets for a New Day* (1970) and *October Journey* (1973)—both published by Randall's Broadside Press in Detroit. Although some of the poems in *Prophets for a New Day* were begun in the thirties and forties, "most of them," according to the poet, were written during the sixties. Brief comment will be made on them in Chapter VI. "For My People," the title poem of her first book, first appeared in *Poetry* in 1937. Told by Owen Dodson at a College Language Association meeting (Howard University, in 1942) that she was winning the Yale Younger Poets Award, she recalls, she "had not even submitted" her manuscript and "thought he was crazy."

She had won, and her volume included a sensitive Foreword by Stephen Vincent Benét, who praised her "Straight-forwardness, directness, reality," and noted that such qualities are "good things to find in a young poet." Benét also observed:

> It is rarer to find them combined with a controlled intensity of emotion and a language that, at times, even when it is most modern, has something of the surge of biblical poetry. And it is obvious that Miss Walker uses that language because it comes naturally to her and is a part of her inheritance.

Indeed "inheritance" is the key word to unlocking the fruits and juices of Margaret Walker's poetic storeroom. Her own experiences, as the daughter of religious parents, of growing up in the South, of being nurtured on the oral tradition, of developing a careful and sympathetic ear for the folk expressions, are all served up again through the poet's "honesty," "sincerity," "candor," and tremendous technical abilities. Margaret Walker's verse does not employ the oblique, abstruse, and learned scalings sometimes evident in Hayden and Tolson. And she is quite at the opposite end of the spectrum from the ladylike lyrics of her predecessors: Anne Spencer, Gwendolyn Bennett and

Alice Dunbar-Nelson. Indeed when measured against the
tradition established by most of her female predecessors,
her work is startling. She certainly bears some kinship to
her forerunner-sisters—especially to Frances Harper in
theme and usage—but her language, lines, and narration
are more related to the work of black male poets Fenton
Johnson, Wright, James Weldon Johnson, Hughes, and
Davis, and white male poets Masters, Lindsay, and Sandburg.

During an exchange with Nikki Giovanni (A Poetic
Equation: Conversations Between Nikki Giovanni and
Margaret Walker, 1974), Margaret Walker said:

> But to get back to this business of language. In the
> twenties and thirties, for the first time we had the use of
> black speech from the streets. We were responsible for
> that particular urban idiom going into the American
> language.

And Nikki Giovanni answered with a perceptive observation:

> It was the first time because we were becoming urban. I
> think one of the things we forget when we start our cri-
> tiques is that we could not have had a street language
> earlier. Speech had been plantation and southern and
> rural. And as we moved to the cities during the migra-
> tion period, we developed a street language.

"I think that's an important point," Margaret Walker
noted, moving on to indebt herself and the whole modern
black poetic folk tradition to Hughes. So it is clear that
Margaret Walker, the Southerner, gleaned from "up"
South (Northern) Blacks the kinds of rich linguistic complements needed to draw the magnificent portraits in For
My People.

The title poem sets the tone of the book and establishes
the poet's intellectual, aesthetical, philosophical, and historical considerations: the acquisition and employment of
knowledge of her past; the exhortation of her people
("The Struggle Staggers Us," but "Out of this blackness
we must struggle forth"); the celebration specifically of
the black folk heritage and language; esteem for her religious (especially supernatural) and spiritual needs.

266   DRUMVOICES

Revealing in both its style and its content, "For My People" is a majestic poem containing the now-famous Whitman tapestry of words and ideas with a Tolsonian ordering of disorder:

> For my people everywhere singing their slave songs repeatedly: their dirges and their ditties and their blues and jubilees, praying their prayers nightly to an unknown god, bending their knees humbly to an unseen power; . . .

Continuing from this first stanza (note the similarity to Fenton Johnson's), the poem views "my people" adding their "strength" to the "gone years" and the "now years." It sees them, as it traverses the physical and spiritual history of Blacks, as "playmates" in Alabama "clay and dust"; as "black and poor and small and different"; as youths who "grew" to "marry their playmates" and "die of consumption"; as "thronging 47th Street in Chicago and Lenox Avenue in New York and Rampart Street in New Orleans"; as "walking blindly spreading joy"; as blundering and groping and floundering"; as "preyed on by facile force of state and fad and / novelty, by false prophet and holy believer"; and "as all the adams and eves."

Finally, in the last stanza, she gives this ringing cry for a more aggressive black push:

> Let a new earth rise. Let another world be born. Let a bloody peace be written in the sky. Let a second generation full of courage issue forth; let a people loving freedom come to growth. Let a beauty full of healing and a strength of final clenching be the pulsing in our spirits and our blood. Let the martial songs be written, let the dirges disappear. Let a race of men now rise and take control.

For My People is a small book (only twenty-six poems) but it is one of the most influential by a black poet.

"Dark Blood" follows the opening poem, reaffirming Margaret Walker's belief in the "forms of things unknown"—as Wright puts it. "Bizarre beginnings in old lands" constituted the "making of me." Luscious, succulent imagery unfolds: "sugar sands," "fern and pearl,"

"Palm jungles," "wooing nights," in contrast to the "one-room shacks of my old poverty." But the "blazing suns" of the poet's conjured-up birthplace will help

> reconcile the pride and pain in me.

Strongly reminiscent of the Harlem Renaissance poets' infatuation with Africa, but ending on the realistic note of the poet's localized "poverty," "Dark Blood" certainly meets Benét's notion of "reality."

The skepticism, the doubt, the scent of sacrilege—seen in poets from Dunbar forward—bring tension to "We Have Been Believers":

> . . . believing in our burdens and our
> demigods too long.

And now (recalling Dunbar's "Sympathy"), the "fists" of the believers "bleed"

> against the bars with a strange insistency.

The strength, begun in the first poem, is carried through "Southern Song" and "Sorrow Home." With incantation and incremental refrain, "Delta" tells of the collective "struggle." Strains of "Believers" course through "Since 1619," in which the poet again retraces the black odyssey:

> How long have I been hated and hating?

The speaker, longing to see the rich "color" of a "brother's face," assails racism, poverty, ignorance, and violence, and laments spiritual desolation. War, poverty, disease, and other heirs of the Depression are the themes of "Today," which speaks of "children scarred by bombs," "lynching," and "pellagra and silicosis."

A different "stride" of this poet is seen in the second section of For My People. "Molly Means," "Bad-Man Stagolee," "Poppa Chicken," "Kissie Lee," "Ralluh Hammuh," "Two-Gun Buster and Trigger Slim," "Teacher," "Gus, the Lineman," "Long John Nelson and Sweetie Pie," and "John Henry" are fresh treatments of authentic stories from black America. "A hag and a witch," Molly Means had seven husbands, and

> Some say she was born with a veil on her face. . . .

The incremental refrain ("Old Molly, Molly, Molly,"
etc.) gives dramatic and psychological thrust to the poem
as Molly's work with the "black-hand arts and her evil
powers" are catalogued. Stagolee, apparently "an all-right
lad,"

> Till he killed that cop and turned out bad,

quite possibly had killed "mor'n one" white man. The
"bad nigger" type found in all black communities is the
portrait drawn of Stagolee:

> Wid dat blade he wore unnerneaf his shirt. . . .

Stagolee mysteriously disappears, though his "ghost still"
stalks the shore of the Mississippi River. Poppa Chicken
was a pimp who, in the American tradition of black-on-
black crime, "got off light" for killing a man and

> Bought his pardon in a year. . . .

Also a black prototype, he had plenty women ("gals for
miles around"), expensive rings and watches, fancy
clothes, displayed a coolness ("Treat 'em rough"), and
when he walked the streets

> The Gals cried Lawdy! Lawd!

Kissie Lee is a throwback to Hard-Hearted Hannah (who
would "pour water on a drowning man,"):

> She could shoot glass doors offa the hinges. . . .

Ralluh Hammuh recalls Dolemite, Shine and others. He
was so "bad" that

> He killed his Maw of fright. . . .

The cultural folk types parade before our eyes, much after
the fashion of "Slim" and other characters in Sterling
Brown's *Southern Road*. Margaret Walker's contribution,
like Brown's, lies in the area of history and linguistics, for
both are accurate chroniclers. But she surpasses Brown in
her search for the verse forms to convey black folk life,
even though, ironically, there is little conscious portrayal
of women in her poems.

Big John Henry tales can be found in practically every

American community. Margaret Walker places her man in Mississippi, where he feasted on "buttermilk and sorghum." As a Big Boy type (Wright, Hughes and others), he assaults the world through physical prowess. He is the best cotton picker, stronger than a "team of oxen," the champion boxer; he can anchor a steamboat with "one hand," is taught by the "witches" how to "cunjer," and is undaunted until a "tenpoun' hammer" split "him open." The ballad, appropriately, is the primary technical vehicle for the poems in this section.

The third section of the book contains six sonnets, capturing remembrances and vignettes. The poet brings her own rhyme scheme, stanzaic pattern and line-stress variations to these pieces. "Childhood" recalls that of all the many human and natural pestilences that invaded the lives of the poor, including the "hatred" that "still held sway,"

. . . only bitter land was washed away.

"Whores" are told that their labors are undignified and warned (a dash of deep woman concern [feminism?]) that as they grow older they will find that their bodies, in this world of turbulence, will neither give "peace" to men nor "leave them satisfied." Ending, rightly it seems, with "The Struggle Staggers Us," *For My People* reminds Blacks that there is room to "stagger" but none to halt:

Struggle between the morning and night.
This marks our years; this settles, too, our plight.

There are few volumes of poetry published since *For My People* that can be considered any *blacker*—in the most complex sense of the word. From the red clay of the children's playgrounds to the teeming treachery of urban fuselages; from the quiet fear to the piercing cry of the hungry; from the deeply (unquestioningly) religious to the iconoclastic and the heretic; from the healthy racial to the good dose of modesty and naïveté—it is all there: a wonderful sensitivity and a rich bank of poetry for all times.

A link to the writers of the Harlem Renaissance, Margaret Walker has had contact with twenties poets Hughes, Bontemps, Fenton Johnson, and Gwendolyn Bennett, as

well as with later bards: Dodson, Hayden, Gwendolyn
Brooks, Margaret Danner, Margaret Burroughs, and Tolson. *For My People*, in the end, stands as the rich digestion (synthesis) of the main currents of the renaissance
and the aesthetic considerations being debated by Locke,
Cullen, Johnson, Brown, and Redding. Margaret Walker
may have produced the volume of poetry many of the
older writers wanted to write. Without being self-effacing
of black humanity, with no lessening or profaning of her
obvious self-love. Sterling Brown, in *Southern Road*,
avoided even mentioning Africa—perhaps because he was
weary of the romantic escapades of some Harlem Renaissance poets. But he deserves no special praise for that
aspect of his "vision."

More critical assessment of Margaret Walker's work is
needed. Barksdale and Kinnamon make important com-
ments in their anthology. Giovanni and Walker, *A Poetic
Equation*, (1974) is extremely helpful in getting to the
grit of the poet's ideas. There are seminal comments in
Paula Giddings' " 'A Shoulder Hunched Against a Sharp
Concern': Some Themes in the Poetry of Margaret
Walker," *Black World* XXI (December 1971), 20–25.
See also Whitlow's *Black American Literature*, Young's
Black Writers of the Thirties, Jackson's essay in *Black Poetry in America*, Gibson's *Modern Black Poets*, Emanuel
and Gross's *Dark Symphony*, *Negro Caravan*, Davis' *From
the Dark Tower*, Redmond's "The Black American Epic:
Its Roots and Its Writers," in Chrisman and Hare, *Con-
temporary Black Thought*, Henderson's *Understanding
the New Black Poetry*, and Gayle's *Black Expression* and
The Black Aesthetic.

Gwendolyn Brooks, the most celebrated black poet of
all time, continues to make her home in Chicago, where
she presides as an elder stateswoman of the new black poetry. She joins Tolson, Hayden, Randall, Margaret Walker,
and others as poets of "transition"—those who helped
continue the literary light of the Harlem Renaissance into
and through the Depression, World War II, the civil
rights struggle, and the Black Power Movement. Born the
daughter of working-class parents in Topeka, Kansas,
Gwendolyn Brooks was reared in Chicago, where she attended public schools, graduating from Englewood High

School in 1934 and Wilson Junior College in 1936. Wilson represented the final step in her formal education, and in 1939 she married Henry Blakely. She has a son and a daughter.

Gwendolyn Brooks began writing poetry at the age of thirteen, and by the time she was in her late teens she had published two mimeographed community newspapers—one being the Champlain *Weekly*. Since the early 1940s her poetry has appeared in numerous publications: *Poetry*, *Black World*, *Common Ground*, *Saturday Review of Literature*, *Negro Story*, *Atlantic Monthly*, and countless others.

Her first book of poetry, *A Street in Bronzeville* (1945), won the Merit Award of *Mademoiselle* magazine, and her second volume, *Annie Allen* (1949), garnered for her a Pulitzer prize (1950) as well as *Poetry*'s Eunice Tietjens Memorial Award. The recipient of a thousand-dollar award from the Academy of Arts and Letters and two Guggenheim fellowships for study (1946 and 1947), Gwendolyn Brooks's awards and citations are so numerous it would take several pages to list them all. She has received over a dozen honorary doctorates, served on special arts and cultural councils, and been listed among the most influential and important Americans in numberless compilations and regional and national acknowledgments. She has won the Poetry Workshop Award, given by the Midwestern Writers' Conference (three times: 1943–45), the Friends Literature Award for Poetry (1964), and the Thermod Monsen Award for Literature (1964). In 1969 she announced that she would award two prizes of $250 each to the best poem and best short story published each year by a black writer in *Negro Digest* (now *Black World*). Institutions where she has taught include Columbia, Elmhurst, and Northeastern Illinois State College, all in Chicago; the University of Wisconsin, the College of the City of New York, and many other public and private schools. For some, however, her crowning achievement was her selection in 1968 as poet laureate of the state of Illinois (succeeding Carl Sandburg).

Other volumes of poetry are *The Bean Eaters* (1960), *Selected Poems* (1963), *In the Mecca* (1968), *Riot* (1969), *Family Pictures* (1970), *Aloneness* (1971), *The*

World of Gwendolyn Brooks (1971, poetry and prose),
and Beckonings (1975). Special publications include *A
Portion of the Field: the Centennial of the Burial of
Lincoln* (1967) and *For Illinois* (1968). The poet has
also written some much-praised poetic fiction: *Maud
Martha, a Novel* (1953), and *Bronzeville Boys and Girls*
(1956). Her work as an editor has been equally impressive: *A Broadside Treasury* (1971) and *Jump Bad: a New
Chicago Anthology* (1971). Her pre-"Black" poetry is
most readily accessible in *Selected Poems*, which contains
her three earlier books and a "New Poems" section.
Selected Poems shows her bridging the stream between the
integrationist plea-bound writers and the firm, acrid, and
adamant voices of the 1960s.

Called the "most careful craftsman since Countee
Cullen," she was (and to some extent remains) greatly indebted to the modernist school of American poetry: Eliot,
Pound, Crane, Ransom, Joyce (influenced, as she says, by
The Dubliners), Stevens, Frost, and Auden. Reading
these poets and the black ones (Dunbar ["a family favorite"], Hughes, Cullen, Johnson, and others of the renaissance) aided her development and provided significant
choices. The results were a bewildering array of technical
proficiencies, which laid a base for the thematic and psychological levels in her poetry. Usually working with what
George Kent calls appropriate "distance," this poet carefully sculptures poetic gems from the granite and the
cheap rock of urban black America's experience: tenement housing, returning unsung war heroes, joblessness,
consumption, murder, endless poverty, love, man-woman
relationships, womanhood, and (especially) motherhood,
nobility of the economically pressed and deep religious devotion. Commenting on the effect of the *distance* and
what Gwendolyn Brooks was able to perceive and achieve
with it, Kent says (*Blackness and the Adventure of Western Culture*) she mastered

> . . . such modernist techniques as irony; unusual con-
> juctions of words to evoke a complex sense of reality
> (Satin Legs Smith rising "in a clear delirium"); squeez-
> ing the utmost from an image . . . ; agility with mind-
> bending figurative language, sensitivity to the music of

the phrase, instead of imprisonment in traditional line beats and meter; experimentation with the possibilities of *free* verse and various devices for sudden emphasis and verbal surprise; and authoritative management of tone and wide-ranging lyricism.

And one is struck, in reading, watching, listening to, or talking with the poet, by her intense yet relaxed love affair with words. Her prose is poetic; her manner is poetic.

In *Report from Part One*, her autobiography, she discusses her life as poet, mother, wife, and traveler. There are valuable insights into the woman who shifted from "Negro" to "Black" in 1967. *Report* also provides her own explication of at least a dozen poems. About poetry writing, she says:

> So much is involved in the writing of poetry—and sometimes, although I don't like suggesting it is a magic process, it seems you really have to go into a *bit* of a trance, self-cast trance, because "brainwork" seems unable to do it all, to do the whole job. The self-cast trance is possible when you are *importantly* excited about an idea, or surmise, or emotion.

Certainly the "trance" quality is found in the early and later Gwendolyn Brooks. One has only to compare the poem "the preacher: ruminates behind the sermon" (*A Street in Bronzeville*) to "Malcolm X" (*In the Mecca*) to see the staying power of the mystic, the seer and the entrancer. *Bronzeville* is a vibrant yet static poetic sculpture. It came in 1945, under the influence of the poet's wide reading and experimentation. James Weldon Johnson had helpfully critiqued her work, the results, she acknowledges, were that she became a surer, more precise poet and critic. The couple in the "kitchenette building" are products of "dry hours and the involuntary plan," who smell "yesterday's garbage" in the hall. After the fifth child has finally emerged from the bathroom.

We think of lukewarm water, hope to get it.

The memorable poems in *Bronzeville* are "the mother," "the preacher," "of De Witt Williams on his way to Lin-

coln Cemetery," "The Sundays of Satin Legs Smith,"
"the ballad of chocolate Mabbie," and selections from a
series of sonnets called *Gay Chaps at the Bar*. "The
mother" recalls abortions:

> You remember the children you got that you did
>   not get,

and pledges her love to the dead children. Even though
she knew them "faintly," she "loved" them "all." Taken
from their "unfinished reach," the aborted lives "never
giggled or planned or cried."

Ruminating "behind the sermon," the preacher—
revealing deepening levels of concern and psychic distress
—wonders how it feels "to be God." The god of the
world the preacher discusses from the pulpit is perhaps
not the god of the "real" world. Consequently the
preacher "ruminates" on whether anyone will

> Buy Him a Coca-Cola or a beer,
> Pooh-pooh His politics, call Him a fool?

Being god has to be lonely, "Without a hand to hold."

De Witt Williams is carried to the cemetery behind the
refrain:

> Swing low swing low sweet sweet chariot.
> Nothing but a plain black boy.

We know he may have been anything but plain. But if he
was just "a plain black boy" we will celebrate the places
where he hung out (pool hall, show, dance halls, whiskey
stores) and was known (47th street, under the "L"). De
Witt's journey is the black American (South to North)
odyssey depicted by Wright, Baldwin, Claude Brown, and
company:

> Born in Alabama.
> Bred in Illinois.
> He was nothing but a
> Plain black boy.

Satin Legs Smith is another *cut* off the block of the black
experience. In immortalizing him, the poet joins a host of
black bards, known and unknown, who have acknowl-

edged the importance and influence of folk culture. Probably like De Witt Williams, Smith comes from a "heritage of cabbage and pigtails." He is reminiscent of Margaret Walker's Poppa Chicken. The analogy, in the opening lines, is to a cat who is "tawney, reluctant, royal." Rising in the morning, Satin Legs relieves himself of "shabby days" when he "sheds" his pajamas. He bathes, puts on the best body scents, and goes to a wardrobe that, when inventoried, sounds like a replay of the whole era of the zootsuiter and the bebopper: diamonds, pearls, suits of yellow, wine, "Sarcastic green," and "zebra-striped cobalt"; wide shoulder padding, ballooning trousers that taper, hats that resemble umbrellas, and "hysterical ties." He is enmeshed in his image and blots out the reminders of poverty and ugliness. He "hears and does not hear"; "sees and does not see." Loving his music and his lady, he takes his date to "Joe's Eats," after which he retires (at home) to her body—"new brown bread . . . soft, and absolute." It is a mosaic-like study complete with the down-home versus Promised Land theme.

"The Negro Hero" ("to suggest Dorie Miller": a World War II navy cook turned hero) "had to kick" white men's "law into their teeth" before he could "save them." Being black, it was not safe, even in the thick and thin of battle when the ship was going down, to come up from the galley and save the white sailors. Instead of jumping overboard, like Shine, and leaving them to their fate, this hero invoked their "white-gowned democracy" and fought at their side despite this hate-freighted statement by a southern white man:

> Indeed, I'd rather be dead;
> Indeed, I'd rather be shot in the head
> Or ridden to waste on the back of a flood
> Than saved by the drop of a black man's blood.

"Negro Hero" symbolically reflects the black American doing his duty, believing in Christianity and democracy, to the best of his American self. As a theme, the idea was losing ground among black writers, but it would be some years before resentment of such "heroics" would be blatantly expressed. Experimental "soldier sonnets" appear in the final section of *Bronzeville* ("Gay Chaps at the Bar"). In "gay chaps at the bar" the soldiers' training does not prepare them to repel air attacks,

> To holler down the lions in the air.

In "the progress" the phrase is questionable when the soldiers hear the march

> Of iron feet again.

The Pulitzer prize-winning *Annie Allen* shows Gwendolyn Brooks sustaining her balance between the modernist influences and her own intuitional phrasings and interest. Some might call it the least *black* of her volumes, especially since it contains the enigmatic and diffusive "THE ANNIAD." And while her "children of the poor" series restates the plight of the "unheroic," she is nevertheless generally more withdrawn than in *Bronzeville*. Yet the titles of both volumes signal her continuing interest in, and empathy with, "everyday people." In her first volume, she had written extensively about women ("the mother," "chocolate Mabbie," "the hunchback"), and she opens *Annie Allen* with "NOTES FROM THE CHILDHOOD AND THE GIRLHOOD." Her neat words and stanzas deal with a neat life in "the parents: people like our marriage." Behind a "white Venetian blind" sit "pleasant custards." "Sunday Chicken" is a humorous comparison between carnivores who eat human flesh and those who eat chicken. Her excavating of poetic jewels from non-hero types takes her through the death of an "old relative" and "the ballad of late Annie," too "proud" to find a man good enough to marry. The reader is encouraged to avoid easy solutions in "do not be afraid of no":

> It is brave to be involved,
> To be not fearful to be unresolved.

And condescending people in high stations are brought low in "pygmies are pygmies still, though percht on Alps." The high and mighty sometimes feel they are better than others, and

> Pity the giants wallowing on the plain.

But unbeknown to the "percht" individuals, there are "no alps to reach."

"THE ANNIAD" contains forty-three 7-line stanzas, adapted, so Miss Brooks says, from the Chaucerian rhyme royal. As a modern poem, it places the author in the middle of the modernist tradition with other black poets: Hayden, Dodson, May Miller, and Tolson, among others. At least one level of complexity is revealed in the appearance of the words and phrases "paradisaical," "thaumaturgic lass," "theopathy," "Prophesying hecatombs," and "Hyacinthine devils sing," and references to Plato, Aeschylus, Seneca, Minnermus, Pliny, and Dionysus. But by the poet's own admission, "THE ANNIAD" is "labored, a poem that's very interested in the mysteries and magic of technique." With Hayden's "The Diver," the poem carries you deeper and deeper into the underbrush of self and psyche. Annie becomes Anniad, the poet's way of giving another unheroic character the stature of the heroic—this time the *Iliad*. When you think of Annie (Anniad), you are told to

Think of sweet and chocolate. . . .

The blurred imagery and perceptions of Hayden's diver are again anticipated in the line

What is ever and is not.

(Remember Satin Legs hearing and not hearing, seeing and not seeing?) Full of magic, history, lore, mythology, supernaturalism, "THE ANNIAD" plunges through the mental and spiritual spheres, and "crescendo-comes,"

Surrealist and cynical.

Anniad is needed hungry, courted, and won, as she descends and ascends the "demi-gloom" of life, of *now* and *then*. Just as you were to

Think of sweet and chocolate

at the beginning of the poem, you are to

Think of almost thoroughly
Derelict and dim and done

as the poem closes. And, perhaps it was all—after all—a
dream as Anniad stands

> Kissing in her kitchenette
> The minuets of memory.

"APPENDIX TO THE ANNIAD" includes the now
famous invention "the sonnet-ballad," in title and type.
The traditional sonnet is enlivened—given a ballad stance
and temperament; the young woman whose soldier-boy-
friend is dead wonders what she can use "an empty heart-
cup for." The achievement of *Annie Allen*, however, is
"THE WOMANHOOD" and especially the five sonnets
on "the children of the poor." Childless people "can be
hard" since they will not, like those with children,

> Hesitate in the hurricane to guard.

In sonnet number two, a mother asks what she can give to
poor children. The fourth sonnet, seeking perhaps to resolve the surreal dream, advises the poor to "First fight.
Then fiddle." There is nothing wrong with rising "bloody,"

> For having first to civilize a space
> Wherein to play your violin with grace.

It is the same unmuted call to militancy rendered by Margaret Walker in the final stanza of "For My People."
   "Beverly Hills, Chicago" takes an interesting look,
through black and poor eyes, at the people who "live till
they have white hair." To say Beverly Hills anywhere is to
evoke images of splendor and richness, of glitter and high
life. The denizens of Chicago's Beverly Hills "walk their
golden gardens" as the poor sight-seers drive through the
neighborhood. Here the "ripeness rots," though "not rag-
gedly." Decadence is neat, says the poet:

> . . . Not that anybody is saying that these people have
>   no trouble.
> Merely that it is trouble with a gold-flecked
>   beautiful banner.

The poem's theme is one that is dear to Blacks in their
daily conversations: that whites, especially rich whites, do
not really live; that they are mannikins, with a fetish for
the well-landscaped life; that they are inhibited and not

free in their expressions. These people, the poet reminds us, also "cease to be," and sometimes

> Their passings are even more painful than ours.

But they often live "till their hair is white." They also make "excellent corpses," as it were, "among the expensive flowers." Nevertheless the poor sight-seers have been changed, noticeably, by what they have seen, and the change is noted in the "little gruff" tones of their voices as they "drive on."

The Bean Eaters finds the poet returning to her transitional breach where she again does battle with problems and enemies of the unheroic. She gathers up the pride, passion, despair, disillusionment, joy, and anguish of "bean eaters" and related gourmets. The book opens with an elegy to her father ("In Honor of David Anderson Brooks, My Father") and, reflecting debts to Margaret Walker, Langston Hughes, the Civil Rights Movement, black music, and the Beat Movement, moves through a tumultuous spectrum of vignettes and perceptions: "My Little 'Bout-Town Gal," "Strong Men, Riding Horses," "We Real Cool," "A Bronzeville Mother Loiters in Mississippi. Meanwhile, A Mississippi Mother Burns Bacon," "The Last Quatrain of the Ballad of Emmett Till," "The Chicago Defender Sends a Man to Little Rock," "The Crazy Woman," and the powerful saga "The Ballad of Rudolph Reed." The death of David Anderson Brooks has left

> A dryness upon the house. . . .

Absence of the man who "loved and tended" gives the poet pause, makes her recall how he translated "private charity" of the old-time religion into "public love."

The " 'bout-town gal" gallivants with "powder and blue dye" while the narrator waits with the moon. Watching western movies, the speaker in "Strong Men, Riding Horses" (not reminiscent of Brown's poem) realizes that Westerns are products of Hollywood, that the strong men are "Too saddled." Meanwhile the speaker has to deal with real life—the fears, the dark—and is "not brave at all." The irony, of course, is that the viewer is often braver. Eating beans "mostly," the "old yellow pair" in "The Bean Eaters" putter around their apartment, recall-

ing their lives "with twinklings and twinges." Desolation
and tragedy of another kind comes to the *dramatis personae* of "We Real Cool," in which the poet employs a
Hughesian jazz pattern with jagged rhythms reminiscent
of beat poetry, Babs Gonzales and King Pleasure. The
poem recites the "live-fast-die-young" pattern of many
urban black youths:

> We real cool. We
> Left school. We
>
> Lurk late. We
> Strike straight. We
> Sing sin. We
> Thin gin. We
>
> Jazz June. We
> Die soon.

The longest poem in *The Bean Eaters* ("A Bronzeville
Mother Loiters in Mississippi. Meanwhile, A Mississippi
Mother Burns Bacon.") is a collage of journalism, day-
dreams, fairy-tale history, and racial horror. The mother of
slain fourteen-year-old Emmett Till (lynched in 1955 in
Mississippi after allegedly making "passes" at a white
housewife) toys over the remains of her son and her damaged faith; at the same time, a white mother muses over
the "crime" and recollects childhood fairy tales of the
"Dark Villain" pursuing the "milk-white maid" (rescued
by the "Fine Prince"). The white mother dares to doubt
the need to lynch young Emmett as she imagines she is
sexually assaulted by the "Dark Villain." The poem includes news reports of the crime, the lynching, as well as
accounts of the trial and the "acquittal." In "The Last
Quatrain of the Ballad of Emmett Till" Emmett's mother
"kisses her killed boy" while sitting in "a red room" and
"drinking black coffee." Unable to describe the mother's
grief, the poet gathers the blurring pain into a delirium-
like metaphor:

> Chaos in windy grays
>   through a red prairie.

Again combining journalism, history and mythology
with "contemporary fact," Gwendolyn Brooks portrays one

of the high points of the civil rights era in "The Chicago Defender Sends a Man to Little Rock" (1957). People in Little Rock, the poet tells us in the opening lines, have babies, comb their hair, and read the papers, like other Americans. She then etches out the contradictions and ironies in the "Soft women softly" who "are hurling spittle, rock." These "bright madonnas," like those with "eyes of steely blue" in McKay's "The Lynching," become "a coiling storm a-writhe." The last line of the poem,

> The loveliest lynchee was our Lord,

has since been repudiated; the poet now feels that the greatest tragedy, the slavery and dehumanization of Blacks, makes for more important and urgent "news" than the crucifixion of a white Jesus.

Later in the same section of the book, a woman who refuses to sing in May because she feels

> A May song should be gay

is admonished after she chooses to sing a "gray" song in November. Critics call her "The Crazy Woman."

One of the more well-known poems in *The Bean Eaters* is "The Ballad of Rudolph Reed," who, along with his wife, son and "two good girls," was "oaken." Rudolph Reed, seeking the Promised Land in the North and riding on the crest of the new push for integration, buys a home in a white neighborhood because he wants to avoid falling plaster and the ghetto roaches

> Falling like fat rain.

But the times are not quite right for integrated housing, and the Reed family experience violence when they move in: Rocks are thrown through their windows the first two nights. The repetition and incrementation are almost ironic in the ballad as Reed, filled with grief and anger when one of his daughters is finally hit with a rock, goes

> . . . to the door with a thirty-four
> and a beastly butcher knife.

He attacks four white men before he is finally slain and kicked by neighbors, who call him "Nigger." It is an un-

pleasant story; but as a chronicle of the themes and consciousness of a poet, it places Gwendolyn Brooks on the
threshold of the new militancy, some of which is unveiled
in the New Poems section of *Selected Poems*. Such poems
as "Riders to the Blood-Red Wrath" and "Langston
Hughes" show her concerned with struggle and the spiral-
ing fury of social unrest. At the same time, she salutes a
white poet, as in "Of Robert Frost," and continues her
practice of mining the unheroic for poetry in a section of
diverse stylistic efforts such as *A Catch of Shy Fish*. The
"riders" (perhaps a parody of the Purple Sage riders)
lurch into the breach of human struggle and social chaos.
They are the freedom riders—seeking what is "reliably
right"—conducting sit-ins, wade-ins, lie-ins, sing-ins, pray-
ins, and voter-registration drives. Carmichael has called
them "shock troops" of the "revolution." One of them
states:

> My scream! unedited, unfrivolous.
> My laboring unlatched braid of heat and frost.
> I hurt. I keep that scream at what pain:
> At what repeal of salvage and eclipse.
> Army unhonored, meriting the gold, I
> Have sewn my guns inside my burning lips.

And he goes on to

> . . . remember kings.
> A blossoming palace. Silver. Ivory.
> The conventional wealth of stalking Africa.

This rider recalls his past, projects his future, and surveys
the state of the world from China to Israel. He is going to
make the "bloody peace" asked for earlier by Margaret
Walker:

> Democracy and Christianity
> Recommence with me.
> And I ride ride I ride on to the end—
> Where glowers my continuing Calvary.

With his "fellows," he intends to see the battle through,

> To fail, to flourish, to wither or to win.
> We lurch, distribute, we extend, begin.

Yet "To Be in Love" is also to extend and "fall" along a golden column

Into the commonest ash.

Diverse, explicit and splendid, the poems in this section achieve balance as the poet salutes two senior bards: Frost and Hughes. Frost has

Iron at the mouth.

And

With a place to stand

he has much more than immediate physical space, but a permanent position on the world's poetry totem. As "merry glory," Hughes

Yet grips his right of twisting free.

His "long reach" encompasses "speech," "fears," "tears," and "sudden death." Hughes's job is not done, and as a "headlight" he must press on

Till the air is cured of its fever.

The poet also returns to her garden of non-heroes in poems about garbage men, the sick, old people, stern women, and "Big Bessie," who "throws her son into the street."

Sculpture, precision, explicitness, and terseness are key words to remember when approaching the poetry of Gwendolyn Brooks. Not primarily of the academy, but often sharing some of its virtues and faults, she has been free to deal primarily with pictures swirling around her during childhood and adulthood in Chicago. Sometimes her poetry about night life and the South carries a forced feeling, since these are not things she is in intimate contact with, but it is always skillful and economical. Her world has not been "wide" in the way that Tolson's and Hayden's have been "wide." But it has been deep and multilayered, complex and womanly, tragic and profound.

Her poetry has not, at this writing, inspired a book-length study, but she has been the subject of much critical treatment. Selected studies will be listed here since bibliographies are widely available. For example, *CLA Journal*, XVII (September 1973) (a special issue on Brooks, Hayden and Baraka) lists a twelve-page bibliography. She is represented in every anthology of Afro-American poetry beginning with *Poetry of the Negro* (1949 ed.) and in many general American anthologies of poetry and literature. Helpful are Kent's "The Poetry of Gwendolyn Brooks" (*Blackness and the Adventure of Western Culture*, 1972); the critical entries in Barksdale and Kinnamon's *Black Writers of America*; Davis' *From the Dark Tower*; Jackson's essay in *Black Poetry in America* (1974); essays in Gibson's *Modern Black Poets*; and *Report from Part One*, the poet's autobiography (1972).

Owen Dodson's first volume of poetry, *Powerful Long Ladder* (1946), was one of the casualties of the disinterest in black poetry during the postrenaissance and war years. The book did not go entirely unnoticed, however, for *Time* magazine described it as standing "peer to Frost and Sandburg and other white American poets who are constantly recited in our schools." *Powerful Long Ladder* appeared in the midst of Dodson's busy (and successful) career as dramatist and teacher. His interest in writing and drama began in his youth in Brooklyn, New York, where he was born and attended public schools. He went to Bates College, obtaining a B.A., and Yale, where he was awarded the M.A. in drama. While a student at Yale, two of his plays—*Divine Comedy* and *Garden of Time*—were produced. Since those years, Dodson's work in drama and other writing has been prodigious. He taught drama at Spelman College in Atlanta and was commissioned to write a play on the *Amistad* mutiny for Talladega College. He directed summer theater at Hampton Institute, the Theatre Lobby Washington, and at Lincoln University. Dodson finally settled at Howard University as drama instructor, later becoming head of the department and remaining there until 1969.

In 1949, he took the Howard University Players on a successful State Department-sponsored tour of Scandinavia and Germany. His novel *Boy at the Window* was published in 1950, and his short story "The Summer Fire" won a *Paris Review* prize (1961) and appeared in the *Best Short Stories* from that publication. He received many other awards and forms of recognition: a Rosenwald

Fellowship, a General Education Board Fellowship, a Guggenheim grant to study and travel in Italy (1953), and a Maxwell Anderson Prize for a verse play. He also wrote the libretto for Mark Fax's opera. He has completed a number of manuscripts in poetry and prose that have never been published. One of his most recent exciting works was *The Dream Awake* (1969), a cultural history of black Americans, released by Spoken Arts and consisting of color films, records, textbooks, illustrations, and other materials that show the range of Dodson's talents and interest. In 1970, his second volume of verse, *The Confession Stone: Song Cycles*, was published, but the poems were written before 1960.

About his work as a poet, Dodson reports with some dispirit in *Interviews with Black Writers*:

> I have written three books of poetry. The first was—I would say—somewhat propaganda, but the third was filled with stories, diaries, and remembrances of Jesus. They are really framed in diaries by Mary, Martha, Joseph, Judas, Jesus, even God. This, I believe, is my most dedicated work. . . . I have written and fought somehow in my writing, but I know now that the courage and forthrightness of writers and poets will change something a little in our dilapidation.

That "first" volume referred to is obviously *Powerful Long Ladder*, but Dodson does not have to deprecate the work, since it will hold him in good stead as a poet. There is not one poem in the book that cannot be aesthetically or stylistically called "poetry." And this is not a claim that many poets can make. Dodson's stylistic influences can be traced to the American modernists. And there is no doubt that, in his recurring despair, he shares sentiments with Eliot, Pound, Auden, and Yeats. Yet, in his lilt and his language, he also pays his debts to Hughes, Dunbar, Cullen (whom he eulogizes), James Weldon Johnson, and the whole web of black folk and spiritual life.

Dodson's note of despair, which pervades the book, is sounded in the opening poem ("Lament"), in which the lynched boy is addressed:

> Wake up, boy, and tell me how you died:
> What sense was alert last. . . .

Relying heavily on his experiences and interests in drama,
Dodson carefully underscores the repulsive act and the
guilt. In an italicized section, he gives details that recall
other poems on the theme:

> *the Mississippi drank itself one night,*
> *the bridge from which you hung threw its arms up,*
> *folded into mud like an old obscene accordion,*
> *the crowd dispersed*
> *counted on its fingers one by one. . . .*

The invisible black viewer of the lynching, going beyond
the actual act to the nature of death itself, gets curious
about the last moments and questions the dead boy:

> Tell me what road you took,
> What hour in the day is luckiest?

The narrator wants a sign ("the acrostic, the cross, the
crown or the fire"), something to make his own way
easier, bearable:

> O, wake up, wake!

We said several strains of black and modern poetry can
be seen in Dodson's work, not the least among them being
the folk idiom. "Guitar" reminds us of similar works by
Sterling Brown. The six-string guitar has a "lonesome"
wail and cannot "hold its own" against the howl of a
Georgia hound. And the guitarist-singer

> *Ain't had nobody*
> *To call me home*
> *From the electric cities*
> *Where I roam.*

An adaptation of the blues motif in style and theme, it
employs incremental refrain and the ambivalent drive-sulk
of the blues troubador. This somber tone of Dodson's per-
sists in such poems as "Sorrow Is the Only Faithful One"
("I am less, unmagic, black"), "Black Mother Praying"
("black and burnin in these burnin times"), and "The
Signifying Darkness," and there are tinges of it even in
celebratory poems such as "Pearl Primus" and "Poem for

Pearl's Dancers." But the grand statement of poetry is always lurking or leading ("Pearl Primus"): "the sun is like a shawl on their backs," and "pistoning her feet in the air." In "Someday We're Gonna Tear Them Pillars Down" a woman complains:

> They took ma strong-muscle John and cut his
> manhood off. . . .

The Blacks in "Rag Doll and Summer Birds" sit in their cabin (like "The Bean Eaters") "waiting for God." The fire in the stove goes out; the newspapered walls, "telling of crimes," curl up, and

> In the Blackness stars are not enough!

Included in *Powerful Long Ladder* are three verse choruses from *Divine Comedy*. Dodson was the first black dramatist to exploit the meaning of the Father Divine phenomenon in verse drama. When a cult leader is gone, the drama contends, the people are forced inward to find a replacement. *Divine Comedy* is bizarre, with shifting uncertainties, horror, violence, religious extremism, and racial intensity. The first chorus asks (in a refrain):

> Cancel us.
> Let doomsday come down
> Like the foot of God on us.

A character called "One" notes:

> We are clear and confused on many issues. . . .

A "Girl" says:

> I dance without legs.

"One" reminds us:

> War, war will bomb your eyes open.

In the "Star Chorus," a "Blind Man" beseeches the others:

> Don't leave the blind to wander
> Where the wind is a wall!

Cullen, one of Dodson's heroes, had suggested that Blacks were not made "eternally to weep" ("From the Dark Tower"), and Dodson has a "Young Man" say

This shall not be forever.

In the section called *Poems for My Brother Kenneth*, Dodson delicately recalls remembrances of his dead brother. The somber tone and weightiness return as the poet, addressing his brother, asks for some answer to the "long tanks" that "creep" and the "dark body of the ruined dark boy." But

There was no reply:
You gave me a smile and returned to the grave.

In *Interviews with Black Writers* Dodson claims that Cullen did not die from disease but "was pushed into death" by "us because we did not recognize the universal quality of what he wanted to say." In his eulogy "Countee Cullen" ("All This Review" section) Dodson bids farewell to his friend, who died in 1946, by likening his plight to that of Socrates:

We hear all mankind yearning
For a new year without hemlock in our glasses.

Later, in "Drunken Lover," we find that this is "the stagnant hour." And Dodson's interest in global oppression is seen in "Jonathan's Song":

Jew is not a race
Any longer—but a condition.

Finally Dodson closes the volume, appropriately, with "Open Letter," wherein he asks for tolerance and understanding in a time of war, hatred, domestic violence, and racism. "Jonathan's Song" had aligned the poet with the Jews being massacred in Germany:

I am a part of this. . . .

So "Open Letter" calls on the universal brotherhood:

Brothers, let us discover our hearts again,
Permitting the regular strong beat of humanity there
To propel the likelihood of other terror to an exit.

The war is almost over, he says, as "planes stab over us."
The word "hallelujah" can be understood in the language
of

> All the mourning children,

and

> The torn souls and broken bodies will be restored
> when war has ceased forever.

Signaling his non-black "brothers," a tone and posture
quickly fading from black poetry, Dodson challenges
them:

> Brothers, let us enter that portal for good
> When peace surrounds us like a credible universe.
> Bury that agony, bury this hate, take our black
>   hands in yours.

Dodson's was the "We Shall Overcome" call, which
would die in the mid-sixties, though a few (Hayden,
Hughes and others) would continue to walk the difficult
tightrope of universal brotherhood.

The Confession Stone: Song Cycles, though published
in 1970, contains work done in the forties and fifties. It is
a strange "cycle," which moves among "The land of the
living and the land of the risen dead." The groupings
(many written to be sung) are "The Confession Stone,"
"Mary Passed this Morning," "Journals of the
Magdalene," "Your Servant: Judas," "Father, I Know
You're Lonely," "Dear, My Son," and "Oh My Boy,
Jesus." The cycles recast biblical stories surrounding Jesus
Christ and the crucifixion, updating them by adding contemporary language (black idiom at times) and technology. In poem I of "Confession Stone," Jesus is quieted
with the words

> shushhh, you need the rest.

Number III asks Jesus if he knows "Lazarus is back." In
V Jesus' mother vows to save him from the cold and icy
Jerusalem ground:

> Let me rock him again in my trembling arms.

"Mary Passed This Morning" contains "letters from Joseph to Martha." Number I is a poetic telegram:

Martha
Mary passed this morning
funeral this evening   stop
Near six o'clock
tell the others   stop
Raising bus fare for you
stop
            signed Joseph

It is clear after a while that Dodson is reliving the life and times of Jesus through black characters; he also uses the old search-for-the-Promised-Land motif (Wright, Ellison, Baldwin, Brown). In number I of "Journals of the Magdalene" the protagonist vows even to "crucify myself" in order

to be with him. Amen.

Writing a letter to Jesus is number I of "Your Servant: Judas." Judas says,

Dear Jesus, I killed myself last night.

The "cycle" is completed as Dodson ends the small volume with the opening poem: "Oh My Boy: Jesus" and the mother saying, in the manner of the preacher in Johnson's "Creation": "rest on my breast."

Of Dodson's frequently anthologized poems, "Yardbird's Skull" (a tribute to saxophone player Charles "Yardbird" Parker) is one of the most enduring and powerful. Parker (1920–55) is also saluted by other poets and writers: Cuney and John A. Williams, to name just two. He is a major figure in the development of jazz, American music and contemporary jazz literature. In statement and style, "Yardbird's Skull" elegiacally captures the psychic and rhythmic layerings and wanderings of "Bird's" horn. When "the Bird" died, Dodson thinks, so did "all the music," and "whole sunsets" were deprived of this great musician's voice. A skull becomes the metaphor for the historical corridors of music, and Dodson's fingering of the skull, like Hamlet of Yorick's, allows him to retrace Bird's journey to greatness: to air; to brotherhood, which sired the music; to soaring birds; to Atlantis, even; and to

Places of dreaming, swimming lemmings.

There has been only slight criticism of Dodson's poetry; Barksdale and Kinnamon write briefly of him. He is in most anthologies of black poetry beginning with Kerlin's *Negro Poets and Their Poems.*

Gwendolyn Brooks's winning of the Pulitzer prize for poetry in 1950 momentarily brought new attention to the poetic activities of Afro-Americans. But though her name hung like anticipation over the decade of the fifties, the period in fact was dominated by fiction writers: "especially the articulate expatriate Richard Wright, Ralph Ellison and James Baldwin. Wright had established a tradition, and many were attempting to follow in his footsteps—including John Oliver Killens, William Attaway and Chester Himes" (Barksdale and Kinnamon). The works of the fiction writers and their accompanying dialogue with black and white critics and each other helped develop "a national, almost global concern for the identity problems of American Blacks." Fiction writers also wrote in a diversity of styles, from "Wright's" school to Demby's explorations of the "consciousness."

However, other poets were writing and publishing in various places during the fifties, but most of their activities were part of the ground swell that would reach a crescendo in the sixties and seventies. Many of them can be found in such anthologies as *Negro Caravan* (1941), *The Poetry of the Negro* (1949), *American Literature by Negro Authors* (1950), *Lincoln University Poets* (1954), *Beyond the Blues* (1962), *Sixes and Sevens* (1962), *Burning Spear: an Anthology of Afro-Saxon Poetry* (1963), and *Soon One Morning: New Writing by American Negroes, 1940–1962* (1963). A recent edition to the body of anthologies treating the poets of this period is *The Forerunners: Black Poets in America* edited by Woodie King, Jr. and introduced by Addison Gayle, Jr. (1975). As individuals and groups, the poets continued to make their work available either to each other or to the small poetry-reading audiences of the period (colleges, schools, churches). Hughes, Hayden, Gwendolyn Brooks, and others, who had established reputations in the forties, continued writing. And the younger or lesser-known poets of this late-transitional stage (Wright, Danner, O'Higgins, Allen/Vesey, Randall, Durem, Holman, Jeffers, Patterson, Atkins, Evans, and others) published in little magazines and won various regional and national writing contests—primarily through schools and colleges.

Opportunity, The Crisis, The Negro Story, Negro History Bulletin, Phylon, and numerous college periodicals continued to provide forums. Some of the poets who appeared in *The Crisis* during the thirties and forties, for example, were Grace E. Barr, Edna Barrett, Milton Brighte, Sophy Mae Bryson, Clarissa Bucklin, Lillian Byrnes, Polly Mae Hall, Alice Ward Smith, Paul A. Wren, Walter Adams, Ethel Collins, Edith M. Durham, and Max Reynolds. Others published in regional magazines or brought out collections of their own works: Noy Joseph Dickerson (*A Scrap Book,* 1931), Thomas Atkins (*The Eagle,* 1936), Leslie M. Collins (*Exile, a Book of Verse,* 1938), William Walker (who published eleven volumes between 1936 and 1943), Olive Lewis Handy, Claude T. Eastman, Nick Aaron Ford (*Songs from the Dark,* 1940), Maurice Fields (*The Collected Poems of Maurice Fields,* 1940), R. F. Boyd (*Holiday Stanzas,* 1940), folklorist J. Mason Brewer (four books of poems), William Holmes Borders (*Thunderbolts,* 1942), Anita Turpeau Anderson (*Pinpoints: Group of Poems and Prose Writings,* 1943), Aloise Barbour Epperson (*The Hills of Yesterday and Other Poems,* 1944), Mary Albert Bacon (*Poems of Color,* 1948), Harrison Edward Lee (*Poems for the Day,* 1954), Willie Ennis (*Poetically Speaking,* 1957), Paul Vesey (*Ivory Tusks,* 1956), and Arthur Wesley Reason (*Poems of Inspiration for Better Living,* 1959).

Among white (and some black) poets, the fifties were aglow with the fervor of the Beat Movement, led by Kenneth Rexroth, E. E. Cummings, Lawrence Ferlinghetti and Allen Ginsberg. Hughes and especially Bob Kaufman played a great part in introducing the beats to the poetic lyrics of jazz and the jagged-lined interpretation of postwar blues of the "lost generation." Another influence on the beats was Russell Atkins, who, with Helen Johnson Collins, founded *Free Lance* in Cleveland (1950). An avant-garde "little" magazine, it played an unsung part in the development of ideas and techniques of the new American poetry. At the dawn of the sixties, the "style" of black life also figured prominently, as always, in the pacing of literary and cultural concerns. The bebop poet Babs Gonzales, along with such jazz-poetry narrators as King Pleasure, influenced the live reading of poetry and signaled a call for re-acculturating the "ear" traditionally used in the silent writing of a poem. As the fifties closed, the precise passion of Gwendolyn Brooks and the troubador's gait of Hughes hurled a dual, though not totally unified, challenge at the coming generation of black poets.

CHAPTER VI

FESTIVALS AND FUNERALS: BLACK POETRY OF THE 1960s AND 1970s

They winged his spirit &
wounded his tongue
but death was slow coming

Who killed Lumumba
What killed Malcolm

festivals & funerals
festivals & funerals
festivals & funerals & festivals & funerals . . .

—JAYNE CORTEZ
From *Festivals & Funerals*

OVERVIEW

The space between festivals and funerals can be infinite or
it can be deathly short. So says Jayne Cortez through the
epic twistings and turnings in her poem. But whatever the
space, or the pace, we all slip, slide, soar, and trip as we
make our way between the polarities (assigned each at
birth) of the kind of life we live and the kind of death we
die. Black poets of the 1960s and 1970s often faced life
and death "straight up": though, as we have seen, black
poets in other times did not cringe from the breach of racial
nightmare, violence, sexuality, unbeautiful language,
wicked or religious folkism, and the demands of music that
each of them seemed to hear—albeit from "different
drummers." To attempt a discussion of contemporary
black poetry is to turn others' tongues into flames: "Blas-
phemy!" "I was the first!" "We started it!" "That anthology was incomplete since it didn't include me!" "It all
began in this place [or that place]!" "His/her poetry is
not black enough!" and so on.

Nevertheless, the "smoke" from the sixties is beginning
to clear and, while more hindsight is needed, there are
important observations that should be made. Hence, in

this chapter, the format will follow preceding ones—but with less biographical-critical data on individual poets. Most serious poets who began writing in the late fifties, the sixties and the early seventies still have much growing and threshing to do. Also, many recent volumes really contain earlier poetry. So it is not easy to evaluate (or even list) black poetry produced over this period. Yet, historically speaking, certain undeniable trends have occurred, and they look roughly like this:

Black poetry since the Harlem Renaissance (see Brown, Redding, Henderson, Jackson) has had cycling currents of "rage" and "fire" though not the sustained gush witnessed in the mid and late sixties;

black poetry after 1945 expressed a belief (see Ray Durem) that white liberals were not really interested in mounting the "final" chariots of fire (or going "all the way") on behalf of Blacks (despite Communist-Socialist pronouncements);

black poetry of the late fifties and early sixties provided a civil-rights ground swell and political climate for the volcanic burst of the later sixties;

in black poetry of the early sixties there was planted the anvil that shaped the stylistic, attitudinal and linguistic character of what is known as the "new black poetry";

current black poetry, despite "evolutions" and "changes," has not radically altered or laid to rest the best work of Dunbar, Hughes, James and Fenton Johnson, Davis, Toomer, Walker, Hayden, Brooks, Tolson, and Dodson;

except for what Stephen Henderson calls "tentative" answers, black poetry defies all definitions (e.g., see statements in Mari Evans' "Black Woman")—splintering off into innumerable directions, styles, forms, themes, considerations and ideas.

This chapter, all above considered (!), will briefly sketch the flow of poetry from the fifties into the mid sixties. Again chronology will be violated, since though many of the poets listed were writing in the forties and fifties, most did not receive substantial attention until the sixties. The sketch will include a general look at transitional poets (older and younger) as their work appears in about a half dozen anthologies (from *I Saw How Black I Was*, 1958, to *Kaleidoscope*, 1967) and what few volumes were being brought out at the time. The examination (see Locke's and Bontemps's divisions of the Harlem Renaissance) then takes up the poets who came to recognition under the banner of the Black Arts Movement and who loosely fall into the category of new black poetry. Older poets— Hayden, Brooks, Randall, Walker, and others—will be briefly revisited to see if the "new" mood wrought any significant changes in their views and/or their poetry. Though we touch upon criticism, this book is *primarily* a historical guide designed to aid readers in their exploration of black poetry. Only a naïve person would attempt, at this stage, a full critique of the poetry of the 1960s and 1970s. However, there are stylistic patterns, similarities, and thematic clusters which will be pinpointed and assessed from time to time. Some of the most provocative recent studies of contemporary black poetry are Henderson and Cook's *The Militant Black Writer in Africa and the United States*, (1969); Joy Flasch's *Melvin Tolson* (1972); Henderson's *Understanding the New Black Poetry* (1973); Sherley Williams' *Give Birth to Brightness* (1972); Gibson's *Modern Black Poets* (1973); and Jackson and Rubin's *Black Poetry in America* (1974).

LITERARY AND SOCIAL LANDSCAPE

Assassinations, high-level political corruption, upheaval, violence, change, clash of ideologies, flaming rhetoric—all describe the contemporary period. Revolutions (of all kinds) mock and mold the world. From Cuba or Vietnam, Harlem to Chile, Pakistan to Watts, Nigeria to Indonesia, Kenya to Berkeley, Jackson State to Kent State— the facts and symbols of change have been dramatic and violent.

Such an overcast, however, has not thwarted major developments in the black sphere where (by the mid fifties) bebop was declining and jazz's greatest contemporary interpreter, Charlie Parker, was dead. But black musicians and vocalists continued probing new forms under the leadership of Miles Davis, John Coltrane, the Modern Jazz Quartet, Wes Montgomery, Ray Charles, Ornette Coleman, Billy Eckstine, Ella Fitzgerald, and Billie Holiday (who died in 1959). Billie Holiday's name and fame again reached a world-wide audience when, in 1972, Diana Ross, formerly of the Supremes, starred in the controversial movie *Lady Sings the Blues*. Saxophonist Coltrane, a major influence on the current generation of musicians and poets, died in 1967. An innovator, he sparked new interests in music with, among other techniques, his "sheets of sound."

The fifties and sixties also witnessed the maturation of rhythm-and-blues, popularized by black radio disc jockeys. Interweaving social commentaries with the news, they anticipated the new oral poetry of the later sixties. Resulting from these broadcasting styles were such programs as "Bandstand" (started in the late fifties). Young white America watched blacks dance, listened to Little Richard and Chubby Checker, and tried to imitate it all on TV and in their homes. This period gave birth to the first white superstar "soul" artist: Elvis Presley. The new black social music, and the dances accompanying it, freed white American youngsters from the prudish and self-righteous inhibitions of their foreparents. But there remain the "exotic" echoes from the twenties.

Generally, American science and industry developed more rapidly than in previous periods. The Soviet Union launched Sputnik, a feat followed by an American-Russian science and space-exploration race, that continues. Telstar paved the way for news coverage of global activities, while biochemical warfare and atomic research have become the nightmares people live daily.

The American literary scene was swamped with political novels, satire, writings on the war, and experimental journalistic prose. The "underground" newspaper emerged as a major vehicle for this new writing. The symbolism and psychology employed in the earlier literature are still present. However, the influence of the writers from the Depression and war years is giving way to gadgetry and a new wave of existential concern. Black, Jewish, Chicano, American Indian, and Asian writers are grabbing more of

the literary stage. This is seen in the new ethnic journals
and publishing companies as well as new interest from established publishers.

Some contemporary Third World (ethnic or colored)
writers of influence include: N. Scott Momaday, Ralph
Ellison, Frank Chin, Chinua Achebe, Ernest Gaines,
James Baldwin, Paul Chan, Albert Murray, Janis Miri-
kitani, Ishmael Reed, James Ngugi, William Demby,
Shawn Hsu Wong, and William Melvin Kelley. During
the contemporary period, many black writers achieved recognition on par with the best writers everywhere. El-
dridge Cleaver's *Soul on Ice* (1968) sold several million
copies, and Reed was nominated in two categories for the
National Book Award in 1973. Among important con-
temporary American poets are Stanley Kunitz, Cyn Zarco,
Robert Hayden, Richard Eberhart, Robert Penn Warren,
José Montoya, Gwendolyn Brooks, Lawson Inada, Karl
Shapiro, Robert Vargas, John Berryman, Henry Dumas,
Víctor Hernández Cruz, Michael S. Harper, Robert Lowell, Daniel Halpern, Richard Wilbur, Paul Vesey, James
Dickey, Imamu Amini Baraka, Sylvia Plath, William Bell,
and James Wright. Hayden received a National Book
Award nomination in 1972 and was elected to the American Academy of Poets in 1975. Many of the black writers,
artists, and poets (some from the pre- and postwar
schools) died during the contemporary period (Tolson,
Bontemps, Robison, Hughes, Wright, Durem, Dumas,
Du Bois, Horne, Rivers, Toomer, Malcolm X). Indeed
death, in one way or another, not only preoccupied writers
(black and white), but was often romantically pursued.
Beat poet Kenneth Rexroth asked, "Why have 30 American poets committed suicide since 1900?" Those poets
not concerned with death were investigating decadence or
the self-destructive elements of society.

The development of contemporary poetry cannot be
viewed properly without understanding the "beat" period.
As a partial product of the bebop era, beat poets emulated
the hip mannerisms and aped the "man alone" (drop-
out) image associated with musicians. Bebop was one way
the black man used to fight the commercialization of his
art. He also used it in playing "Something," in the words
of Thelonious Monk, "they can't play" (*they* meaning

whites). Important beat poets were Lawrence Ferlinghetti, Rexroth, Allen Ginsberg, and Gregory Corso, among the whites, and Bob Kaufman, LeRoi Jones, Russell Atkins, A. B. Spellman, and Ted Joans, among the Blacks. The beat movement, which nurtured occultism, rejection of the Establishment and an existential view of life, was centered in New York's Greenwich Village and the San Francisco Bay area. It died in the early sixties.

Kaufman is viewed by many as the unsung patriarch of the era. Some critics say major white poets of the movement enthusiastically took their cues from Kaufman's innovations, but were not so quick in recognizing his influence. As a kind of spiritual heir to Toomer, Kaufman is a complex, sometimes fragmented, but brilliantly original poet. His work, like that of many of his contemporaries, is influenced by Eastern religious thought and the occult. Stylistically, Kaufman has the breadth and dexterousness of Whitman coupled with the best techniques of modern poetry. He passionately experiments with jazz rhythms in poetry and often invokes jazz themes, moods, and musicians.

Many beat poets and enthusiasts later joined or were spawned by the civil rights struggle, which was intensified by several things: Martin Luther King's Montgomery bus boycott in 1955–56; sit-ins and other dramatizations of segregation and discrimination; the challenges to Jim Crow in travel in 1961 (CORE); the widening activities of SNCC (1961–64) and the March on Washington (1963). Other significant activities inflamed and inspired the hearts and imagination of black American youth especially. The Muslims' (Nation of Islam's) growth to fifty thousand members by 1963 and the Congressional action on civil rights legislation were two seemingly unrelated but strategically important events. The growing influence of the Muslims suggested that many more Blacks no longer believed America was sincere in its pledges to implement changes even when they became law. Reinforcing their distrust were the continued acts of violence against Blacks, night ridings in the South, and harassment of Blacks in public places and their homes. With memory of a contemporary history of lynching that began with Emmett Till's murder, Blacks reeled under the killings of Chaney,

Goodman and Schwerner, Malcom X, Medgar Evers,
King, the Kennedy brothers, and the three Black Panthers
killed by police in a Chicago apartment.

By 1966, however, black-power signs and slogans had
begun to replace the "We shall overcome—black and
white together" exclamations. Young black Americans,
wearing Afro hairdos and African jewelry, attended cultural festivals, back-to-Africa rallies, black-power conferences and poetry readings, and read community news published in revolutionary broadsides and tabloids. Rhetorical
forays by H. Rap Brown and Stokely Carmichael, young
SNCC officers, set off a flurry of state and national laws
against inciting to riot and the transporting of weapons
across state boundaries. Cities of all sizes ignited, setting
the stage for gun battles between police and the often
imagined "snipers." These conflagrations were repeated in
scores of cities after Dr. King was assassinated in 1968.
Watts poet Quincy Troupe captured the shock and horror, and chronicled the "official" reaction, in his poem
"White Weekend":

> The deployed military troops
> surrounded the White House
> and on the steps of the Senate building
> a soldier behind a machine gun
>
> 32,000 in Washington & Chicago
> 1,900 in Baltimore Maryland
> 76 cities in flames on the landscape
> and the bearer of peace
> still lying in Atlanta. . . .

In the last stanza, Troupe noted with curdling irony:

> Lamentations! Lamentations! Lamentations!
> Worldwide!
> But in New York, on Wall Street
> the stock market went up 18 points. . . .

At this writing, fallout from the black revolution rever-
berates around the globe. Black journalist Thomas Johnson reports Irish revolutionaries sing, "We Shall Overcome." Posters and emblems commercialize everything
from African hair styles to the raised clenched fist—the in-

itial 1960s symbol of black unity and defiance. A wave of black movies—sometimes called blaxploitation—beginning with such white experimental films as *Putney Swope* (1969) and given impetus by Melvin Van Peebles' *Sweet Sweetback's Baadasssss Song* (1971), is capturing a multi-million-dollar theater patronage. Black movies retrieved the crippled movie industry from the brink of disaster. Meanwhile, the murder, incarceration, and political harassment of black men and women make them heroes and heroines in black communities—yet ironically symbolize the torment and "genocidal schemes" of America (see Samuel Yette's *The Choice*).

Crisscrossed by paradoxes, political contradictions, social revolts, and religious ambivalences, the black community is nevertheless regenerated by its singers and performers. Black popular music has not only reached unprecedented audiences, but unprecedented money-making capabilities. Rhythm-and-blues, which died about 1965, gave way to "soul"—"I'm a Soul Man," Sam and Dave announced in the late sixties. The Impressions told lovers that you "gotta have soul," and Bobby Womack reminded listeners that the "Woman's Gotta Have It"—presumably "Soul." Black recording companies are rapidly developing; e.g., Motown (Detroit). Curtis Mayfield's soundtrack album *Superfly* (1972) sold more than 22 million copies, and Marvin Gaye's *What's Going On* (1971) set records for album sales. Recently, however, Stevie Wonder has surpassed them all. Literally dozens of singing groups—modeled on the quartets and ensembles of the fifties—are releasing albums regularly. These folk or "soul" poets have become more "conscious" in recent years, and many now drape their songs with political messages and exaltations of blackness. Much of this new wave came on the heels of severe criticism by Baraka, who admonished the singers for doting on unrequited love. Too many, he said, are preoccupied with such themes as "my baby's gone, gone."

Black-consciousness activity, and creativity in general, now flourish. Related involvement includes: development of black acting ensembles; opening of free schools and black universities; establishment of black national-ist/cultural communes; increase in the number of black bookstores and African boutiques; establishment of black-studies programs on white and black campuses and, in

some cases, quota systems for enrolling black students; the
escalation of black demands for "cream of the crop" jobs
such as TV announcing and the hosting of variety shows;
expansion and creation of new roles for black newspapers,
magazines and radio stations; formation of the black
Congressional caucus and similar units in other professional and legislative bodies; and, finally and importantly, new engagement with Africa and her problems and
possibilities. Indeed, future trips to Africa—to the
"mother country" or "homeland"—are discussed at all age
and social levels. Much of this renewed interest is understandable in light of the emergence during the contemporary period of several African nation-states and the increased fraternization among Africans and Afro-Americans.
Malcolm X, canonized today by great numbers of black
students and intellectuals, did much to foster this current
interest in Africa. Shot to death at a rally in Harlem in
1965, Malcolm had already been expelled from the Nation
of Islam and had formed a splinter group known as the
Organization of Afro-American Unity. His *Autobiography
of Malcolm X* (with Alex Haley, 1965), which (as he
predicted) he did not live to see in print, chronicles his
odyssey as Malcolm Little, hustler "Detroit Red," Malcolm X, and El-Hajj Malik El Shabazz. He has been
lionized by Carmichael, H. Rap Brown, Ossie Davis, Baraka, and various other scholars, activists and artists. Black
poets, especially, have found Malcolm (and Coltrane)
limitless sources of inspiration. A partial indication of Malcolm's impact on poets can be seen in *For Malcolm:
Poems on the Life and Death of Malcolm X* (1967), edited by Dudley Randall and Margaret G. Burroughs. In
"El-Hajj Malik El Shabazz," Robert Hayden noted:

> He X'd his name, became his people's anger,
> exhorted them to vengeance for their past;
> rebuked, admonished them,
>
> Their scourger who
> would shame them, drive them
> from the lush ice gardens of their servitude.

At the First World Festival of Negro Arts, held in
Dakar, Senegal, in 1966, Hayden was awarded the Grand

Prize for Poetry. A major event, the festival was attended
by experts, scholars, artists, and enthusiasts of black arts
who gathered for twenty-four days to hear papers and discussions, view art exhibits, cultural performances, and give
preliminary direction to the Black Arts Movement. Presid-
ing over the festival was President Senghor (Senegal), one
of the architects (with Césaire and Damas) of *Négritude*,
African-oriented publications such as *Présence Africaine
and Black Orpheus* have renewed their interests in black
American writers. Likewise, black American journals and
popular magazines (*Black World, Journal of Black Poetry,
The Black Scholar, Essence, Encore, Ebony, Jet*, etc.)
have begun to publish more materials by and about Africans.

The revolution in black arts was signaled by many
events including the First Conference of Negro Writers,
in March of 1959. Langston Hughes was an important
figure there—as he was at the Dakar gathering seven years
later. The First American Festival of Negro Art was held
in 1965, and the Second AFNA took place in November
of 1969 in Buffalo, N.Y. Interlacing these and other conferences, symposia and conventions, were exciting developments and experiments in New York, Chicago, Watts,
Philadelphia, Atlanta, Baton Rouge, St. Louis, Cleveland,
Detroit, and Washington, D.C.

During these cycles of social turmoil and artistic up-
surge, writers and poets often aligned themselves with ideological positions and regional movements. Consequently,
black arts communes and regional brands of black consciousness grew concurrently. Splits between older civil
rights workers and black nationalists were paralleled by
splits between older writers and younger practitioners of
black arts. The splits were not always clear-cut, however,
for many older activists and poets joined the new mood in
spirit, thematic concern and personal lifestyle, while some
of the younger writers retained the influence of the earlier
moods. Complicating things even more were the variants
on the dominant themes of each camp. Gwendolyn
Brooks, Randall, Margaret Danner, Margaret Walker, and
John Oliver Killens are among the older group of writers
who vigorously took up the banner of the new mood.
Younger writers whose works reflect some "tradition" in-

clude Henry Dumas (*Poetry for My People*, 1970 and
Play Ebony Play Ivory, 1974), Conrad Kent Rivers (*The
Still Voice of Harlem*, 1968, etc.), Julia Fields (*Poems*,
1968), Al Young (*Dancing*, 1969, etc.), and Jay Wright
(*The Homecoming Singer*, 1972), to name just a few.
(The creative promise of this period was dealt a severe
blow by the untimely deaths of Dumas and Rivers in
1968.) These poets are deeply influenced by the moods
and preoccupations of the period (self-love, racial injustice, violence, war, and black consciousness and history)
but they work along tested lines and experiment within
careful and thought-out frames of reference. Most of the
writers of the period (their styles and ideologies notwithstanding) have found themselves engulfed at one time or
another in heated debates over questions related to the
"black aesthetic," the relationship of writer to reader,
black versus white audiences, and the part politics should
play in their life and work. At this writing, these discussions continue in most sections of the black world.

The flurry of ideological and aesthetical debate among
the poets (and other writers) has often been precipitated
or attended by critical writings, historical studies, social es-
says and public political statements. Some of the individ-
uals associated with initiating the plethora of rhetoric on
the question of a black aesthetic (and related issues) are
Ron Karenga, Gwendolyn Brooks, Baraka, Addison Gayle,
Hoyt Fuller (*Black World*), Edward Spriggs, Saunders
Redding, Ralph Ellison, Larry Neal, Ernest Kaiser, Mel
Watkins, Ron Welburn, Dudley Randall, Lerone Bennett,
Jr., Nathan Scott, James Emanuel, Toni Cade-Bambara,
John Henrik Clarke, Don L. Lee, Ed Bullins, and Stanley
Crouch. A number of timely studies, literary and cultural,
by black and by white writers, aided in whetting or pro-
longing the critical thirsts. Some of these important and/
or controversial writings are Cook and Henderson, *The
Militant Black Writer: in Africa and the United States*
(1969); Gayle, Jr., ed., *Black Expression* (1969) and *The
Black Aesthetic* (1971); Jahn, *Muntu: the New African
Culture* (1961) and *Neo-African Literature: a History of
Black Writing* (1968); O'Daniel, ed., *Langston Hughes:
Black Genius* (1971); Wagner, *Black Poets of the United
States: Paul Laurence Dunbar to Langston Hughes*
(1963, French edition; 1973 English trans. by Douglas);

Bennett, *Before the Mayflower* (1962); Ellison, *Shadow and Act* (1966); Henderson, *Understanding the New Black Poetry* (1973); Éditions Présence Africaine, *Colloquium on Negro Art: First World Festival of Negro Arts, 1966* (1968); Bone, *The Negro Novel in America* (1965); Roscoe, *Mother Is Gold: a Study in West African Literature* (1971); Cruse, *The Crisis of the Negro Intellectual* (1967); Margolies, *Native Sons: a Critical Study of Twentieth-Century Negro American Authors* (1968); Lee, *Dynamite Voices: Black Poets of the 1960's*, Vol. I (1971); Baraka, *Blues People* (1963), *Black Music* (1967), *Home: Social Essays* (1966), and *Raise Race Rays Raze* (1971); and Williams, *Give Birth to Brightness* (1972). A number of black critics, artists, and activists heatedly denounce whites who research or criticize black literature, saying that only those who have lived the black experience can write about it. Another group holds that whites can report on black writing if they are sincere and sympathetic.

The Black Arts Movement, as the contemporary period is sometimes called, took place in the shadows of what many black social critics have termed the "second Reconstruction." Hence, much of the writing is a revolt against political hypocrisy and social alienation. In the angriest poetry, authors shower disdain and obscenities on the "system" and whites in general. Refusing "integration" even if offered, younger poets deride American values and attitudes. "Unlike the Harlem group," Hayden noted, "they rejected entry into the mainstream of American literature as a desirable goal." Of course, more than a few of the older poets were writing in the sixties and are writing today. Many of them, however, were sometimes laid aside by young readers who were unable to separate "poetry" from the fiery declamations of Carmichael, Brown and innumerable local spokesmen and versifiers. Often the poets exchanged superficial indictments, indulged in name-calling and, as groups or individuals, began rating each other on their "levels of blackness," even though no criteria existed then and none exist today for such judging. Much of the dispute centered around the question of who "started" the Black Arts or the New Black Poetry Movement. While it is true that there *are* leading lights of the new movements, it is misleading and false to say that one

geographical region of the country or one group of persons
is solely responsible for either the main (or major) writing
output or for kicking off any tradition of Blacks writing
about themselves. Such a stand would dismiss the Afro-
American musical past, on the one hand, and distort the
historical development of the creative writing and
thought, on the other. Anyway, the question of *who*
started *what* is not that significant.

During the sixties and into the seventies, literally hundreds of black poets started writing and publishing—in
tabloids, magazines, broadsides, anthologies, and individual collections. Also showcasing the new poetry were the
new publications: *Umbra, Black Dialogue, Soulbook,
Black World* (formerly *Negro Digest*), and *The Journal of
Black Poetry*. Significant clusters of poets developed in
geographical regions. And the atmosphere was enhanced
by a number of African thinkers, artists, poets, and novelists who arrived in America to teach, lecture, perform, and
travel. The importance of this interaction among Blacks
from various parts of the globe cannot be overemphasized.
Black writers and students now read African, West Indian
and Afro-Latin writers. Hughes acquainted American
audiences with African literature in his anthologies: *An
African Treasury: Essays, Stories, Poems by Black Africans*
(1960) and *Poems from Black Africa* (1963). In 1969,
Trinidadian Wilfred Cartey edited *Whispers from a Con-
tinent: the Literature of Contemporary Black Africa*.
Marie Collins compiled *Black Poets in French* (1972) and
Keorapetse Kgositsile edited *The World Is Here* (1973).
Other scholars and writers also wrote critical studies or
edited anthologies of African and Caribbean literature.
Black writing received a significant boost when, in 1971,
Senghor and Afro-Cuban poet Nicolás Guillén were nominated for the Nobel prize for literature—thus fulfilling
James Weldon Johnson's 1922 prophecy that the first
black writer to achieve substantial international fame
would not come from the United States. Heightening the
feeling of the period was Charles Gordone's winning of
the Pulitzer prize for drama (*No Place to Be Somebody*,
1970). Among foreign-born black writers now publishing
or living in the United States are Nigerian novelist-poet
Achebe, exiled South African poet Kgositsile, Nigerian

poet-playwright Wole Soyinka, Ghanaian poet Kwesi Brew, South African critic Ezekiel Mphahlele, Nigerian poet-playwright Ifeanyi Menkiti, Martinican poet-playwright Césaire and Guianese poetscholar Damas. The writers fraternize, exchange ideas and compare styles. Mphahlele, for example, has written critical studies of black American writing (*Voices in the Whirlwind*, 1972), while Gwendolyn Brooks has praised African writing ("Introduction," Kgositsile's *My Name Is Afrika*, 1971). South African poet Mazisi Kunene wrote the "Introduction" for Césaire's *Return to My Native Land* (1969 translation). Ghanaian poet Kofi Awoonor (*Ride Me Memory*) has published three books in the United States. Several Afro-American expatriate artists and writers returned to America during the current period for either temporary or permanent residence.

Added to all the activities and changes was the establishment of black publishing houses (Broadside Press, Third World Press, The Third Press, etc.) and hundreds of news organs and literary journals. A number of important anthologies have also been published. Some of the more notable ones include Pool, *Beyond the Blues*, 1962; Breman, *Sixes and Sevens*, 1962; Bontemps, *American Negro Poetry*, 1963; Hill, *Soon One Morning: New Writing by American Negroes, 1940–1962*, 1963; Hughes, *New Negro Poets*, 1964; Hayden, *Kaleidoscope*, 1967; Abrahams, *Black Voices*, 1968; *New Black Voices*, 1972; Jones and Neal, *Black Fire*, 1968; Major, *The New Black Poetry*, 1969; Jordan, *Soulscript*, 1970; Abdul and Lomax, *3000 Years of Black Poetry*, 1970; Randall, *The Black Poets*, 1971; King, *Black Spirits*, 1972; and Adoff, *The Poetry of Black America*, 1973. In addition to these and other nationally distributed anthologies, many collections of black literature were compiled and published in various regions.

Some of the older and younger names linked to the current period are Lucille Clifton (*Good Times, Good News About the Earth* and *An Ordinary Woman*), Pinkie Gordon Lane (*Wind Thoughts*), Harper (*Dear John, Dear Coltrane, History Is Your Own Heartbeat*), Cuney (*Puzzles*), Troupe (*Embryo*), Sterling Plumpp (*Half Black Half Blacker*), Jayne Cortez (*Pissstained Stairs and the*

Monkey Man's Wares, Festivals and Funerals), Nikki
Giovanni (*Black Judgment, Black Feeling, Black Thought,
Re: Creation*), Reed (*catechism of a neoamerican hoodoo
church*), David Henderson (*De Mayor of Harlem*), Arthur Pfister (*Bullets, Beer Cans & Things*), Baraka (*Black
Magic*), Jon Eckels (*Home Is Where the Soul Is*), Bon-
temps (*Personals*), Hayden (*Selected Poems, Words in
the Mourning Time*), Lee (*Think Black, Black Pride*),
Sonia Sanchez (*Homecoming*), Randall (*Cities Burning
and More to Remember*), Crouch (*Ain't No Ambulances
for No Nigguhs Tonight*), Hughes (*The Panther and the
Lash*), Atkins (*Heretofore*), Norman Jordan (*Destination:
Ashes*), May Miller (*Into the Clearing*), Austin Black
(*The Tornado in My Mouth*), Tolson (*Harlem Gallery*),
Emanuel (*Panther Man*), Vesey (*Ivory Tusks*), Mari
Evans (*I Am a Black Woman*), Julia Fields, Stephany
(*Moving Deep*), Etheridge Knight (*Poems from Prison*),
Gwendolyn Brooks (*In the Mecca, Riot, Family Pictures*),
Roy Hill (*49 Poems*, etc.), Ray Durem (*Take No Prison-
ers*). Far from being exhaustive, this list is merely repre-
sentative of the period's great poetic output.

Many of the poets also write children's stories (Evans,
Jordan, Clifton), fiction (Reed, Young) and criticism
(Neal). Many also are anthologists (Troupe, Randall)
and a large number write plays. The list grows and
changes constantly, especially in view of the constant un-
folding of surprises. Suffice it to say that the contemporary
mood of black poetry is multileveled and complex. There
are generalities; one is that most of the poets unreservedly
saturate their work with obvious black references and cultural motifs. There is also an anti-intellectual flavor, as
many poets turn their backs on academic or Western
forms. This is revealed in a general disregard for the esoteric, literary and sometimes obscure allusions employed in
much white poetry. There are exceptions, of course—nota-
bly in the special Islamic symbolism of Muslim poets
(Marvin X, Askia Touré, Baraka, Sonia Sanchez, and
others). These exceptions can also be seen in works of
poets who explore African ancestor cults, Voodoo, mysticism, and African languages (Reed, Touré, Dumas, Norman Jordan, Sun Ra, K. Curtis Lyle, Kaufman). Generally, though, black poets are framing allusions, images and

symbols in the more concrete cultural motifs, as indicated
in a line from Redmond's "Tune for a Teenage Niece":
"spiced as pot-liquor."

THE VOICES ON THE TOTEM

"SOON, ONE MORNING": THRESHOLD OF THE NEW BLACK POETRY

> My Blackness is the beauty of this land.
> —LANCE JEFFERS

Richard Wright called Blacks "America's metaphor," and
Lance Jeffers referred to them as "the beauty of this land."
Both stances were taken well in advance of the "black
pride" poetry of the sixties and seventies. Margaret Walker's discussion of her playmates in the Alabama "dust"
(1937) is not self-deprecating; and Gwendolyn Brooks's
portrait of Satin Legs Smith (1945) is far from being
simply unhappy. These are only four randomly selected
poetic affidavits of Blacks viewing themselves "positively"
before the advent of the new black poetry. We could, of
course, bring up hundreds of examples, from the poetry of
Phillis Wheatley through that of Hughes. But the point,
already made, is simply that one is seriously remiss in looking at recent black poetry without considering its history.

The poets who wrote and published between 1945 and
1965, for example, did not work in sealed chambers of
tunneled vision. Each group, each cluster of concern,
evolved from some of what had been written or said before. Some of these poets were heavily influenced by white
writers, teachers and critics. However, the best of them applied their knowledge and tools to the service of the black
literary tradition. Others were under the direct tutelage of
Blacks (Paul Vesey studied with James Weldon Johnson,
Joyce Yeldell with Robert Hayden) and became part of a
continuing line of black thought and writing (Vesey in
turn taught Arthur Pfister). Whatever their make-up or
their mission, the poets as a group show great facility with
language, depth of insight and passionate concern for their
collective and individual hurts as Blacks and as humans.

The works of these forerunner poets, and those of their

older pen-fellows, can be found in several anthologies: *Poetry of the Negro* (1949, 1970); the bilingual *Ik Zag Hoe Zwart Ik Was* (*I Saw How Black I Was*, 1958); *Beyond the Blues* (1962); *American Negro Poetry* (1963); *Burning Spear* (1963); *Sixes and Sevens* (1963); *Negro Verse* (1964); *New Negro Poets: USA* (1964, 1966); *Poets of Today* (1964); the bilingual *Ik Ben de Nieuwe Neger* (*I Am the New Negro*, 1965); and *Kaleidoscope* (1967). Also of interest to students of this and the previous area is a new anthology edited by Woodie King, Jr., *The Forerunners: Black Poets in America*, 1975. Bontemps and Hughes edited *Poetry of the Negro* in 1949, the first major collection since Cullen's *Caroling Dusk*. It was revised by Bontemps in 1970, after Hughes's death. Interestingly, some of the 1949 entries have been deleted, and the table of contents has been altered to include new entries such as Randall, Evans and Durem in chronological sequence. Arna Bontemps, a Harlem Renaissance poet who did not publish a volume until 1963 (*Personals*), also edited *American Negro Poetry*, a task that gave him the opportunity to pick the best from the past as well as the present. *I Saw How Black I Was* and *Beyond the Blues* were published in Holland and England, respectively, and edited by Rosey Pool, with the assistance of Paul Bremen. Dr. Pool (1905–73), a native of the Netherlands, came across Cullen when she was preparing a paper on American poetry in 1925. This discovery led to a life-long interest in black culture and poetry. During 1959–60 she toured the United States on a Fulbright travel grant, spending several months visiting and lecturing at twenty-seven black colleges and universities. Her work in black poetry has drawn mixed reactions from cautious black writers and critics. But her importance in helping to bring attention to black poets, despite cries of "exploitation," is undeniable.

Even more controversial is Bremen, who appears to fancy himself as an English Jean-Paul Sartre; he originated the Heritage Series—"devoted entirely to the works of Afro-American authors"—with Hayden's *A Ballad of Remembrance* in 1963. Since that time, Bremen, who edited *Sixes and Sevens* and *You Better Believe It: Black Verse in English* (1973), has released more than twenty volumes of Afro-American poetry. Randall's Broadside

Press serves as the American distributor of the slim books, which have included the aesthetical and historical range of black poetry: Horne (*Haverstraw*, 1963), Bontemps, Rivers (*The Still Voice of Harlem*, 1968; *The Wright Poems*, 1972), Evans (*Where is all the Music?* 1968 but withdrawn "at the author's request"), Atkins (*Heretofore*, 1968), Lloyd Addison (*The Aura & the Umbra*, 1970), Audre Lorde (*Cables to Rage*, 1970), Randall, (*Love You*, 1970), Reed, whom Bremen calls "the best Black poet writing today" (*catechism of a neoamerican hoodoo church*, 1970), James W. Thompson (*First Fire: Poems 1957–1960*, 1970), Dodson, Harold Carrington (*Drive suite*, 1972), Clarence Major (*Private Line*, 1971), the "first non-American contributor"—Mukhtarr Mustapha (*Thorns and Thistles*, 1971), Durem (*Take No Prisoners*, 1971), and Hayden (*The Night-Blooming Cereus*, 1972). Bremen notes that both Mari Evans and Raymond Patterson ordered their books withdrawn because they "were suspicious of the contract terms." In addition to such "suspicion," felt also by other black poets, there is great resentment of Bremen's fast-draw critical evaluations of the poetry—which are often caustic, ridiculous and narrow, and reflect a lack of the broader concerns of black poetry. He calls Durem, for example, one of the first "black" poets. His statement about Reed, coming as it did in 1970, does violence to both the author and the critical atmosphere in which black poets grapple every day. He says Dumas was born in the "incredibly named town" of Sweet Home, Arkansas. Nevertheless (alas!), one wonders where these black poets might have gotten published if such "necessary diseases" as Bremen did not exist.

Negro Verse, edited by Anselm Hollo, has no introduction or foreword, but it does include a dozen blues and gospel song-poems. *New Negro Poets* was edited by Hughes with a Foreword by Gwendolyn Brooks. Use of the word "new" in the title exemplifies the kind of spirit that was in ascension at the time. Gwendolyn Brooks is also her usual terse and definitive self:

At the present time, poets who happen also to be Negroes are twice-tried. They have to write poetry, and they have to remember that they are Negroes. Often

they wish that they could solve the Negro question once
and for all, and go on from such success to the composition of textured sonnets or buoyant villanelles about the
transience of a raindrop, or the gold-stuff of the sun.
They are likely to find significances in those subjects not
instantly obvious to their fairer fellows. The raindrop
may seem to them to represent racial tears—and those
might seem, indeed, other than transient. The golden
sun might remind them that they are burning.

There is an attitude in this statement that the Gwendolyn
Brooks of 1968 will reject: "poets who happen also to be
Negroes." But she reflects Cullen in the "dark tower" and
his ruminating on the "curious thing" of the black poet.
She also presages the twistings and turning in Jayne Cor-
tez's "Festivals & Funerals." And, in introducing the
"New Negro Poets," she informs the reader, ". . . here
are some of the prevailing stars of an early tomorrow."

Walter Lowenfels' decision to include "20 Negroes" in
Poets of Today was spurred in part by his recognition
(along with Shapiro) that "most general anthologies of
American poetry exclude Negroes." An authority on
Whitman, Lowenfels shared an award with E. E. Cummings in the thirties and has helped a number of black
poets get additional exposure: Dumas, Troupe, Patterson,
Redmond, Carrington, Major, Reed, Harper, Hayden, and
many others. Lowenfels' was the first new white-edited anthology to include such a substantial number of Blacks.
There were eighty-five poets in all. One of the most important of these new anthologies is *Burning Spear*, which
contains the work of the Howard poets: Walter DeLegall
(1936–), Lance Jeffers (1919–), Al Fraser, Oswald
Govan, Percy Johnston (1930–), Nathan Richards,
Le Roy Stone (1936–) and Joseph White. *Burning
Spear*, subtitled *an Anthology of Afro-Saxon Poetry*, was
an outgrowth of the Dasein Literary Society, at Howard
University, which established *Dasein: a Quarterly Journal
of the Arts* in 1961. Johnston, its founder, served as publisher, while DeLegall was editor. Their connection with
the older group of poets and scholars is evident in the ad-
visory board: Sterling A. Brown, Arthur P. Davis, Owen
Dodson, and Eugene C. Holmes. Fraser, Govan, Jeffers,
Stone, and White were contributing editors. Poets in the

inaugural issue of *Dasein*, which doubled as a memorial to Richard Wright, were Delores Kendrick, Clyde R. Taylor, Jeffers, William Jackson, Vernon A. Butler, Robert Slaughter, Laura A. Watkins, Govan, Fraser, Delores F. Henry, R. Orlando Jackson, DeLegall, Johnston, and Stone.

There is no single unifying thread running through either *Dasein* or *Burning Spear*, but black influences and subjects are clearly imbedded. *Burning Spear*, for example, is published by Jupiter Hammon Press, another connection—in name—to the tradition of black poetry. In a back-cover note, the eight contributors are called "a new breed of young poets who are to American poetry what Charlie Parker, Dizzy Gillespie, Thelonious Monk and Miles Davis are to American jazz." After this important analogy, the statement continues:

> These eight Afro-Saxon poets are not members of a literary movement in the traditional sense of the word, because they do not have in common any monist view about creativity or aesthetics. Collectively, however, they are indifferent to most critics and reviewers— since criticism in America is controlled and written in the main by Euro-Americans.

Poems by DeLegall, Jeffers, Johnston, and Stone also appear in *Beyond the Blues* and in numerous "little" magazines. And all the poets participated in reading-lecture programs leading up to the wider interest in poetry in the later sixties and seventies. DeLegall (Philadelphia), a mathematician and electronic data-processing specialist, has published in many anthologies and quarterlies, and has read his poetry and lectured at various eastern and southern colleges. Fraser (Charleston) is a political scientist specializing in African affairs. Along with DeLegall, Stone, Govan, Johnston, and Richards, he has been recorded reading his poetry at the Library of Congress. Fraser has cultivated a coffee-shop audience for his readings and has appeared before college groups. He is a philosopher-mathematician.

One of the older members of the group, Jeffers (San Francisco) is credited with having "influence" on the Howard poets. He has taught English and writing at half a dozen American colleges and universities. His first volume of poetry was *My Blackness Is the Beauty of This Land*

(1970), and his second, *When I Know the Power of My Black Hand,* was brought out in 1975. Both are published by Broadside Press. Jeffers has also written novels, short stories and criticism. Johnston (New York) currently teaches at a college in New Jersey and with Stone "co-authored the revolutionary verse pamphlet *Continental Streamlets.*" Also a playwright, Johnston published a pamphlet of his poetry, *Concerto for Girl and Convertible,* in 1960 and was considered the leader of the Howard poets. White is a native Philadelphian whose work appeared in *Liberator, Poets of Today,* and other places. He has been a technician for FAA and has written short stories as well as successful prose poems.

As a group, the Howard poets (listed above) represent one of the toughest intellectual strains in contemporary black poetry. Maybe the fact of their having such diverse interests, backgrounds, and training aided in their vitality, virtuosity and power. To be sure, these are "conscious" poets; but—avoiding slogans and sentimental hero-worship —they present precise analyses and interpretations of their world. Most of them grew up in the bebop era and so their subjects quite naturally include Miles Davis, Lester Young, Charles "Yardbird" Parker, Clifford Brown, Sonny Rollins, Thelonious Monk, and other makers and contributors of that period. A concern for civil rights and black struggle merges with an awareness of the "bomb," middle-class pretensions, history, mythology, religion, and the various trends in poetry: modernity, beat poetry, jazz, and folk lyrics.

DeLegall celebrates the black presence ("My Brownskin Business") and satirizes a pretentious Howard coed ("Requiem for a Howard Lady") who is "cultured" and performs every social amenity perfectly. She wears "High-heeled tennis shoes"; but he hopes, near the poem's end, that the president of The Universal Institute of Eugenics will send a

New species of female

who will be robed in clothes of "sincerity" and who can be called "A Woman." In "Psalm for Sonny Rollins" he announces that he is

Absorbed into the womb of the sound.
>   I am in the sound
>   The sound is in me.
>   I am the sound.

Rollins, the Harlem pied piper, will lead his listeners to "truth," "Zen," "Poetry," and "God."

After "The Blast" (nuclear bombing), Fraser says, there will be

. . . no I, no world, no you.

And Govan also writes convincingly, as in "The Lynching":

He was soaked in oil and the match thrown.
He screamed, he cried, he moaned,
he crackled in his fiery inhuman dance.

Govan's interests span the turbulence in "Hungary," space exploration ("The Angry Skies Are Calling"), and "Prayer," wherein he asks "Christ" for

a new dawn's light!

Jeffers is a living example of the helpless plight of many a black American writer. Although he had been writing for several decades, his work was "white"-listed by anthologists and his poetry did not appear in book form until the seventies. "My Blackness Is the Beauty of This Land" stands as a rebuff to those who say black poetry was recently "invented." Jeffers' poem, written in the fifties, is at once defiant, proud and turbulent:

My blackness is the beauty of this land,
my blackness,
tender and strong, wounded and wise. . . .

The narrator, after the fashion of Margaret Walker, chronicles the hurts, the happinesses, and the hungers of Blacks. These he stands against his "whiteness" and the perversions of larger America. "Black Soul of the Land" mines the same vein: rich reliance on the well-deep strength of the black past. The "old black man" in Geor-

gia is "leathered, lean, and strong." And these are secrets
that "crackers could not kill":

    a secret spine unbent within a spine,
    a secret source of steel,
    a secret sturdy rugged love,
    a secret crouching hate,
    a secret knife within his hand,
    a secret bullet in his eye.

The poet asks the old man to pass on his source of
strength so that he, and his fellows, will be able to "turn
black" the soul of the nation

    and America shall cease to be its name.

Jeffers gathers up a fury of love, anguish and commitment
in other poems: "Her Black and African Face I Love,"
"The Man with a Furnace in His Hand," "Negro Freedom Rider," "Her Dark Body I Cluster," "Black Man in a
New Day," and "Prophecy."

Johnston echoes Jeffers, though in a different voice and
style, in many of his poems. But Johnston's primary concern is with black music and musicians. "To Paul
Robeson, Opus No. 3," celebrates the multifaceted
talents of the man whose song "stood Brooklyn on its
feet." "In Memoriam: Prez" is a magnificent tribute to
the president of jazz: Lester Young, whose music continues to "ignite the heart." In "Fitchett's Basement Blues,
Opus 5," Johnston wonders why everytime

    I want Coltrane or Sonny all
    I get is Brubeck. . . .

"Dewey Square," with its "beat" repertoire and interests
in contemporary everyman, is a poetic summary of the
collective history of Johnston's generation. Words for
"unkinking hair," recollections of radio shows, reminders
of relief and WPA, and Duke Ellington, all leave Johnston
with the knowledge that nothing

    Has changed but my postal zone.

In other pieces, he surveys the current and past black musical scene: "'Round 'Bout Midnight, Opus 17," "Varia-

tion on a Theme by Johnston," and "To Bobby Tim-
mons."

"Black Is My Reward," Richards says, noting,

Sorrow came, and I left the world. . . .

An experimentalist, his "Do Not Forget to Remember"
includes a "prelude" and an "interlude." Like the other
poets, he writes primarily in free verse (almost no rhyme),
and in the foregoing poem he constantly repeats, "A petal
falls." The Howard poets all touch grief and anguish, as
does Richards in "God Bless This Child and Other Children . . . Requiem." In syntax and vocabulary, it loosely
resembles the beats and Kaufman and Atkins. Words
and phrases like "matronymic diva," "sepiacenic martyr,"
"albumenic hawk," "womb-prize," and "black aegis" convey the mystical and eerie sense implied in the repetition
of "sleep" and the innovative typography of the poem.

Also experimental and original is Le Roy Stone. His
study of Miles Davis' "Flamenco Sketches" is separated
into five parts: *ouvert, selim, cannons, enart,* and *bill.* New
York is "red in weeping" and Chicago is "Black-draped"
as Miles utters in "mutes." The music captures the

Dissonant nostalgia of one kiss

of a Spanish lady as it weaves in and out of trans-
continental experiences and locations. The poet reveres
Davis' use and knowledge of world music. Finally, the
music is asked to

Comment
on a cloud of oriental ninths
comment!

In "Notes from the Cubicle of a Disgruntled Jazzman"
Stone becomes a verbal maestro, ripping in "changes," rat-
tling up "thirteenths," storming the "minor mode," and
whipping up "passing tones"—all "with impunity."

Joseph White's "Black Is a Soul" repeats "down" as the
persona drops into "depths," "the abyss," and the
"infinite,"

Where black-eyed peas & greens are stored. . . .

This poignant revelation is made in the end:

> I raise my downbent kinky head to charlie
>> & shout
> I'm black. I'm black
> & I'm from Look Back.

We think immediately of such titles as *Think Black* (Lee) and "Say It Loud—I'm Black and I'm Proud" (James Brown) even though this poem preceded them by several years—to say nothing of Joseph Cotter, Jr.'s "Is It Because I'm Black?" But White can also do light and touching things, as in "Picnic" and "Day Is Done," which places "music in the air" as he prepares for bed and his "woman" sets her hair. His ironic, satirical "Inquisitive" displays the range of these poets. The narrator wonders where "Gods" and "buddhas" hide if the earth and sky are both visible to man.

Little critical attention has been given the Howard group or any of the other poets writing during this period. But they are legion, including well-known as well as unfamiliar names: Johnson Ackerson, Charles Anderson (1938–), Eugene Redmond (1937–), Julian Bond (1940–), John Henrik Clarke (1915–), Leslie M. Collins (1914–), Katherine Cuestas (1944–), Margaret Danner (1915–), Gloria Davis, Durem, Mari Evans, Micki Grant, Julia Fields (1938–), Gordon Heath, Horne, Ted Joans (1928–), Naomi Madgett (1923–), James C. Morriss (1920–), O'Higgins, Patterson, James Randall (1938–), Peter T. Rogers, John Sherman Scott, Carmell Simmons, James W. Thompson (1935–), Vesey, Sarah Wright (1929–), Joyce Yeldell (1944–), Robert Earl Fitzgerald (1935–), Calvin Hernton (1932–), Lula Lowe Weeden (1918–), Lillie Mae Carter, Gloria C. Oden, Mose Carl Holman 1919–), Alfred Duckett (1918–), J. M. Gates, James Emanuel (1921–), Lerone Bennett, Jr. (1928–), Sarah Webster Fabio (1928–), Hoyt Fuller (1927–), Carl Gardener (1931–), Ossie Davis (1922–), Zack Gilbert (1925–), Herbert Clark Johnson (1911–), Bette Darcie Latimer (1927–), Oliver La Grone (1915–), Rivers, Bruce McM. Wright, Pauli Murray (1910–), Roy Hill, Sam Cornish (1938–), Yvonne

Gregory (1919–), Frank Yerby (1916–), Nanina
Alba (1915–68), Frank London Brown (1927–62),
Isabella Maria Brown (1917–), Catherine Carter
(1917–), Ernest J. Wilson, Jr. (1920–), Mary Carter
Smith (1924–), James P. Vaughn (1929–), Robert J.
Abrams (1924–), Roscoe Lee Browne (1930–),
William Browne (1930–), Oliver Pitcher (1923–),
Ishmael Reed (1938–), Adam David Miller (1922–),
David Henderson (1942–), Don Johnson (1942–),
Thurmond Snyder, A. B. Spellman (1935–), Mance
Williams, Tom Dent, LeRoi Jones (1934–), Vivian
Ayers, Helen Morgan Brooks, Solomon Edwards
(1932–), Ed Roberson, Vilma Howard, George Love,
Allen Polite (1932–), Lloyd Addison (1931), Hart
Leroi Bibbs, Durwood Collins (1937–), Bobb Hamil-
ton, May Miller, Stanley Morris, Jr. (1944–), Quandra
Prettyman.

In anthologies this non-exhaustive list was often intermingled with early poets (as far back as Phillis
Wheatley), elder ones (Johnson, McKay, Dunbar), and
spiced with a good offering of post-Harlem Renaissance
poets (Walker, Brooks, Tolson, Hayden). Such names as
Fuller, Bennett, Jr., Holman, Yerby, Davis, and Clarke
fall in the category of part-time poets—most of whom un-
dertook full-time duties as novelists, editors, lawyers, or
teachers. Other important movements parallel to this
phase were the emergence of literary magazines (*Free
Lance, Phylon*), especially on black college campuses;
black newspapers' renewed interest in verse; establishment
of poets in residences at southern black colleges; the
flowering of regional "movements" or writing collectives—
such as those in New York's Greenwich Village (*Yungen,
Umbra*, etc.), Cleveland's Karamu House and *Free Lance*
(Casper Leroy Jordan, Atkins), Howard's *Dasein* group,
the Detroit poets, and Georgia Douglas Johnson's home-
based workshops in Washington, D.C.[1] Not all these de-

---

[1] Development of a black listening audience was a central aim in
most of these activities. For example, on June 16, 1957, young poets
Calvin Hernton and Raymond Patterson read together at 316 East 6th
Street in New York City. A favorite New York gathering place for
readings was the Market Place Gallery (2305 Seventh Avenue), where
Roscoe Lee Browne was featured in the late fifties. In July and

velopments occurred exclusively among black poets, however, for there also were racially mixed writing communes
and editorial staffs. Julia Fields, for example, was in residence at the Bread Loaf Writers' Conference in New
England and studied for a while in Scotland. Redmond,
who won writing awards and published in little magazines
between 1960 and 1965, worked with the staffs of the
Three Penny Broadside (Southern Illinois University) and
Free Lance (Washington University). Other poets and
their outlets were Dumas (*Trace, Anthologist*), Patterson
and Jones (*Floating Bear, Yungen*), Gloria C. Oden (*Urbanite, The Poetry Digest, The Half Moon*), Rivers
(*Kenyon Review, Antioch Review, Ohio Poetry Review*),
Spellman (*Kulchur, Metronome, Umbra,*), Mance
Williams (*Blue and Gold*), and Audre Lorde (*Venture*).
Margaret Danner published a series of poems in *Poetry*
magazine as early as 1952, and in 1956 became an assistant editor.

Of these parallel movements and developments, one
other deserved special notice. Though not on a par with
the Howard poets, the *Umbra* Workshop participants
aided in the production and distribution of black poetry in
the early sixties. Centered in New York's Lower East Side
and Greenwich Village, the *Umbra* poets were founded by
Tom Dent (New Orleans), Calvin Hernton (Chattanooga) and David Henderson (New York). The workshop, which also involved artists and fiction writers, published the first issue of its *Umbra* quarterly in 1963. Other
issues came out in 1964, 1967–68 (an anthology), 1970–
71 (tabloid anthology) and 1974–75 ("Latin Soul" issue).
Dent first served as editor, and Henderson, who now di-
rects the publication from Berkeley, took over in 1967.
Others attracted to the *Umbra* workshop were Reed, Rol-
land Snellings (now Askia Touré), Norman Pritchard,
singer Len Chandler, dancer Asaman Byron, the Patterson
brothers (Charles and William), painters Gerald Jackson
and Joe Overstreet, Lennox Raphael, Dumas, James

August of 1960 a number of black poets read there: Lloyd Addison,
Robert J. Abrams, Browne, Phil Petrie, Allen Polite, Sarah Wright, Hil-
ton Hosannah, M.D., and Browne in a special reading of the works of
Hernton. Others associated with the series included John Henrik Clarke
and Langston Hughes.

Thompson, Julian Bond, Sun Ra, Durem, Steve Cannon, and Joe Johnson. The promise of the *Umbra* group was damaged by two events. One was a failure to print an interview (conducted by Raphael and others) with Ralph Ellison. The second, resulting in a serious split among members, was a controversial anti-Kennedy poem-letter by Durem. President Kennedy had just been assassinated when the Durem piece was approved by the editors. Hernton, Dent and Henderson decided it was in bad taste. Others, according to Henderson, wanted the poem printed and subsequently "kidnaped Pritchard, who was treasurer, threatening him with bodily harm." The incident is viewed as one of the near-fatal blows to the *Umbra* group. Later Snellings, the Pattersons, and others went uptown to work with Jones's newly formed Black Arts Repertory and School.

The work of *Umbra* contributors ranges from the occasional and humorous Bond to the serious Durem. Poems by Durem, Henderson, Hernton, Dent, and Thompson also appear in the early anthologies along with work of other "Village" poets, such as G. C. Oden, Spellman, Jones (Newark) and Joans (Cairo, Illinois). Some are also represented in two later anthologies: *Black Fire* (1968) and *The Poetry of Black America* (1973). Though racial consciousness is not blatantly evident in these poets, the protest is there, especially in the works of Durem, Henderson, and Hernton. *Umbra* made clear its twofold aim in the inaugural issue:

> *Umbra* exists to provide a vehicle for those outspoken and youthful writers who present aspects of social and racial reality which may be called "uncommercial" but cannot with any honesty be considered non-essential to a whole and healthy society. . . . We will not print trash, no matter how relevantly it deals with race, social issues, or anything else.

Dent views "Love" as a "blue tom" lurking "icily" in the darkness. Henderson sees a "Downtown-Boy Uptown" and asks:

Am I in the wrong slum?

His "Sketches of Harlem" include the "GREAT WHITE WAY" and a small black boy confusing the moon and the sun. Durem, who ran away from home at age fourteen, was born in Seattle. While still in his mid-teens he joined the Navy and later became a member of the International Brigades during the Spanish Civil War. Hughes tried to find a publisher for his works as early as 1954. Of himself Durem said: "When I was ten years old I used my fists. When I was thirty-five, I used the pen. I hope to live to use the machine gun. . . . The white North-American has been drunk for four hundred years." His work does not have the finish of a Hayden or Brooks, but he provides an exciting shot in the arm for this period of black poetry (though Bremen's title "first black" poet, is unwarranted). *Take No Prisoners* (1971) contains many of Durem's memorable poems and a "Posthumous Preface" signed in 1962 although he died in 1963. "White People Got Trouble, Too" surveys the plight of whites following the Depression, recession and war, and notes that such an intrusion in the affairs of whites does not equal slavery. After all, life (or history) calls for

One tooth for one tooth.

Most of Durem's poems are short, satirical, ironical, and musical, as in "Broadminded":

Some of my best friends are white boys.
When I meet 'em
I treat 'em
just the same as if they was people.

He writes of black history, slavery, social inequities, prison life, and "pale poets" to whom he confesses his poetry is not "sufficiently obscure" to meet white critical standards. Strangely, *Take No Prisoners* does not include "Award"— "A Gold Watch to the FBI Man (who has followed me for 25 years)"—which traces the agent's surveillance of the narrator through the "blind alleys" of Mexico, the high Sierras, the Philharmonic, L.A., Mississippi, and other places of violence and mayhem. But it is not all over, the agent is told, for in the end

I may be following you!

The work of Village poets was highlighted by the versatile and prolific LeRoi Jones (Imamu Amiri Baraka), A.

B. Spellman, and Ted Joans. Before his new, black stance
of the mid and late sixties, Jones published in little avant-
garde magazines (editing several himself) and was
identified as the most talented Black among the beats. His
two volumes *Preface to a Twenty Volume Suicide Note*
(1962) and *The Dead Lecturer* (1964) show him as a
hip, arrogant, musically involved cat with a tough intelligence. His influences at the time, as he noted, were the
great Spanish poet Federico García Lorca, Williams,
Pound, and Charles Olson. He was an adventurer in style
with an elliptical and sometimes sacrilegious posture. This
aesthetic philosophy was shared by the Black Mountain
poets: George Oppen, Robert Creely, Robert Duncan,
Denise Levertov, Paul Blackburn, Edward Dorn, Ginsberg, Corso, Gary Snyder, and Michael McClure. A music
critic for such magazines as *Downbeat, Jazz,* and *Metronome,* and with an intense interest in black music, Jones
nurtured a careful "ear" in his verse. Hence, the belief
that Jones "suddenly became black" is indefensible. In
"Lines to García Lorca" he uses a section of a "Negro
Spiritual" as an inscription. The poem is typical of Jones's
ability to merge numerous ideas, symbols and images in
one poem. Lorca's death is lamented as Jones uses excerpts
from the Catholic Mass, reflects on his childhood,
explores mythology, gathers bits of poetic confetti from
nature, and hears Lorca "laughing, laughing"—maybe
mocking his killers—

Like a Spanish guitar.

In "Epistrophe" he finds that peering out the window is
"such a static reference." So he wishes "some weird-look-
ing animal" would come by. In the title poem from his
first volume—*Preface*—he adjusts to the way "ground
opens up" and takes him in whenever he goes out to
"walk the dog." Life is as monotonous as the "static reference" of window watching:

Nobody sings anymore.

Ted Joans, another Village poet closely identified with
the beats, published *Beat* (1961), *All of Ted Joans*
(1961), *The Hipsters* (1961) and other volumes. His
most widely known poem from this period is "The .38,"

with its debts to Hughes (which he acknowledged), Whitman and the beats. Beginning every line with the phrase "I hear," Joans narrates the murder of an unfaithful wife and lover by her husband:

> I hear it coming faster than sound the .38
> I hear it coming closer to my sweaty forehead the .38
> I hear its weird whistle the .38
> I hear it give off a steamlike noise when it cuts
>   through my sweat the .38
> I hear it singe my skin as it enters my head the .38
> I hear death saying, *Hello, I'm here!*

As a group, Joans, Jones and Spellman can be carefully compared to the Howard poets. They are in the same age range, and their themes and interests are similar.

Spellman, like Jones, studied at Howard University and has been a disc jockey on FM radio stations. His book reviews and articles on jazz have appeared in *Kulchur*, *The New Republic*, *Jazz*, and *The Nation*. In 1964 his first volume of poems, *The Beautiful Days*, was published. He has also published a book-length study of black music (*Four Lives in the Bebop Business*, 1966). In "Zapata & the Landlord," the "thief," the speaker says, is running in "circles." The poem is a humorous treatment of revolutionary struggle in a Latin American country. In "What Is It," Spellman applies a similar technique. This time a cat "hides in your face," in the corners of the mouth and in "that strange canyon" behind the eyes. "A Theft of Wishes" is experimental in its use of jagged lines and shifts between the tangible and surreal worlds. In the end we are told that

> home
>   is where we make
>
>   our noise.

Another poet who joins this "irreverent" generation is beat innovator Kaufman of the San Francisco Bay area. His first works came out as broadsides from Ferlinghetti's City Lights Books: "The Abominist Manifesto," "Second April" and "Does the Secret Mind Whisper?" Kaufman's poetry, conveying protest through understatement and irony, is marked by unusual and surreal images. His books are *Solitudes Crowded with Loneliness* (1965) and *Golden Sardine* (1967). *Solitudes* was published in French, "immediately" achieving "a notoriety rare among books of poetry by foreign poets" (jacket, *Sardine*). Leading French magazines reviewed the book, publishers noted, adding, "Today in France Kaufman is considered among the greatest Negro-American poets alive in spite of his continuing exclusion from American anthologies, both hip & academic." Kaufman's themes are racial memory ("African Dream"), jazz ("Walking Parker Home," "West Coast Sounds—1956"), other poets and writers ("Hart . . . Crane," "Ginsberg," "Camus: I Want to Know"), incarceration (a series of thirty-four verses in *Jail Poems*), history, mythology, and religion. In "The Eyes Too," he says,

My eyes too have souls that rage. . . .

A "Cincophrenicpoet" meets with "all five" of himself and a vote is taken to "expel" the "weakest" one, who resents it and soars over all limits

to cross, spiral, and whirl.

Somewhat typical of Kaufman's elliptical constructions and wacky imagery is "Heavy Water Blues":

The radio is teaching my goldfish Jujitsu
I am in love with a skindiver who sleeps underwater,
My neighbors are drunken linguists, & I speak
    butterfly,
Consolidated Edison is threatening to cut off
    my brain,
The postman keeps putting sex in my mailbox,
I put my eyes on a diet, my tears are gaining
    too much weight.

In this form and style, Kaufman is not only related to the beats but to Jones, Joans, Spellman, Atkins, and the gifted young Los Angeles poet K. Curtis Lyle.

Among the older poets who did not come into prominence until the 1960s were Vesey (Columbus, Ohio), Holman (Minter City, Mississippi), Bruce McM. Wright (Princeton, New Jersey), O'Higgins (Chicago), Duckett (Brooklyn), Atkins (Cleveland), Emanuel (Nebraska),

and Randall (Washington, D.C.). The poets, and others
of their generation, are not similar enough to be labeled a
"school" or a "movement," but they came of age during
the integration push, when words like "identity" and "humanity" engendered more philosophical discussion than
they do today. These are the men who went to World
War II, opposed lynching and attended northern white
graduate schools. Most were part-time poets, pursuing academic or professional careers.

Vesey, as poet and professional, bridges the middle passage between Africa and Afro-America. At Fisk University
he studied creative writing under James Weldon Johnson,
then went on to law school at Harvard. While he was
studying at the Sorbonne, in Paris, some of his poems
were published, through the intercession of Richard
Wright, in the French magazine *Présence Africaine*.
Vesey was helped greatly in the interpretation and dis-
semination of *négritude*. Paul Vesey (birth name Samuel
Allen) is the name under which he published his bilingual
volume of poems *Elfenbein Zähne* (*Ivory Tusks*, 1956,
Germany). Vesey works with skill and precision. "The
Staircase" is a poem on which, he says, "I would rest my
case, I think, and that of the Negro in this land" (*Blues*).
The poem studies the black predicament through the
plight of a man for whom the "stairs mount to his eternity." Perhaps, like Sisyphus, the stair is purposefully
"unending" since the rotten floor, the "dripping faucet"
and the "cracked ceiling" also remain. The man is joined
by a "twin," who later goes "exalted to his worms." Vesey
also writes an elegy for Dylan Thomas ("Dylan, Who Is
Dead"), a praise poem for baseball legend Satchel Paige
("American Gothic"), and a powerful piece ("A Moment, Please") interweaving two different ideas and
themes: one viewing the universe and the general circumstances of man, the other viewing the specific reality of
being black and called "nigger" by two adolescent girls.
"To Satch" is reminiscent of Tolson's tribute to Louis
Armstrong. Speaking in the poem, Satchel Paige says one
morning he is going to grab a "handfulla stars," throw
three strikes to burn down the "heavens,"

And look over at God and say
How about that!

M. Carl Holman's work is among the few entries for poetry in *Soon, One Morning*. But he is also represented in other anthologies. He has led an active life as a civil-rights fighter (information officer of the United States Commission on Civil Rights), editor (Atlanta *Inquirer*), writer, and teacher. Currently, he is president of the National Urban Coalition. While a student at Chicago University, he won several awards for writing. Holman, whose poetic subjects range from complex psychic meditations to racial pride, is very good indeed but much overlooked. The leisure class finds clocks "intrude too early" in "And on This Shore." The general indifference is also captured:

Across the cups we yawn at private murders.

"Picnic: The Liberated" examines the shifting uncertainties with which leisured Southerners must live. The tension of everyday southern life lies underneath the merriment of the picnic grounds, where men rotate the liquor in "dixie cups" and "absently" discuss "civil rights, money and goods." Yet as the "country dark" comes in and they return to sprinklered yards and "mortgaged houses," they do not know they are

Privileged prisoners in a haunted land.

However this same poet can hear "Three Brown Girls Singing" through the "ribs of an ugly school building." Celebrating the black musical past, Holman has them

Fuse on pure sound in a shift of April light. . . .

Bruce McM. Wright, now a federal district judge in New York, was a Lincoln University poet and, with Hughes and Cuney, edited *Lincoln University Poets* (1954). He served overseas in World War II, later receiving law training at Fordham. While he was in the Army in Wales, he published a volume of his poetry, *From the Shaken Tower* (1944). "The African Affair" finds McM. Wright on a safari to find out what "Black is." He discovers it in "prisons," in the "devils dance," where "deserts burn," the middle passage, and areas where "conscience cannot go." His search carries him deep into Africa, where "traders shaped my father's pain." In "Four Odd Bodkins for My Analyst," one finds that "outraged flesh of secret guilt" has come from the pressures of "circumstance" and "need." Finally, in "When You have Gone from Rooms," there are "never blooming petals" and "never burning suns."

O'Higgins was called by Bontemps a member of the "tribe of wandering poets." After studying with Brown at Howard, O'Higgins won Lucy Moten and Julius Rosenwald fellowships in writing. He later served in World War II, after which he coauthored, with Hayden, *The Lion and the Archer* (1948). O'Higgins' style is less formal than either Holman's or McM. Wright's. He is closer to Vesey, especially in such poems as "Young Poet" and "Two Lean Cats," in which the rain fell like "ragged jets" and made a "grave along" the street. The lean cats, running in "checkered terror" into a poolroom, find that a "purple billiard ball" makes the color scheme explode. The much anthologized "Vaticide" ("For Mohandas Gandhi") sees Gandhi "murdered upright in the day" and left with his flesh "opened and displayed." But, likening Gandhi's death to Christ's, the narrator says such a person who created the "act of love" knows the guilty carry his "death to their rooms." Gandhi's "marvelous wounds" contain the sun and the seas.

Different, yet similar, these poets sought through their individual voices to deal with man's current and past hurts. Atkins, for example, saw the "swollen deep" rise higher as he "went walking," in section two of "Fantasie." A "restless experimentalist with a very high regard for craftmanship," (jacket, *Heretofore*) Atkins was a founder of *Free Lance* (1950), which Conrad Kent Rivers called the "oldest black-bossed magazine around." Between 1947 and 1962, Atkins' poetry appeared in numerous journals and other outlets. A few are *View, Beloit Poetry Journal, Minnesota Quarterly, Naked Ear,* and *Galley Sail Review.* His volumes of poetry are *Phenomena* (1961), *Psychovisual Perspective for Musical Composition* (1958), *Two by Atkins* (*The Abortionist and the Corpse: Two Poetic Dramas Set to Music* (1963), *Objects* (1963), and *Heretofore* (1968). Atkins' aesthetic ideas are often as complex as the poetry itself. His early training was in music and literature; and he said in *Sixes and sevens,* that he was trying for "egocentrical phenomenalism: an objective construct of properties to substantiate effect as object." He

searches after the "designed imagination." In "Night and
a Distant Church," he moves "Forward abrupt" then "up"
through a series of intermingling "mmms" and "ells" with
words like "wind" and "rain." There is more than a hint
of Tolson's ability to meander among Greco-Roman and
Afro-American traditions in Atkins' poetry. But he is
unique. "At War" informs the reader that beyond the
"turning sea's far foam" the "ephemera" of a "moment's
dawn"

> sudden'd its appear. . . .

Later in the same poem, after allusions to Hemingway, the
silence splits:

> Listen a moment—Sh! Listen—!
> that hurrying as of a shore of
> fugitives.

Once Atkins's technique is understood, however, his poetry can be enjoyed for its witty, wacky, yet serious philosophical musings. In "Irritable Song," he inverts, reverses
and convolutes regular syntax:

> Or say upon return
> Coronary farewell
> Leaves me lie. Ugh!
> Dare, sir? Be nay'd
> Tomorrow, tomorrow
> in today?

Atkins writes of the fine arts, John Brown's raid on
Harpers Ferry, black heroes ("Christophe"), the "Train-
yard at Night," and the Cleveland lakefront.

At the other end of the stylistic and thematic pole is
Randall, a librarian by training and trade who, as we shall
see in our discussion of poets of the late sixties, figures
prominently in the development of an audience for the
new black poetry. Randall also served in World War II
and writes poems about the war, love, violence, art, and
the black presence. His well-known "Booker T. and
W.E.B.," digesting the Washington-Du Bois controversy,
was seen by Du Bois, and this pleased Randall. The poem
first appeared in *Midwest Journal*, 1952. Randall has also
written about and translated Russian poetry. With Margaret Danner he coauthored *Poem Counterpoem* (1966),

and his *Cities Burning* appeared in 1968. *More to Remember* (1971) pulls together Randall's poems from "four decades." His work has been published in *Umbra, Beloit Poetry Journal,* and other places. He initiated the Broadside Series (posters) in 1965 with his own "Ballad of Birmingham." The series grew quickly, laying the foundation for his Broadside Press, the most significant black poetry press in America. Randall's work of this period has the stamp of formality. He writes in ballad and free-verse forms, but he had a tightness that would be relaxed in the late sixties. "Legacy" chronicles the hurt, physical and mental, of a land "Lit by a bloody moon." But the one who is "moulded from this clay" vows:

> My tears redeem my tears.

"Perspectives" recasts the time-immemorial theme of *we only pass this way once.* There is no need to complain about discomfort, the poem says, because even the mountains—in their hugeness—are dissolved "away" by the seas. Randall's *Pacific Epitaphs* are recollections of the war. The short pieces are epigrammatic and haiku-like. Here is a poignant one ("Iwo Jima"):

> Like oil of Texas
> My blood gushed here.

Prominent in a group of Detroit poets (Margaret Danner, Oliver La Grone, Naomi Long Madgett, James Thompson, and others), Randall often enmeshes himself in a sense of personal injury over his people's history. This tendency, and a debt to the black poetic tradition (especially Sterling Brown), can be seen in "The Southern Road," in which the "black river" serves as a "boundary to hell." The country is "haughty as a star,"

> And I set forth upon the southern road.

The variety of styles and themes found in these poets is found also in younger poets of their generation: Patterson, Addison, Browne, Redmond, Jay Wright, Anderson, Hernton, and Polite come readily to mind. Of these poets, Patterson is particularly interesting. His "Black All Day" yielded from its second line the title for *I Saw How Black I Was.* Also a Lincoln University poet, Patterson won an

award for his poetry while still an undergraduate. A native
New Yorker, he studied political science and English and
has worked as a counselor for delinquent boys and as an
English instructor. Patterson said in *Sixes and Sevens* that
his first poem was written during World War II as the
"outgrowth of a Cain-and-Abel conflict without the dire
consequences." "Three Views of Dawn" includes the
"silken shawl of night," the disappearance of "corner
specters" and the "splitting" of "stillness." The musical
"Tla Tla" presents free verse spiced with alliterative language of landscape, season and nature. In "Alone," the
protagonist "keeps poems warm" as he watches over the
sleeping lovers as well as the "numb"

who wake and weep.

Patterson did not publish a book until 1969; and its title,
26 Ways of Looking at a Black Man, shows the
influence of Imagists and modernists (see Stevens' *13
Ways of Looking at a Blackbird*). It also reveals much
about the black poet's ability to forge and merge his academic training with his own indigenisms. The speaker in
"Black All Day" is "looked" into "rage and shame" by a
white passerby; but he vows that "tomorrow"

I'll do as much for him.

Patterson constructs a solid poetic foundation, "stone on
stone," as he paints precise portraits of "the brave who do
not break" when provoked ("You Are the Brave"), or the
"lost," the "tireless and raging soul" ("Envoi"). In the
work of Patterson and the younger group of the period
one finds anger or protest, though the general tendency is
toward experimental verse that pinpoints the surest and
richest human feelings. As black poets, their subjects more
often than not reflect this fact. But they do not shun variety.

Phillis Wheatley had been the best-known female poet
until the mid-nineteenth century, when Frances Harper
took up the banner of fame though not necessarily of skill.
A new mood was later evidenced in the work of Angelina
Grimké, Georgia Douglas Johnson (the most famous female black poet after Frances Harper), Gwendolyn Bennett, Anne Spencer, Alice Dunbar-Nelson, Helene John-

son (a young spark in the Harlem Renaissance), Margaret Walker, and Gwendolyn Brooks. Between the forties and sixties, the number of publishing women poets increased significantly. Yet poetry in the United States has remained under the supervision of whites (men); and since women in general have not had the range of opportunities open to men, certainly the black woman went the worst way of that flesh! But the list of black women poets of the period is still impressive: Gloria C. Oden (Yonkers, New York), Nanina Alba (Montgomery), Margaret Danner (Pryorsburg, Kentucky), Mari Evans (Toledo), Julia Fields (Uniontown, Alabama), Vivian Ayers (Chester, South Carolina), Audre Lorde (New York), Naomi Long Madgett (Norfolk), Pauli Murray (Baltimore), Sarah Wright (Witipquin, Maryland), May Miller (Washington, D.C.), and Yvonne Gregory (Nashville), among the dozens of infrequently appearing regional names.

In 1952—two years after Gwendolyn Brooks won the Pulitzer prize—G. C. Oden, who uses her initials "as a way of being anonymous," received a John Hay Whitney Opportunity Fellowship for *The Naked Frame: a Love Poem and Sonnets.* She has worked as a senior editor of a major publishing house and currently teaches English at a college in Baltimore. In the fifties, she joined the Village poets in New York, where she read her poetry in coffee shops, reviewed books and worked on a novel. Her poetry has also appeared in *The Saturday Review* and *The Poetry Digest.* Noting that she appeals "primarily to the intellect," Hayden (*Kaleidoscope*) compared her to Cullen, adding that she "is concerned with poetry as an art expressing what is meaningful to everyone, not just a vehicle for protest and special pleading." Although G. C. Oden uses a variety of forms, her poems are usually crisp and tart. "The Carousel" in an empty park

rides me round and round,

and the darkness drops for her as she observes her surroundings with explicit word-choices: "sight focusses shadow." In "Review from Staten Island" an item in view is "spewed up from water." Later, we are told: "One gets used to dying living," and "even the rose disposes of summer." We hear the dislocated woman in ". . . As when emotion too far exceeds its cause" (phrase from Elizabeth

Bishop). Retreating from heartbreak, she admits that she too knew "love's celestial venturing":

I, too, once trusted air
that plunged me down.
Yes, I!

Nanina Alba is similarly terse and poignant. *The Parchments* (1963) and *The Parchments II* were published before her death in 1968. She taught English, music and French in public schools and was for a long time a member of the English Department at Tuskegee Institute. "Be Daedalus" makes use of Greek mythology to draw a subtle analogy between Blacks and Icarus' "unwise" actions. Death comes as a "tax" for "parching" the sun:

Suns can be brutal things.

"For Malcolm X" recalls "History's stoning."

Margaret Danner is richly sensitive. Born in Detroit, she has spent the greater part of her life in Chicago, where she was once editor of *Poetry*. Her poems in that publication in 1952 prompted the John Hay Whitney Fellowships Committee to offer her a trip to Africa. And in 1962 the literary group with which she identified in Detroit was the subject of a special issue of the *Bulletin of Negro History*. She has published four volumes: *Impressions of African Art Forms in Poetry* (1962), *To Flower* (1962), *Poem Counterpoem* (with Dudley Randall, 1966) and *Iron Lace* (1968). A former poet-in-residence at Wayne State University, she founded Boone House, a lively center for the arts in Detroit, and a similar cultural program in Chicago: Nologonya's. She employs African terminology and themes; but she can also write delightfully in other veins, as in "The Elevator Man Adheres to Form." The "tan man who wings" the elevator reminds her of "Rococo art." Struck by his elegance—and "Godspeedings"—the poet wonders why so intelligent and artful a "tan" man has to run elevators. It is a meticulous poem, subtly exposing the lie that *education qualifies you*. She finally wishes the elevator man's services could be employed

toward lifting them above their crippling storm.

Far From Africa: Four Poems is a sheet of sights, sounds
and suggestions carrying the reader across "moulting days"
in "their twilight" ("Garnishing the Aviary"), "lines" of
"classic tutu" ("Dance of the Abakweta"), "eyes low-
ered" from "despair" ("The Visit of the Professor of Aesthetics") and

a bed of green moss, sparkling as a beetle. . . .

Mari Evans is another kind of transitionalist—shifting
from civil rights poetry of the early phase to, finally, a
more obvious politically "black" stance of the later period.
She has worked as a civil service employee, TV-show
hostess and producer, and instructor of writing. Sometimes
referred to as a spiritual, if not technical, heir to Gwendolyn Brooks, Mari Evans employs irony, suspense, and
rich folk idioms in free verse. "The Rebel," pondering her
own death and funeral, wonders if "Curiosity / seekers"
want to know whether she has really died or just wants to
cause "Trouble." There are humor and satire in "When in
Rome" as the poet interlaces (In the manner of Vesey's
"A Moment, Please") two different conversations. The
black maid, "Mattie dear," is allowed to eat "whatever"
she likes. Alternating the maid's silent responses with the
recitation of a menu from the middle-class environment
("Rome"), the poem incidentally records the traditional
soulfood items the maid craves. "The Emancipation of
George-Hector" ("the colored turtle") shows a growing
impatience with one-step-at-a-time social-change policy.
The turtle used to stay in his "shell" but now he peeks
out, extends his arms and legs, and talks. But this same
poet can wax philosophical, and sentimental. "If there be
Sorrow," it should be for the things not yet dreamed, realized or done. Add to these the withholding of love, love
"restrained." In "Shrine to what should Be," an audience
is asked to "sing" songs to "nobility," and "Righteous-
ness." The children should bring "Trust," the women
"Dreams," the old men "constancy." Ironically the audience is told to ignore tears that fall like a "crescendo,"
and constantly as "a soft black rain." Her tribute to
gospel singers is telling in ". . . And the Old Women
Gathered." One cannot (despite "Rome") escape one's
self, the poet says, as she notices that the "fierce" and
"not melodic" music lingered on even as "we ran."

Julia Fields, a truly searching spirit, studied at Knox College (Tennessee), in England and in Scotland, and has taught high school and college. Her work appeared in *Umbra, Massachusetts Review* and other journals. Along with Margaret Walker, Tom Dent, Alice Walker, Pinkie Gordon Lane and Spellman, she is among the few good black poets who now voluntarily live in the South. Her first book, *Poems*, was brought out by Poets Press in 1968, the same year she received a National Council on the Arts grant. She is substantially represented in R. Baird Shuman's *Nine Black Poets* (1968), and her *East of Moonlight* was published in 1973. She also writes short stories and plays. Her main poetic subjects are racism, death, love, violence and history. "The Generations" come and go, and in between there are "The wars." And in between them are the seasons, flowers, "lavender skies," dawns, "Sombre seas," and the "embryonic calm." "Aardvark" has achieved "fame" since "Malcolm died," and the poet muses:

> Looks like Malcolm helped
> Bring attention to a lot of things
> We never thought about before.

She again salutes this martyr in "For Malcolm X," whose "eyes were mirrors of our agony." In "No Time for Poetry," the reader is advised that midnight is not the time to beseech one's muse: the "spirit" is "too lagging" and there is too much "calm." But the morning is ideal, since it carries "vibrations of laughter" and has no "orange-white mists." As a "woman" listening, near the "broken-hinged door," to a man talk of war ("I Heard a Young Man Saying"), the narrator "somehow planned on living." And the "bright glare of the neon world" sends "gaswords bursting free" in "Madness One Monday Evening."

Pauli Murray and Sarah Wright are poets who also write in other genres. Pauli Murray pursued training for law while she won academic awards and fellowships for her writing. A civil rights pioneer, she published one volume of verse (*Dark Testament*, 1969) and a family history (*Proud Shoes*, 1956). In "Without Name," she is revealed as a formal but excellent craftsman. There are no names for true feeling: let the "flesh sing anthems to its arrival." Sarah Wright, known as a novelist (*This Child's Gonna Live*), coauthored *Give Me a child* in 1955, with

Lucy Smith. About black writers she said (1961), "My motto is tell it like it damn sure is." In "Window Pictures" she sees "black outlines in living flesh." "Urgency" views the relationship between drivers and traffic lights. "God" is "thanked" that the car stops so the passenger can "glory" a while in the "time-bitten punctuation" of the "pause."

Vivian Ayers, the daughter of a blacksmith, attended Barber-Scotia College (Concord, North Carolina) and Bennett College (Greensboro), where her major interests were drama, music and dance. She published a volume of poems (*Spice of Dawns*) and an allegorical drama of freedom and the space age (*Hawk*) that was performed at the University of Houston's Educational Television Station. Currently she lives in Houston, where she edits a quarterly journal, *Adept*. "Instantaneous" features a man being "stunned" by the bolt of "crossing-firing energies" and grabbed up in a blaze

resonant as a million hallelujas—.

And a man inhabits another man who, dying, gasps faintly:

"My god—*this is God. . . .*"

Somewhat different in mood is Naomi Long Madgett, who moved to Detroit from Virginia in 1946 to teach at a high school. She holds a master's degree from Wayne State University. Associated with the Detroit group of poets, she has published four volumes: *Songs to a Phantom Nightingale* (1941), *One in the Many* (1956), *Star by Star* (1965, 1970), and *Pink Ladies in the Afternoon* (1972). Currently she teaches English at Eastern Michigan University and runs the newly established Lotus Press. One of its first projects was *Deep Rivers: a Portfolio: 20 Contemporary Black American Poets* (1974), which includes a teacher's guide prepared by Naomi Madgett. Editors for *Deep Rivers* include Leonard P. Andrews, Eunice L. Howard, and Gladys M. Rogers. The twenty poets included are Paulette Childress White, Jill Witherspoon, William Shelley, G. C. Oden, Naomi Madgett, Patterson, La Grone, Pamela Cobb, Pinkie Gordon Lane, Etheridge Knight, Randall, Hayden, Thompson, Margaret Walker, June Jordan, Gerald W. Barrax, Audre Lorde, Redmond,

Harper and Kaufman. Naomi Madgett's "Simple" ("For Langston Hughes") is realistically humorous. Simple sits in a bar, wanting to talk to someone, when he is approached by a hand-out seeker who needs to change his clothes "but my lan'lady bolted the door." But Joyce, watching, will tap "impatiently" and leave the bar with Simple wondering what "he wanted to say." In "Mortality" we learn that of "all the deaths" this one is the "surest." Some deaths are merely "peace" but vultures "recognize" the "single mortal thing" that holds on to life, and they wait hungrily for the time

When hope starts staggering.

Man must come to grips with the things of this world, we are told in "The Reckoning":

And why and how and what, and sometimes even if.

Poems from *Trinity: a Dream Sequence* convey uncertainties and fears of women and humans. One character has been besieged by "dream and dream again" ("4") and a naked day "corrodes the silver dream," but the music will not "cease to shiver" ("18"). "After" is a lamentation for "mortals" without "wings" to fly away from the "purple sadness" of night. And "Poor Renaldo" is "dead and gone wherever people go" when they "never loved a song." But even "hell" must have "music of a sort." Finely sculptured, like the others, the poem turns to more sorrow near the end. Renaldo, though dead, is "still unresting."

Audre Lorde's early work reflects great skill and control. In the early sixties she wrote:

I am a Negro woman and a poet—all three things stand outside my realm of choice. My eyes have a part in my seeing, my breath in my breathing, all that I am in who I am. All who love are of my people. I was not born on a farm or in a forest, but in the centre of the largest city in the world—a member of the human race hemmed in by stone, away from earth and sunlight. But what is in my blood and skin of richness, comes the roundabout journey from Africa through sun islands to a stony coast, and these are the gifts through which I sing, through which I see. This is the knowledge of the sun, and of how to love even where there is no sunlight. This is the knowledge and the richness I shall give my children proudly, as a strength against the less obvious forms of narrowness and night. (Letter accompanying poems submitted to *Sixes and Sevens*.)

She thus gives a balanced account of herself as woman, Black and poet. And all these dimensions she handles quite well in her poetry. She has published three volumes: *The First Cities* (1968), *Cables to Rage* (1970) and *From a Land Where Other People Live* (1973), which was nominated for a National Book Award. In her early poetry she reflects on "Oaxaca" (in Mexico), where the "land moves slowly" under the "carving drag of wood." The drudging field work goes on while the hills are "brewing thunder," and one can observe

All a man's strength in his sons' young arms. . . .

"To a Girl who knew what side Her Bread was Buttered on" describes the girl as a "catch of bright thunder" apparently guarded by (and guardian of) bones. Ordered to leave the bones, she watches as they rise like "an ocean of straw" and trample her overseer "into the earth." The "Nymph" is brought "forth in the moonpit of a virgin." In "How Can I Love You" the scorned suitor "comes like a thin bird"—instead of like the magnificent Phoenix— later to become "great ash." No wonder, the speaker confirms,

that your sun went down.

The "Moon-minded the Sun . . ." assures that

The light that makes us fertile
shall make us sane.

And we hear that the "year has fallen" in "Father, the Year. . . ." Audre Lorde's work cuts sharp paths of light across the ignorance and confusion around her. This is true of "And Fall shall sit in Judgment," which examines love, concluding that "in all seasons" it

is false, but the same.

Another much-neglected poet is May Miller, of Washington, D.C., whom Gwendolyn Brooks acknowledged as

"excellent and long-celebrated" (Introduction, *The Poetry
of Black America*). Her work can be found in three volumes: *Into the Clearing* (1959) and *Poems* (1962), and
she is one of three poets represented in *Lyrics of Three
Women* (1964). Currently a member of the Commission
on the Arts of the District of Columbia, she has been a
teacher, lecturer, and dramatist and has published her
poetry in a number of magazines: *Common Ground, The
Antioch Review, The Crisis, Phylon,* and *The Nation.*
"Calvary Way" shows a Christian influence with a twist
of irony and gore. Mary is asked how she felt, "womb-
heavy with Christ Child," as she tasted the "dust" of an
"uncertain journey." Recalling the Crucifixion, the poem
finally asks Mary: "Were you afraid?" The "roaches are
winning" in "The last Warehouse," where humans seek
to "abnegate survival laws" and kill roaches until they are
"saturated with their decrease." The characters in "The
wrong side of Morning" were shaken from a "nightmare of
wings" and "mushrooms of huge death" as the poet power-
fully assembles images and layered meanings. "Procession"
employs the dramatic technique (made famous by Brown
and others) of interlacing the formal English of the poem
with italicized black expletives and refrains such as "*Ring,
hammer, ring!*" It is the procession of Christ, but the
reader easily understands, noting the black idioms, that it
is also a black procession through the labyrinths of slavery
and racism. There is a series of such juxtaposed contradictions as "Time is today, yesterday, and time to come,"
"moving and motionless," and "infinite takes familiar
form," while "we seek conviction." Christian mythology
pervades May Miller's work (though she black-bases it).
In "Tally," the subjects "lay there drained of time" and
empty like the "bulge of hour glass" while "Lucifer
streaked to reality."

The deaths of Dumas and Rivers left voids and created
still more anxieties, coming as they did (1968) in the
midst of racial turbulence. However, by the mid-sixties
both poets had written a great deal of poetry and a great
deal about themselves. Rivers died an unnecessary death
in what has been called an "impulsive" act. Dumas was
shot to death by a white policeman in a New York sub-
way. Both deaths occurred within months of each other.
Rivers was born in Atlantic City, New Jersey, and at-

tended public schools in Pennsylvania, Georgia and Ohio.
His college days were spent at Wilberforce University,
Chicago State Teachers College and Indiana University.
In high school (1951) he won the Savannah State poetry
prize. Rivers was greatly influenced by Hughes, Wright
and his uncle Ray McIver. His five books, two of them
published posthumously, are *Perchance to Dream, Othello*
(1959), *These Black Bodies and This Sunburnt Face*
(1962), *Dusk at Selma* (1965), *The Still Voice of
Harlem* (1968) and *The Wright Poems* (1972, with an
Introduction by friend-novelist Ronald Fair). *Ohio Poetry
Review, Kenyon Review,* and *Antioch Review* were only a
few magazines in which his work appeared. Responding to
a request (1962) to comment on himself as black man
and poet, Rivers said, among other things:

I write about the Negro because I am a Negro,
and I am not at peace with myself or the world.
I cannot divorce my thoughts by the absolute
    injustice of hate.
I cannot reckon with my color.
I am obsessed by the ludicrous and psychological
    behavior of hated men.
And I shall continue to write about race—in spite
    of many warnings—
until I discover myself, my future, my real race.
I do not wish to capitalize on race, nor do I wish
    to begin a Crimean War:
I am only interested in recording the truth
squeezed from my observations and experiences.
I am tired of being misrepresented.

Adding to the statement, Rivers said, ". . . beauty and
joy, which was in the world before and has been buried so
long, has got to come back."
But Rivers saw little "beauty and joy" through his own
mind's eye. His poetic landscape is often bleak and filled
with deep psychic yearnings and wanderings through the
ambivalences of black-white relations. There are also torment and brooding. In these, he bears some kinship to
Dumas. For both delve deeply into psychology but are at
the same time accessible. Rivers spent much time research-
ing his past and reading from the great volumes of world

literature. During the mid sixties in Chicago he participated in discussion groups—involving Fair, David Llorens
and Gerald McWorter—out of which grew the now well-
known Organization of Black American Culture (OBAC),
a prominent vehicle for area black arts programs. Rivers
talks about his own death in several poems. "Postscript" is
a poem that "should not have been published." The narrator says he was "living and dying and dreaming" all at
the same time in Harlem. And, toying with his own fate
in the wake of Wright's "sudden death," he recalls the
elder writer's "prophecy" that he too "soon would be
dead." The theme of death—often oral, spiritual or
physical, as in Hayden—can be found in such pieces as
"The Death of a Negro Poet," "Prelude for Dixie," "Four
Sheets to the Wind," "Three Sons," "Asylum" and all of
The Wright Poems. In "Watts," he digests generations of
fear, horror, history and anguish, into epigrammatic fury
—and with a deceptively apparent ease:

> Must I shoot the
> white man dead
> to free the nigger
> in his head?

In a weak assessment of Rivers' poetry, Haki Madhubuti
(Lee) said this poem "asks a revolutionary question" (*Dynamite Voices, Vol. I*). Such a "question," of course, is
one that continually turns or revolves. But, semantics
aside, the comment is blind to Rivers' own battle with the
deep fears and sores caused by America's racial nightmare.
He knew that neither simple-minded answers nor verbal
slapstick would make these hurts disappear. Also, such
criticism violates the poem, robbing the poet of his many-
layered concerns and analytical powers. Rivers is not all
somber and bleak, however; in "The Still Voice of
Harlem," he announces:

> I am the hope
> and tomorrow
> of your unborn.

Even amid the contradictions and uncertainties of
racial/political ping-pong ("In Defense of Black Poets"):

> A black poet must remember the horrors.

Especially since

Some black kid is bound to read you.

The "Note on Black Women" asks that they teach the
poet "honor," "humor," and "how to die," presumably
the reborning death. *The Wright Poems* is an elegiac
sheet. "To Richard Wright" exclaims, almost with defeat:

To be born unnoticed
is to be born black,
and left out of the grand adventure.

Another "Wright" Poem refers to the novelist as

young Jesus of the black noun and verb.

Other poems find the poet wandering or searching
through the "spirits" or "bones" of Wright. In "A
Mourning Letter from Paris," Rivers recalls knowing and
feeling "Harlem's honeyed voice." Several of his
previously unpublished poems were printed in the September, 1975 issue of *Black World*.

Often similar in feeling and theme to Rivers but almost
never in voice and form, is the work of Henry Dumas,
whose "*Négritude* ranges across time and space" (Cleveland *Plain Dealer*). Born in Sweet Home, Arkansas, Dumas
moved to New York when he was ten years old and completed public schools in that city. He attended the City
College of New York and Rutgers between stints in the
Air Force and other activities. Active on the little-magazine
circuit, he won a number of awards and helped establish
several publications. At the time of his death, he was
teaching at Southern Illinois University's Experiment in
Higher Education in East St. Louis. In 1970, SIU Press
published two posthumously collected volumes: *Poetry for
My People* and "*Ark of Bones*" *and Other Stories*, edited
by Hale Chatfield and Redmond. Random House reissued
both works in 1974, the poetry retitled *Play Ebony Play
Ivory*, edited by Redmond. Though there have been no
full-length critical studies of Dumas's poetry, Jay Wright
and Baraka assessed him in the SIU volume, and Wright's
Introduction is retained in the new edition. Wright, him-

self a major poet of this era, identifies the linguistic concerns and musical range of Dumas:

> None of this is perverse, intellectual play. It is indicative of Dumas' sense of history. In "Emoyeni, Place of the Winds," he writes "I see with my skin and hear with my tongue." . . . The line, I suggest, asserts some elementary truth about Dumas', and not alone Dumas', poetic techniques. This book . . . is grounded in that line. What Dumas means is that there *are* racial and social determinants of perception, ideas that he was just beginning to develop. The mind articulates what the senses have selected from the field, and this articulation is, in part, determined by what the perceiver has learned to select and articulate. . . . In "[I] hear with my tongue," Dumas asserts that the language you speak is a way of defining yourself within a group. The language of the Black community, as with that of any group, takes its form, its imagery, its vocabulary, because Black people want them that way. Language can protect, exclude, express value, as well as assert identity. That is why Dumas' language is the way it is. In the rhythm of it, is the act, the unique manner of perception of a Black man.

Writing with the removed passion of the friend that he was, Wright makes vital statements not only about Dumas but about the entirety of black creativity, perception and aesthetic stance in the world. Indeed Dumas jutted all these antennae from his poetry, which he wrote to maintain "our precious tradition." Linguistically, Dumas's base is formal English, a blend of black African languages, Arabic, and Gullah from the islands off the Carolinas and Georgia. His cosmos is shaped by the rich textures of black religious and spiritual life, especially old-time church services and elements of Voodoo. Wright notes: "The blues and gospel music, particularly, were his life breath. Only Langston Hughes knew more, or at least as much, about gospel and gospel singers. . . . Music seemed to Dumas to be able to carry the burden of direct participation in the act of living, as no poem, that was not musically structured, could. . . ."

"Dumas was searching for an analogous structure for poetry." And as a poet, he musically combines the past, present and future, often inseparably, as in "Play Ebony Play Ivory":

> for the songless, the dead
> who rot the earth
> all these dead
> whose sour muted tongues
> speak broken chords,
> all these aging people
> poison the heart of earth.

Curses and curdles, mysticism, blessings and warnings abound ("Rite"):

> Vodu green clinching his waist,
> obi purple ringing his neck,
> Shango, God of the spirits,
> whispering in his ear,
> thunderlight stabbing the island
> of blood rising from his skull.

Later in this same poem, the *word-force* takes precedence over all; what must come, *must come*:

> No power can stay the mojo
> when the obi is purple
> and the vodu is green
> and Shango is whispering,
> Bathe me in blood.
> I am not clean.

His intercontinental, intergalactic soarings call forth any and all devices at his command. He explores the dense rhythms ("of perception") as in "Ngoma," in which he compares the belly of a pregnant woman to the drum head. The husband/doctor listens to the baby's heart; the drummer listens to the voices/feet of the ancestors:

> *aiwa aiwa*
> it is the chest-sound
> same that booms my chest
> *aiwa aiwa*
> a strong sound running

> like feet of gazelle
> *aiwa aiwa*

The poem's crescendo, with its built-in antiphony (and call and response), merges goatskin and woman's belly in the incantatory roar of life and living:

> the goat-skin sings the boom-sound louder
> louder sings the goat-skin louder
> the goatskin sings the boom-sound louder
>   sings the goat-skin louder louder
> louder boom the goat-skin boom-sound louder
>   louder louder

The rich, experimental structure and language, couched in several "traditions," is seen everywhere in this major voice ("from *Jackhammer*"):

> The jackjack backing back and stacking stone
> city-stone into cracked hydraulic echoes of dust.

Or ("Root Song"):

> Once when I was tree
> flesh came and worshipped at my roots.

Or ("A Song of Flesh") love, maddened flight and need:

> When I awoke,
> I took the sleeping mountains of your breasts
> tenderly tenderly
> between my quivering lips
> and I guillotined the stallions,
> drowned the eagles,
> and drove the tiger fish back
> into the sea of your heart.

There are also "many" poets in Dumas. A combination of Whitman, Dunbar, Toomer, Hughes and Walker, coupled with the best of the riming poets of the sixties, produces this sanguine and humorous black truth ("I Laugh Talk Joke"):

> i laugh talk joke
> smoke dope skip rope, may take a coke
> jump up and down, walk around

```
drink mash and talk trash
beat a blind boy over the head
with a brick
knock a no-legged man to his
bended knees
cause I'm a movin fool
never been to school
god raised me and the devil
praised me
catch a preacher in a boat
and slit his throat
pass a church,
I might pray
but don't fuck with me
cause I don't play.
```

There are epic poems such as "Mosaic Harlem" and
"Genesis on an Endless Mosaic," a blues series, experiments in African forms (using spontaneity and ritual),
and such mystical/exploratory poems as "Thoughts/Im-
ages," "Kef," "Ikefs" and "Saba." In one, "Saba"
("Out"), Dumas uses bizarre imagery and musical typography to render that which is hard to describe:

```
sx waterings
          streams
striking aorta
          vibraphones
sx veinings
          myriads
of flagella flucksing rite.
```

Dumas possessed a boundless love for the acoustical leap
and the dramatic "implosion" (as he put it) of ideas in
poetry. What influence his ideas will have on black poetry
remains to be seen. We can only speculate on what would
have been the influence/impact of his work, much of it
written in the early and mid sixties, had it been available
in a collection when the initial thrust of the new black poetry occurred. The American temperament (disfavoring
black writers telling their truths) kept Dumas and Rivers
running. Dumas sought his peace in the deep well of his
own folk culture and in occasional poetic excursions into

mysticism, Africa and Voodoo. Rivers buried himself in the "identity" issues and brooded over his plight as a brilliant Black in a country where the two adjectives together are neither believable nor legitimate. But both left us legacies. For a cogent and far reaching assessment of Dumas' poetry and achievement, see Clyde Taylor's "Henry Dumas: Legacy of a Long-Breath Singer" (*Black World*, September 1975).

"GRIEFS OF JOY": THE POETRY OF WINGS AND THE BLACK ARTS MOVEMENT

No, nothing remains the same
And my spirit reaches out to you
my love
without apologies
without embarrassment
with only the thought that this is
right for us
that moving towards you is like
touching leaves in autumn. . . .
. . . .
our minds and spirits
interlocked like death.
          —PINKIE GORDON LANE, "griefs of joy"

One major difference between the cultural/political upsurges of the twenties and the sixties/seventies was location: the renaissance was centered literarily, if not always geographically, in Harlem; but its recent successors can be found in every North American community with a substantial black population. Another difference was in degree of artistic-political consciousness. To be sure, the cultural and political arms of the renaissance were, on occasion, interlocked. But such marriages never reached the current state of "wholeness" and "continuity."

In the early days of this period there were (are) "stars" of the new black poetry, but the glitter often attended activities "outside" the poetry. Or, put differently, the stars sometimes put "outside" topical stimuli "inside" what is no longer defensible as "poetry." This often meant that the star poets had no connection whatever with a black literary or folk poetry tradition as such. Instead, theirs was a "tradition" of immediacy and transiency, political urgency, and newspaper headlines, combined with high-school-type punch-lining. This is not to say good poetry (however it is defined) was (is) not being written or that charlatans were always "on the take." There is much evidence to support the belief that dozens of these sooth-sayers were sincere and honest—and had chosen what appeared to be the "simplest" and "fastest" vehicle for expressing thoughts about "revolution" and "black togetherness" or raising the "collective consciousness." Such a situation was not helped by the learned poet-activists who sometimes advised young writers to give up "Western" influences and a "white" language. These advisers usually stopped short of suggesting ways in which young poets and writers might assimilate another language into their works. Yet this need to identify and institute an alternative language is a pressing one. In the meantime, impressive contributions toward such a realization have been made by beacons like James Weldon Johnson, Melvin Tolson, Margaret Walker, Henry Dumas, Ishmael Reed, Jayne Cortez, and others.

However, the insincere versifiers usually fell by the wayside in a short time, paving the way, like the Phoenix bird, for still more soap box mounters. At the same time, a number of poets—whose wits and crafts were not about them in the early phase—took to the woodshed to become much better handlers of the word. All this occurred, Larry Neal notes, against a "panorama of violence." Indeed, by the late sixties, black communities all over the United States had been turned upside down by police and spokesmen/supporters of the black revolution. Such young shock troopers as Carmichael, Rap Brown, Charles Koen, Ron Karenga, Huey Newton, and Eldridge Cleaver had already forced the "old-time" black leadership to take a back seat. Now, with father having destroyed son (cf. Williams, Baldwin), the poets were free to declaim, proclaim and exhort. This trend alone shocked the general poetic tradition—since it created a flood of polemicists and pamphleteers who could/would not discuss poetry in its historical contexts. It caused further shock by labeling itself "black" and renegotiating its own "roots." (The word "black" has appeared throughout the history of black poetry, but before the sixties it was not used as a categorical reference to poetry written by Afro-Americans.) Hence, much of the new black poetry has been viewed as non-poetry or antipoetry (in a traditional literary context), because, among other things, it does not depend primarily on subtlety and recondite references. It remains to be seen what impact this particular feature of black poetry will have on the literary (or literacy) trends in Afro-America. Jackson (*Black Poetry in America*) for example, begins his own discussion of the new black poetry by building a convincing analogy between the rise in black literacy and the popularity of the new poetry. Henderson (*Understanding the New Black Poetry*) assures his readers that black readers or listeners clearly "understand" what their poets are saying and are participating more and more as judges of *black* aesthetic qualities in the poetry and the poets' deliveries. But while this chapter will conclude with a few broad critical observations, the immediate aim is to continue the sketch of the poetry's development, interpolating from time to time pertinent critical and illuminating data.

There are dozens of ways to approach the new black poetry. One could, for example, examine its theme, structure and saturation (Henderson), or its several types (Carolyn Rodgers; see bibliography). Starting with important names is another way; the black-aesthetic approach (Gayle, Fuller) is another way. Then there is the magic of black poetry (Baraka, Touré, Reed, Neal, Dumas). Music is also a favorite approach (Crouch, Harper, Jayne Cortez). One could go on and on, but the poetry has been written, and one place to start is with its emergence.

New York certainly played a key role in the new movement, but it did not, as we said earlier, play *the* key or only role. Areas of the East (Philadelphia, Boston, Baltimore, Washington, D.C.) enhanced the boom. Midwest centers were Cleveland, Chicago, Detroit, East St. Louis-St. Louis, and Kansas City, to name some. Related events also took place in the South, where there was another "rising" in Atlanta, Nashville, Jackson, Baton Rouge, Tuskegee, Houston, and Toogaloo. The West added richly, from Los Angeles, the San Francisco Bay area, Sacramento, and Seattle. Developments related to the po-

etry include numerous black arts activities (connected to
cultural or nationalist programs) at settlement houses,
community centers, museums, centers for the dissemina-
tion of ideologies, anti-poverty projects, and educational
institutions. Support also came in the form of a plethora
of black-oriented tabloids, journals, flyers, posters, books,
pamphlets, and records. Of great importance were the new
black bookstores, African curio shops, the painting of
walls of "respect" (Cleveland, Akron, Chicago, St. Louis,
New York, Newark), art exhibits, weekly festivals and jubilees, writers' conferences, writing workshops, the flood of
liberation flags (black-green-red), black-oriented TV talk
and variety shows, and other physical or cultural symbols
(special unity handshakes, and African clothes, hairdos
and jewelry). New York was an important showplace
for the new consciousness. It had the residue of the
postrenaissance years (the Schomburg Library and
Micheaux's Bookstore) in Harlem as well as numerous surrounding black communities. New organizations such as
Barbara Ann Teer's National Black Theater, the New
Lafayette Theater, and various new Harlem cultural projects flowered in the amazed light of such older institutions
as *Freedomways* magazine (Clarke and Kaiser), which has
published many of the new poets: Touré (Snellings),
Madhubuti (Lee), Henderson, Clarence Reed, Welton
Smith, Lloyd T. Delaney, W. D. Wright, Joanne Gonzales, Mari Evans, and others. *Freedomways* also offers
lively reviews and commentaries on poetry, literature, and
the black arts scene.

From the variegated atmosphere of New York gushed
forth a tide of black poets, some having made their mark
earlier in other areas: Henderson, Larry Neal (1937–),
Reed, Patterson, Sun Ra, June Jordan (1936–), Sonia
Sanchez (1935–), S. E. Anderson (1943–), Albert
Haynes (1936–), Hernton, Quintin Hill (1950–),
Ai (Florence Anthony) (1947–), Howard Jones
(1941–), Baraka, Audre Lorde, John Major (1948–),
N. H. Pritchard (1939–), N. J. Loftis, Lennox Raphael
(1940–), James Arlington Jones (1936–), John A.
Williams, Lebert Bethune (1937–), Lethonia Gee,
Bobb Hamilton, Q. R. Hand, Yusef Iman, Ray Johnson,
Odaro (Barbara Jones, 1946–), Clarence Reed, Sharon

Bourke, Yusef Rahman (Ronald Stone), Barbara Sim-
mons, Lefty Sims, Welton Smith (1940–), Spellman,
Edward Spriggs (1934–), Clarence Major (1936–),
Kali Grosvenor (1960–), Lorenzo Thomas (1944–),
Doughtry Long (1942–), Richard Thomas (1939–),
Jay Wright (1935–), Ted Wilson (1943–) , Lloyd
Addison (1931–), Kattie M. Cumbo (1938–), James
Arlington Jones (1936–), Jayne Cortez (via Watts),
Emanuel, Calvin Forbes (1945–), Alexis Deveaux
(1950–), Nikki Giovanni (via Fisk, 1943–), Tom
Weatherly (1942–), Ron Welburn (1944–), Djan-
gatolum (Lloyd M. Corbin) (1949–), Mae Jackson
(1946–), Joe Johnson (1940–), Julius Lester
(1939–), Elouise Loftin (1950–), Judy Simmons
(1944–), Felipe Luciano (1947–), Gylain Kain,
Charles Lynch (1943–), L. V. Mack (1947–),
Rhonda Mills, (1951–), Jodi Braxton (1950–), David
E. Jackson (1950–), Larry Thompson (1950–),
K. W. Prestwidge. The New York black arts scene (poetry
specifically) was all a-whir with the excitement of publishing and poetry reading at an infinite number of gatherings.
Joining these younger writers were older, often revived,
ones. Hughes oversaw much of the proceedings until his
death in 1967. And there were old, as well as new, outlets
for the poetry, which was being read at the Apollo, Car-
negie Hall, New Lafayette Theater, Slug's East, Liberty
House, and in countless community centers and churches.

Most of these poets were not native New Yorkers; and a
great number were not even there during the height of the
Black Arts Movement—but in such outlying areas of the
city as Bridgeport, (Youth Bridge) Yale, Fredonia, Brock-
port, Rutgers, Brooklyn, Boston (Elma Lewis's Center for
Afro-American Culture and Black Academy of Arts and
Letters). But while they had separate black arts programs,
most looked to the movement in New York for inspiration
and direction. In addition to the *Umbra* Workshop there
were the Harlem Writers Guild (Clarke, Killens), Frederick Douglass Creative Arts Center Poetry Workshop, the
Afro-Hispanic Workshop, Workshop for Young Writers,
the Columbia Writing Program (Killens) and Black Arts
Repertory and Theatre/School (Baraka, Snellings).

Among the new journals available to the poets were and are *Umbra* (1963), *Soulbook* (1964), *Black Dialogue* (1965), *Journal of Black Poetry* (1966) (ironically, the last three were begun on the West Coast), *Pride* (1968), *Black Theatre* (1969), *Cricket* (1969), *Black Creation* (1969), *AfroAmerican: a Third World Literary Journal* (1973, Syracuse), BOP (*Blacks on Paper*, Brown University, 1974), *Continuities: Words from the Communities of Pan-Africa* (City College of New York, 1974), *Impressions* (1974), *Cosmic Colors* (early 1970s), *Obsidian* (Fredonia, 1975).

During a speech at Howard University's First National Conference of Afro-American Writers (November 1974), Touré, recounting the tumultuous years and developments, said those responsible for the "black arts and aesthetic movement" were "activists as well as artists." It seemed so, for this particular pattern was most obvious as LeRoi Jones returned to Newark (renaming it "New Ark") and changed his name to Imamu Amiri Baraka, reflecting the great influence of the Nation of Islam on him and his new interests in African culture. Having founded the Black Arts Repertory Theatre and School "to re-educate the nearly half a million Harlem Negroes to find a new pride in their color," he went on to establish Spirit House (Newark) and such other institutions as Spirit House Players and Movers, the African Free School (with its Kawaida doctrine), Jihad Publications, Committee for a Unified Newark, and to help launch several national black political conventions. He was a founder (1970) of the recently strife-ridden Congress of African Peoples.

During the 1967 riots (insurrections) in Newark, Baraka was arrested with several companions and charged with possession of two handguns and ammunition. Between his arrest and the trial, "Black People!" was published in *Evergreen Review*. Baraka seems to have been convicted on the strength of the poem, since the judge cited it in the courtroom. The poem openly encouraged looting, theft, murder of whites, and general insurrection: "What about that bad short you saw last week"; "You know how to get it, you can get it, no money down, no

money never"; "he owes you anything you want, even his
life"; "Up against the wall motherfucker this is a stick
up!"; "Smash the window at night"; "Let's get together
and kill him my man":

> . . . let's get together the fruit
> of the sun, let's make a world we want black
>   children to grow and learn in
> do not let your children when they grow look
>   in your face and curse you by
> pitying your tomish ways.

It was the kind of call and rage that characterized
Baraka's (and many other black poets') verse between
1965 and 1969. Baraka was later acquitted, but a number
of related developments occurred. Impressed by the U.S.
organization of Ron Karenga (whom he met while teaching at San Francisco State College in 1967), Baraka returned to Newark and organized the Black Community
Development and Defense Organization (BCD). His
efforts eventually aided in the election of a black mayor
(Kenneth Gibson). These developments were having
great impact on regional and national black political/
poetry scenes. Baraka's picture posters (with bandages
from the 1967 scuffle with Newark police) began appearing on walls of cultural centers, dormitories and
homes. But many observers were somewhat wary of
Baraka, having seen him go through the "changes" from
beat poet to Harlem and black arts, into Newark and political work. (For great insight into all this, see Theodore
Hudson's *From LeRoi Jones to Amiri Baraka*, 1973. Yet
Baraka's influence was felt in most centers of the new
black poetry—and even in places where his poetry had not
actually been read; or, if read, not fully understood and
digested. It was not unusual to hear a black youth quote a
few lines from a poster poem or from a live reading, but
who, when questioned about Baraka's works, did not know
the name of a single one.

After *The Dead Lecturer*, Baraka (also playwright) published *Black Magic: Poetry, 1961–1967* (1969), *In Our
Terribleness* (1970), *Spirit, Reach* (1972), as well as
numerous essays and stories. With Neal he coedited *Black*

Fire (1968), which, along with Major's *The New Black
Poetry* (1969), showcased the new poetry. In the Foreword to *Black Fire*, Baraka called black artists "the founding Fathers and Mothers, of our nation. We rise, as we
rise (agin). By the power of our beliefs, by the purity and
strength of our actions." Using his strange new grammar
and syntax, he viewed the poets and writers as:

> The black artist. The black man. The holy man. The
> man you seek. The climber the striver. The maker of
> peace. The lover. The warrior. We are they whom you
> seek. Look in. Find yr self. Find the being, the
> speaker. The voice, the back dust hover in your soft
> eyeclosings. Is you. Is the creator. Is nothing. Plus or
> minus, you vehicle! We are presenting. Your various
> selves. We are presenting, from God, a tone, your own.
> Go on. Now.

He thus set the "tone" for poets/philosophers, reiterating
at the same time much of what was being said in other
writings across the nation.

Neal, a perceptive critic and balanced theoretician, published two volumes: *Black Boogaloo: Notes on Black Liberation* (1969, Journal of Black Poetry Press, Foreword by
Jones) and *Hoodoo Hollerin' Bebop Ghosts* (1975). His
Afterword to *Black Fire* is tantamount to Hughes's famous "declaration" of the twenties. Presenting "artistic
and political work" from what must be "called a radical
perspective," *Black Fire* should be read "as if it were a
critical re-examination of Western political, social and artistic values." Challenging and exhorting other writers,
Neal continued:

> We have been, for the most part, talking about contem-
> porary realities. We have not been talking about a re-
> turn to some glorious African past. But we recognize the
> past—the total past. Many of us refuse to accept a trun-
> cated Negro history which cuts us off completely from
> our African ancestry. To do so is to accept the very
> racist assumptions which we abhor. Rather, we want to
> comprehend history totally, and understand the man-
> ifold ways in which contemporary problems are affected
> by it.

Speaking against the hindsight of psychology and turbulence, Neal added:

> There is a tension within Black America. And it has its roots in the general history of race. The manner in which we see this history determines how we act. How should we see this history? What should we feel about it? This is important to know, because the sense of how that history should be felt is what either unites or separates us.

Finally, he sums up what can be called the credo or *modus operandi* of the new black poetry and the Black Arts Movement:

> The artist and the political activist are one. They are both shapers of the future reality. Both understand and manipulate the collective myths of the race. Both are warriors, priests, lovers and destroyers. For the first violence will be internal—the destruction of a weak spiritual self for a more perfect self. But it will be a necessary violence. It is the only thing that will destroy the double-consciousness—the tension that is in the souls of black folk.

It was the kind of challenge that sent many a newly blackened poet or activist into the long night of the soul to purge himself of real or imagined enemies of his people.

Poetically speaking, however, it was Baraka's "Black Art" that set much of the pace, form and violent tone in the new black poetry:

> Poems are bullshit unless they are
> teeth or trees or lemons piled
> on a step. Or black ladies dying
> of men leaving nickel hearts
> beating them down. Fuck poems
> and they are useful, wd they shoot
> come at you, love what you are,
> breathe like wrestlers, or shudder
> strangely after pissing. We want live
> words of the hip world live flesh &
> coursing blood. Hearts Brains
> Souls splintering fire. We want poems

like fists beating niggers out of Jocks
or dagger poems in the slimy bellies
of owner-jews. Black poems to
smear on girdlemamma mulatto bitches
whose brains are red jelly stuck
between 'lizabeth taylor's toes. Stinking
Whores! We want "poems that kill."
Assassin poems, Poems that shoot
guns. Poems that wrestle cops into alleys
and take their weapons leaving them dead
with tongues pulled out and sent to Ireland. Knockoff
poems for dope selling wops or slick halfwhite
politicians Airplane poems, rrrrrrrrrrrrrrrr
rrrrrrrrrrrrrrr . . . tuhtuhtuhtuhtuhtuhtuhtuhtuh
. . . rrrrrrrrrrrrrrrr . . . Setting fires and death to
whities ass. . . .
. . . .
We want a black poem. And
a Black World.
Let the world be a Black Poem
And let All Black People Speak This Poem
Silently
or LOUD

"Black Art" was often cited as the sanguine em-
bodiment of the black aesthetic and a rejection of white
culture and lifestyle. Poems, Baraka states, must not only
have guts and earthiness (like Blacks), but they must also
be weapons and shields against racism, police, merchants,
hustlers, crooked politicians and status-climbing black
bourgeois. Above all, they should exalt blackness ("sons,"
"lovers," "warriors," "poets," and "all the loveliness here
in this world.") These, then, are the dominant themes in
much of the new poetry and the philosophies stated (with
radical divergences) from coast to coast. Baraka's purge extends through such poems as "Poem for HalfWhite College Students," "The Racist," "Little Brown Jug" ("WE
ARE GODS"), "W.W." (attack on wig-wearing
women), "CIVIL RIGHTS POEM" ("Roywilkins is an
eternal faggot"), "Ka 'Ba," and finally, in "leroy," his last
will and testament:

When I die, the consciousness I carry I will to
black people. May they pick me apart and take the

useful parts, the sweet meat of my feelings. And leave
the bitter bullshit rotten white parts
alone.

But there are also sensitive love poems in the later period,
poems caught up in the stressed life of blackness ("Sterling Street September"): "the beautiful black man, and
you, girl, child nightlove, . . . :

We are strange in a way because we know
who we are. Black beings passing through
a tortured passage of flesh.

In his Foreword to *Black Boogaloo*, Baraka says of the
world: "the soldier poets will change it" (though Baraka
was probably referring to himself). What Neal's volume
changed has not yet been ascertained but it certainly contains ambitious and successful poetry. His debt to the
older generation of poets, artists and thinkers can be seen
in such poems as "Queen Mother's Sermon," "The Middle Passage and After," "Love Song in the Middle Passage," "Garvey's Ghost," "Lady Day," "Harlem Gallery:
from the Inside," and "Malcolm X—an Autobiography."
Making use of mysticism, chant and musicographic inter-
polations, Neal (cf. Dumas) is effective—moving, sensing
and feeling:

Olorum
Olorum
Olorum. . . .

The horror of "The Middle Passage and After" is seen in
the "Decked, stacked, pillaged" slaves. "Long Song in
Middle Passage" views the

Red glow of sea-death mornings.

Other poems ("Songs," "Jihad," "Kuntu," "Orishas") reveal Neal's interests in supernaturalism, African philosophy and the allusive, mystical powers inherent in the
"word." He seeks poetically to implement the ideas he
stated in *Black Fire* and a special, black issue of *TDR*
(*The Drama Review*) in summer of 1968. The issue,
edited by *TDR's* contributing editor Bullins, compiled
ideas and plays rooted in what was then called the "new"

consciousness; also featured was work by Sonia Sanchez and Adam David Miller.

Neal's "The Black Arts Movement" was a blueprint for black arts and political change. Echoing statements in *Black Fire*, he argued against "any concept of the artist that alienates him from his community," and noted:

> Black Art is the aesthetic and spiritual sister of the Black Power concept. As such, it envisions an art that speaks directly to the needs and aspirations of Black America. In order to perform this task, the Black Arts Movement proposes a radical reordering of the western cultural aesthetic. It proposes a separate symbolism, mythology, critique, and iconology. The Black Arts and Black Power concept both relate broadly to the Afro-American's desire for self-determination and nationhood. Both concepts are nationalistic. One is concerned with the relation between art and politics; the other with the art of politics.

But his idea of a "separate" aesthetic was not embraced by all black poets, artists, or intellectuals. Neither was there complete agreement (or understanding) among its own proponents. For example, Spriggs, a versatile artist and thinker, led a boycott of Major's *The New Black Poetry* on the grounds that it was being brought out by a white publisher (International Publishers). But Spriggs had not objected, earlier, to use of his work in *Black Fire*, also published by whites (Morrow). His position statement appeared in *The Journal of Black Poetry* (Fall 1968):

> how in the hell are the black publishers ever going to get off into it if not by the assistance of the writers? how are distributorships ever going to mature with the publishers if the highly marketable works of wm kelly, j. killens, ja wms, 1 neal, e bullins, leroi j, or the like never comes their way? does the concept of black power and black arts extend that far? i say yea, i say yea, yea.

Spriggs joined a large number of critics and practitioners of the black arts—Touré, Neal, Crouch, Fuller, Bullins, Lee, Gonçalves—in the controversy over black writers' roles and responsibilities. Despite the controversy, however, Major's anthology appeared as a kaleidoscopic offering of the new black poetry. Major included a perceptive and fitting Introduction:

> THE INNER crisis of black reality is often studded in these poems by the swift, vividly crucial facts of social reality; which consists in part, anyway, of all the implications and forces of mass media, the social patterns, the bureaucratic and mechanical mediums of human perceptions, even of the quickly evolving nature of the human psyche in this highly homogenized culture, in all of its electric processes and specialist fragmentation. Black reality, in other words, is like any other reality profoundly affected by technology. The crisis and drama of the late 1960s overwhelms and threatens every crevice of human life on earth. These poems are born out of this tension.

In his own poetry, Major surveys Vietnam, alienation, impending world destruction, black history, music, mythology, and personal excursions into dreams. He published *The Dictionary of Afro-American Slang* (1970), *Swallow the Lake* (1970), *Symptoms and Madness* (1971), *Private Line* (1971), *The Cotton Club* (1972), and *The Syncopated Cakewalk* (1974), as well as novels and essays. He has also directed the Harlem Writers Worshop. In the acknowledgments to *Poetry*, Major indebts the anthology to many influences: Lowenfels, Reed, Raphael, Art Berger, Smith, Fuller, Nat Hentoff, Randall, Atkins, Bremen, Young, and David Henderson. Major's "Down Wind Against the Highest Peaks" is typical of his style: angled and sharp twisted language, spacings that replace punctuation, tidbits of world knowledge applied to the racial statement (satire or exhortation), and experimental typography. Recalling his "passage," he sees "Tonto Sambo Willie," noting that even Mexico— "an asskissing nation"—now has the "super-blonde" on its "billboards."

In the midst of all these events, the poets vigorously promoted programs that extended their concepts and visions. Spriggs and Ahmed Alhamisi were corresponding editors of the *Journal*; Baraka, Major, Mazzam Al Sudan (now El Muhajir), and Neal became contributing editors. Editor-at-large Bullins was later joined by Touré. In the

seventies, Ernie Mkalimoto was added as a contributing
editor, with Major's name disappearing. Major, Randall,
Neal, Spriggs, Bullins, Baraka, and Alhamisi have all
served as guest special editors. An important influence on
(and outlet for) the new poetry, the *Journal* was "in
many ways born of *Soulbook* and *Dialogue*" (Gonçalves,
now Dingane, *Journal* editor). The magazine continues to
print the newest poetry, zeroing in on such other areas as
the West Indies (Summer 1973), and printing lively news
and announcements as well as reviews and criticism. Its
Spring 1968 issue, for example, was dedicated to Joseph T.
Johnson, Los Angeles poet who had recently been killed.
Abdul Karim edited *Black Dialogue* with Spriggs, Touré,
and Gonçalves serving as associate editors. Relocating in
New York in the late sixties, *Dialogue*'s new editorial
board included Spriggs, Nikki Giovanni, Jaci Early, Elaine
Jones, S. E. Anderson, and James Hinton. Alhamisi and
Carolyn Rodgers became Midwest editors; Spellman, Julia
Fields, and Akinshiju became editors for the South; and
Joans and Kgositsile took over as Africa and at-large edi-
tors. *Soulbook*'s editorial board now includes Hamilton,
Alhamisi, Carol Homes, Baba Lamumba, Zolili, Ngqondi
Masimini, and Shango Umoja. Among the administrative
staff is Donald Stone (Rahman), whose work appears in
Black Fire and all the journals.

Along with Spriggs, Touré, and Larry Miller (Katibu),
Rahman aided Baraka at Spirit House. His "Tran-
scendental Blues," full of chant/song and line experimentation, fuses the world of black music (and musicians) with the "strife riddled concrete bottoms of
skyscraper seas." Rahman's influences, obvious in his
name, are seen in his statement that a "riff" so high and
grand "Could be Allah." Finally, winding the poem into a
tribute to the black woman ("Bitter bit her bitterness
humming"), he rejects Christians and whites and warns
that

My spears shall rain. . . .

The Islam influence is also seen in other poets of the
period: Spriggs, Touré, Baraka, Iman, Neal, Alhamisi,

Dumas, Marvin X, Sonia Sanchez, who along with Nikki Giovanni emerged as one of the most popular poets of the era. These women poets and others—Audre Lorde, June Jordan, Mae Jackson, Kattie M. Cumbo, Jayne Cortez, Alexis Deveaux, Elouise Loftin, Odaro (Barbara Jones)— helped create a new wave of excitement about the possibilities and potentials of poetry by black women.[2] Adding to this healthy storm of active interest are such new black magazines as *Encore* and *Essence*. The most famous woman poet is Nikki Giovanni, a profound thinker and provocative speaker, whose skills and insights do not always extend into her poetry. Her route to New York was by way of Tennessee and Fisk University, where she was a member of Killens' Writers Workshop. Fame came in the late sixties, after she penned a series of volatile prose-like statements that were startling; even more so, coming from a woman. In the sixties, she privately published her poetry which was later brought out by Broadside Press and larger publishers. Her volumes include *Black Feeling, Black Talk, Black Judgement* (1970), *Re-Creation* (1970), *My House* (1972) and a book of poems for children, *Spin a Soft Black Song* (1971). Her anthology of black women poets, *Night Comes Softly*, was released in 1970, and she has recorded albums, written an autobiography, and published a series of "conversations" with Margaret Walker. Highly controversial among the new poets, she has been accorded numerous accolades: a Woman of the Year award; subject of features in *Ebony* and *Essence*; appearances on the Johnny Carson and Mike Douglas shows; a much-sought-after speaker on the college lecture circuit; recipient of an honorary doctorate from Wilberforce University and labeled the "Princess of Black Poetry" by Ida Lewis, *Encore* editor.

Denounced as an "individualist" by Madhubuti (Lee) and praised by Margaret Walker and Addison Gayle, Nikki Giovanni has rejected the label "revolutionary." Her singing of "God Bless America" on national television, after receiving the "Woman of the Year award,"

---

[2] See, as related reading, Andrea Benton Rushing's "Images of Black Women in Afro-American Poetry" (*Black World*, September 1975).

prompted letters to black publications questioning her sincerity. Some saw contradictions in the actions of the woman who, during the sixties, wrote "Of Liberation":

Dykes of the world are united
Faggots got their thing together
(Everyone is organized)
Black people these are facts
Where's your power. . . .
Honkies rule the world
The most vital commodity in america
Is Black people
Ask any circumcized honkie. . . .

The final stanza of this "poem" warns:

Our choice now is war or death
Our option is survival
Listen to your own Black hearts.

"Concerning One Responsible Negro With Too Much Power" echoes other themes in the new black poetry. The "responsible negroes" are "scared" and on the run. She tells them that

your tongue must be removed
since you have no brain
to keep it in check

In "Reflections on April 4, 1968," she calls Dr. King's assassination "an act of war." In "The Great Pax Whitie" she paraphrases a section from Genesis, in the Bible, noting that the first word was "Death"; "death to all niggers." Occasionally a line of interest jutted through what was otherwise only vertical prose. The pants of "Beautiful Black Men," for example, "hug what i like to hug." There is the characteristic repetition and emotion-freighted language, as in "True Import of the Present Dialogue, Black vs Negro":

Nigger
Can you kill
Can you kill
Can a nigger kill
Can a nigger kill a honkie

Can a nigger kill the Man . . .
Can you stab-a-Jew . . .
Can you run a protestant down with your
'68 Eldorado . . .
Can you piss on a blond head. . . .

The poem continues, reciting names of the "enemy" and cataloguing crimes and wrong-doings visited on Blacks, finally asking:

Learn to kill niggers
Learn to be Black men.

Much of what Nikki Giovanni was saying in the sixties moved black youth—it was not always safe or chic to disagree even if you wanted to—and some of it was admirable. But these things do not make her work defensible as poetry. "My Poem" and "Poem for Aretha" are certainly worthy, even noble, subjects that fall leisurely down the page, angling here and there but revealing nothing of the insight into human beings or poetic power that one finds in a poem by Helene Johnson, Margaret Walker, Gwendolyn Brooks, or Jayne Cortez. Her poetry lacks lyricism and imagery, and her forced themes show her as a vicarious revolutionary. "Nikki-Rosa," her most often quoted poem from the early period, is an exception to the rule. It has a believable, conversation-like language (characteristic of her poetry), and its details honestly tap the inner reaches of the collective black experience, as she unfolds the story of family fun and misfortune:

your biographers never understand
your father's pain as he sells his stock
and another dream goes
And though you're poor it isn't poverty that
concerns you. . . .

My House is a newer Giovanni. The venom has lessened, though some of the rampage is evident in "On Seeing Black Journal and Watching Nine Negro Leaders 'Give Aid and Comfort to the Enemy' to Quote Richard Nixon." There is no stunning improvement in style, language or technique. The poems deal with love, the city, childhood (always her rites of woman-passage), Africa and

Afro-American culture. Yet her promise and potential can
be glimpsed in "Africa I":

> on the bite of a kola nut
> i was so high the clouds blanketing
>   africa
> in the mid morning flight were pushed
> away in an angry flicker
> of the sun's tongue. . . .

Nikki Giovanni's importance, reminiscent of Frances
Harper's, in her personal influence (especially her great
drama on albums and in public), which has inspired many
young black women to write about themselves and their
world. But some of them, such as Mae Jackson, who won
Black World's Conrad Kent Rivers Award, have yet to
show the "stuff" of poetry in their writings. Mae Jackson's
Can I Poet with You was published in 1969 by Black Dialogue Publishers. Nikki Giovanni wrote the Introduction,
and Mae Jackson, in turn, dedicated the book to her.
Poet is full of the "complaints" that quickly became monotonous in the poetry of the sixties. In themes and
usages, the poems resemble Nikki Giovanni's work. "To a
Reactionary," "To the Negro Intellectual," and "Note
from a Field Nigger" are familiar in the sometimes confused and disturbed annals of the new poetry.

Sonia Sanchez, closely identified with the new poetry
and the new consciousness, alternates between terse, explicit verse and the sprawling, prosaic meanderings that
often serve the auditory demands of the new audiences.
Formerly married to the poet Etheridge Knight, she has
actively worked as playwright, poet and teacher. Her books
are *Homecoming* (1969), *We a BaddDDD People*
(1970), *It's a New Day: Poems for Young Brothas and
Sistus* (1971), *Love Poems* (1973), and an anthology
from her Young Writers Workshop at the Countee
Cullen Library in New York, *Three Hundred and Sixty
Degrees of Blackness Comin at You* (1972). "Malcolm" is
a lament and a night-filled memory for her:

> Yet this man
> this dreamer,
> thick-lipped with words

    will never speak again
    and in each winter
    when the cold air cracks
    with frost, I'll breathe
    his breath and mourn
    my gun-filled nights.

Her "for unborn malcolms," however, is another approach. Constricting words and structure, and attempting to achieve a black street speech, she tells Blacks to "git the word out" to the "man/boy" murderer who is taking a "holiday." Blacks are "hip to his shit" and when "blk/princes" die again white "faggots" "will die too." An experimentalist, Sonia Sanchez added her own unique voice to the flood of angry, cynical and derisive language in the new verse ("definition for blk/children"):

    a policeman
            is a pig
    and he shd be in
            a zoo
    with all the other piggy
            animals.   and
    until he stops
        killing blk/people
    cracking open their heads
    remember.
        the policeman
      is a pig.
            (oink/
             oink.)

She also joined the poetry of black love and man-woman unity, seeking through her particular style and voice to heal wounds of doubt, mistrust and loneliness. In "to all sisters," she says "hurt" is not the "bag" black women "shd be in." They are advised to love the black man who makes them "turn in/side out." Her journey has carried her from the fiery declamations of the revolutionary to the quiet turbulence and beauty of *Love Poems*—being, maybe, among the first of the new poets to fulfill Randall's prediction that black poetry would "move from the declamatory to the subjective mode."

June Jordan published *Who Look at Me* (1969), *Some Changes* (1971), the anthology *Soulscript* (1970), and a volume of poetry by students in her Brooklyn creative writing workshop, *The Voices of the Children* (1970). Her latest volume of poetry is *New Days: Poems of Exile and Return* (1974). Concise, analytical, and allusory, her poetry is in a free-verse style characteristic of practically all the recent black poetry. "Uncle Bull-boy" relates the death of a man whose eyes "were pink with alcohol." The living brother (uncle) reminisces, in the manner of black men, about their sharing of street talk, expensive shoes, and alcohol. And finally:

> His brother   dead from drinking
> Bull-boy drank to clear his thinking
> saw the roach inside the riddle.
> Soon the bubbles from his glass
> were the only bits of charm
> which overcame his folded arms.

Audre Lorde's "Rites of Passage" (for "MLK Jr") eulogizes Dr. King:

> Now rock the boat to fare-thee-well.

and remembers him this way:

> Quick
> children kiss us
> we are growing through dream.

Much of Audre Lorde's recent work concerns young people; even the title of her latest book *From a Land Where Other People Live* (1973), carries the awe and dream of the child's world. She writes now about teachers, man-woman relations, seasons, dreams: "As I Grow Up Again" and "Black Mother Woman," who thinks of her own mother's strength when "strangers come to compliment" her:

> I learned from you
> to deny myself
> through your denials.

Among the younger New York women poets, Judy Simmons, Alexis Deveaux, and Elouise Loftin sing out.

Judith's Blues (Broadside) was published in 1973. The poems submerge themselves in the troubled human psyche ("Schizophrenia") and explore the "Youth Cult," "Women," and "Daffodils"—although the titles do not reveal the poet's pithy searchings. Reflecting Judy Simmons' study of psychology, the poetry yields its meaning as the multiple layers of tensions and insights are uncovered. In "Schizophrenia" the "animal squats," next to the "piano" in a "corner," with an abnormal number of legs, arms, and a mouth that stretches from "forehead to abdomen." But the poet assures herself that if she does not lose control

it won't come back
inside of me.

Elouise Loftin's poetry (*Jumbish*, Emerson Hall, 1972; and *Barefoot Necklace*, Jamima House, 1975) has youthful, zesty imagery, indicative perhaps of the ease of these new technicians of the language. "Rain Spread" informs:

Last night threw her legs
open to me. . . .

She has the new woman sensibility, a good knowledge of the social landscape, and the cynicism often found among today's young, gifted and black. "Gettin caught" displays her humor and wit:

if they catch you
with your pants down
offing your guard
or peeing for free
if they catch you
doing something crazy
with quotes around it
and try to make you
feel
like you been
catched
you must be doing some
thing ok.

Spirits in the Streets (1973) is Alexis Deveaux's strange but fascinating prose-poetry account of growing up in

Harlem. A West Indian mother, despairing over a husband's misuse of his wife and children, complains:

> lord why he beat that woman so? and them
> children god only know what's gonna happen to
> them. eatin poison. has lye. eat you up inside
> jesus have mercy. you can't be too careful with
> children. you got to watch them every second.
> The world is so evil honey you know what i
> mean? merciful jesus shame them with the last word.

These examples represent only a fraction of the new poetry being written by younger (and older) New York-area
poets. Others are Katherine Cuestas, Phillip Solomon,
Gayle Jones (1949–), Stephen Kwartler, Wesley Brown,
Debra Gilliam, Vanessa Howard, Fatisha (*Sapphire Longing in the Blue Dust*), and Glen Thompson, to name
some. Poets who were launched in the earlier period also
published new items. Henderson's *Felix of the Silent Forest* (1967) was introduced by Jones; his mimeographed
The Poetry of Soul bears no date. He also published *De
Mayor of Harlem* in 1970, the same year he moved to
Berkeley. Essentially a Harlem poet, Henderson surveys
everything from the "Harlem Rebellion, Summer 1964" to
"Harlem Anthropology."

The transitions and outreachings of these poets are also
evident in Touré, who in 1968 went to teach black studies
at San Francisco State College. His works are *Juju* (1970,
Third World Press) and *Songhai!* (1972), the latter published by Songhai Press and introduced by Killens. Touré's
"Soul-gifts" are amply spiced with philosophy, black history, black music, Islamic influences, and "Juju," which
says Coltrane's horn is "cascading fountains of blood and
bones." *Songhai!* ranges from satire of Diana Ross and
Dionne Warwick to castigations of insincere activists.
The magical power of words is used to structure the ideal
black society. Touré's list of influences (see Foreword to
book) explains much about some of the black poetry
emanating from the New York area: Neal, Dumas,
Baraka, Gonçalves, Coltrane, Pharoah Sanders, Cecil
McBee—all preachers. "Poets of a Nation-in-Formation."

Related developments of the New York movement can
be seen in such projects as the *Ghetto '68* (Sol Battle) an-

thology of the Workshop for Young Writers in Harlem; *Wakra*, a new, Boston-based journal devoted to the examination "of events, the arts, ideas"; *Betcha Ain't* (1974), Celes Tisdale's anthology of "Poems from Attica"; a new anthology of young poets, *We Be Poetin'* (1974), by Tisdale; and *Writers Workshop Anthology*. No unifying thread runs through the work of New York-area poets except that of a relentless acceptance and pursuit of their blackness. One notes, however, that mysticism, examination of the occult, cosmic-musical forms and subjects, and the influence of Islam are more evident than in the poetry of other regions. But these are, of course, generalities that await more hindsight and research before they can be finalized and presented as significant phenomena on the larger tapestry of the poetry. Finally, for the New York area, the fire of the oral tradition was ignited by the dramatic, incantatory (drum-accompanied) declamations of "the Last Poets" and "the Original Last Poets." Along with Gil Scott-Heron, their impact on the black masses has been tremendous. With the exception of Gil Scott-Heron (who has awesome talents), these new *griots* have temporary standing. Scott-Heron combines blues, jazz and street conversation into an impressive ritualistic vehicle of protest and exhortation.

During the New York resurgence a number of things were going well for black poetry in Pennsylvania. Lincoln University—which produced Tolson and Hughes—delivered another group of diverse poets during this period: Carl Greene, Mary Louise Horton, Everett Hoagland, S. E. Anderson, Kathy Benjamin, Scott-Heron, Bernadine Tinner, Rita Whitehead, and others. Hoagland is a Broadside poet (*Black Velvet*, 1970), and Scott-Heron (*Free Will, Pieces of a Man*, etc.) is a recording poet-singer. Converging at points like the Muntu black artist group—founded by Neal, C. H. Fuller, theoretician Jimmy Stewart and Marybelle Moore—Philadelphia poets found various kinds of assistance. Other Philadelphia poets are Carl Greene (1945–), Lucy Smith from the older school, F. J. Bryant, Jr. (1943–), Mark Traylor, Clarence Maloney (1940–), Pat Ford, Joseph Bevans Bush, Janet M. Brooks, Carol Jenifer, and Don Mizell. Works by some of these youthful poets are in *Black Poets Write On: an*

Anthology of Black Philadelphia Poets (1970), published by the Black History Museum Committee. Harold Franklin's Introduction states: "A BLACK POET *IS* A KIND OF WARRIOR"—thus linking Philadelphia sentiments to those in New York and Boston. The Black Butterfly, Inc., a cultural center, was one of the several crossroads for various cultural/political activities in Philadelphia. Its founder was Maloney (now Chaka Ta), whose *Dimensions of Morning Sky* was published in 1964 in Pamplona, Spain. "Good Friday: 2 A.M." celebrates a "sultry brown girl" who "seems a superior animal." This "sepia siren" also holds the "semen" of a "vivid passion." Philadelphia poets explore city life and Africa, and exalt blackness. There is, too, the rage and vehemence often found in New York and Chicago poetry. "Cool Black Nights" (by Traylor, who died at age twenty-two) also captures driving street rhythms and rough rhymes:

> them hard-looking
> >hard-talking
> >hard-loving
> Cool black dudes

and

> them fine-looking
> >fine-walking
> >fine-talking
> >fine-loving
> them fine soul sisters. . . .

In Pittsburgh there was born the short-lived *Black Lines: a Journal of Black Studies* (1970). It published such Pittsburgh-area poets as Ed Roberson, August Wilson and Joanne Braxton, as well as such poets from the Midwest as Al Grover Armstrong and Redmond. The University of Pittsburgh Press opened up to black poets that same year, publishing Harper (*Dear John, Dear Coltrane*, 1970; *Song: Can I Get a Witness*, 1973), Roberson (*When Thy King Is a Boy*, 1970, and *Etai-Eken*, 1975) and Gerald Barrax (*Another Kind of Rain*, 1970). Roberson's poetry makes use of the gamut of techniques and styles—from neat drama to slanted spacings and slashes. In "mayday" there is an "underside of heaven" and the warning from one misunderstood that he is "armed" to fight the final

kindling of your dreaming.

"Othello Jones Dresses for Dinner" is a satirical look at the "Guess Who's Coming to Dinner" theme. After dating a white woman, the narrator assures her parents that he is "well mannered." Roberson adds his voice to a growing group of Pittsburgh poets that includes Kirk Hall (1944–).

Poetic talent has always been sired to the south in Washington, D.C., where Sterling Brown continued to teach into the early seventies. Howard, by now leading all black universities in the new consciousness, was the scene of a number of significant disturbances that nudged the school toward a new image. While Howard's poetic history can be traced through the early days of Sterling Brown (and into the Howard poets), the school has produced a number of younger writers: Clay Goss, Richard Wesley, E. Ethelbert Miller (*Andromeda*, 1974), and Paula Giddings. Its new image was deepened and broadened by the appointments of the Guianese poet Damas and Stephen Henderson (English chairman at Morehouse), who heads the Institute for the Arts and Humanities. However, the Howard drama was staged against a series of developments in the surrounding communities: Federal City College (Scott-Heron), Center for Black Education (Garrett), New Thing in Art and Architecture (Topper Carew), The New School of Afro-American Thought (Gaston Neal), Drum & Spear Bookstore (and Press) and the D.C. Black Repertory (Robert Hooks).

In addition to Damas and Henderson, the institute has added Madhubuti (Lee), Killens, Goss, Brown, Arthur P. Davis, and Ahmos Zu-Bolton. Already, the program's service to poets has been invaluable. Selected for special honors have been Baraka, Gwendolyn Brooks, Joans, and Dodson. A number of poets were also featured in the institute's First Annual Symposium: Lucille Clifton, Goss, Scott-Heron, Adesanya Alakoye, Miller, and Mari Evans. Touré, Johnston, and Kgositsile were guests for a program examining the African cultural presence in the Americas. Several poets have been invited to read and be recorded for the permanent audio/video library: Jayne Cortez, Crouch, Davis, Sarah Webster Fabio, Harper, Jeffers, Joans, Redmond, Sonia Sanchez, Scott-Heron, Bruce St. John, Margaret Walker, and Jay Wright.

In 1968 Gaston Neal said his "philosophy" was "to purge myself of the whiteness within me and link completely with my black brothers in the struggle to destroy the enemy and rebuild a black nation." He appeared to be working at that task for a while before the Afro-American school closed. In "Today" he said the tone of his life resembled a "growl mingled" with

the groan of the past . . .

and he lamented the jungles, which had been

deflowered by napalm. . . .

Karl Carter, another D.C. poet, appears in *Understanding the New Black Poetry*. He evokes the spirits of the "Heroes" of Orangeburg, Jackson, Memphis, New York, and Nashville, recalling that during a riot in Nashville he was

Riding somewhere in my mind with Eldridge
    Cleaver. . . .

"Roots" is an unsuccessful attempt to fuse the drama of colloquial black language with a formal English narrative about his grandmother.

Other poets living or publishing in the D.C. area during the sixties and seventies were Bernadette Golden (1949–   ), Helen Quigless (1945–   ) and Corrie and Roberta Haines. Beatrice Murphy (1908–   ), who over the years has contributed greatly to the growth and development of black poetry, has edited three important anthologies: *Negro Voices* (1938), *Ebony Rhythm* (1947), and *Today's Negro Voices* (1970). Her own volumes of poetry are *Love Is a Terrible Thing* (1945) and, with Nancy Arnez, *The Rocks Cry Out* (Broadside, 1969). Her poetry has moved from a traditional meter to a traditional free verse, dealing in the new phase with tensions caused by overemphasizing "white" and "black," and war. She is currently director of the Negro Bibliographic and Research Center and serves as managing editor of its publica-

tion *Bibliographic Survey: the Negro in Print*. Poetry by
D.C.-area poets can be found in *Transition*, a journal of
Howard's Afro-American Studies Department. Editors are
Miller, Iris Holiday, Ella Harding, and Veronica Lowe.
The Hainesses co-authored *As I See It* (1973). Many D.C.
poets are also found in *Synergy: D.C. Anthology*, edited
by Zu-Bolton and Ethelbert Miller (Energy Black South
Press, 1975).

Adjacent to the District of Columbia, in Baltimore,
more height is added to the black poetry totem. Lucille
Clifton (1936–   ), Sam Cornish (1938–   ) and Yvette
Johnson (1943–   ) have produced poetry that stands with
the best contemporary verse. *Good Times* (1969), *Good
News About the Earth* (1972) and *An Ordinary Woman*
(1974) are volumes by Lucille Clifton, who also writes
children's books. She currently teaches at Coppin State
College in Baltimore, where she lives with her husband
and six children. Even her titles suggest something about
her spirit and temperament. In the swamp of depression
and bleakness, it is indeed warming to hear someone proclaim Good News! The "Eldridge" of the 1960s is compared to a meat "cleaver" that will not "rust or break."
And there are humor, irony and truth in "Lately" in
which the "always drunk" delivery man says:

> "I'm 25 years old
> and all the white boys
> my age
> are younger than me."

While some sing good times in the kitchen, there are also
other acknowledgments: "Malcolm," "Eldridge," "Bobby
Seale," and student participants in demonstrations at Jackson and Kent states. *Good News About the Earth* gives
black and contemporary settings to biblical stories. Most
are unique, like the very womanly "Mary":

> this kiss
> as soft as cotton
>
> over my breasts
> all shiny bright
>
> something is in this night
> oh Lord have mercy on me

i feel a garden
in my mouth

between my legs
i see a tree

An Ordinary Woman is consciously woman, and the
poems, like those in other volumes, deal with everyday—
"ordinary"—things. However, Lucille Clifton has become
more of the mystic and the seer, using surreal and allusory
imagery, as in "Kali," "The Coming of Kali," "Her Love
Poem" and "Salt." Finally, there is "God's Mood":

He is tired of bone,
it breaks.
He is tired of eve's fancy and
adam's whining ways.

Cornish is a poet, teacher and editor. His books include
In this Corner (1964), *Beneath the Window* (n.d.,
1965?), *People Angles* (1967), *Winters* (1968), *Your
Hand in Mine* (for children, 1970) and *Generations*
(1971). With W. Lucian, he edited *Chicory: Young
Voices from the Black Ghetto* (1969), which developed
into a series still being published by the Enoch Pratt Free
Library (Community Action Program). Current editor of
Chicory is Melvin Edward Brown. Cornish has much
stylistic ammunition and is a precise navigator of language.
He tells "MIDDLE CLASS GIRLS WITH CRIPPLED
FINGERS WAITING FOR ME TO LIGHT THEIR
CIGARETTES":

your fingers
folded in your
lap

control the serpent
in your eyes

your face
never staring

with a smile
in your ruffled
collar

your eyes
populate the brick
with restless stares.

The influence of Cornish and others can be seen in *Express Yourself* (1973), an "anthology of student writings" from Edmondson High School, and *I Speak* (1973), poems by students at Coppin State College—"the Coppin poets."

The Baltimore and D.C. poets continue the long arm of poetry that embraces the South, where many poets now live: Spellman, Jeffers, Margaret Walker, Alice Walker (1944–), who recently moved from Mississippi to New York, Pinkie Lane, the BLKARTSOUTH poets (New Orleans), the Ex-Umbra poets (North Carolina Central University), Betty Gates (Miles College, Alabama), Gerald Barrax (1933–), (North Carolina State University), Ladele X (Leslie Powell), Leo J. Mason (Atlanta) and Lorenzo Thomas. The region receives and gives new blood to poetry through a continual flow of poets and teachers to and from the South. Some well-known older names are Johnson (James), Braithwaite, Tolson, Hayden, Jeffers, and Vesey. Among younger poets who have taught in recent years in the South are Audre Lorde (Toogaloo), Redmond (Southern), Wright (Toogaloo and Talladega), Spellman (Morehouse), and Kgositsile (North Carolina A & T). The South has also undergone dramatic changes as a result of the Black Consciousness Movement. Symbols are everywhere: the Free Southern and the Dashiki theaters in New Orleans, SUDAN South/West poetry-music theater group in Houston, the Theater of Afro-Arts in Miami, and Atlanta's Black Image. In Atlanta, Spellman organized the Center for Black Art, which publishes *The Journal Rhythm* (1970). Stone became editor, Ebon (Sigemonde Kharlos Wimberli) poetry editor, and Spellman editor of essays and features. The summer (1971) issue of *Rhythm* was also a memorial to Donald L., Graham (1944–71), poet-theoretician who succeeded Killens as director of the Writers Workshop at Fisk. Graham, who was also a musician, had published three books: *Black Song, Soul Motion,* and *Soul Motion II. Rhythm* said he "was running one of the baddest workshops in the South" and "teaching at the Revolutionary People's college in Nashville at the time of his death." Also in Atlanta is the influential Institute of the Black World.

Margaret Walker, a long-time teacher at Jackson State College in Mississippi, hosted in 1973 the bicentennial celebration of the publication of Phillis Wheatley's *Poems.* Her own poetry, however, has changed somewhat from the stance she took in *For My People.* Yet *Prophets for a New Day* (1970) and *October Journey* (1973) are difficult to judge against her other work, since she turned to the novel in the fifties and sixties and several poems in *October* were published in journals between 1930 and 1960. *Prophets* is a chronicle of the Civil Rights Movement. She writes about "Birmingham," "Street Demonstration," "Jackson, Mississippi," the March on Washington, and the biblical prophets: "Jeremiah," "Isaiah," "Amos" and "Joel." But the "new" prophets (Malcolm, Medgar Evers, Andy Goodman, Michael Schwerner, James Chaney) fought "oppression" in Louisiana, Mississippi and Georgia. *October* is in a quieter mood, employing a variety of verse forms, including the ballad in "Harriet Tubman." Margaret Walker's own unique sonnet is seen in "For Mary McLeod Bethune" and "For Paul Laurence Dunbar." And the earlier poet is suggested in "I want to Write":

I want to write songs of my people.

Alice Walker, novelist and poet, until 1974 shared the state of Mississippi (Jackson) with Margaret Walker. Her volumes are *Once* (1968) and *Revolutionary Petunias* (1973), the title of which, judging from other statements she has made, is probably a pun. Her poems range over her own civil-rights activities and general experiences, and include some satire. A poem in *Once* relates the story of the young black man who wanted to integrate a white beach in Alabama—in the "nude." She announces her debts in the dedication to *Petunias*: George Jackson, "heroes and heroines, and friends of early SNCC," Bob Moses, and Fannie Lou Hamer. These poems (written in personal tones) deal with history, folk strength and the stuff the black South is made of: "romance" that "blossomed" in pews at funerals; women with fists that "battered" doors ("Sunday School, Circa 1950"); a "back-woods woman" who kills her husband's murderer, then reminds her executors to water the *petunias*. And she also writes of a different kind of "Rage":

The silence between your words
rams into me
like a sword.

Yet another Mississippian and poet is Julius Eric Thompson, a history teacher at Toogaloo. *Hopes Tied Up in Promises* was published in 1970 and aims at lifting the new consciousness above mere "hopes." Thompson writes about being a black man in Mississippi, "Delta Children," Martin Luther King and "Black Power." There is also a series of poems on Africa.

In Louisiana, much new poetry has been flowing from the pens of young and old poets alike. Zu-Bolton, now residing in the District of Columbia, still edits *Hoodoo* magazine through Energy BlackSouth Press, in De Ridder, Louisiana. He formerly coedited *The Last Cookie*, based in De Ridder, San Francisco, and Geneva, New York. *Hoodoo I*, dedicated to two black students killed by policemen on the campus of Southern University in November of 1972, contained work by Lorenzo Thomas, May Miller, Pinkie Lane, Kalamu Ya Salaam, Jerry Ward, and other South-based poets. *Hoodoo 2 & 3*, a double issue published in 1975, contains work of more southern poets: Arthenia Bates Millican, Alice Walker, and Charles Rowell, as well as selections from the broader world of black writing. Energy BlackSouth Press will soon publish *A Niggered Amen*, Zu-Bolton's first volume of poems.

Under the guidance of the late English chairman, Melvin A. Butler, Southern University established the short-lived *Black Experience*, the first issue of which contained several poems by Alvin Aubert, a Southern alumnus who now resides in New York and edits *Obsidian: Black Literature in Review*. Aubert's *Against the Blues* (1971) surveys blues, love and his Louisiana heritage. Pinkie Lane, new English Department head at Southern, published *Wind Thoughts* (1972) as well as several broadsides: *Two Poems* (1972), *Poems to My Father* (1972), and *Songs to the Dialysis Machine* (1972), all brought out by South

and West, Inc., of Arkansas. South and West is also the
publisher of the annual *Poems by Blacks* (1970, 1971,
1972), for which Pinkie Lane has become permanent editor.

Butler inaugurated the annual Black Poetry Festival in
1972. In the program notes of the first festival, he stated:

> The Black Poetry Festival provides a rare opportunity to
> bring together professional and apprentice poets in an
> effort to define and legitimize all forms of Black poetic
> talent as a prelude and postlude to defining and legit-
> imizing the reality of Black people. Hopefully, the re-
> sults of our efforts will be a better understanding and a
> greater appreciation of the lives, aspirations and achieve-
> ments of Black people.

The festivals have attracted a number of poets including
Madhubuti, Sonia Sanchez, Gwendolyn Brooks, Randall,
Redmond (writer-in-residence, summers, 1971–72),
Primus St. John, Zu-Bolton, Knight, Aubert, Jayne Cortez,
Lucille Clifton, Troupe, Kalamu Salaam, Neal, Mari
Evans, Audre Lorde, and Irma McLaurin. The programs,
which included student poets and musicians, have inspired
a Poetry Writing Workshop under the supervision of Row-
ell, an English instructor.

The first three volumes of *Poems by Blacks* contain a
rich lode of southern poets: Leon E. Wiles (Philander
Smith College), Elijah Sabb (Little Rock), Booker T.
Jackson (Little Rock), Mary Gibson (Talladega College),
Eddie Scott (Memphis), Electa Wiley (Shreveport),
Otis Woodard (Memphis), Harry Bryce (Lemoyne Owen
College), Arthur Pfister (Tuskegee Institute, *Beer Cans
Bullets Things & Pieces*, 1972), Ollie Cox (Fayetteville,
North Carolina), Upton Pearson (Jackson, Mississippi),
Linda Hardnett, Jacquelyn Bryant (Meridian), Arthenia
Bates (Baton Rouge), Lois Miller (Baton Rouge),
Dennis Harrell (Tallahassee), Barbara Jean Knight
(Memphis), T. J. Reddy, and Kathleen Reed (Shreve-
port). Although Pinkie Lane did not edit the first two
issues of *Poems* (she did edit vol. III), she acted as ad-
viser, and her own work was substantially represented. She
is a gifted word manipulator, with consummate skill and
poetic passion.

North of Baton Rouge, in New Orleans, the Free Southern Theater had burned out by the late sixties, but out of
its workshops came *Nkombo,* which carries the work of
BLKARTSOUTH writers. Tom Dent, one of the
founders of FST, and Salaam now jointly edit the publication. Some BLKARTSOUTH poets are Isaac Black, Dent,
Salaam, Renaldo Fernández, Nayo (Barbara Malcolm),
Raymond Washingon, and John O'Neal. Again, no single
thread ties these poets together—except the "movement"
in the South. But their concerns for the movement are
often expressed better outside of poetry. In 1969
BLKARTSOUTH published individual volumes of poems
by Salaam (*The Blues Merchant*), Fernández (*The Impa-
tient Rebel*), Nayo (*I Want Me a Home*) and Washington (*Visions from the Ghetto*). "Racist Psychotherapy" is
Black's blueprint for Afro-American salvation. He advises
Blacks to spend less time rapping and drinking and more
time working for the cause. In "Ray Charles at Mississippi
State," Dent says:

> I hear people waiting for the riot to begin in their
>   hearts. . . .

Of "The Blues," Salaam says:

> "it is not submission."

But too much of his work is speechy. Salaam has also published *Hofu Ni Kwenu: My Fear Is for You* (1973),
which received a mixed review from Rowell in the September 1974 issue of *Black World.* And he is an editor of
the New Orleans-based *Black Collegian,* a valuable publication. Fellow BLKARTSOUTHerner Nayo writes a "Bed-
time Story": an exchange between mother and son about
"revolution." Answering the son's question, "When we
gonna have the revolution?" the mother says "Soon, son."
The other poets castigate Whitey and praise Blacks. But,
ironically, they write very little about southern life. Dent
currently leads the Congo Square Writing Workshop.
There are also writing workshops at Dillard and Xavier
universities.

Julia Fields, currently living in North Carolina, brought
out *East of Moonlight* in 1973, but one of her most eloquent testimonies is "High on the Hog," which es-

tablishes her right to have "caviar" or "shrimp soufflé" over "gut" or "jowl." Some menus and political stances are overexoticized by revolutionaries, she says, and she has "earned" the right to do what she likes. She has even heard "Mau Maus" screaming and "romanticizing pain." But she has paid her dues and had enough pressures from both sides of the color line. The subtle dart, but direct power, of Julia Fields suggests a healthy future for black poetry.

From Nashville came the echo of John Oliver Killens' Writers Conferences at Fisk University, the most important one taking place in the spring of 1967. Hayden, who had been at Fisk since the forties, left in 1968 after a series of brushes with proponents of the black aesthetic. The 1967 conference (probably the straw that broke the camel's back for Hayden) is seen by some as a major juncture in the new black writing. Gwendolyn Brooks talked about it in her autobiography, Margaret Walker discussed it with Nikki Giovanni in their published "conversations," and Hoyt Fuller wrote glowingly of it in Black World. Writers attending the conference were David Llorens, Fuller, Ron Milner, Clarke, Bennett, Margaret Danner, Nikki Giovanni, Randall, Lee, Margaret Walker, Sonia Sanchez, Jones, and Margaret Burroughs. Probably held in the South for symbolic reasons, the conference provided the first real "new" national dramatic arena for old and young writers. Gwendolyn Brooks (a "Negro" then, she has said) recalls being "coldly respected" after just having flown to Nashville from "white white South Dakota." However, she was among the first (with Randall and Fuller) to take up the banner of the black aesthetic and the causes of the young writers. Such action, of course, was displeasing to a number of white and black poets, not the least among them Hayden, who refuses to acknowledge the existence of a "separate" aesthetic for Blacks (Kaleidoscope, 1967, and Black World poll, January 1968).

Although the Fisk example has been followed by dozens of black colleges all over the South, Midwest and East, there is still no monolithic stand on "directions," but some writers keep trying to give them anyway. One indication of the healthy diversity among black writers is the journal Roots, published at Texas Southern University.

Editors are Tommy Guy, Jeffree James, Turner Whorton,
and Mance Williams. Lorenzo Thomas is also associated
with the publication. Volume I, number 1 contains essays,
art and the works of several poets, most of them Southerners. The poetry, devoid of monotonous theme or style,
represents a broad range of interests in linguistics, subjects
and forms. M'lo, in "a love supreme," says, "all my eyes
gazed forever backwards." In "she'll never know," Mickey
Leland writes of various aspects of the social and physical
landscape, including the "Kinky haired boys" who build
"arsenals of straw." Clarence Ward notes in "Hanging
On" that the rent has gone up, eviction is imminent,
there is no food for the baby, and

Hanging on aint easy. . . .

J. ahmad j.'s title "Hard Head Makes a Soft Ass" implies
the poem's statement. And fantasy eternalizes, "like a
good high," for Tommy Guy in "Brother."
The themes of unity, self-esteem, the African
"motherland," and anger remain in the new poetry as the
Midwest and West contribute immensely to its brilliance
and the controversy. Ohio, for example, represented a
unique gathering of diverse views on the new consciousness, attracting a number of poets to aid the work of
Norman Jordan (1938–   ), Atkins, James Kilgore (all
from Cleveland) and Hernton. Now at Oberlin, Hernton
succeeded Redmond as writer-in-residence there a year af-
ter Quincy Troupe began a residency at Ohio University.
Sarah Webster Fabio has also taught at Oberlin during
Hernton's leave of absence. However, Cleveland-area activ-
ity was spurred by a long tradition of black writers includ-
ing Dunbar, Hughes, Chesnutt (one of the founders of
Karamu House) and Atkins. This continuum produced
Jordan and a host of younger poets: Anthony Fudge,
Larry Howard, Larry Wade, Art Nixon, Clint Nelson,
Robert Fleming (*Ku Wais* magazine), Alan Bell, Roland
Forte, Ted Hayes, Elmer Buford, and Bill Russell of the
Muntu poets. Other participating writers-artists were
Clyde Shy, Ameer Rashid, and Anetta Jefferson. Support
for poets and their activities came from various places: the
Cleveland *Call and Post*, Afro-Set Black Arts Project,
United Black Artists. Free Lance, and Karamu House

where Jordan's plays were produced before and during his stint as playwright-in-residence there.

Kilgore writes out of a strong tradition of black humanism nurtured in religious homes. His volumes are, *The Big Buffalo and Other Poems* (1969), *Midnight Blast* (1970), *A Time of Black Devotion* (1971), and *Black Bicentennial* (1975). The poems exposed the contradictions in American democracy and survey the "High Rise Dreams" of Blacks caught in the urban-renewal scrabble. *Devotion*, dedicated to Coretta Scott King, vibrates with concern for black students, Third World survival, and a fascination with Frantz Fanon.

A different kind of poet, Jordan is sometimes angry, cynical and violent, other times prophetic and mystical. He has published three volumes: *Destination: Ashes* (1967, 1971), *Above Maya* (1971) and, with Marcia Gage, *Two Books* (1974). Dedicated to the "Community," *Destination* contains Jordan's best and most memorable poems. In Cleveland he emerged as a major force in the new black poetry, uniting the older tradition, symbolized by *Free Lance*, and the Muntu poets. *Destination*, first published privately by Jordan, was later brought out by Third World Press (Chicago) with an Introduction by Lee, who said he "learned" that Hughes had no need to "re-write and revise." (!) Anyway, *Destination* chronicles Jordan's own development from the period of civil rights through black power. His poetry is all free verse, usually easily accessible narrative making ample use of *dramatis personae* from every walk of black life. There are alcoholism, violence, poverty, loneliness, and exaltation of blackness. "I Have Seen Them" describes those on relief, hungry and cold, praying for "miracles." Nellie Reed used to be a girl about town, "Laughing and dancing," but now, at twenty-six, she is dead and her ghost "trembles" in a wine bottle (in the alley) "needing a fix." Jordan also spoofs "High Art and All That Jazz":

> Fuck you and your
> damn verbs
> let me tell it like
> it is
> *nasty* and *funkey*.

"Feeding the Lions" (1966) is his most anthologized poem. The "army" of brief-case-carrying social workers invades black neighborhoods each morning, passes out checks, moves quickly from one door to another, and, after filling its quotas, leaves "before dark." There are also poems about mysticism, religion, mythology and karma, including drawings of eyes, triangles and circles—all reflecting the many influences on Jordan's work and the approaching new mood (*Above Maya*). But *Destination*, with its short, epigrammatic verses and parables, sees through allusory, romantic "unity" near the end and mounts an attack on revolutionary charlatans, backsliders of the movement and those who view violence as the only solution to racism. Yet "Cosmic Witchdoctors" reaffirms his faith in black writers working far into a "liquid night"; they provide the foundation

for tomorrow's liberation.

Jordan's belief in the mystical, magical powers of the word can be seen in the name *Vibration*, a Cleveland magazine with which he was closely associated. It is "Dedicated to the Resurrection of the Mentally and Spiritually Dead."

Ohio poets found outlets for their work in *Vibration* and other journals: *Black Ascensions* (Cuyahoga Community College), *Proud Black Images* (Ohio State University) and *Lifeline: When America Sings She Croaks* (Oberlin). Oberlin students also produced a special black issue of the college's *Activist* magazine; it contained poems by both students and well-known poets. Fudge, a staff member of *Black Ascensions*, published *Migration* in 1972. Cleveland poet, Elmer Buford, penname B. Felton (1934–), brought out *Conclusions*, with an Introduction by Atkins, who praised the young poet for not consciously engaging in the "disfigurement of perceptions" to polemicize a "constricted kind of 'relevance.'" In "An Elegy to Eternity," Felton, a vibrant and versatile poet, says:

Tear-ducts swell, bursting in a
      delight of flood and fury.

Garfield Jackson, a young prize-winning poet, is one of the editors of *Proud Black Images*. Many young and older

Ohio poets are included among its pages: Forrest Gay, Dianne Gould, Jackie Toone, Ebrahim Aljahizz, Mohssen Aslam (Chris Jenkins), Battuta Lukamba Barca, Linda Callender, Beverly Cheeks, Antar Sudan Mberi, Leatrice Emeruwa, Roslyn Perry Ford, Ray Montgomery, Kilgore, Jordan, and others. Although the journal's title sets a conceptual pace and places it in the stream of the new consciousness, there is no unifying theme or idea in the poetry. John Whittaker calls "Singers, Dancers" the "doers of initial deeds" and

Implementers of the inevitable Black life.

Hernton, who attended Ohio schools, became writer-in-residence at Central State University in the sixties. He published *The Coming of Chronos to the House of Nightsong* in 1963, and since then he has written many books and articles on America's social/sexual hangups. One of his most powerful poems appeared in the first issue of *Confrontation: a Journal of Third World Literature* (summer 1970) founded and edited by Troupe at Ohio University. "Street Scene" shows Hernton playfully looking at the identity question along with other things. When he meets and speaks to his "dream" on the "street," he receives this answer:

"Go to hell, sonofabitch."

Confrontation also publishes other Ohio poets; yet its concerns are broad, as seen in the names of contributing editors: Damas, Sergio Mondragon, Fernando Alegría, Neal, Redmond, Tam Fiori, David Henderson, Melvin Edwards, and Wilfred Cartey. Other Ohio communities also showed indications of the new consciousness. Cincinnati's first black arts festival was organized by Nikki Giovanni in 1967, and out of this effort grew The New Theater. Herbert Martin (1933–   ), *New York the Nine Million and Other Poems* (1969), made an immeasurably valuable contribution to the understanding of black poetry when he organized the Paul Laurence Dunbar Centennial in 1972 at the University of Dayton.

Indiana heaved forth precious words from Gary, Indianapolis, Purdue, Terre Haute, and other areas. Mari

Evans organized arts and consciousness programs in Indianapolis and Bloomington. *I Am a Black Woman,* containing poems written over several years, unfortunately did not find a publisher until 1970. However, the book deservedly received the Black Academy of Arts and Letters Second annual Poetry Award. She has been closely identified with activities in Chicago, where Third World Press publishes her writings for children. Her title poem is a spiritual, psychological, and historical journey of the black woman, whose "trigger tire/d fingers" now

> seek the softness of my warrior's beard. . . .

A major poem, it combines the best of the modernists' techniques with a quasi musical score so as to give the impression of someone singing or humming along with the reader. Mari Evans scans other fields of black life, writing about lonely and dejected women, self-pride, violence, black unity, and Africa. In "Who Can Be Born Black" she joyously and defiantly asks:

> Who
> can be born
> black
> and not exult!

Also closely associated with the Chicago and Detroit movements is Etheridge Knight (1933–   ), who was serving a twenty-year term in Indiana State Prison when *Poems from Prison* (1968) appeared, with a Preface by Gwendolyn Brooks. She called his poetry

> Vital. Vital.
> This poetry is a major announcement. . . .
> And there is blackness, inclusive, possessed and given;
> freed and terrible and beautiful.

Her own version of the black aesthetic was expressed in the same statement: "Since Etheridge Knight is not your stifled *artiste,* there is air in these poems." Knight roams the deep crevices of black spiritual and psychic worlds as he combines the language of the prison subculture with the rhythms of black American street speech. He bounces or drives hard—a poetry of "hard bop"—looking at prison life, love and ancestry. Exceptional pieces are the folksy "Hard Rock Returns to Prison from the Hospital for the Criminal Insane," the mystical and mythical "He Sees Through Stone," the genealogical "The Idea of Ancestry," the innovative *haiku* sections, and "On Universalism," which warns against applying "universal laws" to Blacks' "pains" and "chains" in America. His technical abilities are poignantly displayed in *haiku* "9":

> Making jazz swing in
> Seventeen syllables AIN'T
> No square poet's job.

Knight, who was later released from prison, also edited *Black Voices from Prison* (1970), and in 1973 Broadside Press published *Belly Song and Other Poems*. He loses his reach when he overintellectualizes in his poetry. And *Poems* is not surpassed by *Belly Song*. The second book has some fine moments, but it sometimes slips into polemics. However, Knight is still stretching out as a poet, currently doing research into oral literature with the aid of a Guggenheim grant. *Belly* shows him pursuing this tradition in "The Bones of My Father," which smile at the moon in Mississippi

> from the bottom
> of the Tallahatchie.

Finally, a number of poets from this general region of the Midwest and South are included in a special black-poetry issue of *Negro American Literature Forum* (spring 1972) edited by Redmond. The *Forum* is published by Indiana State University School of Education and edited by John Bayliss, an Englishman. It regularly reviews black literature.

Chicago is a Midwest heart and has a long tradition of black arts, going back to, and before, Count Basie's opening at the Sunset Club, in 1927. However, some of the more recent forces helping to shape the new poetry movement there are South Side Community Arts Center, the formidable Johnson Publications, Kuumba's Workshop and Root Theater (Francis and Val Ward), the DuSable Museum of African American History (Margaret Burroughs), Organization of Black American Culture, Insti-

tute of Positive Education and Third World Press
(Madhubuti), *Free Black Press*, Afro-Arts Theater, Malcolm X College, Oscar Brown, Jr., *Muhammad Speaks*
(now *Bilalian News*), Ellis's Bookstores, Chicago *Defender*, and Philip Cohran (Artistic Heritage Ensemble).
Much of the new poetry scene generates from OBAC and
Gwendolyn Brooks. Fuller, former *Black World* managing
editor, is also adviser to OBAC's Writer's Workshop. In
a 1969 (fall) issue of *Nommo*, the workshop's journal,
Fuller said:

> Black is a way of looking at the world. The poets of
> OBAC, in revealing their vision, celebrate their
> blackness. In this moment in history, what might under
> different circumstances be simply assumed must neces-
> sarily be asserted. And the OBAC poets know—if others
> do not—that pale men out of the West do not define
> for mankind the perimeters of art. This they want all
> black people to know.

In the journal's winter issue of the same year, Fuller said
OBAC members were "seeking" to be "both simple and
profound." They display an "imaginative representation
of their experiences," but they also seek "to be revolutionary." In the first quote, Fuller's tone, carrying the
battle-baiting phrase "even if others do not," seemed to
have been a signal for, among others, Don L. Lee
(1942–   ), to continue his own relentless attacks on all
fronts. There are no sacred cows, as Lee sees it, and since
"others do not" know what the youthful Chicago Blacks
presumably *did* know, Lee's assignment seems to have
been to teach them. Gwendolyn Brooks concurred with
most of this feeling, embracing as it were a "new" blackness and (unfortunately) engaging in self-deprecation: "It
frightens me to realize that, if I had died before the age of
fifty, I would have died a 'Negro' fraction." Lee, following
the examples of Randall and Baraka, began Third World
Press—a valuable vehicle for the new poets—and changed
his name in the early seventies to Haki R. Madhubuti. He
also established the Institute for Positive Education, which
publishes *Black Books Bulletin* (with himself as editor).
Other poets included in the editorial staff are Sterling
Plumpp (1940–   ), Johari Amini (Jewel Latimore)

(1935–   ), Emanuel, Sarah Webster Fabio, the late
David Llorens (who launched Lee's national career in
Ebony, March 1969), and Dudley Randall. OBAC was
founded in 1967; poets of varying temperaments were attracted to it and to Gwendolyn Brooks's workshops:
Carolyn   Rodgers   (1943–   ),   Walter   Bradford
(1937–   ),   Carl   Clark   (1932–   ),   Mike   Cook
(1939–   ), James Cunningham (1936–   ), Ronda Davis
(1940–   ), Sam Greenlee, Philip Royster (1943–   ),
Peggy   Kenner   (1937–   ),   Madhubuti,   Linyatta
(1947–   ), Sharon Scott (1951–   ), Sigemonde Wimberli (Ebon) (1938–   ), and a continuous stream of
newly arriving poets. Other Chicago-area poets are
Stephany Fuller (1947–   ), Eugene Perkins, Irma
McLaurin, Lucille Patterson, Jerrod, Zack Gilbert
(1925–   ), Alicia Johnson (1944–   ), Ruwa Chiri,
Robert Butler, and Barbara McBain (1944–   ).

The work of many Chicago-area poets can be found in
*Nommo, Black Expressions, Black World, Black Writers'
News, Muhammad Speaks,* and in the anthologies *A
Broadside Treasury* (1971) and *Jump Bad: a New Chicago
Anthology* (1971), both edited by Gwendolyn Brooks.
They can also be found in numerous other nationally distributed anthologies and journals. *Black World,* as name
and concept, was a concession won by Chicago-area artists
and activists who protested against the old name, *Negro
Digest,* in the late sixties. Until April of 1976, when Johnson Publishing Company ceased publishing it, Fuller
guided *Black World's* new image through the choppy
waters of controversy and change. But many readers have
been critical of *Black World's* particularized stands, its
lack of "open" forum on some issues, and its tendency to
circumscribe individuals and groups. Nevertheless the journal has been an indispensable aid to black poets and writers, printing their work, identifying anthologists, noting
books published, and serving as facilitator and conduit for
prizes and contact. At the same time, however, the Afro-
American community faces the challenge of producing a
journal that can reflect its new sophistication and thought.

Among all new poets, Madhubuti is second only to
Nikki Giovanni in the number of accolades and the com-
mercial attention he and his poetry have received. A

sampling of critics, poets, and scholars who feel he is one of the greatest of the new poets would have to include Stephen Henderson, Fuller, Gwendolyn Brooks, Margaret Walker, Paula Giddings, Baraka, Mari Evans, Randall, and Gayle. Gwendolyn Brooks has said he physically resembles Jesus Christ, and her Introduction to *Jump Bad* hails him as "the most significant, inventive, and influential black poet in the country." Overlooking, for the moment, the prerequisite of reading "all" the poetry in the "country" before making such a statement, it is paradoxical in view of the "collective" policy—and the anti-individualist positions—that allegedly form the cornerstone of the Chicago poetry scene.

Madhubuti has published five volumes of poetry: *Think Black!* (1967), *Black Pride* (1968), *Don't Cry, Scream* (1969), *We Walk the Way of the New World* (1970), *Directionscore: Selected and New Poems* (1971) and *The Book of Life* (1973). His *Dynamite Voices, Vol. I* (Broadside Press), published in 1971, is a study of fourteen black poets of the sixties; but, like his other criticism, it reveals that he is a hazy thinker who lacks discretion and a firm understanding of the black poetry tradition. He spends an entire page, for example, illuminating and apparently advocating the use of the word "motherfucker." And any book about the sixties should not come off the press without examining the poetry of LeRoi Jones/Imamu Baraka. Madhubuti attributes the fathership of the new black poetry to Baraka but does not discuss the man's poetry. There are other, incredible flaws in the book, for which this young poet's mentors must share some blame. As a critic, he did not (could not!) cultivate the "distance" of a Johnson, Brown, Redding, or Henderson, and consequently—lacking discipline and training—could not really *see* the poetry. The book's redeeming values, such as they are, possibly reside in its incidental information and bibliography.

As a poet, Lee fares better, employing wit, irony, understatement and signification (e.g., "In the Interest of Black Salvation": "Jesus saves—S&H Green Stamps"). But there are excellent poets in Chicago who have been dwarfed by his political image (Plumpp, Cunningham, Rodgers, Gilbert, etc.) His themes range from what Arthur P. Davis has called "The New Poetry of Black Hate," through love

and black pride, to the haggard pontifications in *The Book
of Life* in which he rearranges sayings and parables stated
better by Aesop, bush Africans, Plato, Baraka, and Tolson.
Like Nikki Giovanni and others, his early work reinforced
the self-love concept, castigated Whitey and encouraged
black unity. Most of his ideas were summed up in the titles *Think Black!* and *Black Pride*; his devices are everyday
conversation (often not well wrought but sometimes quite
startling), signification, and musical rhythms ("The
Wall"). These he adjusts in an often effective typography
which moves in parallel columns vertically or horizontally
on the pages. In introductions to his books and in "critical" articles, Madhubuti tries to give "directions" to black
writers—as he does in much of his poetry. "First Impressions on a Poet's Death," an elegy for Conrad Kent
Rivers, has irony and chronicles the often un-talked-about
causes of premature black deaths. Some may die of "too
much" sex and drink, he says, but "poets who poet"

> seldom
> die
> from
> overexposure.

But he can unknowingly dabble with the most complex aspects of black life, as in "The Self-Hatred of Don L. Lee,"
where, after studying black history, he learns to love the
"inner" person and hate (with vehemence)

> my light
> brown
> outer.

Certainly a profound and tragic dilemma is stated here,
since hating one's color will not change it and since one
has to live with it for the rest of one's life. It is a good
poem for studying the so-called "solution" that some
black writers claim to have "found" to the identity problem.

One of his most famous poems is "Don't Cry, Scream."
Praised highly by Stephen Henderson, the poem paraphrases the heretical rantings of Ron Karenga, who encouraged Blacks to renounce the blues. A tribute to Col-

trane (see much better ones by Harper, Touré, and Troupe), it is largely graphic (hieroglyphics?) with occasional areas of intelligibility. Then there is this salient self-disgust:

> i cried for billy holiday.
> the blues. we ain't blue
> the blues exhibited illusions of manhood.

Even the German Janheinz Jahn knew better. How could Coltrane have "evolved" without the blues? And certainly, today, Madhubuti must face the question: if the blues were destructive, then how did he "make it"? Indeed, how did anyone "make it" without the "bridge" of survivalisms necessary to "cross over"? Madhubuti's influence on the new poetry has been substantial, however, though in most instances the influence has been in the area of politics rather than poetry. With other "stars" of the new black poetry, he has helped to popularize it.

Carolyn Rodgers' volumes are *Paper Soul* (1968), *Songs of a Blackbird* (1969), *2 Love Raps* (pamphlet) (1969), *Blues Gittin Up* (1972) and *How I Got Ovah* (1975). *How I Got Ovah* and Sherley Anne Williams' *The Peacock Poems* (1975) were both nominated for the National Book Award in 1976. Womanly and convincing, Rodgers writes of young women, love, revolutionaries, and music. In "Phoenix" she recalls traveling "with the wind" and hearing the many voices.

> screaming blooddrops of time.

"Jazz" describes "three" at the bar, the clicking and clinking of drinking glasses,

> and the murmur of thick mouths. . . .

"Rebolushinary x-mas/eastuh julie 4/etc. etc. etc." is a satire on "militants." And she tells us that

> bits of me splintered into a mirror

in "Look at My Face a Collage." These ideas and themes, and many others, can also be found in the poetry of Johari Amini, Plumpp and Cunningham. Johari Amini's books include *Images in Black* (1967), *A Folk Fable* (pamphlet) (1969), *Let's Go Somewhere* (1970), and *A Hip Tale in*

Death Style (1972). She relies heavily upon black colloquialisms, usually achieving success. But she has other
ranges, as can be seen in "Brother," which longs for the
"soil" of black people, where they can feel the

universe shudder. . . .

Plumpp's works are *Portable Soul* (1969), *Half Black,
Half Blacker* (1970) and *Steps to Break the Circle*
(1975). A Southerner with a background in psychology,
he has also written a provocative study called *Black Rit-
uals* (1973). His interests are seen in such titles as "From
Manless Sisters to Big Bad Rappers," "Black Messages"
("believe in us"), "Living Truth" ("black history . . . a
banned epic"), and "Egypt (for Black Motherhood)":

an everlasting sunrise awoke. . . .

One of the most perceptive, skillful, and innovative
poets is Cunningham. His one volume is *The Blue Narrator* (1974), and he has been published widely in periodicals. "The City Rises" as

a sad stiff wooden place. . . .

"St. Julien's Eve: for Dennis Cross" wonderfully mixes
the senses; the narrator is "stabbed" in the "ear" by
Brahms, and then there follows great poetry:

the wind-man tearing at the bridge

as a man stands wondering

why does the river
float up to the sky. . . .

A Tolsonian thrust, "Rapping Along with Ronda Davis"
is a delightful combination of

Moon beams & yams

and shows Cunningham's ability to place disparate order-
ings in his poetic vise. "A Street in Kaufman-ville: or a
note thrown to carolyn from rodgers place" is a study of
the "fragments" of Bob Kaufman in whom the past sees

a madness unlike my own. . . .

And arriving "From the Narrator's Trance,"

a song thumbed down a cruiser for a ride. . . .

Cunningham also writes of other poets and artists. In conducting his fascinating experiments with the language, he celebrates the wide span of the hybrid Afro-American heritage. Certainly, here is a poet to be closely watched.

Among other Chicago poets who have published volumes are Gilbert, *My Own Hallelujahs* (1971); Chiri, *An Acknowledgment to My Afro-American Brother* (1968); Perkins, *Black Is Beautiful* (1968); Wimberli (Ebon) *Ghetto Scenes* (1968) and *Revolution* (1968) ("a new Black voice to alarm the establishment"—Perkins); Margaret Burroughs, *What Shall I Tell My Children Who are Black* (1968); Greenlee, *Blues for an African Princess* (1971); Lucille Patterson, *Moon in Black* (1974); Stephany, *Moving Deep* (1970); Royster, also a master drummer, *The Black Door* (1971); Kgositsile, *Spirits Unchained* (1969) and *For Melba* (1970); Butler, *Black Visions,* (1968); and Jerrod, *To Paint a Black Picture* (1969). A yet newer group, not all Chicagoans, have been published in Third World Press's New Poets series: Angela Jackson, *Voodoo/Love Magic* (1974); Damali (Denise Burnett), *I Am That We May Be* (1974); Fred Hord, *After Hours* (1974); and Sandra Royster, *Women Talk* (1974). These young poets deal with a wide variety of subjects, though with a narrower variety of forms; mostly, however, they are concerned with revolution, self-pride, heterosexual relations, and black life in urban America.

Among the many good things that have emerged from Chicago is the "new" Gwendolyn Brooks, who, as we saw in Chapter V, has always been solid in her blackness and wonderfully magic in her poetry. The Brooks of *In the Mecca* (1968), *Riot* (1969), *Family Pictures* (1970), *Aloneness* (1971), and *Beckonings* (1975) is not drastically different from her former self. In *Report from Part One* (1972), her autobiography, she apparently approved the use of a Madhubuti Preface that tells more about his own reading and writing problems than it does about this great woman's poetry. Madhubuti complains about her complex verse; but her poetry has never been "easy" to read (probably never will be), and *Riot* continues that tradition of toughness, a poetry that yields meaning after many readings. She employs mythology, history, sarcasm and dramatic dialogue to reveal white middle-class pomposity even in face of a "Riot"; she later juxtaposes the art of Bing Crosby and Melvin Van Peebles, and surveys love. The "Black philosopher" is the thread that spines the section called The Third Sermon on the Warpland. There are traces of her terse, earlier style, particularly her unique word-sound progressions:

> as her underfed haunches jerk jazz.

And a white liberal, observing a riot, asks

> "But WHY do These People offend *themselves?*"

adding that it is time to "help."

Family Pictures contains the snapshots of her new young heroes, the people who helped her become "Black." But despite well-meaning salutes to Kgositsile, Lee, Bradford, and young Africans, there is a monotony of praise. However, no one is perfect, and she is apparently struggling as hard with commitment as she is with the new poetry. In "Speech to the Young. Speech to the Progress-Toward," dedicated to her own children, the sensitive mother-poet gives advice that many another young person might accept and cherish:

> Live not for The-End-of-the-Song.
> Live in the along.

Such caution comes at an important juncture, when the world is moving right along, to use a cliché, and leaving behind those too mired in their own "self-revelations" to look, listen and learn. And one crowning salute to this great lady of black letters was an impressive anthology of poetry and testimonials, *To Gwen with Love: a Tribute to Gwendolyn Brooks* (1971), assembled by Madhubuti and others.

Chicago poets were only a skip from Gary, Indianapolis, Detroit, St. Louis, Cleveland, and Kansas City, and the closeness allowed for interchanges on all levels. Motown's poetry output, like that of other communities, was interwoven with related symbols and expressions of the new consciousness: Margaret Danner's Boone House for the Arts, Reverend Cleage's Shrine of the Black Madonna, Motown Records, Broadside Press, Vaughn's Bookstore, and area black-studies projects. The poetry hub for the

late sixties and seventies, of course, is Randall's Broadside
Press. Randall has changed as a poet and person, he says,
in ways that perhaps parallel the changes in Gwendolyn
Brooks. A "father" figure among some new black poets, he
publishes dozens of them (over one hundred, at this writing), releases new books of his own poetry, serves as distributor of Breman's Heritage Series, and travels widely as
lecturer, teacher, librarian, and translator of Russian poetry.

A formalist by training and temperament, Randall described his new poetic stance in a statement in *Modern
and Contemporary Afro-American Poetry* (Bell, 1972):

> My poetics is to try to write poetry as well as I can. I
> think I have said elsewhere that the function of the
> poet is to write poetry. My earlier poetry was more for-
> mal. Now I am trying to write a looser, more irregular,
> more colloquial and more idiomatic verse. I abhor
> logorrhea, and try to make my poems as concentrated as
> possible.

Indeed Randall has tried to do just that—moving from a
traditional to a loose conversational verse. This he attempts in such volumes as *Love You* (1970) and *After
the Killing* (1973). When Randall is describing a girl in
an African village or the "Miracle" of love, he is genuine
and strong. But such poems as "Green Apples" and
"Words Words Words" pit him against his mettle. These
and other pieces are merely vertical prose, appearing as
sketches and letters. But he is primarily a librarian, publisher, and editor whose service to black poets has been
and remains invaluable. This is seen not only in his production of their work, but in the many anthologies he has
edited. With Chicagoan Margaret Burroughs, he coedited
Malcolm: Poems on the Life and Death of Malcolm X
(1967), a foresightful and commanding work. Randall
also edited *Black Poetry* (1969) and *The Black Poets*
(1971), the latter unbalanced and apparently quickly
put together, since it has practically no introduction and
contains no bio-bibliographical material on the poets. In
addition to Randall and Margaret Danner, other poets
in this upper-midwest area are James Randall (1938–   ),
James   Thompson   (1936–   ),   Richard   Thomas
(1939–   ), William Thigpen (1948–71), Naomi Mad-

gett, Hayden, Rocky Taylor (Tejumolá Ologboni)
(1945–   ), Pearl Cleage Lomax (1948–   ) (now living in
Atlanta), Malaika Wangara (1938–   ), Ahmed Alhamisi
(1940–   ), A. X. Nicholas (*Woke Up This Mornin':* the
Poetry of the Blues and *The Poetry of Soul*), Reginald
Wilson (1927–   ), Sonebeyatta (1956–   ), Carolyn
Thomas (1944–   ), Leaonead Bailey (1906–   ), Melba
Boyd (1950–   ), Shirley Woodson (1936–   ), Jill
Witherspoon (1947–   ), La Donna Tolbert (1956–   ),
Stella Crews (1950–   ), Darnell Hawkins (1946–   ), and
Frenchy Hodges (1940–   ). Some of their works can be
found in *Ten, A Broadside Treasury, The Black Poets* and
in the small individual volumes regularly published by
Broadside Press. An important volume from the area is
poet-editor Alhamisi's *Black Arts: Anthology of Black Cre-
ations* (with Kofi Wangara, 1969). For further details on
Detroit and other Broadside poets see *Broadside Authors
and Artists* (Leaonead Bailey, 1974).

James Randall has published *Don't Ask Me Who I Am*
and *Cities and Other Disasters* (1973). His poetry is intense, commanding and dramatic. In "Network News" we
are told:

For years he'd watched the growing madness of
   the State.

There is irony and pathos, as in "Street Games," in which
a boy is

black as the ancient curse of Africa. . . .

A different kind of poetry is written by Ologboni, who in-
termingles drum rhythms, incantatory meditations and
sharp establishment-directed barbs in *Drum Song* (1969),
introduced by Gwendolyn Brooks. The poet is also a
painter, who tells us in "Untitled" that the night contains

indifferent stars. . . .

Hayden has been teaching at the University of Michigan, his alma mater, since the late sixties, when he left
Fisk. His *Words in the Mourning Time* (1970) anticipates the theme of Jayne Cortez's overpowering "Festivals
& Funerals." He seeks a place where man will no longer be
called nigger, gook, kike or honkie, but "man." There are

frightening poems and terrifying images in *Words* as
Hayden surveys the "Sphinx" ("my joke and me"),
"Soledad" ("cradled by drugs, by jazz"), "Kodachromes
of the Island" ("fingerless hands") and "El-Hajj Malik
El-Shabazz" ("the waking dream"). "Zeus over Redeye"
reflects on the poet's visit to the Redstone Arsenal. It is an
intense drama, joining other great poems as a major statement on our times. Western man's inverted and predatory
mythic totem, his depravity, his quixotic movements and
blur-causing speed, the human "loom" of tension—all are
staged against the backdrop of the missile arsenal, where
death machines bear the names of ancient Greco-Roman
mythological figures. Such naming allows "new mytholo-
gies" to "come to birth." Among terms associated with
Hayden's nightmarish world of visible/invisible and anticipated violence are dragon, hydra, basilisk, tulips, corollas,
Zeus, Apollo, Nike, and Hercules. The missiles tower
("stasis") like

> a sacred phallic grove. . . .

Apparently the guides at the arsenal cannot satisfactorily
answer questions about the missiles' destinies and dangers:

> Your partial answers reassure
> me less than they appall.
> I feel as though invisible fuses were
> burning all around us burning all
> around us. Heat-quiverings twitch
> danger's hypersensitive skin.
> The very sunlight here seems flammable.
> And shadows give
> us no relieving shade.

Dismal and final, Hayden's poem adds its own particular tone, style and language to the lengthening totem of
the new black poetry. For, despite his disagreements with
the black aestheticians, there is no doubt that "Zeus"
reaffirms a belief expressed by younger, sometimes louder,
poets: that the Western world is doomed to destruction at
its own hands (will "off itself," a younger poet might
say). In fact, the theme of an approaching *end* is quite
"American" in poetry, still being preached by white poets
and spokesmen: from Bob Dylan to Billy Graham.

Rich contributions have also been made by poets and artists in southern Illinois and Missouri. East St. Louis and St. Louis, though situated in two different states and separated by the Mississippi River, have a mutual history that goes back to before the days of the famous *Dred Scott* case. These black communities, alternately warring and loving, worked closely together during the height of the Black Arts Movement. Poets and artist were drawn to or supported by BAG (Black Artists Group), House of Umoja, The Blacksmith Shop of Black Culture, the Black Liberator Project, the House of Truth, Impact House, the Experiment in Higher Education at SIU, Sophia House, Katherine Dunham's Performing Arts training Center (EHE-SIU), Black River Writers, and the Southend Neighborhood Center. Some of the poets from this area are Bruce Rutlin (Ajule) (1941–), Rhea Sharlem Grant, Sherman Fowler (1943–), Redmond, the late Cynthia Conley (Sister Zubenia, who later joined OBAC), Saundra Reynolds (1951–), Arthur Dozier, Bobb Elliott (1942–), Austin Black (1928–) (who went to Los Angeles), Fred Horton, Arthur Brown (1947–), Dwight Jenkins, Romenetha Washington (1938–), Marlayne Simpson (1954–), Donald Henderson, Henry Osborne, Jon Wilson, Vincent Clark, Gloria Walker (1948–), Vincent Terrell (1945–), Jerry Herman, Reginald Allen Turnage, Wayne Loftin (1949–), Derrick Wright (1950–), Gregory Anthony (1946–), Katherine Dunham (1912–), Nate Johnson, and others.[3]

Writings by these poets are included in *Sides of the River: a Mini-Anthology of Black Writings* (Redmond, 1969), Betty Lee's *Proud* magazine (which also offers prizes), the Mill Creek *Intelligencer*, a special issue of *Sou'wester* (fall 1968, selected by Redmond), *The Black Liberator*, *The Creator* (1969), *Tambourine* (1966, White and Schwartz), *Collection* (1968), Volume I of *Poems by Blacks* (1970). Dumas, who taught for a year at East St. Louis (EHE-SIU, 1967–68), and Redmond cosponsored writing programs in the Rap-Write Now

---

[3] A new St. Louis Writers Workshop, guided by Shirley La Flore, includes Marci Howell, Candalaria Silva, Patricia Williams, Wale Amusa, Geraldine Cole and Debra Anderson.

Workshops and Black River Writers group. *Collection* was student-produced under Dumas's supervision, with Fowler and Linda Stennis serving as editors.

Elliott writes, in "The Dream Time," about the "spirochete womb" of the mother of the universe, the Phoenix, and the death "fashioned at the end" of five hundred years. Great Phoenix that she was, the mother of the universe now leaves the dreamer

> With only her great murky sexuality. . . .

Elliott is a dreamer and surrealist, but Black ushers in a different temperament with his *The Tornado in My Mouth* (1966). He has the irreverence of the beats, the funkiness and drive of the hard boppers, and the sexuality of one in hot pursuit. "Asexual Flight" says

> to the burning cove
> island of remiss
> banish your love
> without a kiss—
> life without love
> a man's last wish.

Another kind of dilemma is presented in "Razor Mama Democracy / the ache in 3-D," in which

> the blue haze hurts

and now the hair is turning "into an aching grey." Black salutes "the gladiator" in "Coeval Drums for Leroi," and in the meantime covers (imagines!) a lot of time and history: "the dead arterial insanity"; "futility in jagged crags"; "Kierkegaard/Sartre"; "like dripping brine"; "over the window of my being"; and finally "Her power in howling winds" brings

A DRUMBEAT FOR LEROI.

"Black & Funky" is subtitled "a hypothetical orgasm," and there is iconoclasm in "DAMN YOUR god!" His "(a poem for MALCOLM X)" is subtitled "the liberated war-horse."

In "Carrying a Stick," Fowler asks:

> Who cares, that I had yesterday's stale gum for
> breakfast?

"Thinking" allows various images to stream and burst forth,

> vomiting tidings
> only the mind can hear.

Student-mother Romenetha Washington writes, in "Rat Race," about the pressures on today's black woman who watches people

> Scurrying from sun to sun. . . .

Also pulled along, she says

> I protest but still I run.

Loftin, a young poet who writes with economy and simplicity, uses irony in summarizing Wright and Baldwin in "Reality":

> out of the cotton fields
>   and burning suns
> to overcrowded cities
>   and shades of slums.

Redmond and Fowler founded Black River Writers publishing company, which brought out *Sides of the River*. Currently under the supervision of Catherine Younge, the press has published Redmond's volumes *A Tale of Two Toms* (pamphlet, 1968), *A Tale of Time & Toilet Tissue* (pamphlet, 1969), *Sentry of the Four Golden Pillars* (1970), *River of Bones and Flesh and Blood* (1971), *Songs from an Afro/Phone* (1972), *In a Time of Rain & Desire* (1973), and an Lp, *Bloodlinks and Sacred Places* (1973). *Consider Loneliness as These Things* was published in 1973 by *Centro Studie e Scambi Internazionali*, in Italy. Redmond, a native of East St. Louis, strives for black familyhood (immediate and extended) in his poetry, though he attempts to do this without forced allegiances, without "disfigurement of perceptions," and by allowing the depth-shaping words to flow naturally. His poetry ranges from such humorous folk portraits as "Invasion of the Nose":

> His nose was his radar,
> His eyes icy darts that moved faster than the speed-of-
>   sound jets.

He could rap like a pneumatic drill
Or croon like Smokey Bill when the occasion arose

to considerations of love under strain, as in "Inside My Perimeter":

Inside my perimeter
Of fears
A unit of guerillas
Strikes at the barbed-wire
Hovels that hoard our love:
That incarcerate our needs—
An insurgent army
Storms the bastille of pride
Shells this façade of custom,
Knells the collapse
Of the straw men inside us—
Accepts the sun,
Allows the contorted face of
Stress to smile again—
To glow again!
Allows Love to Live.

Elsewhere in the larger area there were/are other goings on in poetry: Iowa, Nebraska and Kansas City, where Wilbur Rutledge (1940–   ) and others associated with the Afro-American Cultural Center, The Black Contemporary Players of Kansas City, and the Black Writers Workshop received assistance and exposure. Also contributing to the arts scene of this area were the Vanguard Bookstore, the HUB Bookstore and the Yates Branch YWCA. Among the poets are Mary Ruth Spicer, Guiou Taylor, Willesse Hester, and Jackie Washington. These and others are included in *Anthology: Black Writers' Workshop* (Kizna, 1970), and Rutledge has published *Jomo* (1971).[4]

At the University of Denver for the year 1974–75, where he substituted for Mphahlele, who took a leave of absence, Kgositsile (1938–   ) embodies Pan-Africanism in fact and symbol. He was born in Johannesburg, South

---

[4] One of the most inventive and talented of midwestern poets, Bruce Rutlin, has not been published widely. Hear his highly original style on Lps: *Ofama: Children of the Sun* (with saxophonist Oliver Lake, 1971) and *Poem of Gratitude* (1972). Rutlin is a St. Louisan.

Africa, and has been exiled in the United States since
1961. In the summer of 1975 Kgositsile went to Tanzania,
where he now teaches at the University of Dar Es Salaam.
His articles, poems and interviews have been published in
various parts of the world, and he has taught at several
American colleges and universities. In addition to books
already mentioned, he has published *My Name Is Afrika*
(1971) and edited *The Word Is Here: Poetry from Modern Africa* (1973). His own aesthetic is stated in his Introduction to the anthology:

> Poetry, the word at its most expressive, can be a prayer,
> an appeal, condemnation, encouragement, affirmation—
> the list of endeavors is endless. And if it is authentic, as
> anything else expressive of a people's spirit, it is always
> social.

This concept he embraces in his own poems, especially in
Africa, in which, in the Introduction, Gwendolyn Brooks
writes that his

> *Art is life worked with. . . .*

His Afro-American brothers incorporated the Africanisms
into their works, and Kgositsile combines his own indigenisms with a mastered fluency in black American idioms. He assays the whole of our tumultuous times (in
Africa and America), intermingling an acquired black
street language with a demanding and stringent form. One
of the most able craftsmen, he writes excellent poems
about children, women, violence, music, Malcolm X,
Lumumba, Gwendolyn Brooks, African dances, Billy Holiday and "The Nitty Gritty," in which the once furious
songs are now

> frozen on battered black lips. . . .

With Gwendolyn Brooks, Madhubuti, and Dudley Randall, Kgositsile authored *A Capsule Course in Black Poetry
Writing* (Broadside Press, 1975).

The poets of the East, South, Midwest and near West
are a bit more than a hop, skip and jump from California,
but many of them were inspired by TV appearances, national magazine coverage, and cross-country tours of the
Watts poets. Born, as it were, between the California sun

and the rebellion of 1965, the Watts Writers' Workshop was initially under the direction of Budd Schulberg. Later, as older writers left and newer ones came in, the supervision of the workshop was assumed by Harry Dolan and Herbert Simmons. Related spheres of culture and influence included the Watts Happening Coffee House, the short-lived *Shrew* magazine, the Watts Repertory Theater, the Aquarian Bookstore, the Sons of Watts, the Black Panthers, Karenga's US organization, and the Frederick Douglass Writers' House, which housed the first Watts writers program. Among those associated with this and other area writing groups were Milton McFarlane, Clyde Mays (1943–), Troupe (1943–), Stanley Crouch (1945–), Robert Bowen, Pamela Donegan (1943–), Emmery Evans (1943–), Fanita (1943–), Lance Jeffers, Lino, K. Curtis Lyle (1944–), Vallejo Ryan Kennedy (1947–), Cleveland Sims (1944–), Leumas Sirrah (1948–), Simmons (1930–), Eric Priestly (1943–), Ojenke (Alvin Saxon, 1947–), C. K. Moreland, Jimmy Sherman (1944–), Johnie Scott (1948–), Ernest Mayhand, James Thomas Jackson (1927–), Fannie Carole Brown (1942–), David Reese Moody (1933–), Edna Cipson (1946–), Jayne Cortez (1938–), Blossom Powe (1929–), Kamau T. Shams Wa Kamra ("word musician"), Sonora McKeller (1914–), Moss Humphrey (1934–), Nola Richardson (*When One Loves*, 1936–), Harley Mims (1925–), Birdell Chew (1913), Lanee Williams, Ridhiana, and others. Their works are found principally in two anthologies: Schulberg's *From the Ashes* (1967) and Troupe's *Watts Poets and Writers* (1968). Other poems are scattered through such periodicals as *Los Angeles Magazine*, *Shrew*, *Confrontation*, and *West*. Troupe's anthology, published by the House of Respect, reflected a major shake-up among the Watts writers, resulting in Troupe and a dozen or so others forming their own group.

Seen as a movement, the Watts group, in quality and quantity, emerges as one of the most powerful on the new black poetry scene (roughly resembling the magnificent Howard group). For although the poetry is not uniformly good or excellent, there is a courage of vision, style and

theme that one looks hard to find in the other groups. This
may be due in part to the migratory patterns of Blacks in
the West—most of these poets were not born in Los Angeles—and the racial kaleidoscope of California. Whatever
the reasons, there is a prismatic range in the poetry that
moves from the earth-woman musicality of Jayne Cortez,
across the allusive and often mystical excursions of Lyle,
to the signifying blues interludes of Crouch, who has also
written some daring and seminal criticism in *Black World*
and the *Journal of Black Poetry. Ain't No Ambulances for
No Nigguhs Tonight* (1972) is the title of both his book
and his Lp recording, which includes "rap" as well as poetry, with liner notes by Lyle. Crouch uses folk forms and
themes intertwined with music and various dramatic techniques. Many of the poems are dedicated to such musicians as Parker and Coltrane; others attempt the complicated spontaneity of live jazz solos. The title poem
anticipates the day of the final riot, when there will not be
"no" ambulances for "no nigguhs." But the poem's hero,
Monkey Junior, "got on his job" like Nat Turner.

Lyle (*Drunk on God and Out of Nowhere*, 1975) says
his influences are Artaud, Octavio Paz, César Vallejo,
Césaire, and others. His poetry is characterized by elliptical phrases and obscure information that he constricts into
frightening, surreal images and states. "Sometimes I Go to
Camarillo & Sit in the Lounge" describes how the poet
stares into "an awning of spirit," viewing the world as

   yellow trumpets of starving blues

yet hearing a Vietnamese mother's "ultra-high-frequency
screams." We are told that "cobalt bullets" smash the
heart of the "lone ranger" in "Lacrimas or there is a need
to Scream." However, Lyle's most famous poem is "I Can
Get It for You Wholesale," a statement on the contemporary political-religious-racial scene. One of the finest
readers of poetry, Lyle has recorded *The Collected Poems
of Blind Lemon Jefferson* (1973), on which he is accompanied by saxophonist Julius Hemphill (of BAG), and
others.

Ojenke has an unlimited range of intellectual and social
concerns as he sculptures his poetry from the diverse ingredients that produced the Afro-American. Reflecting his
great knowledge of Greco-Roman classics, "Black Power"
has the lyre of "Black Orpheus" pierce

the dark solitude of a Hadean world. . . .

He then wanders into ancient Greece and Nigeria in the poem. In "Watts" there is a commotion caused by lightning and famine,

assassinating tin people and whole grass-blades?

Later on, Diogenes, Socrates and the oracle of Delphi enter the poem. But these characters come to Watts only to find people escaping into a "toxicant" and fleeing from

some too-true truth. . . .

Ojenke also wrote an Introduction to Evans' book *The Love Poet* (1971). About Evans' reading ability, Ojenke said: "Emmery is crying slyly into your ear." "Roaches" depicts a scene familiar to some:

two roaches dance across the room to the tune
  of poverty. . . .

Scott is one of the more well known of the Watts poets. In "The Fish Party," he says:

The fish are gathering again tonight. . . .

And fish-watchers, ignorant of the world's problems, get their charges from trying to guess what the fish will do. During the conversation, Scott talks parenthetically about war and poverty, but all is exclamatorily interrupted:

Hey, look? Goldie has just eaten Jesus up!

"Watts, 1966" is a poem millions heard on national TV. It has the familiar theme of black rage and white indifference. But Scott closes it on memorable lines:

The man named Fear has inherited half an acre,
and is angry.

Other Watts poets deal with love, violence, contemplation of freedom, and music. Many left Watts after the late sixties. Troupe went to Ohio University (to edit *Confrontation*) and later published *Embryo* (1973) and *Ash Doors and JuJu Guitars* (1976), and coedited *Giant Talk: An Anthology of Third World Writings* (1975), after moving to New York. Lyle taught for several years at

Washington University in St. Louis, and recently returned
to Los Angeles. Jayne Cortez went to New York, where
she has lived and written since the late sixties. Her three
books are *Pissstained Stairs and the Monkey Man's Wares*
(1969), *Festivals and Funerals* (1971), and *Scarifications*
(1973). She has also recorded an Lp, *Celebrations and
Solitudes* (1974). Her themes and styles are broad, but
mostly they embrace music as aspect and form. Africa as
struggle and spirit is also a dominant theme in her poetry.
Pissstained is especially rich in its interweavings of music
and indexes of struggle. "The Road" is "where another
Hank moans" and is

> Stoney Lonesome. . . .

"Lead" describes the kind of hard life that is "cracklin hot
at sunrise." Lead, of course, is Leadbelly, whom the "nigguhs" desperately want to hear

> spit the blues out.

Her struggles are more than simple "contrivances" as they
chronicle the hardships and good times of Dinah, Bird,
Ornette, Coltrane, "Fats" Navarro, Clifford Brown, and
others—a veritable poetic tapestry of black expression in
defiance of death, from one who would ("Hungry Love")

> . . . eat mud to touch the root of you. . . .

Among other Southern California poets are Robert Bowen
(1936–   ), Sherley Anne Williams, Arthur Boze
(1945–   ), Kinamo Hodari (1940–   ), Dee Dee McNeil
(1943–   ), Bill Thompson and Lance Williams. A popular Watts counterpart of The Last Poets of New York
are the Prophets of Watts, who have recorded several Lps.
  Northern California also reflects the varied interests and
backgrounds of black poets and writers. Indeed, a listing
of poets and writers from the general San Francisco Bay
area reads like a national convention: Gonçalves
(1937–   ), Reed, Al Young (1939–   ), Harper
(1938–   ) (now at Brown), Ntozake Shange (1948–   ),
Conyus (1942–   ), Clyde Taylor, Víctor Hernández Cruz
(1949–   ), Angelo Lewis (1950–   ), L. V. Mack
(1947–   ), Miller, Thulani Nkabinde (1949–   ),
Lawrence McGaugh (1940–   ), Cecil Brown, El Muhajir
(Marvin X), (1944–   ), Leona Welch, Joyce Carol

Thomas (1938–), Joseph McNair (1948–), David Henderson (1942–), Jon Eckels, Glen Myles (1933–), George Barlow (1948–), Ernest Gaines, Herman Brown (Muumba), Pat Parker, De Leon Harrison (1941–), Sarah Webster Fabio (1928–), William Anderson, Maya Angelou (1928–) and Alli and Macheweo Aweusi (*Words Never Kill*, 1974). Bay-area activity in the arts has been heightened and enhanced by the San Francisco Afro-American Historical and Cultural Society, bookstores such as More, Marcus and New Day (Gonçalves), activities of Black Panthers and similar groups, the DEEP Black Writers Workshop, the Rainbow Sign cultural center in Berkeley, Nairobi College, and numerous other cultural and literary projects. Poems by many of these bards are included in Miller's *Dices or Black Bones* (1970), *Journal of Black Poetry*, *Yardbird Reader* (a semiannual edited by Reed, Young, Brown and Myles), *Umbra Blackworks* (Henderson, all issues, especially 1970–71), and other nationally distributed anthologies and periodicals.[5]

Reed, a strange and original writer, has published three volumes of poems: *catechism of a neoamerican hoodoo church* (1971), *Conjure: Selected Poems, 1963–1970* (1972), *Chattanooga* (1973), and four novels. Volumes of poetry and more fiction are forthcoming. His work has drawn a curious mixture of adjectives from critics: "brilliant," "cute," "jumbles and puzzles," "important," "bad comics" and so on. Indeed, Reed writes his poetry themes into his novels and his fiction themes into his poems, thus revealing an arresting literary continuum. In this service, he employs dialects, Voodoo, the occult, whimsicality, wit, mysticism, satire, which he obviously enjoys, all reinforced by assorted library information and street expressions. He violates time barriers, placing an ancient Greek figure in a contemporary poem, or vice versa. His verse forms are experimental, roughly recalling the beats and other past stylistic irreverencies. But a close reading will show him in the tradition of Dunbar, Toomer, and Tolson. There are no sacred cows for Reed, who sometimes lambasts black nationalists and white liberals in the same poem. Gener-

---

[5] The works of many Northern California writers can also be found in a special "Arts & Literature" issue of *The Black Scholar*, June 1975.

ally, his techniques work (some are astonishing); but he often spends too much time attacking real or created antagonists and having fun at the expense of his readers. His titles alone are good enough to keep you slapping your thigh or scratching your head: "Report of the Reed Commission," "I am a cowboy in the boat of Ra," "There's a whale in my thigh," "The feral pioneers," "The Black Cock," "Gris Gris," "And the Devil Sent a Ford Pinto, Which She also Routed." In 1973 Reed became the first black writer to be nominated for a National Book Award in two categories.

Gonçalves (Dingane), an occasional poet, is unique in his intellectual-typographical approach to ideas (see *Black Fire*), but his service to black poetry has been more obvious in his work as founder-editor of the *Journal of Black Poetry*. He also served as poetry editor of *Black Dialogue*. A quiet, but steady, influence on the new black poetry, he has written some of the most informed criticism to come out of the period. Currently he runs/operates New Day Bookstore in San Francisco, where the *Journal* and its press are headquartered. Among poets published by the press are Neal and Welton Smith (*Penetration*, 1971), a virtuoso poet who was born and raised in San Francisco. Smith's "Malcolm" ends discussing the kinds of tracks tears make and telling the reader:

in my heart there are many
unmarked graves.

There are also word gifts in "the danger zone," "If I could hold You for Light," "for a sorceress" ("you keep changing me into air") and "Black Mother" ("an odd ecstasy moving"); these join blues, excursions through city streets, and thoughts on Africa.

Young and Harper both teach writing, at Stanford and Brown respectively, and both use music aesthetically and stylistically. Young has published *Dancing* (1969) and *The Song Turning Back into Itself* (1971), as well as novels and articles. His poetry satirizes militants, salutes white and Third World poets, and incorporates legends into a broad linguistic base. There is a consistency of interest, as seen in the titles of his books. In "Erosong" he finds himself dancing "naked" though

All my shores had been pulled up. . . .

"Yes, the Secret Mind Whispers," dedicated to Kaufman, calls poetry a "tree"

forever at your door. . . .

Young ranges over the whole of the life experience, writing about squirrels, jazz musicians, Spain, Stockholm, nighttime and sorrow.

However, his poetry is stylistically different from that of Harper, who left California in 1970. Harper's volumes are *Dear John, Dear Coltrane* (1970), *History Is Your Own Heartbeat* (1971), *Photographs: Negatives: History as Apple Tree* (1972), *Song: I Want a Witness* (1973), *Debridement* (1973) and *Nightmare Begins Responsibility* (1974). Praise for his poetry has come from a wide spectrum of eminent critics and poets, primarily academicians, including Gwendolyn Brooks and Hayden. Critic M. L. Rosenthal recently singled out Harper and Baraka as examples of black poets contributing to the new American poetry scene (New York *Times Magazine*, November 24, 1974). Laurence Lieberman has also praised Harper, who received nominations for the National Book Award as well as the Black Academy of Arts and Letters' First Annual Poetry Award. Harper has kept a consistency of tone that critics particularly admire, and though his poetry sometimes lacks metaphorical tension (funk?) to ignite the important statements he makes about black music, there is a firm intelligence at work. His themes are illusion, pained creativity, war, racism, jazz, nature, history, death, and the mythological evolution of mankind. Much of his poetry is personal, confessional, and he interweaves a medical vocabulary into some of it. He often includes chants, hums, and names of songs and musicians. His musico-poetic concerns can be seen in these lines from "Dear John, Dear Coltrane":

Why you so black?
cause I am
Why you so funky?
cause I am
Why you so black?
cause I am

Why you so sweet?
cause I am
a love supreme, a love supreme. . . .

Harper, Reed, Gaines, and Young are included in O'Brien's *Interviews with Black Writers.*

El Muhajir (Marvin X) is another kind of poet, Islam-influenced and adamantly black: *Fly to Allah* (1969), *Black Man Listen* (1969), *Woman—Man's Best Friend* (1973). Each book salutes Allah and contains some occasionally well-turned poetry intermingled with proverbs, parables and songs. He praises Elijah Muhammad and Tommy Smith, and announces, "Bigger Thomas Lives!" In "The Origins of Blackness" he says,

Black is not a color

but

All colors come from Black. . . .

Myles and Eckels are also at different ends of the poetic spectrum, while McNair is in the middle. Myles published *Down & Country* in 1974 as a collage of his drawings and poems. He surveys contemporary life, his upbringing on "Bebop and blues in Phoenix," and his experiences as an artist and art student. Eckels has moved from poetry of anger and protest to "poetry written by a human being, for human beings." His books include *Black Dawn, This Time Tomorrow, Black Right On, Home Is Where the Soul Is* (1969), *Our Business Is in the Streets* (1970), and *Fire Sign* (1973), which gives its name to his press. In his early phase, Eckels wrote about "Black Is," "Hell, Mary," "In Memory of Marcus," "A Responsible Nee-grow Leader," and other poems, also coining an interesting term:

Western Syphilization. . . .

Fire Sign, "for the free and will be," shows a thematic and cultural breadth as he writes love poems and salutes freedom in general. McNair, a cosmic and religious poet who bridges African spirituality and his own psychic revelations, has published *Earthbook* (1972), *Juba Girl* (1973), and *An Odyssey* (1976). Certainly the world will hear more from this gifted young writer.

Among Northern California women poets, the multi-talented Maya Angelou is primarily a prose and script writer, but has published two books of poems: *Just Give Me a Cool Drink of Water 'fore I Die* (1971), which was nominated for the Pulitzer prize, and *Oh Pray My Wings Are Gonna Fit Me Well* (1975). Her poetry mirrors its musical and folkloristic influences. Pat Parker's poetry can be found in an excellent little volume called *Child of Myself* (1972) and *Dices* (1970). She uses her own woman-feelings to assess current upheaval. "Brother" reveals contradictions in the love-but-hurt approach some black men take toward their women. The "system" she has just been struck with, she says,

> is called
> a fist.

Other of her poems deal with humor and tragedy in husband-wife relations. In "A Moment Left Behind" she asks,

> Have you ever tried to catch a tear?

"From Deep Within" says that the way of a woman is turbulent with many forces and colors of feelings, but

> A woman's body must be taught to speak. . . .

Pat Parker's work searches behind the cosmetics and the vogue to the true disturbances. So does the work of Joyce Carol Thomas, whose two books *Bittersweet* (1973) and *Crystal Breezes* (1974) were published by Fire Sign Press and whose *Blessing* (1975) was brought out by Jocato Press. Her poems are about women's moods, church, black music, children and love. There is a modern feel and texture in her lines, which economize without displaying abruptness or undecipherable code. Yet her strength is unmistakable, as in "I Know a Lady":

> I know a lady
> A careful queen
> She bows to no one

Her will is a
Fine thread of steel. . . .

In these poems, and the works of Pat Parker and Leona
Welch, one sees a strong health and future in Bay area
women poets. *Black Gibraltar*, Leona Welch's first book,
was published in 1971. Here and there, one finds subdued
rage and impatience before racism and ignorance; but her
poetry also exalts the black woman and speaks in low
tones to men. Her language ranges from folk expressions
to formal examinations of love. "Status Quo" is the study
of a Black with "class" and dignity:

Got my white poodle by the leash.

Less able than the other women, in her poetry she salutes
a number of heroines including women in her family and
Nikki Giovanni.

Finally there is the much-traveled Sarah Fabio, instru-
mental in black-studies development in Northern California but now living in Iowa. She published two volumes, *A
Mirror: A Soul* (1969) and *Black Is a Panther Caged*
(1972), and then, without notice, brought out seven volumes (!), all in 1973: *Soul Is: Soul Ain't, Boss Soul* (also
the name of her Lp), *Black Back: Back Black, Jujus & Jubilees, My Own Thing, Jujus/Alchemy of the Blues*, and
Together / to the Tune of Coltrane's Equinox. Her earlier
poetry is more formal, reflecting her vast reading-thinking
range; but the later work shows that she had joined the
new poetry movement completely. Her most memorable
poem is "Evil Is No Black Thing," in which she converts
all dark things traditionally associated with evil into
lighter colors or allows them to be revealed in a broader
context, in which they invariably become good. Her recent
voluminous efforts deal with experimental blues poems,
rap styles, folk narratives, and attempts to reconstruct
black oral history. These things she does quite well on her
albums and in live readings; but much of the work in the
new books is excessively conversational and burdened
with contrived hipness.

Erzulie and Things (1975) is coauthored by poets
Ntozake Shange and Thulani Nkabinde. Ntozake's play,

For Colored Girls Who Have Considered Suicide/When The Rainbow is Enuf (a choreopoem), originally produced by Woodie King and the New Federal Theater in 1976, later opened to excellent Reviews at the Anspacher/Public Theater in New York. And Ms. Thulani's work also appears in *Jambalaya: Four Poets* along with the poems of Lorenzo Thomas, Ibn Mukhtarr Mustapha (Sierra Leone) and Cyn Zarco. *Jambalaya* is edited by Steve Cannon with an introduction by Cruz. Cruz writes poetry marked by brevity. *Snaps* (1969) and *Mainland* (1973) show him relying on his Puerto Rican heritage, his relationships with other poets (often black), New York City and other urban areas, and Spanish mythology. Now living in the Bay area, Cruz often interpolates bilingual phrases into his poems. Barlow (*Gabriel*, 1974) has done impressive and promising work in the area of urban language and Afro-American history. B. Rap published *Revolution Is* (1969) and *Metamorphosis of Supernigger* (1973). Meanwhile, a young inmate at Vacaville Medical Facility, Herman Brown (Muumba), published *Some Poems and Things* (1971). Young Sacramento poet Clarence McKie Wigfall has shown strengths in *The Other Side* (1970), and another Sacramentan, Wes Young, brought out *Life Today* (1970) and *Rambling and Things* (1972). Young black poets were also published in Grant High School's *Omnibus*. Redmond, who has taught at California University, Sacramento, since 1970, conducts writing workshops on campus and such community sites as the Oak Park School of Afro-American Thought. Keith Jefferson (1951–   ), a Kansas city-born poet and a member of the Henry Dumas Writing Workshop of Sacramento, recently published *The Hyena Reader* (1975). Several poets are working and studying at Black Arts West in Seattle; and poet Primus St. John teaches at Portland State University (Oregon). His first volume, *Skins on the Earth*, was published in 1976.

REFLECTIONS ON THE NEW BLACK POETRY

Such terms as "Armageddon," "chariots of fire," "smoking sixties," "get down on Whitey," and "warrior priests" are often used by critics attempting to describe and define the new black poets. To be sure, there was much verbal fire and brimstone; but few of the poets had time to stay "mounted in a chariot of fire," as Blyden Jackson put it. Indeed, when the landscape is viewed in its wholeness, one notes that some who mounted "chariots" often were not poets at all. Even the most verbal and popular of the new poets—Nikki Giovanni, Baraka, Sonia Sanchez, Madhubuti—denounced poetry as a luxury that could be ill afforded during a "revolution," admitting in the meantime, perhaps, that theirs was a particular brand of oratory not striving for poetry in a traditional sense. At the same time, the black poetry tradition has these men and women, and others, to thank for snatching it from the brink of obscurity and giving it a prominence it had never before enjoyed. This chore alone has earned them an important "place" in the poetic scheme of things—albeit a "place" yet to be designated. This place may also be altered by Baraka's recent renunciation of an exclusively Pan-Africanist position and his embracing of a Marx-inspired "scientific socialism."

There are myriad problems and conflicts in the writings and lives of many of the new poets. Some, suffering from the "disfigurement of perceptions," do not always portray a correct sociological picture of Blacks, let alone a correct poetic one. Anxious to "saturate" themselves in the new blackness, they disguise their own confusion in half-baked theories about Afro-American life; this results in a poetry that is often riddled with confusions, inaccuracies, and oversimplifications of the black experience. A further result, and this is ghastly, is that star-makers view the poetry through an inverted lens, so that a popular "latex brand" receives a final stamp of approval while the deeper, searching, and more profound poetry (Dumas, Patterson, Cornish, Cortez, Jordan, Lorde, Rivers) is downplayed. Such an inversion provides black and white readers with an extended "disfigurement," muddying the already doubled vision rather than clearing it up, as Neal had predicted. Adding to this confusion are a cadre of black critics who parade essentially political, parochial, and ideological defenses under the banner of a black aesthetic. Both McKay and Rivers said, "No white man can write my story," but, during the contemporary period, some beleaguered black readers and teachers have asked, "Where is the Black writer who will write it?"

Contrary to popular belief, it takes a lifetime to understand the complex phenomenon called the black experience. And those few young writers (and spokesmen) who seemed to have mastered aspects of it often spent years in prison (Malcolm, Knight, Harold Carrington), which allowed them time to reflect, develop and experiment. Even Gwendolyn Brooks had "time" to work out ticklish questions in the areas of art, politics, and poetry. Unlike Frances Harper and other female poets, she did not teach or go on a temperance-league lecture circuit during her early years. That she cultivated and protected her "distance" is evident in the superior quality of her work, which does not shun the salient themes of the new poetry: black pride, Africa, black music, self-love, black heterosexuality, violence, mistrust of whites, destruction of the Western world, and self-determination.

Yet those opposing the black aesthetic do not always have a clean slate, since they are often "shored up" by personal experiences with whites. Among the opponents of the "separate" aesthetic for Blacks, Hayden and Redding are most vocal. However, both have maintained close associations with academy-trained/oriented white critics and writers. Hayden must ask himself why black poets should not subscribe to a black aesthetic if he subscribes to the aesthetic of the Baha'i faith—"the only one," he has said, "to which I willingly submit." Black culture possesses the possibilities and potentialities for a new religion, one that could even replace or modify the Christian force (mystique) behind black strivings and aspirations; this is a prospect that should not be too lightly dismissed.

That some new poets do wade into the intense intellectual and psychological realm of blackness, however, is seen in Jayne Cortez's "Festivals & Funerals." Musical, daring, ambivalent, complex and technically dexterous, it summarizes the uncertain world of blacklife. Like Hayden's "Zeus" and Gwendolyn Brooks's "Riot," it fluently captures the suspense and hyperactivity of the contemporary world. The polarities—*festivals* and *funerals* —are archetypal and mythological, since they at once tap

DRUMVOICES

the unexplored and state what is known. The poem is also
an emotional barometer of the 1960s. Its healthy ambivalence, couched in the "invisible" world and "cyclical
nightmare" of the black experience, becomes allegorical as
the poet celebrates heroes, sung and unsung, all of whom
are dead in one way or another.

> They winged his spirit &
> wounded his tongue
> but death was slow coming.

The "slow" death is both the agony and the ecstasy, as it
were, nestled somewhere between the dope needle ("rusty
rims of a needle") and the "cultural vaginas" that
"rushed" through

> streets urging men to die for shame.

The poet has "lost a good friend" whom she loved; but he
has been shipped back to her "C.O.D." with "thorns on
his casket":

> collect on death
> collect on death
> collect on death.

This "friend" soon becomes the many dead black spokesmen whose blood has been "consumed by vultures":

> Who killed Lumumba
> What killed Malcolm.

The above lines join other nuances of a frightening refrain
which laments the loss of all friends; death and dope and
violence and consumption have devoured them:

> There are no tears
> we have no friends
> that is the word
> . . . .
> we are alone.

The world of "cadillacs and cocaine" is populated by
festivals and funerals, poets that scream "kill run kill,"
"dashikis in the wind," "the flesh of Patrice" and "the
blues." Blacks know that ever-hovering death is as close as

the juke joint or the church. In the urban maze of mind and place, the driving pace will perform its ecstatic operation even when dope, false idols, political oppression and all else fail. Black girl, black boy, alone ("we are alone"), without friends in a hostile country or living in one owned by foreigners. In Africa or America the fates of Blacks are dramatically similar:

Who killed Lumumba
What killed Malcolm.

It is a pressure cooker without a back door, or valve to let off steam. The rush of the poem's language complements the "rush" of black life, which is necessitated by oppression but which, in turn, results in an enormously high number of deaths.

From among the many good poets of this era will emerge a few great ones, though the emergence has been somewhat retarded by the popular renunciation of "art" and "ideas." But it cannot be restrained too long, because there are both urgency and breadth in much of the new thought and poetry. It is paradoxical to send black students to Western schools—to be trained on "heavy" philosophy and technology—and then ask them to reduce all their knowledge and training to complaints and focusless rantings. For, surely, if black thought and literature cannot be called on to function in their traditional capacities —to train, develop and stimulate the faculties—then the "battle for the minds of black people" has already been won by the other side. Finally, since Blacks as a people are profoundly tragic, comic or heroic, then their ideas and their poetry should reflect these tendencies profoundly and with consummate power. For we have not always roamed the "streets and alleys of other men's minds" (Thurman); and a true and honest black poetry will not be afraid to be "great" or to stand alongside whatever else of greatness there is in this world.

CHAPTER VII

CONCLUSION: AFTERTHOUGHTS

As promised in our Preface, we have tried to avoid forcing our research and findings into manicured paradigms and neat frames. However, *Drumvoices* does advance theories and theses—many of them well known and some of them original—for this study has been termed a critical history; and one must take *stands*. Indeed, the poets have taken their own stands, as individuals and groups, since to project an inner self to the public is to assume a stance: to work out one's systems of beliefs, perceptions, relationships, and values within the function or framework of poetry and poetics. Such stands have always represented critical choices for poets. And for Afro-American poets they have created a unique crisis-continuum in that so many "unusual" factors attend their written "commitments." One factor was the apparent self-mockery that initially accompanied the poets' use of written English. For the early bards, there was the simple—but grave—task of "proving" their ability to employ literary skills; this test, alas, was conducted by "liberal" slavemasters, while many states made black literacy a crime punishable by imprisonment, beating and, in some cases, even death.

There was much confusion and misdirection of values and energies in the earlier poetry: the poets were neither encouraged nor allowed to retain an African flavor (let alone language). The Christianization of slaves had aided in the development of a ghastly "duality"—or wall between the African and himself—which cluttered the poets' self- and world-views, indeed sending most black intellectuals into psychic chaos. This tendency, called a "veil" by W. E. B. Du Bois, held Afro-American poetry in a state of moral limbo up through the beginning of the twentieth century. And though there were exceptions (Horton, Whitfield, Whitman, Frances Harper), anyone with proper background study can understand the isolationism and alienation of a Phillis Wheatley or a Jupiter Hammon, who refused freedom for himself but advocated it for young Blacks. One need only read David Walker to discover the boundaries of Negro "freedom" in the "free" states of early America.

In the meantime, a folk tradition—on the plantations, among escaped slaves, out of the minstrel era—was also developing. This folk strain in the poetry (separated by Wagner from the "spiritualist" vein) has survived as a conscience, more or less, of Afro-American letters, philosophy, and art. And even though such critics as Wagner make false distinctions between the folk and the literary (or spiritual) realms, all but a few of the "intellectual" poets have delved into the folk roots and origins in one way or another. This fact is not as obvious in such poets as Countee Cullen, Claude McKay, or Jean Toomer as it is in, say, Paul Laurence Dunbar, James Weldon Johnson, Sterling Brown, and Langston Hughes—but it can be identified. At the same time, however, the ambivalent attitude toward the Christian God and white people is as evident in the folk poets as it is in those steeped in book theology.

Examination of the artificial boundaries established between folk (oral, gestural) poetry and literary (intellectual, book) poetry has not been pursued with enough intensity by critics and writers. Just because Europe and larger America have depreciated communal art forms does not mean that Afro-America has to follow suit! Or does it? And, as we stated in the beginning of Chapter VI, the social-communal value of the poetry has yet to be viewed in the context of black reading trends and habits. For we know Blacks place great emphasis on the dramatic presentation of a poem. Witness the magnetism and charisma of poets at live readings and the development of a national black audience for poetry via such vehicles as Ellis Haizlip's TV show "Soul." All the foregoing statements tie in with our opening remarks about *stands* taken by poets. For, if the transliteration, if you will, of the thought or impulse to the page results in a reduction of poetic intensity, then the silent reading of the poem cuts a similar nerve contact between reader and the originating idea or instinct. One has only to hear such an "intellectual" poet as Robert Hayden read his own works to understand this principle. Our point, then, is that much of

the strait-laced poetry of the early periods has less meaning for us when it is not delivered in its natural environ-
ments of church services, abolitionist rallies, choir-singing,
dances or social activities. For example, one should avoid
listening to a poor reader present dialect poems of Dunbar, Davis, or Corrothers.

A number of devices and themes are central to Afro-
American poetry. And while there have been instances
(Wheatley, Hammon, Ann Plato, the Creole poets) of
poets' being immune to the social whirlwind, most Afro-
American poets have been *in* that whirlwind. Hence, patterns of segregation in America turned a "curse" into a
"blessing" (to paraphrase Alain Locke) and provided
black poets with private languages, forms, styles, and tones.
From the ditties, blues, spirituals, dozens, sermons, and
jokes, the poets fashioned an endless stream of poetic
forms and fusions (Tolson dressed the Pindaric ode in a
blues form). And that same, segregated pattern gave these
poets their ominous themes and their grave tones and
temperaments, which, coupled with their crisp insight into
America's contradictions and paradoxes, allowed them to
project, to prophesy, and to refine their "duality" into one
of the most powerful aesthetical tools available to any
group of writers. Hence the Afro-American poet has his
own private (cultural) symbols and themes as well as
those of the larger world. For example, most black poets
have written poems about lynching, but most Euro-
American poets have not. Themes related to slavery, job
discrimination, the ambivalence of a Christian God, psychic tumult in a white world, homelessness and rest-
lessness, poverty reinforced by oppression, racism, prejudice, rivers and trains, castration, plus the landscape of
terror and fear resulting from a web of social inequities,
all, in one way or another, work themselves into Afro-
American poetry.

Though certain forms and themes have historically
dominated Afro-American poetry, unique variations and
divergent approaches characterize the use of them.
Outside of the dominating clusters, however, the poets
display myriad other interests, themes and preoccupations.
Many of these trends stem from black family units that
have existed for hundreds of years—even if such a fact is

obscured by a socio-media representation with all its accompanying pathological emphases. (Any young Black's critical analysis of white culture includes his own unstated or implied cultural preferences.) True, Africans in the new land have lived the *nightmare* amid talk of an American Dream; and, understandably, the darker poets' songs are full of unpleasantries and recollections of that nightmare. But the end of black poetry can never be self-pity, chauvinism, ideology, rhetoric, or complaint (Baraka says, "The End of Man Is His Beauty"). Thus Margaret Walker, amid her sisters' use of "safe" female subjects and her brothers' trips to the altar of the white literati, is able to celebrate black life (*For My People*). Robert Hayden transcends artificial barriers between himself (and us) and nature and enters the flower (*Night-Blooming Cereus*), as does Henry Dumas in *Play Ebony Play Ivory* and Pinkie Gordon Lane in *Wind Thoughts*. Other examples of such diversity and sensitivity abound: Owen Dodson (*Powerful Long Ladder*), Langston Hughes (*The Dream Keeper*), Alice Walker (*Once*), Raymond Patterson (*26 Ways of Looking at a Blackman*), Joyce Carol Thomas (*Blessing*), and the cross-spread of almost any anthology.

We have said the poet takes a stand not inherent in, say, the musician's, when he commits his thoughts to paper. And over the past few years of social change and unrest, the black poet whose aesthetic or religious position was not aligned with that of vested interest groups came up before many a *strange* court, at which times his own feelings and sensibilities were often neutralized in favor of the "popular latex brand." Serious critics and "cultural stabilizers" need to examine such "one-way" approaches to poetry/criticism, especially as they have occurred over the past ten years. We mention this "side" show of the contemporary poetry scene because its presence has often dirtied the waters of "open" thought and either crippled or destroyed many a budding talent. In a few cases, it has even muffled a rich or significant voice. However, it is time the critical flood gates were "opened" completely and honestly. Only in this way can Afro-American poetry continue to breathe the breath of the ancestors.

Finally, as winds of change shift, speed up, or slow down, and the "tradition" congeals, readers and poets must ask about ultimate designs and inherent missions. As the drum stands at the crossroads of traditional African and Afro-American culture, so the poet should stand at the center of the drum. Most poetic principles, and the language associated with them, rely on the vocabulary of sound and music. Music is the most shared experience—the most vital commodity—among Afro-Americans. And poetry is music's twin. Both the metaphysical and the metaphorical word stem from and return to the drum: life, love, birth, and death labored out in measured rumble or anxious cacophony. Between the *lines* are the rattle of choruses, the whine (hum) of guitars, and the shriek of tambourines, framed by rivers that will not run away. And the drumvoices urging us to cross them, cross them.

BIBLIOGRAPHICAL INDEX

This bibliography is designed to serve the needs of beginning and advanced students of black poetry. It is not intended to be exhaustive, since so many bibliographies repeat the same items. Nor has there been any attempt to cite the numerous single collections of poems, because check lists and specialized bibliographies are available. Moreover, most anthologies, critical studies, and histories list such collections—in selected bibliographies and biographies. Since many black poets publish privately or with small and relatively unknown publishing houses, the student will want to examine regular listings and reviews in periodicals such as *Black World, Journal of Black Poetry, Freedomways, Black Books Bulletin, The Black Scholar, CLA Journal, Black Creation, Small Press Review, Obsidian: Black Literature in Review,* and others. Some of the small black publishers list titles on inside covers of their books; and scores of records and tapes of readings, films, broadsides (single poems), pamphlet publications, and tracts can be obtained from individual poets and the small houses. Recently, such larger recording companies as Folkways, Flying Dutchman, and Motown have begun to record and distribute black poetry. However, the task of locating and developing a check list for the myriad publications and publishing activities of black poets still awaits some serious student of black literature. In the meantime, there are a number of important bio-bibliographical works one can consult: *Afro-American Writers* (Turner), *Living Black American Authors* (Shockley and Chandler), *Broadside Authors and Artists* (Bailey), *Index to Black Poetry* (Chapman), and *Black American Writers Past and Present: a Biographical and Bibliographical Dictionary* (Rush, Meyers, and Arrata).

GENERAL RESEARCH AIDS

Adams, Russell L. *Great Negroes, Past and Present.* Chicago, 1964.
The Arthur B. Spingarn Collection of Negro Authors. Washington, D.C., 1948.

Bailey, Leaonead. *Broadside Authors: An Illustrated Biographical Directory.* Detroit, 1971.

Baskin, Wade; and Runes, Richard N. *Dictionary of Black Culture.* New York, 1973.

Bontemps, Arna. "The James Weldon Johnson Memorial Collection of Negro Arts and Letters." *Yale University Library Gazette,* XVIII (October 1943), 19–26.

———. "Special Collection of Negroana." *Library Quarterly,* XIV (c. 1944), 187–206.

Brignano, Russell C. *Black Americans in Autobiography: an Annotated Bibliography of Autobiographies and Autobiographical Books Written Since the Civil War.* Durham, N.C., 1974.

Burke, Joan Martin. *Civil Rights; a Current Guide to the People, Organization and Events.* New York, 1974.

Chapman, Abraham. *The Negro in American Literature and a Bibliography of Literature by and About Negro Americans.* Stevens Point, Wis., 1966.

Chapman, Dorothy H., comp. *Index to Black Poetry.* Boston, 1974.

Culver, Eloise Crosby. *Great American Negroes in Verse, 1723–1965.* Washington, D.C., c. 1965.

Davis, Lenwood G. "Pan-Africanism: a Tentative Check List of Books, Periodicals, Articles." *Black World,* XXII (December 1972), 70–96.

Deodene, Frank; and French, William P. *Black American Fiction Since 1952: a Preliminary Checklist.* Chatham, N.J., 1970.

———. *Black American Poetry Since 1944, a Preliminary Checklist.* Chatham, N.J., 1971.

Dictionary Catalog of the Jesse E. Moorland Collection of Negro Life and History. 9 vols. Boston, 1970.

Dictionary Catalog of the Schomburg Collection of Negro Literature and History. 11 vols. Boston, 1962, 1967.

Drzick, Kathleen; Murphy, John; and Weaver, Constance. *Annotated Bibliography of Works Relating to the Negro in Literature and to Negro Dialects.* Kalamazoo, Mich., 1969.

Du Bois, W. E. B.; and Johnson, Guy B. *Encyclopedia of the Negro: Preparatory Volume.* Rev. ed. New York, 1946.

———. *A Select Bibliography of the Negro American.* 3rd ed. Atlanta, 1905.

Guzman, Jessie P., ed. *Negro Year Book.* Tuskegee, Ala., 1947.

Houston, Helen Ruth. "Contributions of the American Negro to American Culture: a Selected Checklist." *Bulletin of Bibliography,* Vol. 26, No. 3 (July–September 1969), 71–83.

Index to Periodical Articles by and About Negroes (formerly *A Guide to Negro Periodical Literature and Index to Selected Periodicals*).

International Library of Negro Life and History. 10 Vols. Washington, D.C., 1967–69.

Irvine, Keith, ed. *Encyclopedia of the Negro in Africa and America.* St. Clair Shores, Mich., c. 1973.

Jahn, Janheinz. *A Bibliography of Neo-African Literature from Africa, America, and the Caribbean.* New York, 1965.

Johnson, Harry A. *Multimedia Materials for Afro-American Studies.* New York, 1971.

Kaiser, Ernest. "The History of Negro History." *Negro Digest,* XVII (February 1968), 10–15, 64–80.

———. "Recent Books." *Freedomways,* each issue.

Major, Clarence. *Dictionary of Afro-American Slang.* New York, 1970.

McPherson, James, et al., eds. *Blacks in America: Bibliographical Essays.* New York, 1972.

Miller, Elizabeth; and Fisher, Mary L. *The Negro in America: a Bibliography.* 2nd ed. Cambridge, Mass., 1970.

Murphy, Beatrice M., et al., eds. *Bibliographic Survey: the Negro in Print.* Washington, D.C., Vols. 1–7 (1965–71).

Porter, Dorothy B. "Early American Negro Writings: a Bibliographical Study." *Papers of the Bibliographical Society of America,* XXXIX (1945), 192–268.

———. *Early Negro Writing, 1760–1837.* Boston, 1971.

———. *North American Negro Poets: a Bibliographical Check List of Their Writings, 1760–1944.* Hattiesburg, Miss., 1945.

Preminger, Alex, et al., eds. *Princeton Encyclopedia of Poetry and Poetics.* Princeton, N.J., 1974.

Puckett, Newbell Niles (ed. Murray Heller). *Black Names in America: History and Meaning.* Boston, 1975.

Querry, Ronald; and Fleming, Robert E. "A Working Bibliography of Black Periodicals." *Studies in Black Literature,* Vol. 3, No. 2 (Summer 1972), 31–36.

Rowell, Charles H. "A Bibliography of Bibliographies for the Study of Black American Literature and Folklore." *Black Experience, a Southern University Journal,* LV (June 1969), 95–111.

Rush, Theressa; Meyers, Carol; and Arrata, Esther; comps. *Black American Writers Past and Present: a Biographical and Bibliographical Directory.* Scarecrow Press, 1975.

Shockley, Ann Allen; and Chandler, Sue P.; eds. *Living Black American Authors: a Biographical Directory.* New York, 1973.

Schomburg, Arthur A. *A Bibliographical Checklist of American Negro Poetry.* New York, 1916. (Schomburg Collection)

Smith, Jessie Camey. "Developing Collections of Black Literature." *Black World,* XX (June 1971), 18–29.

Toppin, Edgar A. *A Biographical History of Blacks in America Since 1528.* New York, 1971.

Turner, Darwin T. *Afro-American Writers*. New York, 1970.

Williams, Ora, comp. "A Bibliography of Works Written by American Black Women." *CLA Journal*, Vol. XV, No. 3 (March 1972), 354–77.

Work, Monroe N. *A Bibliography of the Negro in Africa and America*. New York, 1928.

Yellin, Jean Fagan. "An Index of Literary Materials in *The Crisis*, 1910–1934: Articles, Belles-Lettres, and Book Reviews." *CLA Journal*, XIV (1971), 452–65.

PERIODICALS

Amistad

The Anglo-African

Bandung—Itl

Black Academy Review

Black Books Bulletin

The Black Collegian

Black Creation

Black Dialogue

The Black Experience

Black Forum

Black Orpheus: A Journal of African and Afro-American Literature.

The Black Position

Black Review

The Black Scholar

Black Theatre

Black World (formerly *Negro Digest*).

BOP (Blacks on Paper)

Chicago Defender

Chicory

CLA Journal

Confrontation: a Journal of Third World Literature

The Crisis: a Record of the Darker Races

Dasein

Douglass' Monthly

Ebony

Encore

Essence

Ex-Umbra

Fire

Freedom's Journal

Freedomways

Harlem Quarterly

Hoodoo Black Literature Series

Impressions

The Journal of Black Poetry

The Journal of Black Studies

The Journal of Negro Education

The Journal of Negro History

Juju

The Liberator

The Messenger

Mwendo

Negro American Literature Forum

Negro History Bulletin

The Negro Quarterly

New York Amsterdam News

Nkombo

Nommo

Obsidian: Black Literature in Review

Opportunity: a Journal of Negro Life

Phylon: the Atlanta University Review of Race and Culture

Players

Présence Africaine: Cultural Revue of the Negro World

Renaissance II

Roots: a Journal of Critical
  and Creative Expression
Soulbook
The Southern Workman

Studies in Black Literature
Tuesday
Umbra
Yardbird Reader

ANTHOLOGIES

Abdul, Raoul, ed. *The Magic of Black Poetry*. New York, 1972.
———; and Lomax, Alan; eds. *3000 Years of Black Poetry*. New
York, 1970.
Adams, William; Conn, Peter; and Slepian, Barry; eds. *Afro-
American Literature: Poetry*. Boston, 1970.
Adoff, Arnold, ed. *Black Out Loud: Anthology of Modern
Poems by Black Americans*. New York, 1970.
———, ed. *I Am the Darker Brother: an Anthology of Modern
Poems by Black Americans*. New York, 1968.
———, ed. *It is the Poem Singing into Your Eyes*. New York,
1971.
———, ed. *My Black Me: a Beginning Book of Black Poetry*.
New York, 1974.
———, ed. *The Poetry of Black America*. New York, 1973.
Afro-Arts Anthology. Newark, 1966.
Alhamisi, Ahmed; and Wangara, Harun K.; eds. *Black Arts: an
Anthology of Black Creations*. Detroit, 1970.
Ambrose, Amanda. *My Name Is Black: an Anthology of Black
Poets*. New York, 1974.
Andrews, Leonard P.; Howard, Eunice L.; and Rodgers, Gladys
M.; eds. *Deep Rivers, a Portfolio: 20 Contemporary Black
American Poets*. Detroit, 1974. (Teacher's Guide by Naomi
L. Madgett)
Arnold, David; Zu-Bolton, Ahmos; and Shifflet, J.; eds. *The Last
Cookie*. Vol. I, No. 1, San Francisco, 1972.
Baker, Houston A., Jr., ed. *Black Literature in America*. New
York, 1971.
Barksdale, Richard; and Kinnamon, Keneth; eds. *Black Writers
of America*. New York, 1972.
Battle, Sol, ed. *Ghetto '68*. New York, 1968.
BCD. *Soul Session*. Newark, 1969.
Benig, Irving, ed. *The Children*. New York, 1971.
Bell, Bernard W., ed. *Modern and Contemporary Afro-American
Poetry*. Boston, 1972.
The Best of 40 Acres Poetry. New York, c. 1972.
*Black Poets Write On! an Anthology of Black Philadelphian
Poets*. Philadelphia (Black History Museum), 1970.
Bontemps, Arna, ed. *American Negro Poetry*. New York, 1963.
———, comp. *Golden Slippers*. New York, 1941.

————, ed. *Hold Fast to Dreams*. New York, 1969.

Booker, Dr. Merrel Daniel, et. al., eds. *Cry at Birth*. New York, 1971.

Boyd, Sue Abbott, ed. *Poems by Blacks*. Vols. I–III. Fort Smith, Ark., 1970–72, 1974. (Starting with Vol III, Pinkie Gordon Lane, ed., annual)

Breman, Paul, ed. *You Better Believe It*. Baltimore, 1973.

Brawley, Benjamin, ed. *Early Negro American Writers*. Chapel Hill, N.C., 1935.

Brooks, Gwendolyn, ed. *Jump Bad: a New Chicago Anthology*. Detroit, 1971.

————, ed. *A Broadside Treasury*. Detroit, 1971.

Brown, Sterling A.; Davis, Arthur P.; and Lee, Ulysses; eds. *The Negro Caravan*. New York, 1941, 1969.

Burning Spear: an Anthology of Afro-Saxon Poetry. Washington, D.C., 1963.

Cade, Toni, ed. *The Black Woman: an Anthology*. New York, 1970.

Calverton, Victor F., ed. *Anthology of American Negro Literature*. New York, 1929.

Cartey, Wilfred. *Whispers from a Continent: the Literature of Contemporary Black Africa*. New York, 1969.

Chambers, Bradford; and Moon, Rebecca; eds. *Right On! Anthology of Black Literature*. New York, 1970.

Chapman, Abraham, ed. *Afro-American Slave Narratives*. New York, 1970.

————, ed. *Black Voices: an Anthology of Afro-American Literature*. New York, 1968.

————, ed. *New Black Voices*. New York, 1971.

Chometzky, Jules; and Kaplan, Sidney; eds. *Black and White in American Culture: Anthology from the Massachusetts Review*. Amherst, Mass., 1969.

Clarke, John Henrik, ed. *Harlem: Voices from the Soul of Black America*. New York, 1970.

Collins, Marie, ed. *Black Poets in French*. New York, 1972.

Coombs, Orde, ed. *We Speak as Liberators: Young Black Poets*. New York, 1970.

Cornish, Sam, and Dixon, Lucian W.; eds. *Chicory! Young Voices from the Black Ghetto*. New York, 1969.

Cromwell, Otelia; Turner, Lorenzo D.; and Dykes, Eva B.; eds. *Readings from Negro Authors*. New York, 1931.

Cullen, Countee, ed. *Caroling Dusk: an Anthology of Verse by Negro Poets*. New York, 1927, 1974.

Cunard, Nancy, ed. *Negro Anthology*. London, 1934.

Cuney, Waring; Hughes, Langston; and Wright, Bruce McM.; eds. *Lincoln University Poets*. New York, 1954.

Danner, Margaret, ed. *The Brass House*. Richmond, Va., 1968.

————, ed. *Regroup*. Richmond, Va., 1969.

David, Jay, ed. *Black Joy*. New York, 1971.

Davis, Arthur P.; and Redding, Saunders; eds. *Cavalcade: Negro American Writing from 1760 to the Present*. Boston, 1971.

Davis, Charles T.; and Walden, Daniel; eds. *On Being Black: Writings by Afro-Americans from Frederick Douglass to the Present*. New York, 1970.

Dee, Ruby, ed. *Glowchild*. New York, 1972.

Dreer, Herman, ed. *American Literature by Negro Authors*. New York, 1950.

Edwards, Gregory; Loftin, Wayne; and Ware, Gregory; eds. *The Black Community Feeling, Thinking, Reacting. . . .* Omaha, Circa, 1971.

The editors of Vantage Press, comps. *New Voices in American Poetry, 1972*. New York, 1972.

Ellmann, Richard; and O'Clair, Robert; eds. *The Norton Anthology of Modern Poetry*. New York, 1973.

Emanuel, James A.; and Gross, Theodore; eds. *Dark Symphony: Negro Literature in America*. New York, 1968.

Feldman, Eugene; and Perkins, Eugene; eds. *Poetry of Prison: Poems by Black Prisoners*. Chicago (Du Sable Museum of African American History), c. 1971.

Ford, Nick Aaron, ed. *Black Insights: Significant Literature by Black Americans—1760 to the Present*. Waltham, Mass., 1971.

Freedman, Frances S., ed. *The Black American Experience: a New Anthology of Black Literature*. New York, 1970.

Gersmehl, Glen, ed. *Words Among America*. New York, 1971.

Giovanni, Nikki. *Night Comes Softly*. Newark, 1971.

Goldstein, Richard, ed. *The Poetry of Rock*. New York, 1968.

Gross, Mary Anne, ed. *Oh, Man, You Found Me Again*. Boston, 1972.

Gross, Ronald; Quasha, George; Williams, Emmett; Colombo, John Robert; and Lowenfels, Walter; eds. *Open Poetry*. New York, 1973.

Haslam, Gerald W., ed. *Forgotten Pages of American Literature*. Boston, 1970.

Hayden, Robert; Burrows, David; and Lapides, Frederick; eds. *Afro-American Literature*. New York, 1971.

Hayden, Robert, ed. *Kaleidoscope: Poems by American Negro Poets*. New York, 1967.

Henderson, Stephen. *Understanding the New Black Poetry (Black Speech and Black Music as Poetic References.)* New York, 1973.

Hill, Herbert, ed. *Soon, One Morning: New Writing by American Negroes, 1940–1962*. New York, 1963.

Hollo, Anselm, ed. *Negro Verse*. London, 1964.

Hopkins, Lee Bennett, comp. *On Our Way; Poems of Pride and Love*. New York, 1974.

Huggins, Nathan, ed. *Voices from the Harlem Renaissance*. New York, 1976.

Hughes, Langston, ed. *The Book of Negro Humor*. New York, 1966.

————, ed. *La Poésie Négro-Américaine*. Paris: Éditions Seghers, 1966.

————, ed. *New Negro Poets: U.S.A.* Bloomington, Ind., 1964.

————; and Bontemps, Arna; eds. *The Poetry of the Negro, 1746–1970*. Rev. ed. Garden City, N.Y., 1970.

Hunter, Paul; Parson, Patti; and Parson, Tom; eds. *The Whites of Their Eyes: Revolutionary Poems*. Seattle, 1970.

Images: an Anthology of Black Literature. Brooklyn, N.Y., c. 1972.

Jackson, Bruce, ed. *"Get Your Ass in the Water and Swim Like Me": Narrative Poetry from Black Oral Tradition*. Cambridge, Mass., 1974.

————, ed. *Wake Up Dead Man: Afro-American Worksongs from Texas Prisons*. Cambridge, Mass., 1972.

Johnson, Charles S., ed. *Ebony and Topaz: a Collection*. New York, 1927.

Johnson, James Weldon, ed. *The Book of American Negro Poetry*. Rev. ed. New York, 1931.

————, *The Book of American Negro Spirituals*. New York, 1925; *The Second Book of Negro Spirituals*. New York, 1926.

Jones, LeRoi; and Neal, Larry; eds. *Black Fire: an Anthology of Afro-American Writing*. New York, 1968.

Jordan, June, ed. *Soulscript: Afro-American Poetry*. Garden City, N.Y., 1970.

Kearns, Francis E., ed. *The Black Experience: an Anthology of American Literature for the 1970's*. New York, 1970.

Keegan, Frank L., ed. *Blacktown, U.S.A.* Boston, 1971.

Kendricks, Ralph, ed. *Afro-American Voices: 1770's–1970's*. New York, 1970.

Kerlin, Robert T., ed. *Negro Poets and Their Poems*. 2nd ed. Washington, D.C., 1935.

King, Woodie, ed. *Black Spirits: a Festival of New Black Poets in America*. New York, 1972.

————, ed. *The Forerunners: Black Poets in America*. Washington, D.C., 1975.

Knight, Etheridge, ed. *Black Voices from Prison*. New York, 1970.

Kramer, Aaron, ed. *On Freedom's Side: an Anthology of American Poems of Protest*. New York, 1972.

Lane, Pinkie Gordon, ed. *Discourses on Poetry*, Vol. 6. Fort Smith, Ark., 1972.

————, ed. *Poems by Blacks* (annual). Fort Smith, Ark., 1973.

Lanusse, Armand, comp. *Creole Voices: Poems in French by Free Men of Color.* Ed. Edward M. Coleman. Centennial ed. Washington, D.C., 1945.

Locke, Alain, ed. *Four Negro Poets.* New York, 1927.

————, ed. *The New Negro: an Interpretation.* New York, 1925.

Long, Richard A.; and Collier, Eugenia; eds. *Afro-American Writing: an Anthology of Prose and Poetry.* 2 vols. New York, 1972.

Lowenfels, Walter, ed. *From the Belly of the Shark.* New York, 1973.

————, ed. *In a Time of Revolution: Poems from Our Third World.* New York, 1969.

————, ed. *Poets of Today.* New York, 1964.

————, ed. *The Writing on the Wall.* Garden City, N.Y., 1969.

Major, Clarence, ed. *The New Black Poetry.* New York, 1969.

Miller, Adam David, ed. *Dices or Black Bones: Black Voices of the Seventies.* Boston, 1970.

Miller, Ruth, ed. *Blackamerican Literature 1760–Present.* Beverly Hills, Calif., 1971.

Miller, Wayne Charles, ed. *A Gathering of Ghetto Writers— Irish, Italian, Jewish, Black, Puerto Rican.* New York, 1972.

Moon, Bucklin, ed. *Primer for White Folks.* New York, 1945.

Moore, Gerald; and Beier, Ulli; eds. *Modern Poetry from Africa.* Baltimore, 1963.

Murphy, Beatrice, ed. *Ebony Rhythm.* New York, 1948, 1968.

————, ed. *Negro Voices.* New York, 1938.

————, ed. *Today's Negro Voices, an Anthology by Young Negro Poets.* New York, 1970.

Nelson, Alice Dunbar, ed. *Masterpieces of Negro Eloquence.* New York, 1914.

Nicholas, A. X., ed. *Poetry of Soul.* New York, 1971.

————, ed. *Woke Up This Mornin!* New York, 1973.

Norfolk Prison Brothers. Introduction by Elma Lewis. *Who Took the Weight?* Boston, 1972.

Osofsky, Gilbert, ed. *Puttin' on Ole Massa: the Slave Narratives of Henry Bibb, William W. Brown and Solomon Northup.* New York, 1969.

Patterson, Lindsay, ed. *An Introduction to Black Literature in America from 1746 to the Present.* Washington, D.C., 1969.

————, ed. *A Rock Against the Wind: Black Love Poems.* New York, 1973.

Perkins, Eugene, ed. *Black Expressions: an Anthology of New Black Poets.* Chicago, 1967.

Pool, Rosey E., ed. *Beyond the Blues: New Poems by American Negroes.* Lympne, Kent, England, 1962.

———, ed. *Ik Ben de Nieuwe Neger.* The Hague, 1964.

Porter, Dorothy, ed. *Early Negro Writing, 1760–1837.* Boston, 1971.

Ragain, Kathy, ed. *Occasional Papers, Plays and Poetry.* Vol. I. Kent, Ohio, 1971.

Randall, Dudley, ed. *Black Poetry: a Supplement to Anthologies Which Exclude Black Poets.* Detroit, 1969.

———; and Burroughs, Margaret; eds. *For Malcolm: Poems on the Life and Death of Malcolm X.* Detroit, 1969.

———, eds. *The Black Poets.* New York, 1971.

Redmond, Eugene, ed. *Sides of the River: a Mini Anthology of Black Writings.* East St. Louis, Ill., 1969.

Reed, Ishmael, ed. *19 Necromancers from Now: an Anthology of Original American Writing for the '70s.* Garden City, N.Y., 1970.

———, ed. *Yardbird Reader,* Vol. 1. Berkeley, 1972.

Robinson, William H., ed. *Early Black American Poets.* Dubuque, Iowa, 1969.

———, ed. *Nommo: an Anthology of Modern Black African and Black American Literature.* New York, 1972.

Rodgers, Carolyn, ed. *For Love of Our Brothers.* Chicago, 1970.

Rollins, Charlemae Hill, comp. *Christmas Gif'.* New York, 1963.

Sanchez, Sonia, ed. *Three Hundred and Sixty Degrees of Blackness Comin' at You.* New York, 1971.

Schulberg, Budd, ed. *From the Ashes: Voices of Watts.* New York, 1967.

Shapiro, Norman R., ed. and tr. *Négritude: Black Poetry from Africa and the Caribbean.* New York, 1971.

Shuman, R. Baird, ed. *A Galaxy of Black Writing.* Durham, N.C., 1970.

———, ed. *Nine Black Poets.* Durham, N.C., 1968.

Simon, Myron, ed. *Ethnic Writers in America.* New York, 1972.

Simmons, Gloria M.; and Hutchinson, Helen D.; eds. *Black Culture.* New York, 1972.

Stanford, Barbara Dodds eds. *I, Too, Sing America: Black Voices in American Literature.* New York, 1971.

Talley, Thomas W., ed. *Negro Folk Rhymes.* Port Washington, N.Y., 1922, 1968.

Taylor, Clyde, ed. *Vietnam and Black America.* Garden City, N.Y., 1973.

Ten: an Anthology of Detroit Poets. Fort Smith, Ark., 1968.

Tisdale, Celes, ed. *Betcha Ain't: Poems from Attica.* Detroit, 1974.

———, ed. *We Be Poetin'.* Buffalo, N.Y., 1974.

Troupe, Quincy, ed. *Watts Poets and Writers*. Los Angeles, 1968.

———; and Schulte, Rainer; eds. *Giant Talk: an Anthology of Third World Writings*. New York 1975.

Turner, Darwin T., ed. *Black American Literature: Poetry*. Columbus, Ohio, 1970.

Vorhees, Lillian; and O'Brien, Robert W., eds. *The Brown Thrush Anthology of Verse by Negro Students at Talladega College*. Athyn, Pa., c. 1932. (Schomburg Collection)

Washington, William D.; and Beckoff, Samuel; eds. *Black Literature: an Anthology of Outstanding Black Writers*. New York, 1972.

Watkins, Mel, ed. *Black Review No. 1*. New York, 1971.

———, ed. *Black Review No. 2*. New York, 1972.

Watkins, Sylvester C., ed. *Anthology of American Negro Literature*. New York, 1944.

Weisman, Leon; and Wright, Elfreda S.; eds. *Black Poetry for All Americans*. New York, c. 1972.

Wertheim, Bill; and González, Irma; eds. *Talkin' About Us*. New York, 1970.

White, Newman I.; and Jackson, Walter C.; eds. *An Anthology of Verse by American Negroes*. Durham, N.C., 1924.

Wilentz, Ted; and Weatherly, Tom; eds. *Natural Process: an Anthology of New Black Poetry*. New York, 1971.

Wood, Clement, ed. *Negro Songs, an Anthology*. Girard, Kan., 1924.

Woodson, Carter G., ed. *Negro Orators and Their Orations*. Washington, D.C., 1925.

Wormley, Beatrice; and Carter, Charles W.; eds. *An Anthology of Negro Poetry by Negroes and Others*. n.p., n.d. Works Progress Administration. (Schomburg Collection)

Young, Al, ed. *Yardbird Reader*, Vol. II. Berkeley, Calif., 1972.

LITERARY HISTORY AND CRITICISM

GENERAL

Adams, William. *Afro-American Authors*. Boston, 1971.

———, ed. *Afro-American Literature: Nonfiction*. Boston, 1970.

Allen, Samuel. "Negritude and Its Relevance to the American Negro Writer." *The American Negro Writer and His Roots*. New York, 1960. Pp. 8–20.

Baker, Houston A., Jr. "Balancing the Perspective: a Look at Early Black American Literary Artistry." *Negro American Literature Forum*. Vol. 6, No. 3 (Fall 1972), 65–70.

———. *Long Black Song: Essays in Black American Literature and Culture*. Charlottesville, Va., 1972.

————. "Utile, Dulce and the Literature of Black America." Black World, XXI (September 1972), 30–35.

Baraka, Imamu Amiri (LeRoi Jones). "The Black Aesthetic." Negro Digest, XVIII (September 1969), 5–6.

Bontemps, Arna. "The Black Renaissance of the Twenties." Black World, XX (November 1970), 5–9.

————. "Famous WPA Authors." Negro Digest, VIII (June 1950), 43–47.

————. "The Harlem Renaissance." The Saturday Review of Literature, XXX (March 22, 1947), 12–13, 44.

————. "The Negro Contribution to American Letters." The American Negro Reference Book. Ed. John P. Davis. Englewood Cliffs, N.J., 1966. Pp. 850–78.

————. "The New Black Renaissance." Negro Digest, XI (November 1961), 52–58.

————, ed. The Harlem Renaissance Remembered. New York, 1972.

Brawley, Benjamin. Early Negro American Writers. Chapel Hill, N.C., 1935.

————. "The Negro in American Literature." The Bookman, LVI (October 1922), 137–41.

————. The Negro Genius. New York, 1937.

Bronz, Stephen H. Roots of Negro Racial Consciousness: The 1920's: Three Harlem Renaissance Authors. New York, 1964.

Brooks, Russell. "The Comic Spirit and the Negro's New Look." CLA Journal, VI (1962), 35–43.

Brown, Lloyd W. "Black Entitles: Names as Symbols in Afro-American Literature." Studies in Black Literature, 1 (Spring 1970), 16–44.

————, ed. The Black Writer in Africa and the Americas. Los Angeles, 1973.

Brown, Sterling A. "The American Race Problem as Reflected in American Literature." The Journal of Negro Education, VIII (1939), 275–90.

————. "The New Negro in Literature (1925–1955)." In Rayford W. Logan, et. al., eds. The New Negro Thirty Years Afterward. Washington, D.C., 1955. Pp. 57–72.

Calverton, Victor F. The Liberation of American Literature. New York, 1932.

————. "The Negro and American Culture." The Saturday Review of Literature, XXII (September 21, 1940), 3–4.

Cayton, Horace R. "Ideological Forces in the Work of Negro Writers." In Herbert Hill, ed. Anger and Beyond: the Negro Writer in the United States. New York, 1966. Pp. 37–50.

Chapman, Abraham. "The Harlem Renaissance in Literary History." CLA Journal, XI (1967), 38–58.

Clarke, John Henrik. "The Neglected Dimensions of the Harlem Renaissance." *Black World*, XX (November 1970), 118–29.

———. "The Origin and Growth of Afro-American Literature." *Negro Digest*, XVII (December 1967), 54–67. (See also *Black Voices* in anthology section)

Clay, Eugene. "The Negro in Recent American Literature." *American Writers' Congress*. Ed. Henry Hart. New York, 1935. Pp. 145–53.

Colloquium on Negro Art: the First World Festival of Negro Art (1966). Présence Africaine Editions, 1968.

Conrad, Earl. "American Viewpoint: Blues School of Literature." Chicago *Defender*, December 22, 1945, p. 11.

Cook, Mercer; and Henderson, Stephen. *The Militant Black Writer in Africa and the United States*. Madison, Wis., 1969.

Cooke, M. G., ed. *Modern Black Novelists: a Collection of Critical Essays*. Englewood Cliffs, N.J., 1971.

Cosgrove, William. "Modern Black Writers: the Divided Self." *Negro American Literature Forum*. Vol. 7, No. 4 (Winter 1973). 120–22.

Cruse, Harold. *The Crisis of the Negro Intellectual*. New York, 1967.

Cullen, Countee. "The Dark Tower." *Opportunity*, monthly column, 1926–28.

Davis, Arthur P. "Growing Up in the New Negro Renaissance: 1920–1935." *Negro American Literature Forum*, II (1968), 53–59.

———. *From the Dark Tower: Afro-American Writers, 1900–1960*. Washington D.C., 1974.

Dickstein, Morris. "The Black Aesthetic in White America." *Partisan Review*, XXXVIII (Winter 1971–72), 376–95.

Du Bois, W. E. B. *The Souls of Black Folk*. Chicago, 1903.

Eleazer, Robert B., comp. *Singers in the Dawn: a Brief Supplement to the Study of American Literature*. Atlanta, Ga., 1934.

Ellison, Ralph. *Shadow and Act*. New York, 1964.

Emeruwa, Leatrice W. "Black Art and Artists in Cleveland." *Black World*, XXII (January 1973), 23–33.

Evans, Mari. "Contemporary Black Literature." *Black World*, XIX (June 1970), 4, 93–94.

Fabre, Michel. "Black Literature in France." *Studies in Black Literature*. Vol. 4, No. 3 (Autumn 1973), 9–14.

Fleming, Robert E. "'Playing the Dozens' in the Black Novel." *Studies in Black Literature*, Vol. 3, No. 3 (Autumn 1972), 23–24.

Ford, Nick Aaron. Annual "Critical Survey of Significant *Belles Lettres* by and About Negroes." *Phylon*: XXII (1961), 119–34; XXV (1964), 123–34.

———. "Black Literature and the Problem of Evaluation." *College English*, XXXII (1971), 536–47.

———. *Black Studies: Threat or Challenge?* Port Washington, N.Y., 1973.

———. "On the Teaching of Black Literature with the Aid of Anthologies." *College English*, Vol. 34, No. 7 (April 1973), 996–1013.

———. "What Every English Teacher Should Know About Black Studies." *The CEA Critic*, Vol. 36, No. 4 (May 1974), 19–27.

Fuller, Hoyt W. "Black Images and White Critics." *Negro Digest*, XIX (November 1969), 49–50.

———, ed. "A Survey: Black Writers' Views on Literary Lions and Values." *Negro Digest*. XVII (January 1968), 10–48, 81–89.

———. "Perspectives." *Negro Digest* and *Black World*, monthly column, through April 1976.

———. "The Negro Writer in the United States." *Ebony*, XX (November 1964), 126–34.

Gayle, Addison, Jr. "Reclaiming the Southern Experience: the Black Aesthetic 10 Years Later." *Black World*, XXIII (September 1974), 20–29.

———, ed. *Black Expression: Essays by and About Black Americans in the Creative Arts.* New York, 1969.

———, ed. *The Black Aesthetic.* New York, 1971.

Gerald, Carolyn. "The Black Writer and His Role." *Negro Digest*, XVIII (January 1969), 42–48.

Gibson, Donald B., ed. *Five Black Writers.* New York, 1970.

Giovanni, Nikki and Margaret Walker. *A Poetic Equation: Conversations Between Nikki Giovanni and Margaret Walker.* Washington, D.C., 1974.

Green, Elizabeth Lay. *The Negro in Contemporary American Literature.* Chapel Hill, N.C., 1928.

Hairston, Loyle. "Is Black Writing American Literature?" *Freedomways*, Vol. 13, No. 1 (First Quarter), 1973, 50–54.

Haslam, Gerald W. "The Awakening of American Negro Literature 1619–1900." In C. W. E. Bigsby, ed. *The Black American Writer.* Deland, Fla., 1969. Vol. II, pp. 41–51.

———. "Two Traditions in Afro-American Literature." *Research Studies, a Quarterly Publication of Washington State University*, XXXVII (September 1969), 183–93.

Hill, Herbert. "The Negro Writer and the Creative Imagination." *Arts in Society*, V (1968), 244–55.

Huggins, Nathan I. *Harlem Renaissance.* New York, 1971.

Hughes, Langston. *The Big Sea.* New York, 1940.

———. *I Wonder as I Wander.* New York, 1956.

———. "The Negro Artist and the Racial Mountain." *The Nation*, CXXII (1926), 692–94.

———. "To Negro Writers." In Henry Hart, ed. *American Writers' Congress.* New York, 1935. Pp. 139–41.

————. "The Twenties: Harlem and Its Negritude." *African Forum*, I (Spring 1966), 11–20.

Isani, Mukhtar Ali. "The Exotic and Protest in Earlier Black Literature." *Studies in Black Literature*, Vol. 5, No. 2 (Summer 1974), 9–14.

Jackson, Blyden. "A Survey Course in Negro Literature." *College English*, Vol. 35, No. 6 (March 1974), 631–36.

————. Annual "Résumé of Negro Literature." *Phylon*: XVI (1955), 5–12; XVII (1956), 35–40.

Jahn, Janheinz. *Neo-African Literature: a History of Black Writing.* New York, 1968.

Jeffers, Lance. "Afro-American Literature, the Conscience of Man." *The Black Scholar*, II (January 1971), 47–53.

Jones, LeRoi (Baraka, Imamu Amiri), *Home: Social Essays.* New York, 1966.

Johnson, Charles S. "The Negro Enters Literature." *Carolina Magazine*, LVII (May 1927), 3–9, 44–48.

Johnson, James Weldon. *Along This Way.* New York, 1933.

————. *Black Manhattan.* New York, 1930.

Keller, Joseph. "Black Writing and the White Critic." *Negro American Literature Forum*, III (1969), 103–10.

Kent, George E. *Blackness and the Adventure of Western Culture.* Chicago, 1972.

————. "Outstanding Works in Black Literature During 1972." *Phylon*, Vol. XXXIV, No. 4 (December 1973), 307–29.

————. "Struggle for the Image: Selected Books by or About Blacks During 1971." *Phylon*, Vol. XXXIII, No. 4 (Winter 1972), 304–23.

Kgositsile, Keorapetse. "Language, Vision and the Black Writer." *Black World*, XXI (June 1972), 25–27.

Kilgore, James C. "The Case for Black Literature." *Negro Digest*, XVIII (July 1969), 22–25, 66–69.

Killens, John Oliver. "Another Time When Black Was Beautiful." *Black World*, XX (November 1970), 20–36.

King, Woodie; and Anthony, Earl; eds. *Black Poets and Prophets; the Theory, Practice and Esthetics of the Pan-Africanist Revolution.* New York, 1972.

Klotman, Phyllis R. "An Approach to the Teaching of Black Literature—or: What's a White Lady Like You Doing in a Class Like This?" *The CEA Critic*, Vol. 34, No. 2 (January 1972), 12–15.

Lamming, George. "The Negro Writer and His World." *Présence Africaine*, Nos. 8–10 (June–November 1956), 324–32.

Lash, John. Annual "Critical Summary of Literature by and About Negroes." *Phylon*: XVIII (1957), 7–24; XIX (1958), 143–54, 247–57; XX (1959), 115–31; XXI (1960), 111–23.

Llorens, David. "What Contemporary Black Writers Are Saying," *Nommo*, I (Winter 1969), 24–27.

――――. "Writers Converge at Fisk University." *Negro Digest*, XV (June 1966), 54–68.

Locke, Alain L. "Dry Fields and Green Pastures." *Opportunity: Journal of Negro Life*, Vol. 28 (Jan. 1940), 4–10, 28.

――――, ed. *The New Negro: an Interpretation.* New York, 1925.

Loggins, Vernon. *The Negro Author: His Development in America to 1900.* New York, 1931.

Margolies, Edward. *Native Sons.* New York, 1968.

Mason, Julian. "Some Thoughts on Literary Stereotyping." *Negro American Literature Forum*, Vol. 6, No. 3 (Fall 1972), 63–64, 70.

Matthews, Geraldine O.; and the African-American Materials Staff of the School of Library Science, North Carolina Central University. *Black American Writers, 1773–1949: a Bibliography and Union List.* Boston, 1976.

M'Biti, John. *African Religions and Philosophies.* New York, 1970.

Mezu, S. Okechukwu, ed. *Modern Black Literature.* Buffalo, N.Y., 1971.

Miller, Ruth. *Backgrounds to Black American Literature.* Scranton, Pa., 1971.

――――. "The Negro Writer and His Relationship to His Roots." *The American Negro Writer and His Roots.* New York, 1960. Pp. 1–8.

Mitchell, Loften. *Black Drama.* New York, 1967.

Murray, Albert. *The Hero and the Blues.* Columbia, 1973.

――――. *The Omni-Americans: New Perspectives on Black Experience and American Culture.* New York, 1970.

――――. *South Again to a Very Old Place.* New York, 1972.

Neal, Larry. "Any Day Now: Black Art and Black Liberation." *Ebony*, XXIV (August 1969), 54–58, 62.

"Our Prize Winners and What They Say of Themselves." *Opportunity*, IV (1926), 188–89.

O'Brien, John. *Interviews with Black Writers.* New York, 1973.

O'Daniel, Thurman, ed. *Langston Hughes, Black Genius: a Critical Evaluation.* New York, 1971.

Redding, Saunders. "American Negro Literature." *The American Scholar*, XVIII (1949), 137–48.

――――. *To Make a Poet Black.* Chapel Hill, N.C., 1939. (Reprint, College Park, Md., 1968)

Rourke, Constance. "Tradition for a Negro Literature." *Roots of American Culture.* New York, 1942. Pp. 262–74.

Sellin, Eric. "Neo-African and Afro-American Literatures." *Journal of Modern Literature*, Vol. 1, No. 2 (1970–71), 249–53.

Shapiro, Karl. "The Decolonization of American Literature." *Wilson Library Bulletin*, XXXIX (1965), 842–53.

Simon, Myron. "Ethnic Writers and Mainstream Literature." *The CEA Critic*, Vol. 34, No. 2 (January 1972), 20–25.

Spingarn, Arthur B. "Books by Negro Authors." *The Crisis*, 1938–65, annual feature.

Studies in the Literary Imagination, Vol. VII, No. 2 (Fall 1974) 1–152. (Special number: The Harlem Renaissance)

Taylor, Clyde. "Black Folk Spirit and the Shape of Black Literature." *Black World*, XXI (August 1972), 31–40.

Thompson, Larry, ed. "Black Words." *Yale Literary Magazine* (special issue), Vol. 139, No. 3 (Fall 1969), 2–40.

Thurman, Wallace. "Negro Artists and the Negro." *The New Republic*, LII (August 31, 1927), 37–39.

Trimmer, Joseph F. *Black American Literature: Notes on the Problem of Definition.* Muncie, Ind., 1971.

Turner, Darwin T. "Afro-American Literary Critics." *Black World*, XIX (July 1970), 54–67.

——. *In a Minor Chord.* Carbondale, Ill., 1971.

——. "The Teaching of Afro-American Literature." *College English*, XXXI (1970), 666–70.

——, Bright, Jean; and Wright, Richard; eds. *Voices from the Black Experience: African and Afro-American Literature.* Waltham, Mass., 1972.

Wade, Melvin; and Wade, Margaret. "The Black Aesthetic in the Black Novel." *Journal of Black Studies*, Vol. 2, No. 4 (June 1972), 391–408.

Walcott, Ronald. "Ellison, Gordone and Tolson: Some Notes on the Blues, Style and Space." *Black World*, XXII (December 1972), 4–29.

Washington, Mary Helen. "Black Women Image Makers." *Black World*, XXIII (August 1974), 10–18.

West, Carole Cannon; and Williams, Allen. "Awareness: Teaching Black Literature in the Secondary School." *Journal of Black Studies*, Vol. 3, No. 4 (June 1973), 445–71.

Whitlow, Roger. *Black American Literature.* Chicago, 1973.

Williams, Kenny J. *They Also Spoke: an Essay on Negro Literature in America, 1787–1930.* Nashville, Tenn., 1970.

Williams, Sherley. *Give Birth to Brightness: a Thematic Study in Neo-Black Literature.* New York, 1972.

Wright, Bruce McM. "The Negritude Tradition in Literature." *Studies in Black Literature*, Vol. 3, No. 1 (Spring 1972), 1–3.

Yellin, Jean Fagan. *The Intricate Knot: Black Figures in American Literature, 1776–1863.* New York, 1971.

Young, James O. *Black Writers of the Thirties.* Baton Rouge, La., 1973.

POETRY

Baraka, Imamu Amiri. "Black Revolutionary Poets Should Also Be Playwrights." *Black World*, XXI (April 1972), 4–6.

Barksdale, Richard K. "Trends in Contemporary Poetry." *Phylon*, XIX (1958), 408–16.

———. "Urban Crisis and the Black Poetic Avant-Garde." *Negro American Literature Forum*, III (1969), 40–44.

Bell, Bernard W. *The Folk Roots of Contemporary Afro-American Poetry*. Detroit, 1974.

Bennett, M. W. "Negro Poets." *Negro History Bulletin*, IX (1946), 171–72, 191.

Berger, Art. "Negroes with Pens." *Mainstream*, XVI (July 1963), 3–6.

Bland, Edward. "Racial Bias and Negro Poetry." *Poetry*, LXIII (1944), 328–33.

Bone, Robert. "American Negro Poets! a French View." *Tri-Quarterly*, No. 4 (1965), 185–95.

Bontemps, Arna. "American Negro Poetry." *The Crisis*, LXX (1963), 509.

———. "Negro Poets, Then and Now." *Phylon*, XI (1950), 355–60.

Braithwaite, William Stanley. "Some Contemporary Poets of the Negro Race." *The Crisis*, XVII (1919), 275–80.

Brawley, Benjamin G. "Three Negro Poets: Horton, Mrs. Harper and Whitman." *Journal of Negro History*, Vol. 2 (Oct. 1917), 384–92.

Breman, Paul. "Poetry into the Sixties." In C. W. E. Bigsby, ed. *The Black American Writer*. Deland, Fla., 1969. Vol. II, pp. 99–109.

Brooks, Gwendolyn. "Introduction." In Arnold Adoff, ed. *The Poetry of Black America*. New York, 1973.

———. "Poets Who Are Negro." *Phylon*, XI (1950), 312.

———. *Report from Part One*. Detroit, 1972.

Brown, Sterling A. "The Blues." *Phylon*, XIII (1952), 286–92.

———. "The Blues as Folk Poetry." *Folk-Say, a Regional Miscellany* (1930), 324–39.

———. "Negro Folk Expression: Spirituals, Seculars, Ballads and Songs." *Phylon*, XIV (1953), 45–61.

———. *Negro Poetry and Drama*. Washington, D.C., 1937.

———. *Outline for the Study of the Poetry of American Negroes*. New York, 1931.

Bush, Roland E. "Negritude: A Sense of Reality." *Black World*, XXII (November 1972), 36–47.

Carter, Lawson; Hayden, Robert; and Phillips, Judson. *How I Write I*. New York, 1972.

Cartey, Wilfred. "Four Shadows of Harlem." *Negro Digest*, XVIII (August 1969), 22–25.

Chapman, Abraham. "Black Poetry Today." *Arts in Society*, V (1968), 401–8.

Charters, Samuel B. *The Poetry of the Blues*. New York, 1963.

Collier, Eugenia W. "Heritage from Harlem." *Black World*, XX (November 1970), 52–59.

————. "I Do Not Marvel, Countee Cullen." *CLA Journal*, XI (1967), 73–87.

Davis, Arthur P. "The New Poetry of Black Hate." *CLA Journal*, XIII (1970), 382–91.

Daykin, Walter I. "Race Consciousness in Negro Poetry." *Sociology and Social Research*, XX (1936), 98–105.

De Costa, Miriam (Sugarman). "Social Lyricism and the Caribbean Poet/Rebel." *CLA Journal*, Vol. XV, No. 4 (June 1972), 441–51.

Echeruo, M. J. C. "American Negro Poetry." *Phylon*, XXIV (1963), 62–68.

Ellison, Martha. "Velvet Voices Feed on Bitter Fruit: a Study of American Negro Poetry." *Poet and Critic*, IV (Winter 1967–68), 39–49.

Ely, Effie Smith. "American Negro Poetry." *The Christian Century*, XL (1923), 366–67.

Emanuel, James A. "Renaissance Sonneteers." *Black World*, XXIV (September 1975), 32–45, 92–97.

Flasch, Joy. *Melvin B. Tolson*. New York, 1973.

Fowler, Carolyn. "A Contemporary American Genre: Pamphlet/Manifesto Poetry." *Black World*, XXIII (June 1974), 4–19.

Furay, Michael. "Africa in Negro American Poetry to 1929." *African Literature Today*, II (1969), 32–41.

Garrett, Delois. "Dream Motif in Contemporary Negro Poetry." *English Journal*, LIX (1970), 767–70.

Garrett, Naomi M. "Racial Motifs in Contemporary American and French Negro Poetry." *West Virginia University Philological Papers*, XIV (1963), 80–101.

Gayle, Addison, Jr. *Claude McKay: the Black Poet at War*. Detroit, 1972.

Gibson, Donald B., ed. *Modern Black Poets: a Collection of Critical Essays*. Englewood Cliffs, N.J., 1973.

Glicksberg, Charles I. "Negro Poets and the American Tradition." *The Antioch Review*, VI (1946), 243–53.

Good, Charles Hamlin. "The First American Negro Literary Movement." *Opportunity*, X (1932), 76–79.

Heath, Phoebe Anne. "Negro Poetry as an Historical Record." *Vassar Journal of Undergraduate Studies*, III (May 1928), 34–52.

Henderson, Stephen. *Understanding the New Black Poetry;*

Black Speech and Black Music as Poetic References. New York, 1973.

Horne, Frank S. "Black Verse." *Opportunity*, II (1924), 330–32.

Jackson, Blyden; and Rubin, Louis D., Jr. *Black Poetry in America: Two Essays in Historical Interpretation.* Baton Rouge, La., 1974.

Johnson, Charles S. "Jazz Poetry and the Blues." *Carolina Magazine*, LVIII (May 1928), 16–20.

Johnson, James Weldon. "Preface." *The Book of American Negro Poetry.* New York, 1931. Pp. 3–48.

Jones, Edward A. *Voices of Negritude.* Valley Forge, Pa., 1971.

Kerlin, Robert T. "Conquest by Poetry." *The Southern Workman*, LVI (1927), 282–84.

———. *Contemporary Poetry of the Negro.* Hampton, Va., 1921.

———. "A Pair of Youthful Negro Poets." *The Southern Workman*, LIII (1924), 178–81.

———. "Present Day Negro Poets." *The Southern Workman*, LXIX (Dec. 1920), 543–48.

———. "Singers of New Songs." *Opportunity*, IV (1926), 162–64.

Kilgore, James C. "Toward the Dark Tower." *Black World*, XIX (June 1970), 14–17.

Kjersmeier, Carl. "Negroes as Poets." *The Crisis*, XXX (1925), 186–89.

Lee, Don L. "Black Poetry: Which Direction?" *Negro Digest*, XVII (Sept.–Oct. 1968), 27–32.

———. *Dynamite Voices: Black Poets of the 1960's.* Detroit, 1971.

Locke, Alain. "The Message of the Negro Poets." *Carolina Magazine*, LVIII (May 1928), 5–15.

Malkoff, Karl. *Crowell's Handbook of Contemporary American Poetry; a Critical Handbook of American Poetry Since 1940.* New York, 1973.

Moore, Gerald. "Poetry in the Harlem Renaissance." In C. W. E. Bigsby, ed. *The Black American Writer.* Deland, Fla., 1969. Vol. II, pp. 67–76.

Morpurgo, J. E. "American Negro Poetry." *Fortnightly*, CLXVIII (July 1947), 16–24.

Morton, Lena Beatrice. *Negro Poetry in America.* Boston, 1925.

"Negro Poetry." In Alex Preminger, Frank J. Warnke and O. B. Hardison, eds. *Encyclopedia of Poetry and Poetics.* Princeton, N.J., 1965. Pp. 558–59. (See also African poetry)

"Negro Poets, Singers in the Dawn." *The Negro History Bulletin*, II (1938), 9–10, 14–15.

Pool, Rosey. "The Discovery of American Negro Poetry." *Freedomways*, III (1963), 46–51.

Ramsaran, J. A. "The Twice-Born Artists' Silent Revolution." *Black World*, XX (May 1971), 58–68.

Randall, Dudley. "Black Bards and White Reviewers." *The Black Position*, Number 1 (1971), 3, 15.

Redding, J. Saunders. *To Make a Poet Black*. Chapel Hill, N.C., 1939; College Park, Md., 1968.

Redmond, Eugene B. "The Black American Epic: Its Roots, Its Writers." *The Black Scholar*, II (January 1971), 15–22.

———. "Five Black Poets: History, Consciousness, Love & Harshness." *Parnassus*, Summer–Fall 1975.

———. "How Many Poets Scrub the River's Back?" *Confrontation*, I (Spring 1971), 47–53.

———. "Introduction." In Lance Jeffers. *When I Know the Power of My Black Hand*. Detroit, 1975.

Richmond, M. A. *Bid the Vassal Soar: Interpretive Essays on the Life and Poetry of Phillis Wheatley and George Moses Horton*. Washington, D.C. 1974.

Rodgers, Carolyn M. "Black Poetry—Where It's At." *Negro Digest*, XVII (Sept. 1969), 7–16.

Rollins, Charlemae. *Famous American Negro Poets*. New York, 1965.

Rushing, Andrea Benton. "Images of Black Women in Afro-American Poetry." *Black World*, XXIV (September 1975), 18–30.

Sheffey, Ruthe. "Wit and Irony in Militant Black Poetry." *Black World*, XXII (June 1973), 14–21.

Sherman, Joan R. *Invisible Poets: Afro Americans of the Nineteenth Century*. Urbana, Ill., 1974.

Stauffer, Donald Barlow. *A Short History of American Poetry*. New York, 1974.

Taussig, Charlotte E. "The New Negro as Revealed in His Poetry." *Opportunity*, V (1927), 108–11.

Taylor, Clyde. "Henry Dumas: Legacy of a Long-Breath Singer." *Black World*, XXIV (September 1975), 41.

Thurman, Wallace. "Negro Poets and Their Poetry." *The Bookman*, LXVII (1928), 555–61.

Tinker, Edward Larogue. *Les Cenelles, Afro-French Poetry in Louisiana*. New York, 1930.

"The Umbra Poets." *Mainstream*, XVI (July 1963), 7–13.

"The Undaunted Pursuit of Fury." *Time*, XCV (April 6, 1970), 98–100.

Valenti, Suzanne. "The Black Diaspora: Negritude in the Poetry of West Africans and Black Americans." *Phylon*, XXXIV (December 1973), 390–98.

Wagner, Jean. *Les poètes nègres des États-Unis: Le sentiment racial et religieux dans la poésie de P. L. Dunbar à L. Hughes*. Paris, 1963.

———. *Black Poets of the United States: from Paul Laurence*

Dunbar to Langston Hughes (translation by Kenneth Douglass). Urbana, Ill., 1973.

Walker, Margaret. "New Poets." *Phylon*, XI (1950), 345–54.
White, Newman I. "American Negro Poetry." *South Atlantic Quarterly*, XX (1921), 304–22.
———. "Racial Feeling in Negro Poetry." *South Atlantic Quarterly*, XXI (1922), 14–29.
Work, Monroe N. "The Spirit of Negro Poetry." *The Southern Workman*, XXXVII (1908), 73–77.

FOLKLORE AND LANGUAGE

Abrahams, Roger. *Deep Down in the Jungle: Negro Narrative Folklore from the Streets of Philadelphia*. Hatboro, Pa., 1964.
———. "Playing the Dozens." *Journal of American Folklore*, 75 (1962), 209–18.
———. *Positively Black*. Prentice-Hall, 1970.
Adams, E. C. L. *Nigger to Nigger*. New York, 1928.
Allen, William Francis; Ware, Charles Pickard; and Garrison, Lucy McKim; comps. *Slave Songs of the United States*. New York, 1867, 1929, 1951.
Andrews, Malachi; and Owens, Paul T. *Black Language*. Berkeley, 1973.
Baratz, Joan C.; and Shuy, Roger W. *Teaching Black Children to Read*. Washington, D. C., 1969.
Brasch, Ida Wales; and Brasch, Walter Milton; comps. *A Comprehensive Annotated Bibliography of American Black English*. Baton Rouge, La., 1974.
Brewer, J. Mason. *American Negro Folklore*. Chicago, 1968.
———. "American Negro Folklore." *Phylon*, VI (1945), 354–61.
———. *Dog Ghosts, and Other Texas Negro Folk Tales*. Austin, Tex., 1958.
Brown, Sterling A. "The Blues." *Phylon*, XIV (1958), 286–92.
———. "Negro Folk Expression; Spirituals, Seculars, Ballads and Songs." *Phylon*, XIV (1953), 45–61.
———. "Negro Folk Expression. ⚡1. Folk Tales and Aphorisms." *Phylon*, XI (1950), 318–27.
Charters, Samuel B. *The Country Blues*. New York, 1959.
Claerbaut, David. *Black Jargon in White America*. Grand Rapids, Mich., 1972.
Conley, Dorothy L. "Origin of the Negro Spirituals." *The Negro History Bulletin*, XXV (1962), 179–80.
Corbett, Edward P. J. "Students' Right to Their Own Language." *College Composition and Communication*, XXV (Fall 1974), 1–32.

Courlander, Harold. *Negro Folk Music, U.S.A.* New York, 1967.
———. *A Treasury of African Folklore.* New York, 1975.
Curtis-Burlin, Natalie. *Negro Folk Songs.* New York, 1918/1919.
Dalby, David. "African Survivals in the Language and Traditions of the Windward Maroons of Jamaica." *African Language Studies* 12, 1971.
———. *Black Through White: Patterns of Communication in America and the New World.* African Studies Program, Terre Haute (Indiana University), 1970.
Davis, Ossie. "The English Language Is My Enemy." *American Teacher* (April 1967).
DeStefano, Johanna S. *Language, Society and Education: a Profile of Black English.* Worthington, Ohio, 1973.
Dillard, Joey Lee. *Black English: Its History and Usage in the United States.* New York, 1972.
Diton, Carl. *Thirty-Six South Carolina Spirituals.* New York, 1928.
Dorson, Richard M., ed. *African Folklore.* New York, 1972.
———. *American Negro Folktales.* New York, 1967.
Dundes, Alan, ed. *Mother Wit from the Laughing Barrel: Readings in the Interpretation of Afro-American Folklore.* Englewood Cliffs, N.J., 1973.
Ellis, A. B. "Evolution in Folklore: Some West African Prototypes of the Uncle Remus Stories." *Popular Science,* XLVIII (November 1895), 93–104.
Fisher, Miles Mark. *Negro Slave Songs in the United States.* New York, 1963.
Georgia Writers' Project. *Drums and Shadows: Survival Studies Among the Georgia Coastal Negroes.* Athens, Ga., 1940; New York, 1972.
Handy, E. C.; and Niles, Abbe; eds. *Treasury of the Blues.* New York, 1949.
Harris, Joel Chandler. *Daddy Jake the Runaway, and Short Stories Told After Dark.* New York, 1889.
Haskins, James; and Butts, Hugh F. *The Psychology of Black Language.* New York, 1973.
Hughes, Langston; and Bontemps, Arna. *The Book of Negro Folklore.* New York, 1958.
Hurston, Zora Neale. *Mules and Men.* Philadelphia, 1935.
Jackson, Bruce, ed. *"Get Your Ass in the Water and Swim Like Me": Narrative Poetry from the Black Oral Tradition.* Cambridge, Mass., 1974.
———. *Wake Up Dead Man: Afro-American Worksongs from Texas Prisons.* Cambridge, Mass., 1972.
Jahn, Janheinz. *Blues and Work Songs.* Frankfurtam Main, W. Germany, 1964.

————. *Negro Spirituals*. Frankfurtam Main, W. Germany, 1962.

Jones, LeRoi. *Black Music*. New York, 1967.

————. *Blues People: Negro Music in White America*. New York, 1963.

Krehbiel, Henry Edward. *Afro-American Folksongs: a Study in Racial and National Music*. New York, 1914.

Labov, William. *A Study of the Non-Standard English of Negro and Puerto Rican Speakers in New York City*. Co-operative Research Report 3288, Vol. 2, 1969.

————. *Language in the Inner City: Studies in the Black English Vernacular*. Philadelphia, 1972.

————. *Sociolinguistic Patterns*. Philadelphia, 1973.

————. *The Social Stratification of English in New York City*. Washington, D.C., 1966.

————. *The Study of Non-Standard English*. Champagne, Ill., 1970.

Landeck, Beatrice. *Echoes of Africa in Folk Songs of the Americas*. New York, 1961.

Leffall, Delores C.; and Johnson, James P.; comps. *Black English: an Annotated Bibliography*. Washington, D.C., 1973.

Loman, Bengt. *Conversations in a Negro Dialect*. Washington, D.C., 1967.

Lomax, John Avery; and Lomax, Alan. *American Ballads and Folk Songs*. New York, 1934.

————. *Negro Folksongs as Sung by Leadbelly*. New York, 1936.

Lovell, John. *Black Song: the Forge and the Flame, the Story of How the Afro-American Spiritual Was Hammered Out*. New York, 1972.

————. "Reflections on the Origins of the Negro Spiritual." *Negro American Literature Forum*, III (1969), 91–97.

Major, Clarence. *Dictionary of Afro-American Slang*. New York, 1970.

Marsh, J. B. T. *The Story of the Jubilee Singers; with Their Songs*, 7th ed., London, 1877.

Matthews, M. M. *Some Sources of Southernisms*. University, Ala., 1948.

McGhee, Nancy B. "The Folk Sermon: a Facet of the Black Literary Heritage." *CLA Journal*, XIII (1969), 57–61.

Morse, J. Mitchell. "The Shuffling Speech of Slavery: Black English." *College English*, Vol. 34, No. 6 (March 1973), 834–43.

Odum, Howard W.; and Johnson, Guy B. *The Negro and His Songs*. Chapel Hill, N.C., 1925.

————. *Negro Workaday Songs*. Chapel Hill, N.C., 1926.

Oliver, Paul. *Blues Fell This Morning: the Meaning of the Blues*. New York, 1960.

————. *Conversations with the Blues.* New York, 1965.

Sandilands, Alexander. *A Hundred and Twenty Negro Spirituals.* Morija, Basutoland, 1951, 1964.

Scarborough, Dorothy; and Gulledge, O. L. *On the Trail of Negro Folk-Songs.* Cambridge, Mass., 1925.

Scarborough, W. W. "Negro Folklore and Dialect." *Arena*, XVII (1897), 186–92.

Shirley, Kay. *The Book of the Blues.* New York, 1963.

Shuy, Roger W. *Cross-Cultural Analysis.* Washington, D.C., 1972.

————. *Discovering American Dialects.* Champagne, Ill., 1967.

————. *Field Techniques in an Urban Language Study.* Washington, D.C., 1968.

————. *Social Dialects and Language Learning.* Champagne, Ill., 1964.

————; and Fasold, Ralph W. *Teaching Standard English in the Inner City.* Washington, D.C., 1970.

Silverman, Jerry. *One Hundred and Ten American Folk Blues.* New York, 1958.

Smith, Arthur L. *Language, Communication and Rhetoric in Black America.* New York, 1972.

————. *Rhetoric of Black Revolution.* Boston, 1969.

————. *Transracial Communication,* Englewood Cliffs, N.J., 1973.

————; Hernández, Delvenia; and Allen, Anne. *How to Talk with People of Other Races, Ethnic Groups and Cultures.* Los Angeles: Trans-Ethnic Education Communication Foundation, 1971.

————; and Rich, Andrea L. *Rhetoric of Revolution: Samuel Adams, Emma Goldman, Malcolm X.* Durham, N.C., 1970.

————; and Robb, Stephen. *The Voice of Black Rhetoric: Selections.* Boston, 1971.

Smitherman, Geneva. "God Don't Never Change: Black English from a Black Perspective." *College English*, Vol. 34, No. 6 (March 1973), 828–33.

————. *Black Language and Culture: Sounds of Soul.* New York, 1975.

Spalding, Henry D., ed. *Encyclopedia of Black Folklore and Humor.* New York, 1972.

Stewart, W. A. "Continuity and Change in American Negro Dialect." *Florida Foreign Language Reporter*, Vol. 6, No. 2 (1968), 3–4.

Sullivan, Philip E. "Buh Rabbit: Going Through the Changes." *Studies in Black Literature*, Vol. 4, No. 2 (Summer 1973), 28–32.

Talley, T. W. *Negro Folk Rhymes, Wise and Otherwise.* New York, 1922.

Thurman, Howard. *Deep River*. New York, 1955.
————. *The Negro Spiritual Speaks of Life and Death*. New York, 1947.
Turner, Lorenzo D. *Africanisms in the Gullah Dialect*. University of Chicago Press, 1949; University of Michigan Press, 1974.
Twiggs, Robert D. *Pan-African Language in the Western Hemisphere*. North Quincy, Mass., 1973.
Twining, Mary Arnold. "An Anthropological Look at Afro-American Folk Narrative." *CLA Journal*, XIV (1970), 57–61.
Welmers, William E. *African Language Structures*. Berkeley, Calif., 1973.
White, Newman I. *American Negro Folk Songs*. Cambridge, Mass., 1928.
Wolfram, Walter A. *A Sociolinguistic Description of Detroit Negro Speech*. Washington, D.C., 1969.
————; and Clarke, Nona H. *Black-White Speech Relationships*. Washington D.C. 1971.
Work, John W. *Folk Song of the American Negro*. Nashville, Tenn., 1915.
————. "Negro Folk Songs." *Opportunity*, I (1923), 292–94.

DISCOGRAPHY AND TAPE INDEX

COLLECTIONS (PHONOGRAPH)

African Drums. Ethnic Folkways Library FE 4502 A/B.
African Origins and Influences. Folkways FA 2691, FE 4500, FE 4530, FS 384.
Afro-American Blues and Game Songs. Ed. by Alan Lomax. Library of Congress Recording AAFS 14.
Afro-American Music. W/Or. James. 2 Asch 702.
Afro-American Spirituals, Work Songs and Ballads. Ed. by Alan Lomax. Folkways FA 2650-59.
A Gathering of Great Poetry for Children, Vol. 2. W/Gwendolyn Brooks. Caedmon TC 1236.
A Hand Is on the Gate. Dir. by Roscoe Lee Browne. Folkways 9040.
American Folk Songs for Children. Perf. by Bessie Jones. Southern Folk Heritage Series. Atlantic 1350.
American Poems of Patriotism and Prose. Incl. James Weldon Johnson. Caedmon TC 1204.
Animal Tales Told in Gullah Dialect. Ed. by Duncan Emrick. AAFS L44-46.
Anthology of Music of Black Africa. Everest 3254/3.
Anthology of Negro Poets. Ed. by Arna Bontemps. (Read by Langston Hughes, Sterling Brown, Claude McKay, Countee

God's Trombones and Selected 20th Century Negro Poetry. Perf. by James Weldon Johnson, Alice Childress, and P. Jay Sidney. Educational Audio Visual 75 R 440.

Head Start Child Development Group of Mississippi. Asch 701.

Jazz Canto—Vol. I. Poetry Jazz Album. Read by Langston Hughes. World Pacific PJ 1244.

John's Island, Its People and Songs. Folkways FS 3840.

Les Ballets Africains de Keita Fodéba, Vol. I. Disques Vogue CLVLX 297.

Margaret Walker Alexander Reads Poems of Paul Laurence Dunbar and James Weldon Johnson. Folkways FL 9796.

Missa Luba. Sung by Joachim Ngoi and Les Troubadours du Roi Baudouin. Phillips PCC 606.

Music Down Home. Ed. by Charles Edward Smith. Folkways FA 2691.

Music from the South. Field Recordings by Frederic Ramsey, Jr. Folkways FP 650-59.

Music of Equatorial Africa. Recorded by André Didier. Folkways FP 4402.

National Poetry Festival. Incl. Gwendolyn Brooks and Langston Hughes. Library of Congress LWO 3868, 3869, 3870.

Negro Blues and Hollers. Ed. by Marshall W. Stearns. AAFS L59.

Negro Folk Music of Africa and America. Folkways FE 4500.

Negro Folk Rhythms. Perf. by Ella Jenkins and group. Folkways FA 2374.

Negro Folk Music of Alabama. Folkways Records P417-418 471-474.

Negro Folksongs and Tunes. W/Elizabeth Cotten. Folkways FG 3526.

Negro Folk Songs for Young People Sung by Leadbelly. Sung by Huddie Ledbetter (Leadbelly). Folkways FC 7533 ※2.

Negro Folk Stories and Music. Folkways 4417/8 4471/4.

Negro Poets Anthology. Folkways 9791.

Negro Poets in USA. Folkways 9792.

Negro Prison Camp Work Songs. Folkways FE 4475.

Negro Prison Songs. Perf. by Mississippi State Penitentiary Prisoners. Tradition Records TLP 1020.

Negro Religious Songs and Services. Ed. by B. A. Botkin. AAFS L10.

Negro Songs, Stories and Poetry for Young People. Folkways Records FC 7110, 7114, 7312, 7003, 7103, 7104, 7533, 7654.

Negro Work Songs and Calls. Ed. by B. A. Botkin. AAFS L8.

The New Black Poetry. Educational Audio Visual IRR 136.

New Jazz Poets. Ed. by Walter Lowenfels. AR Records BR 461 (Broadside).

Spoken Anthology of American Literature: the 20th Century.
Incl. James Weldon Johnson and Countee Cullen. University
of Arizona Press Records R63-1127.

*Spoken Arts Treasury of 100 Modern American Poets Reading
Their Poems,* V. 13. W/Gwendolyn Brooks. Spoken Arts
1052.

*Spoken Arts Treasury of 100 Modern American Poets Reading
Their Poems.* Read by James W. Johnson, Langston Hughes,
Countee Cullen, Owen Dodson, Gwendolyn Brooks. SA-P-18.

The Story of Jazz. Written and Narrated by Langston Hughes.
Folkways FC 7312.

Struggle for Freedom. Folkways FH5717, FH5511, FD5525,
FH5502, FH5522, FD5252, FH5523, FC7752.

Today's Poets, Vol. IV. Incl. Robert Hayden. Scholastic Records
FS11004.

Tough Poems for Tough People. Incl. Don L. Lee's, Etheridge
Knight's poetry. Caedmon Records, Inc. (1971).

Values in Literature. Incl. James Weldon Johnson. Houghton-
Mifflin 2-26409.

*Walk Together Children: the Black Scene in Prose, Poetry and
Song.* Read and Sung by Vinnie Burrows. Spoken Arts SA
1030.

The Weary Blues. Written and Narrated by Langston Hughes.
Verve VSPS-36.

World Famous Negro Spirituals. Perf. by Fisk Jubilee Singers.
Folkways FA 2372.

SINGLE POETS (PHONOGRAPH)

Angelou, Maya. *The Poetry of Maya Angelou.* GWP Records
ST2001.

Braithwaite, Edward. *Islands.* Argo PLP 1184/5.

———. *Masks.* Argo PLP 1183.

———. *Rights of Passage.* Argo PLP 1110/1.

Brooks, Gwendolyn. *Gwendolyn Brooks Reading Her Poetry:
w/Introductory Poem by Don L. Lee.* Caedmon TC 1244.

Brown, Elaine. *Seize the Time.* Read and Sung by Elaine
Brown. Vault 131.

Brown, Sterling. *Sterling Brown Reads His Poetry.* Folkways FL
9790.

———; and Hughes, Langston. *The Dixie Belle. Sterling
Brown and Langston Hughes Reading from Their Works.*
Folkways 9790.

———; and Hughes, Langston. *16 Poems.* Folkways 9794.

———; and Hughes, Langston. *Works of Sterling Brown and*

Langston Hughes. Read by authors. Folkways FP 90.

Burroughs, Margaret G. *What Shall I Tell My Children Who Are Black?* Sound-A-Rama SOR 101.

Cortez, Jayne. *Celebrations and Solitudes*. Strata-East Records, Inc. SES-7421.

Crouch, Stanley. *Ain't No Ambulances for No Nigguhs To-night*. Flying Dutchman FDS 105.

Cullen, Countee. *To Make a Poet Black*. Caedmon S-1400.

Dodson, Owen. *The Dream Awake*. Spoken Arts SA1095.

Fabio, Sarah Webster. *Boss Soul*. Folkways FL-9710.

―――. *Soul Ain't: Soul Is*. Folkways 9711.

Giovanni, Nikki. *Like a Ripple on a Pond*. Niktom 4200.

―――. *Truth Is on Its Way*. Right-On Records RR 05001.

Hughes, Langston. *Black Verse*. Buddah 2005.

―――. *Did You Ever Hear the Blues?* Big Miller's renditions of. . . . United Artists UAL 3047.

―――. *The Dream Keeper and Other Poems of Langston Hughes*. Read by Langston Hughes. Folkways FC 7104 (new no. FP 104).

―――. *Langston Hughes Reads and Talks About His Poems*. Spoken Arts SA 1064.

―――. *Poems by Langston Hughes*. Read by Langston Hughes. Asch Records 454.

―――. *The Poetry of Langston Hughes*. Caedmon (1968).

―――. *Ruby Dee and Ossie Davis Read from Selected Poems of Langston Hughes*. VTC 1272 (Caedmon 1272).

―――; and Danner, Margaret. *Writers of the Revolution*. Black Forum BB 453.

Johnson, James Weldon. *Four Readings from God's Trombones*. By James W. Johnson. Musicraft Album ⧣21.

―――. *God's Trombones*. Read by Bryce Bond. Folkways FL 9788.

―――. *God's Trombones*. Read by Harold Scott. United Artists UAS 5039.

Jones, LeRoi. *Black and Beautiful . . . Soul and Madness*. Jihad Productions Jihad 1001.

―――. *Sonny's Time Now*. Jihad Productions Jihad 663.

The Last Poets. *At Last: The Last Poets*. Blue Thumb BTS 52.

―――. *Chastisement*. Blue Thumb BTS 39.

―――. *The Last Poets*. East Wind Associates, Douglas 3.

―――. *Right On!* Juggernaut Records Jug St. LP 8802.

―――. *This Is Madness*. The Last Poets II. Douglas Communications Stereo Z0583.

Lyle, K. Curtis. *The Collected Poems of Blind Lemon Jefferson*. Mbari Production Company.

Redmond, Eugene B. *Blood Links and Sacred Places*. Black River Writers 110-13.

Rutlin, Bruce. *Ofama: Children of the Sun*. Black Artists Group.
———. *Poems of Gratitude*. Black Artists Group.
Sanchez, Sonia. *Sanchez*. Folkways 9793.
Scott-Heron, Gil. *Free Will*. Flying Dutchman Stereo FD 10153.
———. *Pieces of a Man*. Flying Dutchman Stereo FD 10143.
———. *Small Talk at 125th and Lenox*. Flying Dutchman Prod., Ltd. FDS-131.
Van Peebles, Melvin. *Ain't Supposed to Die a Natural Death*. A & M SP 4223.
———. *As Serious as a Heart Attack*. A & M SP 4326.
———. *Brer Soul*. A & M SP 4161.
Walker, Margaret. *The Poetry of Margaret Walker Read by Margaret Walker*. Folkways FL 9795.

SINGLE POETS (TAPE)

NOTE: Many of the educational and cultural institutions at which black poets have read maintain audio and/or video tapes of readings.)

Brooks, Gwendolyn. *Family Pictures*. Broadside Voices.
Eckels, Jon. *Home Is Where the Soul Is*. Broadside Voices.
Emanuel, James A. *Panther Man*. Broadside Voices.
———. *The Treehouse and Other Poems*. Broadside Voices.
Harper, Michael S. *History Is Your Own Heartbeat*. University of Illinois Press.
Hodges, Frenchy Jolene. *Black Wisdom*. Broadside Voices.
Jeffers, Lance. *My Blackness Is the Beauty of This Land*. Broadside Voices.
Kgositsile, Keorapetse. *Spirits Unchained*. Broadside Voices.
Knight, Etheridge. *Poems from Prison*. Broadside Voices.
Lee, Don L. *Don't Cry, Scream*. Broadside Voices.
———. *Readin' and Rappin'*. Broadside Voices. LP-BR-1.
———. *We Walk the Way of the New World*. Broadside Voices.
Murphy, Beatrice M.; and Arnez, Nancy L. *The Rocks Cry Out*. Broadside Voices.
Randall, Dudley. *Cities Burning*. Broadside Voices.
———; and Danner, Margaret. *Poem Counterpoem*. Broadside Voices.
Sanchez, Sonia. *Homecoming*. Broadside Voices.
———. *We a BaddDDD People*. Broadside Voices.
Stephany. *Moving Deep*. Broadside Voices.
Walker, Margaret. *Prophets for a New Day*. Broadside Voices.
X, Marvin. *Black Man Listen*. Broadside Voices.

INDEX

R